# Chinatown Film Culture

# Chinatown Film Culture

## The Appearance of Cinema in San Francisco's Chinese Neighborhood

KIM K. FAHLSTEDT

Rutgers University Press
New Brunswick, Camden, and Newark, New Jersey, and London

Library of Congress Cataloging-in-Publication Data

Names: Fahlstedt, Kim K., author.
Title: Chinatown film culture: the appearance of cinema in San Francisco's Chinese neighborhood / Kim K. Fahlstedt.
Description: New Brunswick: Rutgers University Press, 2020. | Includes bibliographical references and index.
Identifiers: LCCN 2019049103 | ISBN 9781978804401 (paperback) | ISBN 9781978804418 (hardback) | ISBN 9781978804425 (epub) | ISBN 9781978804432 (mobi) | ISBN 9781978804449 (pdf)
Subjects: LCSH: Motion picture audiences—California—San Francisco—History. | Chinese—California—San Francisco—Social life and customs. | Chinese in motion pictures. | Motion picture theaters—California—San Francisco—History. | Motion pictures—Social aspects—California—San Francisco. | Chinatown (San Francisco, Calif.)—Social life and customs.
Classification: LCC PN1995.9.A8 F34 2020 | DDC 302.23/43—dc23
LC record available at https://lccn.loc.gov/2019049103

A British Cataloging-in-Publication record for this book is available from the British Library.



∞ The paper used in this publication meets the requirements of the American National Standard for Information Sciences—Permanence of Paper for Printed Library Materials, ANSI Z39.48-1992.

www.rutgersuniversitypress.org

Manufactured in the United States of America

For Cissi, Joshi, and Boris

## Contents

# Preface

In January 1909, a promotional handbill appeared in *Billboard*, one of the foremost U.S. entertainment trade publications. Hidden among commentaries and film ads, the handbill offered brief information about the opening of a new San Francisco movie theater. This type of advertisement was not unusual in the U.S. nickelodeon era. In fact, the contents of the bill were completely ordinary, except for one thing: very few, if any, of *Billboard*'s contemporary readers, could understand what was on offer. The handbill, announcing the opening of the Oriental Theatre on San Francisco's Grant Avenue, was written in Chinese (see figure 19 in chapter 6).

For most *Billboard* readers who took notice, the Chinese ad provided an exotic example of the rapid popularization of the film medium as public amusement. Beyond its quality as a pictographic curiosity, the ad provided information about location, opening hours, the price of admission, and a couple of characterizing adjectives about the types of films on display. These were crowned with an offer for reduced tickets for families. But, more important, this "curiosity" announced the existence of a Chinese American movie audience in one of the leading trade magazines of the U.S. entertainment industry.

Three years later, on the eve of December 12, 1912, fifty-five film exhibitors braved the Indianapolis cold and huddled in the ballroom of the Claypool Hotel for the first convention of the Indiana section of the Motion Pictures Exhibitors' League. After opening remarks from a local banker and the organizer of the event, a man of considerable stature took the floor. M. A. Neff, of Cincinnati, Ohio, had formed the organization about a year earlier to protect the interests of moving picture men from arbitrary legislators, frightful censors, and the court of public opinion. Neff declared that the avalanche-like proliferation of moving pictures in the United States during the past couple of years surpassed that of any other form of business. Yet, as he continued to address the crowd, he spoke of China and the ongoing revolution there that sought to replace its totalitarian form of government with modern Western-style democracy.

As reported by *Motography,* Neff declared that "China, bowed down by the tyranny of a despotic government for centuries, has learned to feel the galling sores of her burden through the medium of the motion picture. It has forced the truth home where millions of books and thousands of devoted men and women have failed." To exemplify, Neff told of a recent meeting with a gentleman, "just returned from China after a stay of two years, who informed him that the moving picture, more than all other forces of civilization was responsible for the present movement to overthrow the old despotic order of things."[1]

Neff, who was convinced that the medium itself would change the course of American society and was no stranger to hyperbole, went on to liken the unity of the nation's film exhibitors to that of Jesus's apostles. Yet for all his belief in the transformative power of cinema, he failed to articulate how the film medium's perceived impact on "backwards" China in actuality provided an unprecedented link to the United States. Although possibly the nation's most well-informed man on matters pertaining to film exhibition, Neff, along with most of his peers, seemed less interested in the transformative role cinema was playing for Chinese communities decidedly closer to home.

The Chinese marketplace has been coveted and fantasized about by American film producers and exhibitors since the realization that there was money to be made in the movie business. This potential, along with the seemingly eternal cycle of racial caricatures produced by Hollywood, has, in turn, been the focal point of most scholarship on Chinese American cinema. More than a hundred years later, as the United States grapples with finding its place in a world order recast by the emergence of a new transformative medium, a world order in which a yet-again "reawakened" China is perceived as playing a central role, the practice and history of Chinese American media culture has remained concealed and fraught by century-old stereotypes.

This book tells a different story. By investigating what lies beyond convoluted historical artifacts and stale perceptions, focusing on the audiences, exhibition, and moviegoing experience in San Francisco's Chinatown in the early twentieth century, it provides a novel, complex, and at times astonishing account of how cinema appeared at the heart of Chinese America.

# Chinatown Film Culture

# Introduction

The role of audiences has played a significant part in historical studies of the emergence of U.S. film culture. In particular, scholars have focused on the importance of immigrant audiences in urban centers. First- and second-generation immigrants, many argue, were a key component in the rapid popularization of small movie houses, from Manhattan's Lower East Side to the Los Angeles Plaza. At the turn of the twentieth century, both geographic locations were adjacent to their respective city's Chinese neighborhoods. Although it has been noted that Chinese Americans were avid moviegoers, the role played by Chinese Americans in histories of the U.S. nickelodeon era is often reduced to an anecdotal mention or a brief bit-part appearance. While such omissions are often justified by a lack of source material and language skills, their recurrence has, inadvertently, situated Chinese American audiences into a place of historical obscurity.

In the past two decades, the historical imagery of Chinese Americans has emerged as a subject of film historical inquiry.[1] This scholarship primarily focuses on the mechanisms of racist representations in films, for example, the yellowface practice.[2] Although it is highly relevant to historical studies of the public image of Chinese in the United States, this concentration on on-screen stereotypes has obscured other—equally important—aspects of Chinese American film culture, such as audience and film production. In recent years, a few film scholars have begun to consider the transpacific exchange of people, ideas, and cultural production that made up vital aspects of life in Chinese America in the nineteenth and twentieth centuries. Denise Khor has investigated Asian American communities in Seattle, Stockton, and Hawaii.[3] Ramona Curry has studied untold transnational histories of Chinese American film production in the silent era, underlining how Chinese communities' participation in U.S. film culture remains principally underexplored.[4] While these excellent and much-needed studies demonstrate the richness of this overlooked area of modern U.S. entertainment history, none of them have considered the Chinese community that, arguably, has had the most cultural impact in U.S. history: Chinese San Francisco.

In the late 1900s and early 1910s, San Francisco's Chinese community had been one of the Bay Area's defining aspects for more than fifty years. The city's Chinatown was the cultural center of a transpacific Chinese community whose population extended along the West Coast, from Los Angeles to Vancouver. Chinese Americans from all over the area went to Chinatown for leisure, which, before the turn of the century, was a mix of Chinese theater and the insalubrious enterprises of the Barbary Coast, San Francisco's notorious red-light district. The neighborhood was destroyed—like the rest of downtown San Francisco—in the devastating 1906 earthquake and fire. When a new Chinatown was built, film exhibition quickly became its most popular form of entertainment. Chinese San Franciscans started to regularly patronize the movie houses of Chinatown and the southern part of the adjacent North Beach area. The non-Chinese managers of the movie houses sought to cater to the Chinese San Franciscan audiences by accommodating the film experience to their tastes. At the same time, these exhibitors attempted to attract tourists from outside Chinatown by utilizing the kind of Orientalist stereotypes that would become emblematic for Hollywood's representations of "Chineseness" in general and San Francisco's Chinatown in particular, as the dream factory began to establish its narrative format in the second half of the 1910s.

This book is about the emergence of cinema as a form of public entertainment in Chinatown. It deepens inquiries into Chinese American film history by locating Chinese Americans as featured participants, rather than bit players, in U.S. film history. As a tributary contribution to broader investigations into early U.S. film culture, it explores the connection between the movie houses of immigrant neighborhoods and the urban space that surrounded them. While earlier studies of the postulated process of "Americanization" of first- and second-generation immigrants at nickelodeon era movie theaters have primarily concentrated on the relationship between screen and spectator, this book suggests that this process saturated the whole moviegoing experience, from the street into the movie theater. The study shows that various spaces of post-quake Chinatown, its movie theaters, and emerging U.S. film culture had the functional dynamics of "transcultural contact zones" and "thirdspaces," in that it facilitated and connected to an alternative public sphere through which Chinese San Franciscans could experience the veritable link between the film medium and modernity culture. As such, the film culture that emerged in and around San Francisco's Chinatown between 1906 and 1915 appears as both inclusive and alienating for Chinese San Franciscans.

The introduction of film culture in San Francisco's Chinatown came at a time when the burgeoning American film industry slowly began to relocate from the East Coast to California. Although by the end of this period Los Angeles would emerge as the new home of the U.S. studio system, the more cosmopolitan city of San Francisco was the state's entertainment hub. Several of the performers, producers, and exhibitors who would eventually make up the foundation of "Tinseltown" started on the San Francisco theater and vaudeville circuit. This study demonstrates how local film exhibition was influenced by and appropriated for Chinese American patrons, while also functioning as fertile soil for a strong brand of Orientalism, which, exported by key showmen such as Sid Grauman, would evolve into central representations of Asiatic otherness in the Classical Hollywood era. More than providing the first comprehensive study of moviegoing in Chinese America, this book also tells a story about a film and entertainment culture marginal from, yet decidedly impactful on, more dominant historical narratives of American cinema.

## Post-quake Chinatown Film Culture?

This book posits that there was such a thing as "post-quake Chinatown film culture." To be of use, this term needs some explanation. What is meant by post-quake Chinatown film culture? And what makes it relevant as a framework for historical inquiry?

Raymond Williams described "culture" as one of the most complicated words in the English language.[5] Williams outlined three prevalent modern usages of the noun "culture": first, as describing a process of "intellectual, spiritual, and aesthetic development"; second, indicating a particular way of life, whether of a people, a period, or, a group; and third, describing the works and practices of intellectual and particularly artistic creativity—often connected to notions of "high culture."[6] Within the humanities, this complexity has sometimes divided scholars into focusing on either the material or the symbolic production of a particular people, period, or both. Williams advised allowing room for the categories to be related, rather than contrasted, while at the same time being stringent and precise in each conceptual usage. In this book, all three of Williams's subcategories apply to the notion of culture, albeit in varying capacities. The first two categories are most prevalent, describing intellectual and aesthetic practices and ways of life in post-quake Chinatown. The third, denoting artistic works and practices, is considered but to a lesser degree.[7] Thus, the culture studied here is in many aspects the same as that often envisaged by the field of cultural studies, dealing with the complex relation of both "material" and "symbolic" production.[8] The 1909 Chinese-language *Billboard* advertisement for the Oriental Theatre provides an example of this kind of overlap between material production and symbolism.

While this study adheres to a cultural studies approach, it does so with film exhibition in Chinatown as its nodal point. The specific focus on *film culture* also needs some deliberation. The object of film history has expanded from the study of films to their context. Scholars such as Robert C. Allen have outlined a shift in focus in studying historical film culture as a set of experiences "associated with but not reducible to films."[9] Examples of such experiences in this study include audience accounts, economic records, distribution practices, marketing strategies, and exhibitor interviews. The notion of Chinatown film culture primarily focuses on the underexplored practices of film exhibition and audiences, and how they related to other contemporary cultural practices and social developments in this specific area. In other words, it provides a spatio-temporal vantage point in Chinatown, from which it is possible to observe and analyze the impact of the emerging American film industry.

Finally, "post-quake" refers to the period after the 1906 earthquake and fire that destroyed large parts of San Francisco and put the city's economic, political, and social infrastructure into a phase of transition. In 1915 the city hosted the Panama-Pacific International Exposition (PPIE) and showcased its rejuvenation to the world. It was also the year in which several of the city's leading film exhibitors began relocating to Los Angeles. These years defined a new path for disreputable San Francisco and ushered in a more modern iteration, primed for tourism and commercial trade. For Chinatown, which was completely razed, the rebuilding of the neighborhood was paralleled by upheaval in China. Between 1907 and 1912, a revolution fueled by ideas of modernization of the political and social system in the old country gradually disrupted and replaced a 1,000-year lineage of despotic rule.

## Salvaged Film History

This study is the result of a seven-year process of analyzing and synthesizing archival objects in conversation with a variety of scholarly disciplines. The best way to describe it is as history salvaged from the margins. There are three general respects in which this is true. First, most of the primary sources used have not been considered previously for this purpose. It would, however, be misleading to describe them as forgotten, as they have been stored, preserved, and to a degree also been made accessible through various archival practices. Second, the history produced here investigates a community that has existed at the fringe of U.S. society. For a long time, Chinese Americans were exempt from the liberties vested in most other U.S. citizens. Third, Chinese Americans have played marginal roles in accounts of U.S. film history. The marginalization can be seen not only through the documented historical experiences of the Chinese American community in the United States but also in the scarcity of such archival materials.

As will be evident throughout this book, a significant amount of the primary sources drawn on have entered into archives for reasons other than the documentation of the history of the Chinese in America. As Nicholas Mirzoeff and Jack Halberstam have pointed out, "Archival research tends to be constrained by the placement of archives according to arcane colonial logics of organization."[10] Whether organized by a colonialist mind-set or not, the archival collections considered for this book have called for unorthodox strategies in order to locate relevant materials. In many cases, they have been categorized and sorted into historical collections on film and media, as well as local history. Several of these sources have been used to relate a different kind of story, one that speaks volumes about the emergence of the film medium and modernity in the United States. If viewed from a different perspective, their contents are, however, more polyphonic. Consulting a volume of *Billboard* from 1909 in search of Chinese American film culture is a rather different experience than looking for mentions of D. W. Griffith. Reading the *San Francisco Call* from 1911 for traces of Chinatown film screenings is a different practice than reading it for information on post-quake San Francisco politics. As archival materials, these sources have led a double life, partly in the historical spotlight, partly in the periphery. Before learning how to decode and contextualize the contemporary language of accounts written about Chinatown entertainment for a non–Chinese American readership, one first needs to figure out ways to find such accounts in archives that have fundamentally deemed such information irrelevant. The necessary methodological approach thus becomes to read not only the contents of the archive, but the archival structure itself, against the grain.

Broadly formulated, this study adheres to a framework of cultural studies developed by film scholars under the umbrella term "New Film History," using methods of historical materialism to investigate relations between cinema and place. The term "New Film History" is a synecdoche for revisionist interventions into established narratives of film history that emerged in the 1980s. Negotiated by a turn to empiricism, debates on the perceptive revolution brought about by cinematic modernity, and a renewed interest in nuancing the experiences of historical film audiences, New Film History fostered a methodological approach that sought to analyze the "generative mechanism of moviegoing within everyday life."[11]

Working with fragments of historical film culture could be described as what Walter Benjamin called redemptive historical materialism. In his labyrinthine text "On the Concept of History," Benjamin tasked the historian with brushing "history against the grain."[12] Equally inspiring and mysterious, the text, written shortly before Benjamin's death, has generated a multitude of interpretations.[13] Benjamin's theses become relevant to the historical materialism of New Film History in that it attempts to assemble and revisit accounts that have been left out of dominant historical narratives. Benjamin opposed the continuum of Rankean historicism as a history of "victors," which sends the vanquished to the margins.[14] Political theorist Ronald Beiner, one of Benjamin's interpreters, has outlined the overriding concern of the theses as that of continuing to wage the fight for the oppressed past: "Where the historicist sees an inert 'chain of events,' the historical materialist sees a broken vessel in need of repair, a ruined past in need of salvation."[15] For Benjamin, such processes of reconnection to a ruined past could be achieved by making "the continuum of history explode."[16] John Kuo Wei Tchen and Dylan Yeats elaborated this notion as a methodological perspective on historical fragments that can inform revisionist histories of oppression, where fragments of a "seemingly distant past" can appear as a "lightning flash in the present." For Tchen and Yeats, such fragments could momentarily disentangle us from past and present structures of power and cause us "to look at our surroundings differently" and help us understand "a new pattern of meaning."[17] Historical materialism as a methodological approach, then, is what guides this inquiry to identify and use overlooked remnants of the past to produce a more nuanced understanding of our shared history, as well as our present moment: "a constellation of past and present through which the present would find an image of itself and thus see more clearly."[18]

Critics have argued that Benjamin's vision of history might be more useful as a guiding principle than a methodological program for historical materialists.[19] Robert C. Allen and Douglas Gomery, doyens of New Film History, argued that historians must reflect their position beyond the classical empiricist notion of collector and arranger of historical materials on a daily basis.[20] Therefore, the approach here warrants further clarification. The primary objective of the method is not to interpret films through their context, but rather the very context in its relation to the exhibition of films—what Richard Maltby has called "writing historical studies of cinema that are not centrally about films."[21] This stance differs from Janet Staiger's text-centered historical materialist perspective on film reception, which primarily departs from specific films in order to cast a wider net on its contemporary reception.[22] Again, the Chinese-language advertisement from *Billboard* provides an illustrative example, as it suggests an exhibition context without mentioning specific films. However, to understand this context, we need to shift our focus toward a decentered and spatialized concept of historical film spectatorship.[23]

An essential aspect of this decentralization is the concept of local histories of film culture, which emphasizes the relation between film exhibition and place. During the past decades, a growing body of film histories has investigated cinema audiences from a local perspective—often attempting to identify and localize place-specific contexts in which audiences experienced cinema. These "microhistories" could then cumulatively build toward a deeper history of moviegoing.[24] Such investigations would, in turn, facilitate more detailed analysis of the manifold shifts and nuances of early film culture in a way that allows for the inclusion of events and tendencies that break away in other directions than those of the general trends.[25]

Generally, the local turn in film studies has given historians a way to critically approach the heterogeneity of historical audiences—a stone that had been left unturned by earlier "grand theory" models of spectatorship.[26] Some concerns have been raised about the changing role of the film historian and about the risk that such inquiries will produce works of scholarly myopia, idiosyncratic microhistories without medium specificity that are unfit for the ambition to inform historical inquiry at the macro level.[27] One could hold similar doubts toward a study that attempts to retrieve meaning from archival objects reduced to a place at the margins of history. However, as argued by Richard Maltby, in order to answer the larger questions about cinema's cultural function and historical audiences in the first decades of the film medium, we need "detailed historical maps of cinema exhibition, amplified by evidence about the nature and frequency of attendance."[28] In this context, the local film history here produced can be regarded as a cartographic contribution, shedding light on a multilayered blind spot of U.S. film history.

Adding to these general perspectives on film exhibition, many local-specific considerations come into play. To paraphrase Joel Frykholm's study of the rise of the feature film and Philadelphia film culture, San Francisco film culture could be seen as a unit of thousands of moviegoers, and thousands of reels of film shown in close to a hundred venues, the film experience of each filmgoer being of some importance to at least him or her, and the existence of each place of exhibition being an important element to at least a certain number of San Franciscans during the period of inquiry.[29] But since it would be virtually impossible to account for every single moviegoing experience a century later, even within the limited spatiotemporal framework of one day at one neighborhood theater known for its incredibly loyal patrons, all of whom identified as being from roughly the same class and with a solidly homogeneous framework of cultural reference, the task of accounting for film experiences within something pronounced as "film culture" could turn into a painstaking practice of collecting personal anecdotes, without being able to connect the dots and provide anything of substantial historical value. The myriad experiences that are representative of the "film culture" of a certain place simultaneously inform and complicate the concept. In this sense, this account is a diachronic balancing act, which, in the words of Barbara Klinger, forces consideration of film culture's fluid, changeable, and volatile relation to history.[30]

## Sources and Strategies

Because a large percentage of the films from the first decades of cinema are lost, most early film historians cannot directly observe the phenomena they seek to explain. Film historians working with this general principle must rely on those artifacts available to the time and scope of the investigation, which often means studying nonfilmic materials. Examples of such materials include production records, newspapers, government documents, and even old premises that once served as movie theaters. The scarcity of films pertaining to the scope of this study and the methods of inquiry developed by film historians working with nonfilmic materials have influenced the approach to the source material in this study. As a result, the source material comes from a wide array of archival collections. The firsthand materials include 16mm, and 35mm films screened with and without live sound accompaniment at editing tables and in movie theaters, digitized versions of silent film viewed on a computer screen and in lecture halls, trade press articles and advertisements, contemporary local newspapers published in multiple languages, address directories, census records, World War I draft cards, censorship materials, old photographs of movie theaters, recent photographs of buildings that used to be movie theaters, posters, postcards, interviews, shipping records, personal letters, government correspondence, maps, city ordinances, state laws, and federal laws.

For a long time, archival research of sources such as the ones listed earlier has necessitated traveling to the archives and repositories where they are preserved.[31] While these sources are preserved in physical archives, their materiality varies considerably. In Shanghai, I did initial searches for relevant material through consulting original copies of local newspapers and municipal records. At Stockholm University and the University of Illinois, publications such as *Young China* and *Motography* could be perused by hand-cranking through them on microfilm. The scanned records available on location at the Library of Congress in Washington, DC, were viewed on editing tables and computer screens. All different repositories generate different physical experiences of archival practice.[32] Such activities have presupposed a scholar with considerable time and funds allocated to being "on the road." Whereas the bulk of the major discoveries linked to New Film History have been made possible by such painstaking tests of patience and economy, developments procured by the proliferation of online archives since the mid-2000s have opened new avenues of making historical documents accessible to a wider variety of researchers, as well as to a broader audience.[33] The possibilities of data mining and new modes of visualization have been championed by some, while others have suggested that the experience of working in the physical archives offers modes of discovery that cannot yet be reproduced by looking at a computer screen.[34] Although both of these approaches are valid in terms of the minutiae of archival work, it is through a close and comparative combination of the two that extensive detective work researching early film history becomes the most effective.

A great deal of the source material is gathered from contemporary trade magazines. Most frequently the reader will encounter material from *Moving Picture World*, *Billboard*, *Variety*, and *Motography*, and to a lesser degree material from the *New York Clipper*, *Exhibitor's Times*, *Film Index*, *Motion Picture News*, *The Nickelodeon* (*Motography*'s predecessor), and *The Rounder*. While journals like *Billboard* and *Variety* covered a wide variety of stage performances, and others like *Motion Picture News* and *Moving Picture World* had a decidedly more film-specific focus, by 1908 they constituted a spectrum of film reporting positioned along the great divide of the U.S. film industry. *Film Index* aligned closely with the "trust," whereas *Billboard* and *Motion Picture News* could be found at the other end, siding with the "independents." According to Richard Abel, the middle-ground position assumed by *Moving Picture World* secured its dominance for many years.[35] While noting the fluctuating self-interests of each journal, I have incorporated the publications, editorials, articles, advertisements, interviews, reviews, film stories, and listings into the investigation with a San Francisco Chinatown-specific perspective. Generally, I have considered trade press material because of what it can tell us about the placement, duration, and look of theaters. Another broad consideration has been to establish the internal dynamics between local theaters and exhibitors, as well as their relation to each trade paper's San Francisco correspondent.

While we can use trade papers like *Billboard*, *Variety*, and *Moving Picture World* to derive some information about Chinese San Franciscan audiences, it is important to note that such observations were often done to underline the "peculiarity" of the theater. Regularly, trade papers singled out the Chinese audience members in their descriptions of Chinatown theaters. Such rhetoric, in general, was in no way specific to the description of Chinese audiences but rather was applied to most other nonwhite moviegoers. However, trade paper accounts of San Francisco Chinatown audiences often evoked an Orientalist terminology that resonated with the mythical iterations commonly found in contemporary sensationalist writings on the area. More than the audiences, the Chinatown movie theaters and the overall exhibition situation often stand in contrast to the rest of San Francisco in the trade press.

Three major local newspapers make up another significant part of the source material: the *San Francisco Chronicle*, the *San Francisco Call*, and, William Randolph Hearst's *San Francisco Examiner*.[36] Such newspapers offered extensive coverage of turn-of-the-century public entertainment. A number of film historians have championed the possibilities of using local newspapers to, in Jan Olsson's words, approach local nuances of "audience composition and civic promotion" in U.S. film culture from 1907 onward.[37] Paul S. Moore has in several publications pointed to the function of the local newspaper as a veritable menu for a city's entertainment output.[38] Richard Abel has underlined the function of newspapers as an independent driving force in the development of early U.S. film culture.[39] As such, local newspapers provide cartes du jour of film culture for both contemporary moviegoers and present-day historians.

As mentioned previously, the Chinatown movie theaters were generally exempt from the daily attention of local newspapers. While Chinatown film exhibition occasionally surfaced in reports of fire hazards, regulation, and charity events, newspapers aimed a more notable focus toward Chinese San Franciscans. Here, the newspapers provide a discursive backdrop for the marginalized social status of Chinese Americans in the Bay Area. Whether the articles portrayed the city's Chinese population in a positive or a negative light, the common denominator for most of them was to corroborate, or belie, the deep-seated racial prejudice against Chinese immigration that had pervaded the region since the 1870s.

The history of organized anti-Chinese campaigns in San Francisco begins with the city's initial rapid growth. The first records of confrontation with Chinese Californians came from the mining camps in the 1850s. The ethnic divide went on to become ingrained in the labor politics of the area.[40] Alexander Saxton noted that from the time of the gold rush, sharply drawn lines divided the Chinese and non-Chinese contingents of California's labor force. The significant growth of the Chinese workforce during the 1870s and 1880s further reinforced these prejudicial boundaries.[41] Between 1863 and 1869, Chinese workers were instrumental in the construction of America's first transcontinental railroad. These often life-threatening jobs were rewarded with minuscule pay. Although the work ethic of the Chinese was commonly held up as second to none, their societal status was among the lowest in America.[42] In 1869, China and the United States signed the Burlingame Treaty, which would encourage immigration across the Pacific. The wording explicitly stated that Chinese in America should be exempt from persecution on the basis of their origin or faith. The same would apply to Americans in China.[43] This edict was blatantly ignored by the anti-Chinese movement that was brewing in California in the 1870s, organized by public agitators like Dennis Kearney, to whom I will return shortly. In 1882, the anti-Chinese lobby succeeded in pushing through the Chinese Exclusion Act, which effectively reversed the Burlingame Treaty and in reality separated Chinese in America from their families back home.

It was not only disgruntled laborers who sought to alienate Chinese immigrants. Some of San Francisco's most powerful men regularly spoke out against the Chinese, while exploiting their labor for personal gain. Historian Gray Brechin located the transformative power behind the emergence of the modern San Francisco within a small elite. Among the wealthy patriarchs of the city were men like Leland Stanford and William Randolph Hearst, both of whom had made their fortune on the American westward expansion.[44]

Stanford gained incredible wealth and industrial influence through the success of the Central Pacific Railroad. William Randolph Hearst, the heir to the famous miner George Hearst, used the wealth of the family enterprise to fund his career as a publisher and politician.[45] While both Stanford and Hearst often publicly assumed an anti-Chinese stance to further their political careers, Chinese American labor was instrumental to the men's financial and political capital. The completion of the railroad sent large numbers of Euro-American and Chinese workers into unemployment. Alexander Saxton found that although Euro-American culture contained widespread anti-Chinese animosity before the transpacific influx of labor to California, it quickly bloomed into a significant regional factor, as the Democratic Party sought to score political points by blaming the lack of jobs on the Chinese workforce.[46]

In 1877, as local unemployment increased dramatically, the San Francisco branch of the Workingmen's Party of the United States agitated fiercely against the city's "coolie labor." Several demonstrations were held at City Hall blocks away from Chinatown. In late July, the tension escalated into riots, and factions of demonstrators transformed into an angry mob that marched on Chinatown, burning down dozens of laundry shops and killing four people.[47] Dennis Kearney, an Irish American laborer who had been among the demonstrators, saw a political opportunity in the wake of the riots. In the fall of 1877, Kearny formed his labor party, the Workingmen's Party of California, and started deliberately targeting Chinese San Franciscans in a violent public uprising against prevailing labor conditions. While local police regularly arrested Kearney and other leaders of the new party, the anti-Chinese message struck a chord. In the 1879 elections, the party won a landslide victory and saw the new mayor, Isaac Kalloch, join their anti-Chinese campaign. In early 1880, demonstrators gathered daily in the "sandlots" around City Hall to coerce employers to dismiss Chinese San Franciscan workers. Several factory owners capitulated to the pressure, and thousands of workers were laid off.[48] Although the Workingmen's Party was initially successful in local politics, its internal structure soon imploded, and by late 1880 the party had disappeared. However, the anti-Chinese sentiment remained active in local politics and public debate.

Anti-Chinese perspectives and attitudes are ever-present when researching local newspapers from the late nineteenth and early twentieth century. These papers offer a discursive realm to follow the local factors that shaped the city's film exhibition culture from nickelodeons to movie palaces, but they also function as records of the socially wide-ranging marginalization of Chinese San Franciscans on a daily basis. Obvious and problematic evidence of this is the dearth of Chinese San Franciscan writings in the English-language papers. While certain San Francisco opinion makers, such as Ng Poon Chew, occasionally were given editorial space in the *San Francisco Call*, Chinese San Franciscans had by 1907 developed their own institutions and platforms of mass communication. Between 1906 and 1915, San Francisco had four Chinese-language newspapers. Like the city's English-language newspapers, they all came with political alliances and internal dynamics. The most influential of these papers during the era was Chew's *Chung Sai Yat Po*. Partial holdings of the Chinese-language newspapers from the period are kept by the Chinese Historical Society of America (CHSA) and at University of California at Berkeley. Chinese San Franciscan newspapers were researched with the assistance of the late Professor Phil Choy.[49] While the Chinese-language newspapers have not been the subject of the same systematic scrutiny as the English ones, our joint preliminary conclusion is that they focused on local social issues and dispatches of developments of the ongoing revolution in China, rather than the Chinatown movie theaters. Local entertainment updates might have been omitted because, although Chinese San Franciscans liberally and regularly visited the area's movie and vaudeville theaters, they were generally owned and managed by non-Chinese proprietors. However, certain events, such as the political flare-up between Republican China, Chinatown luminaries, and the organizers of the PPIE regarding the Chinatown concession at the Joy Zone, the exposition's entertainment section, were commented on extensively in the local Chinese press. Such accounts have been analyzed in translation.[50] On a secondhand basis, well-known studies like Yong Chen's *Chinese San Francisco* and lesser-known studies, such as Yumei Sun's 1999 dissertation and Erica Y. Z. Pan's monograph on the immediate effect of the 1906 earthquake and fire on Chinatown, employ a wide variety of accounts from local Chinese newspapers, which have been carefully incorporated partly to offset the inevitable bias of English-language sources.[51]

Nonetheless, the situation uncovers a source-based bias. Scholars such as Rey Chow have discussed how the tangible Western academic bias regularly makes itself known through traditions of thought and language used to appropriate non-Western cultures. This academic act of colonialism has also been discussed as a form of academic tourism.[52] Given the often deeply rooted personal connections and the political movement for Asian American civil rights that charged and energized postcolonial and Asian American studies in its initial stages, this is a complicated issue. While such aspects matter a great deal, especially in terms of the multitudinous marginalization of the Chinese in San Francisco, claims of cultural primacy to a history so inherently complex and multivocal as Chinatown's also risk becoming essentialist and historically reductive. In her categorization of scholarly works within the field of Chinese American studies, Sucheng Chan argued that the tangible division in the field was one of the driving forces behind revisionist studies, rather than ethnic polarization between scholars.[53] Although there exists no singular "correct" way to write Chinese American history, Chan's observation reminds us that the development of the field is deeply indebted to the Asian American movement and that its efforts to regain the dignity and respect the Chinese American community has been denied in the past should continue to guide inquiries into the field.

My national perspective (if there is such a thing) is neither Chinese nor Chinese American. From this vantage point, the research and writing of this study were also, in a sense, conducted from the margins. These margins are, of course, significantly different from the ones outlined for the subject of this study, and can be traced in varying access to sources, language thresholds, and academic affiliations rather than in the social, institutional, and historical marginalization that has been the experience of many Chinese Americans.[54] Further, the many different locales and people I encountered during this project have influenced its development greatly; as such, it is transnational in the most literal sense of the word.[55] The notion of transnationality in the field of cinema studies has spawned a plethora of meanings and usages. This study broadly adheres to Miriam Hansen's approach to transnational film history as a way of tracking "which cinemas in different geopolitical locations and constellations engaged with the contradictory experience of modernity." For Hansen, this approach bore the promise of finding "resonances across violent divisions and asymmetrical conditions of wealth and power," but also "the shared concern, on the part of filmmakers and audiences alike, with modern life . . . a concern that included . . . the as yet unrealized promise of a more humane and just society."[56] However, the emergence of transnational perspectives does not necessarily debunk biases and traditional assumptions in Western scholarly views of marginalized cultures. The methodological focus of this book, emphasizing the transcultural contact zones and thirdspaces of San Francisco's turn-of-the-century entertainment culture, heeds calls for decolonization of many of the cultural assumptions on which Western scholarship stand.[57] This structural deprogramming is one for the *longue durée*—a process to which this study can hopefully offer a modest contribution.

## Toward a Chinatown Film History

The era between the nickelodeon boom and the emergence of the feature film has been defined as transitional, not only in terms of the industrial relocation from the commercial centers of the East Coast to the convenience of the West Coast, but also in terms of what Jan Olsson called "the complex web of transformations and negotiations" that pervaded film culture throughout the period.[58] While making inroads into the underinvestigated local film history of San Francisco, this book remains focused on Chinatown. As a consequence, some of the founding figures of early San Francisco film culture, like the Miles brothers, and G. M. "Broncho Billy" Anderson, remain peripheral. Other, lesser-known "players," like Ben Michaels, shoulder more important roles, given their involvement in the emergence of film exhibition in the Chinatown and North Beach area.

Throughout this work, I continually establish and elaborate the links between symbolism employed in marketing strategies in post-quake Chinatown film exhibition and contemporary representations of Chinatown in films. Cinematic representations of Chinatown were plentiful on U.S. screens during the period of study. However, it is not within the scope of this investigation to contribute an exhaustive sweep of Chinatown imagery in transitional era filmmaking. The analysis operates on the fundamental principle that Orientalist stereotypes abound in cinematic imagery of Chinatown and "Chineseness" during the era.[59]

On a related note, while this book continuously grapples with contemporaneous discursive representations of "Chineseness" and how they relate to post-quake San Francisco film exhibition, it does not provide a systematic study of the frequency of such representations on Chinatown movie screens. The research material unearthed tells us a great deal about exhibition practices in Chinatown theaters, but it rarely mentions specific titles of the films on display. Therefore, I have refrained from speculating on the frequency of "Chinatown films" shown in Chinatown theaters, while considering the impact of specific screenings and certain films when such material has been available.

The significant scholarly attention directed toward the place of the audience during cinema's first decades has provided a stepping-stone for this exploration. Earlier cultural histories of film stressed the importance of the working class for the establishment of the film theaters in major U.S. cities.[60] Others argued that middle-class audiences were just as integral in the establishment of the film medium in the United States.[61] Revisionist attempts to recategorize the film audience's place and mobility in localized social settings have led to vigorous debate.[62] One major point of contention has been whether the audience makeup of a particular theater could be determined by the socioeconomic status of the people inhabiting the neighborhood of the theater's location.[63] This otherwise productive and instructive correspondence was unsuccessful in establishing a correlation between divisions of class and ethnicity, or the appearance of movie theaters in certain neighborhoods. To avoid confusion about implied causal relations between demography and moviegoing habits of the population of certain areas of San Francisco, I consider research findings of municipal reports, public surveys and court statements against how such a correlation was *perceived* in local newspapers and the trade press. The ambition is to create an adequate synthesis of "hard data" and "soft accounts" that are representative of the period but that also further the direction of this study.

While indubitably fraught with San Francisco–specific structures of Euro-American hegemony—such as capricious safety regulations, overinflated rates for Chinese renters, and Orientalist imagery visible both on- and off-stage and on screens at theaters—the Chinatown movie theaters were also spaces where many Chinese San Franciscans regularly encountered films presented in a context engineered to satisfy their preferences as an audience. Sometimes this study follows familiar narratives of Orientalist imagery and ethnic polarization; at other times it encounters emerging strategies of resistance to marginalization from Chinese San Franciscans. Most of the time, however, this study of Chinatown post-quake film exhibition offers insights into a set of complex cultural and social processes. As evidenced in the work of Rebecca Solnit, whose creative approaches to the historical-cultural-social geographies of San Francisco often transport the reader to spaces unfit for binary interpretation, these "third" histories deserve attention in their own right.[64]

American studies scholar Ruth Mayer has charted how transmedial representations of Chinatowns could be understood as a complex network interlinking real and imaginary spaces in Western modernity.[65] In an essay from 2011, she argued that spatial representations of Chinatown found in the various incarnations of Sax Rohmer's supervillain, Fu Manchu, can be conceptualized as "complicated and contorted responses to a changing national and urban geography."[66] While taking her examples from source material that deals in the self-perpetuating mythical representations of Chinatowns, Mayer couched her argument in political geographer Edward Soja's concepts of the fragmentary state of the turn-of-the-century urban metropolis.

The analytical directions of both Mayer's and Miriam Hansen's ideas of alternative and unmappable spaces ultimately diverge, and their empirical materials are often on opposing sides of the common cinema studies divide between textual and contextual analyses. However, they arrive at a shared junction, which pertains to notions of urban space and the transnational flows of people and ideas commonly associated with turn-of-the-twentieth-century globalism. For Hansen, the alternative public site offered by the cinema had close ties to Michel Foucault's notion of heterotopia. Foucault discussed heterotopia as contrasting utopia: "real places—places that do exist and that are formed in the very founding of society—which are something like counter-sites."[67] In Hansen's early cinema rendition of the concept she wrote that "the cinema participated in the upheaval of traditional coordinates of space and time, it also offered a refuge in which the violence of the transition could be negotiated in a less threatening, playful, and intersubjective manner."[68]

Hansen continued, "The aesthetics of disjunction not only contested the presumed homogeneity of dominant culture and society in the name of which immigrants were marginalized and alienated, but also lent the experience of disorientation and displacement the objectivity of collective expression. It is in this sense that the notion of the cinema as a heterotopia converges with the concept of an alternative public sphere—as a medium that allows people to organize their experience on the basis of their own context of living, its specific needs, conflicts, and anxieties."[69]

While Hansen's notion focused on screen-audience interactions, the limited archival records describing such interactions offer little information about specific films. The notion of Chinatown film theaters as spaces in which members of marginalized communities could organize their experience of modernity is better understood using the notion of thirdspace, which, rather than focusing on the "violence of transition," emphasized the liminality and the productive potential of the shared experience of moviegoing.[70] The investigation of movie theaters as possible alternative spaces for a particular marginalized audience leads to an exciting intersection where historical film studies crisscross with vectors emerging from the scholarly fields of postcolonial theory, Asian American studies, and critical studies of space.

While various notions of thirdspace have struck a chord within cinema studies, the term has yet to find widespread usage in studies of film history.[71] Most employments understand the term as a strictly mental space. Soja, however, initially attempted a wider framing of the concept, echoing Foucault's notion of heterotopias and Henri Lefebvre's concept of "lived space."[72] Going beyond distinctions of the mental and material, Soja sought to address the "socio-spatial dialectic" of thirdspace, a dimension in which "both mental and material spaces, the real and imagined," interacted.[73] The idea to approach the history of Chinatown with the concept of thirdspace evokes the work of John Kuo Wei Tchen and Dylan Yeats, who cited historical thirdspaces as fruitful entry points to more nuanced understandings of the convoluted history of Chinese America, claiming that the employment of the concept was not to create an opposite truth, but rather "to break with what we imagine we know and believe by finding a third space where differences are understood as gradations rather than starkly as 'us' versus 'them.'"[74] Homi Bhabha touched on similar grounds in his writings on historical moments of cultural difference and the fringe spaces of modernity.[75] Bhabha described his interest in the process of hybridity as not so much to establish from which two "original cultural moments" a new enunciation would emerge, but rather, to investigate the "third space" that enables its emergence: "This third space displaces the histories that constitute it, and sets up new structures of authority, new political initiatives, which are inadequately understood through received wisdom."[76] Bhabha's third space offered "in-between" spaces, which provided "the terrain for elaborating strategies of selfhood—singular or communal—that initiate new signs of identity, and innovative sites of collaboration, and contestation, in the act of defining the idea of society itself."[77] In approaching the shared experiences of moviegoers, this book attempts to locate instances of liminality in San Francisco Chinatown moviegoing and investigate cultural differences as factors in the construction of culture. As such, the notion of thirdspace here might be better understood in tandem with what some scholars have termed "transcultural contact zones."[78]

In the early 1940s, Cuban historian and anthropologist, Fernando Ortiz introduced and developed the notion of transculturation as opposed to the term "acculturation," which implied the "acquisition of culture in a unidirectional process."[79] In his masterwork, *Cuban Counterpoint: Tobacco and Sugar*, Ortiz suggested the notion of transculturation as a way to study the formation of new cultural manifestations, emphasizing both the destruction of cultures and the creativity of cultural unions.[80] In later years, Mary Louise Pratt has elaborated on the various processes of transculturation as taking place in "cultural contact zones," which she describes as "social spaces where disparate cultures meet, clash, and grapple with each other, often in highly asymmetrical relations of domination and subordination—like colonialism, slavery, or their aftermaths as they are lived out across the globe today."[81] The idea of locating the interactional spaces beyond fixed and binary categorizations of cultural identity echoes Edward Said, who in *Culture and Imperialism* issued a plea to study cultures "contrapuntally."[82] In light of Pratt's work, Sebastian Jobs and Gesa Mackenthun offered a further definition of the transcultural contact zone as where "people living in in-between cultures constantly having to juggle their lives between different cultural codes could shape the character of these contact zones in carving out a space of agency that is also potentially a site of change."[83] For this study, the notions of transculturation and contact zones offer productive approaches to investigate local and regional offspring of dominant and residual cultures from decentralized points of view. The aim is to acknowledge and go beyond these fixed perceptions in order to, paraphrasing Fernando Coronil, treat "binary oppositions not as fixities, but as hybrid and productive," reflecting their transcultural formation and their transitional value in the flow of transnational film history.[84]

To conclude, this study's approach to the in-between and cultural borderlands space of post-quake Chinatown does not set out to identify some hidden or "alternative" state of fixed identification. Rather, the notions of thirdspaces, contact zones, and alternative public spheres are mobilized to understand cultural phenomena in which the negotiation of the perceived cultural differences in San Francisco's Chinatown entered areas and situations that are not adequately described by using the common binaries set up by notions of "Orientalism," "ethnic polarization," "anti-Chinese forces," or "Chinese American resistance." While most of the fragmentary glimpses into Chinatown film culture assembled and analyzed for this study could be described by using one or several of these terms, many of them also tell stories about a more complex cultural landscape, in which cultural differences played a central role in everyday life.

For such an openness to emerge, it is the place of the historian to function as a bricoleur and facilitator to locate, or *salvage*, a perspective that, in the words of James Hay, re-emphasizes the "*site* of film practice as a spatial issue or *problematic*."[85] Tchen and Yeats commented that such a break "is necessary both to debunk the Western colonial tradition and also to demonstrate that once decolonized, it is a varied history full of alternative pasts, presents, and futures that can engage with different cultures, traditions, and visions."[86] This book aims to make a microhistorical contribution to this intellectual direction.

## Structure of This Book

Given the lack of previous scholarly coordinates and points of reference regarding the subject matter at hand, I have divided the book into three parts, each of which corresponds to a thematic approach. While some research material might reappear in different parts of the book, it does so from different points of view. Therefore, one exhibitor's activities on Broadway might be analyzed in light of a post-quake San Francisco legislator's approach to film in part I, only to reappear as an example of pandering to Chinese American audiences in part III. As such, the parts and their thematic approaches are particular and interrelated at the same time. The general idea is to present the reader with a detailed and careful view, without having to chop the tree down and separate the roots from the limbs.

In the absence of previous exhaustive investigations of the emergence of film exhibition in San Francisco, part I outlines a tentative history of early film culture in the city, from the first cinematic experiments and the medium's public breakthrough in the city, to the important and contested role cinema came to play after the earthquake and fire. Before Hollywood, San Francisco was California's hub of public amusement. Performers and exhibitors traveled from the East and the West to try their luck in a cosmopolitan entertainment culture that ranged from highbrow to infamously seedy. The first chapter, titled "Bold Visions and Frontier Conditions," shows how moving pictures at first played a supporting role in this multifaceted operetta. But the 1906 earthquake and fire destroyed many of the city's most famous establishments and created a void in the live entertainment output. The ruination and displacement of theaters, producers, and performers coincided with a nationwide proliferation of cheap movie theaters. As the city began to rise, the nickelodeon craze arrived. The availability and affordability of film exhibition soon made moviegoing San Francisco's most popular form of amusement. Movie houses began popping up all over the area, from the downtown entertainment center of Market Street to neighborhood theaters in the Mission District, the Fillmore District, and in Chinatown. The broad public interest in movies, in turn, quickly generated a business climate pervaded by equal measures of bold opportunism and innovation. Drawing on a wide range of archival materials, this chapter provides a rudimentary cartography of some of the key coordinates in this landscape.

Chapter 2, titled "'If I Had the Power to Do So I Would Destroy Them with My Own Hands,'" after an incendiary proclamation by a San Francisco minister, investigates the interaction between the public, politicians, and film exhibitors at the height of the Progressive Era. By concentrating on the operation and strategies of two key figures, San Francisco mayor James "Sunny Jim" Rolph, and a young theater impresario Sid Grauman, this chapter shows how film exhibition became the focal point of local policies of public reform, social improvement, and cultural uplift, conceived of in tandem with the anticipation of, and formulated in preparation for, the PPIE—widely seen as the new and improved city's reopening to the world. Both Rolph and Grauman would go on to achieve great historical stature, and both were instrumental in how local film culture became closely connected to new and residual notions of the city's dangerous spaces, where Chinatown loomed large in the background.

Building on the foundational understanding of San Francisco and its film culture around the turn of the century, we take the streetcar from bustle of Market Street, along Kearney, up to Chinatown. Part II approaches Chinatown film culture by investigating the appearance of film exhibition and movie theaters in the neighborhood. Its first chapter, "'The Most Cosmopolitan City in the World,'" contextualizes Chinatown in San Francisco through a historiographical and geospatial orientation. At the heart of this chapter is the contradiction between the importance of the transpacific Chinese influence to the city of San Francisco and the systematic marginalization of the city's Chinese inhabitants. This set of contradictions runs like a thread throughout the history of the city's development from a Spanish missionary hamlet to the modern outpost of the American West. As Chinese Americans were gradually excluded from participation in U.S. society, they created strategies of survival, ranging from community organization and resistance to systemic oppression, to aspects of everyday life, such as shopping and going out. While the Chinese American community anchored many social and cultural activities in the traditions of the homeland, these activities were also appropriated to fit the local circumstances of diasporic living. As outside voices increasingly described Chinatown as an unwanted and dangerous foreign colony, the neighborhood was simultaneously a tourist attraction for the middle class. These contradictions and strategies serve as a critical foundation to understand the infrastructure of Chinese San Francisco and its people around the time when cinema became a popular public amusement in that city.

Chapter 4, titled "'Eyes Darting Around, Spirit Dashing About,'" after a line in a contemporary poem by an unknown Chinese San Franciscan, charts the emergence of movie theaters, film exhibits, and cinematic spectatorship in

Chinatown and North Beach in the period between 1906 and 1915. Drawing on a wide variety of accounts of moviegoing and exhibition practices, it maps the location and operation of each theater individually, but also consider the internal dynamics and relations between the theaters. Issues of placement, competition, ownership, and funding are investigated in relation to audience demography and changing regulations on public safety and health concerns. While these theaters were the first to make film exhibition available and accessible to Chinatown, they were preceded by a rich history of local public amusements hinging on the circulation of actors, plays, and cultural traditions across the Pacific, such as the Chinese theater and opera. This historical context provides a spatially grounded perspective to explore the patterns and idiosyncrasies of Chinatown film culture, its relation to contemporary U.S. film exhibition, but also its connection to transpacific cultural exchange.

As the revolutionary winds blowing across the Pacific and the project to rebuild imbued Chinatown with a renewed sense of nationalism and local pride, other aspects of the newly constructed neighborhood reinforced its public image as an exotic foreign colony, closely aligned with notions of Chinatown as one of San Francisco's main tourist attractions. Although the rejuvenation of Chinatown was built by and paid for by local and overseas investors, the visual appearance of the neighborhood was primarily designed by non-Chinese architects. Chapter 5 investigates how such aspects were mirrored in local film culture, as theaters and exhibitors routinely employed manifestations of Orientalism as a marketing strategy. I approach this local manifestation through the notion of the "Chinesque aesthetic," a description borrowed from a contemporary architect commenting on Chinatown's new appearance to address how post-quake Chinatown film culture encompassed a locally specific brand of Orientalism. The notion of the Chinesque aesthetic, which also lends its name to the title of this chapter, returns us to Sid Grauman, one of the main propagators of this aesthetic in the post-quake era. A case study of the various displays of "Chineseness" at PPIE locates a juncture in the parallel operation of these seemingly contradictory cultural vectors, as an emerging Chinese American resistance began to openly contest such public displays of the Orientalist Chinatown underworld fantasy.

Part III shifts the focus from exhibitors and movie theaters to their functions in the Chinese San Franciscan community. From here, I explore multiple dimensions of what Chinatown film culture meant to Chinese American audiences: as a physical space for film experiences, as a symbol of Chinatown's modernization, as an emblem of Chinatown vice, and as a manifestation of U.S. Orientalism. Chapter 6, titled "'Where the People Aren't All American,'" after the writings of young Italian American author Adriana Spadoni, looks closely at how these dimensions manifested in the design, operation, marketing strategies, and social space of the Chinatown and North Beach movie theaters.

It investigates how Chinese San Franciscans became the theaters' key audience group, sought out by non-Chinese exhibitors. By creating a place-specific film culture, shaped to the customs and tastes of Chinatown audiences, the post-quake movie theaters afforded the Chinatown community an exceptional site for Chinese American appropriation of film culture. Albeit propelled primarily by business competition and local efforts of cultural translation and interpretation, the Chinatown and North Beach entertainment scene created urban sites of transcultural exchange and hybridity that were available to and inclusive of Chinese Americans like no other place in the city or the country.

Chapter 7, "Chinatown Modernity," approaches Chinatown film culture and audiences through the prism of a Chinese diaspora undergoing a fundamental transformation, closely tied to the ongoing societal shifts spurred on by the Xinhai Revolution on the Chinese mainland. The rapid rebuilding of the "new Chinatown" coincided with political developments in China, as well as with the coming of age of second and third generations of Chinese immigrants, many of whom had grown up in exclusionist-era San Francisco. Chinatown film culture and movie theaters here appear as contested sites of modernity—a material and symbolic battleground for conflicting attitudes and perceptions of a generational chasm within the community. The investigation of political rallies and importation of documentary-style films showing images of the ongoing revolution in China also considers instances when local movie theaters and films functioned as communal spaces beyond the individual screen-spectator or business-consumer interaction.

The concluding chapter engages with the trajectories and implications that emerge from this study. By locating the thirdspaces of local film exhibition and how they entangled the film medium with Chinese American modernity and the Chinesque aesthetic, it points out how post-quake Chinatown film culture contained competing visions for the place of Chinese Americans in U.S. society. While the Orientalist imaginary of Chinatown would move on to new, powerful realizations mediated by the stereotyping machinery of Classical Hollywood cinema, the political awakening and local resistance to anti-Chinese sentiments fortified its transpacific connections to movements of similar ambition in China. The discussion also highlights how the notion of Chinatown modernity challenges historical assumptions of modernity as an inherently Western cultural and social force.

Finally, this is a study that continually deals with accounts of historical contradiction. Some of these enunciations are loud, racist, and unsophisticated, whereas others are multivocal, transcultural, and complex. Some of them speak of an environment that functioned as repositories for Orientalist stereotypes that produced and even exported new Yellow Perilist sentiments. Some formulate a Chinatown film culture that provided Chinese San Franciscans both material and perceptual sites to experience, affect, and claim ownership of the film medium. Other voices speak of hybridity and transculturation, rooted in the cosmopolitan locality of early twentieth-century San Francisco. This book is an attempt to collate these parallel articulations as locally coexisting social and cultural processes. As such, Chinatown film culture, as it appears here, goes beyond standardized historical imagery and tells a story alternative to and transgressive of established narratives of U.S. film history.

# Part I

# Early Film in San Francisco

# 1

# Bold Visions and Frontier Conditions

## The Emergence of Film in San Francisco

Historical scholarship on the early film culture in San Francisco is, lamentably, scarce. Geoffrey Bell's *The Golden Gate and the Silver Screen*, published in 1984, provided a historical introduction to film production in the Bay Area.[1] Jack Tillmany's mapping of San Francisco movie theaters focuses on developments of neighborhoods and cinema architecture from a century-long perspective.[2] Although significant in their own right, these studies provide us with little insight into local film culture during the nickelodeon boom and the transitional era. Therefore, the first part of this book provides a discursive mapping of San Francisco moving image culture between the years 1879 and 1917. The first period, between 1879 and 1906, will be awarded less consideration than the second, from after the earthquake and fire up until late 1917.

The two chapters in part I are bound by two seminal events that "happened" to the city in the early twentieth century: the 1906 earthquake and fire and the 1915 Panama-Pacific International Exposition (PPIE). San Francisco historians, such as Gray Brechin and Sarah J. Moore, have foregrounded the razing and rebuilding of the city as essential to the experience of modernity.[3] The destruction was vast and devastating, but it also offered an unprecedented opportunity to rebuild the city virtually from scratch. While many of the ideas of raising a Paris of the West from the ruins of old San Francisco eventually proved too impractical, the spirit of renewal and sophistication resided in visions of the city throughout the early 1910s. For the modern vision of San Francisco, the earthquake provided a distinct point of departure, while the PPIE offered a rare and eventually tangible horizon for modern life. These two events, more than any other, conditioned the development of film culture in San Francisco during the nickelodeon and transitional eras.

While part I provides an unprecedented exploration of the emergence of cinema in San Francisco, the chapters are both written to inform the investigation of Chinatown that follows. In other words, this account of San Francisco film culture slants toward Chinatown. The focus makes the historical hierarchization of people and places of exhibition appear different than would a more holistic account of the city's early film culture. As a consequence, figures of established importance to U.S. film history, like Eugene Roth, the Miles Brothers, and Gilbert "Broncho Billy" Anderson, are not given extensive consideration beyond a mere mention, since their involvement in Chinatown film history was negligible. Some well-known characters of the early film industry, like Sid Grauman, are cast in a different light, given their considerable involvement in the Chinatown exhibition scene. It is also necessary to bring people previously obscure in U.S. film history to the forefront, given their prominence in the Chinatown film scene. Because this chapter focuses on the importance of these people's respective involvement in the San Francisco film scene at large, it does not discuss Chinatown and the adjacent North Beach area in depth. Instead, these two areas function as a destination toward which we detour, through the city, in space and time.

Before we consider the first decades of film culture in San Francisco, it may be useful to revisit the notion of "film culture" briefly. The employment of the term is to enable a perspective on film history that includes consideration of film exhibition, distribution, and production and how they functioned in local contexts and public discourses. These interrelated strands are commonly referred to in U.S. film history as the three areas of control and power interest during the establishment of the U.S. film industry on the West Coast in the 1910s. This chapter considers how these three intertwined strands of film industry connect to the local setting of San Francisco in general, and Chinatown in particular, during a period of significant upheaval.

Finally, in studies on early film culture, the experience of modernity in the late nineteenth and early twentieth centuries is intrinsically linked to the technological and perceptual developments of cinema in the early 1900s.[4] This link runs like a current through these chapters' cartographic endeavor to locate movies against the dynamism of modern post-quake city life. By investigating a range of institutions that continually shaped the flux of film culture, from the meeting rooms of city planners to the street corners of nighttime entertainment, I seek answers to a set of fundamental questions about the emergence of cinema in San Francisco. How did the grand visions of the post-quake city impact the development of film culture? Why were some theaters more popular than others? Why were some theaters visited more frequently on a weekday, and where did people go on the weekend, and why? For whom was going to the movies a recurring part of the daily routine, and for whom was it an unusual event? Let us begin.

## Pre-quake Film Culture

Although Los Angeles holds the central position as the transformative power of U.S. film history, the history of film culture in San Francisco predates that of its southern cousin to a considerable degree. While the invention and first public exhibitions of film are most commonly dated to around 1895, a historicization of San Francisco's film culture has to take into account the photographic experiments of Eadweard Muybridge in the late 1870s, conducted under the auspices of San Francisco tycoon Leland Stanford. Muybridge made his most famous efforts to capture and reproduce real-life movement on photographic plates in the Palo Alto area, today recognized as the fountainhead of technological development in the twenty-first century. Muybridge's revolutionary inventions made it possible to study real-life movement in a progressive state of arrest. Albeit not the first invention that anticipated the coming of the film medium, it was one of the most conspicuous. In the words of Rebecca Solnit, it was as though Muybridge "had grasped time, made it stand still, and then made it run again, over and over."[5] The now iconic strip of images of a horse midstride made its public debut at the San Francisco Art Association in 1880, on Pine Street, just a couple of blocks away from Chinatown. Up until the 1906 disaster, San Francisco's main entertainment area started around Chinatown's Portsmouth Square and ran with the streetcar along Kearny Street, all the way down to Market Street. It was at the junction of these two streets that the first public showing of film occurred some fifteen years later.

In 1894, Peter Bacigalupi, a phonograph salesman and penny arcade proprietor, bought five Edison kinetoscopes from the Holland Brothers for $2,500.[6] San Francisco–born Bacigalupi had spent the past decade building a small entertainment emporium in Peru. In the early 1890s, he was involved in several scandals, among them the death of the young wife of a well-known San Francisco steamship captain.[7] The events forced him to leave South America and go back to his native city. Upon his return, Bacigalupi went back into the entertainment business. He set up a storefront operation in the *San Francisco Chronicle* building on the corner of Market and Kearny Streets. From there, he continued with entertainment parlors on Market and Stockton Streets and in the old Bella Union Theater on Kearny, on the border between the Barbary Coast and Chinatown. While Bacigalupi briefly attempted to expand his business to Los Angeles, San Francisco remained his home base.[8] The headquarters of this little emporium lay on Mission Street, between Third and Fourth Streets.[9]

Although others had taken over the torch from Muybridge, the city still remembered his remarkable moving pictures. With the coming of Edison's kinetoscope, the *Chronicle* evoked Muybridge's exhibit at the Art Association: "The invention will be greatly developed, and it is not impossible that it will prove an invaluable aid to chemists, who, with its assistance, can watch processes too rapid for the human eye to note."[10] News about the novel and improved variety of moving pictures traveled quickly, and soon people lined up outside to pay ten cents to catch a glimpse of the visual wonder.[11]

In 1897, Adolphus W. Furst, a middle-aged former auctioneer, opened a motion picture theater on Market Street, across from the east end of Grant Avenue.[12] Furst named the place after its Lubin Cineograph, a combined camera/projector. During the next few years, the Cineograph became a staple in San Francisco's nightlife.[13] Historians regard Furst's movie house as one of the first in the whole nation to show films exclusively.[14] According to an article in the *Moving Picture World*, the two-story building started as a vaudeville and moving picture theater. Films were shown on the ground floor, where there was no seating. Tickets for the stage show and the films were sold separately, the five-cent price of admission for films being the cheaper. After some time, Furst scrapped the vaudeville, and the theater continued as a film-only establishment.[15] Just like Bacigalupi's entertainment parlor, Furst's moving-picture theater attracted spectators from all over the San Francisco area, most of them drawn to the novelty of the medium.[16] In 1902, Furst branched out and opened another Cineograph theater in Los Angeles, before moving there permanently in 1906.[17]

In 1898, former vaudeville actor David "D.J." Grauman and his son, Sid, opened the Unique Theater on Market Street, close to the corner of Mason Street. The young Grauman was inspired to work in moving pictures after working as a janitor at Furst's theater for a time.[18] According to Grauman's biographer Charles Beardsley, the building in which the family business started was known as the Hoodoo Store, "because everybody who set up there had bad luck."[19] However, the luck was turning for the Graumans, whose initial business model was to buy and screen foreign films from companies like Pathé and Gaumont, distributed by Bacigalupi, among others. D. J. Grauman, in an interview with *Moving Picture World*, recalled that Edison's material was of low quality compared with the foreign films. He also related that the greatest pre-quake sensation at the Unique Theater had been Georges Méliès's film *A Trip to the Moon*.[20] The Graumans soon opened another theater, the Lyceum, on 310 O'Farrell. Both theaters ran vaudeville and films, using a Bioscope projector. Despite Beardsley's claim that the Graumans' theater was an instant and long-lasting success, local newspaper reports on the family's pre-quake dealings suggest that the initial years included considerable struggles and that D. J. Grauman had to make a financial settlement with another local showman as late as January 30, 1906, in order not to lose the Unique Theater.[21]

The year 1902 was when America's first film exchange came into existence, originated by three brothers from Cincinnati, Ohio, with the family name of Miles. The Miles Brothers' road to San Francisco film culture took a long, but not uncommon, detour through Alaska, where they shot films of the gold rush in 1900. It was Harry, the eldest, who came up with the idea of the film exchange as a way of maximizing the profits for screenings of their films. He started renting out films to the local vaudeville houses from a storefront located in the Tenderloin neighborhood, on 116 Turk Street, conveniently located just a block away from Market Street.

Although initially conceived as a strategy to get the most out of the local film circuit, the Miles Brothers' exchange system—which rented rather than sold film copies—provided an early model for what would become the nationwide practice of how to distribute and screen film. According to Charles Musser, the gradual transformation from sales to rentals was one of the fundamental elements of the U.S. film industry between the years 1903 and 1904, as "the separation of distribution from exhibition and the treatment of a reel of film as a standardized interchangeable commodity had commercially revolutionary implications for the film business."[22] In late 1903, the Miles Brothers opened an office across the street from the Biograph Company in New York City. The film exchange started selling old Biograph reels at a bargain price to its out-of-town business contacts, many of them located back home in California. Around the same time, the Percival Waters' Kinetograph Company started renting film reels to Boston theaters.[23] National film distribution was taking off. Richard Abel has noted that within a matter of months "ads for selling agents and rental exchanges suddenly appeared."[24] The proverbial snowball was in motion.

In 1905, the Miles Brothers expanded their San Francisco business concerns to operate amusement parks and nickelodeons. Soon they moved to a larger space, including a big studio and one of the most technologically advanced film laboratories in the country.[25] The Miles Brothers were doing very well and advertised their transcontinental film exchange service—operating from both sides of the United States—in elaborate style in *Billboard* and *New York Clipper*.[26] Their former manager James Sciaroni later reminisced in *Moving Picture World* about this period: "At one time San Francisco was quite a distributing center for films, shipments being made as far as New Orleans and Chicago."[27]

FIG. 1 Advertisement for the Miles Brothers film exchange. *Billboard*, August 8, 1905, 48. (Image courtesy of Proquest Historical Newspapers)

The same year, Pathé announced the Miles Brothers as the exclusive West Coast selling agents for their popular films.[28] In early 1906, the Miles Brothers took out an advertisement in *Billboard* that commented on the rising popularity of films, especially in the vaudeville theaters where, they claimed, films had been screened after the last performance as an exit cue for audiences.[29] This change was attributed to a better quality of films produced by a better quality of people. The advertisement read, "What a change has come over the Moving Picture Turn in Vaudeville and everywhere. Three or four years ago, when the Moving Pictures came on in the Vaudeville Theatres, you would see over half the audience would put on their wraps and take their departure. Notice the present day Vaudeville audience. They all stay now until the last 'Good Night' slide is thrown. The answer is easy. Some of the best brains of the country are now devoted to turning out the finest things in Moving Pictures."[30]

During the year of the earthquake, the Miles Brothers' business was the only one listed under "Moving Pictures" in the *Crocker-Langley* directory.[31] While the Miles Brothers, Bacigalupi, and the Graumans were not the only San Franciscans trying to make a profit from the popularity of moving pictures, the city was slow to catch on to the "nickelodeon boom" that was taking place in the eastern United States in 1905.[32] According to Sciaroni, "Vaudeville and moving pictures seemed to have started here first and spread to the east, but the Nickelodeon idea originated there and came to the coast later."[33] Other than Bacigalupi, the Edison Company regularly sent kinetoscope films to two other local companies: Bullard & Breck, on Post Street, and the Novelty Motion Picture Company, on Market Street.[34] Moving pictures were shown in some live theaters, such as the Central on Market Street, the Orpheum on O'Farrell Street, and the California on Bush Street.[35] All of them were easily accessible from the Market and Kearny Street streetcars. While the Orpheum was an example of a more upscale vaudeville theater using films in their repertoire, the California's main output was risqué vaudeville acts and burlesques, complemented by motion picture crime dramas, such as Biograph's *River Pirates* (G. W. Bitzer, 1905).[36] William L. Wright and Gustave Walter's Animatoscope had been an attraction at the Chutes Amusement Park since 1902.[37] Exhibitors also incorporated films with stereopticon views for educational purposes, given at the Academy of Sciences Hall on Market Street and the Metropolitan Hall on Fifth Street.[38] Similar multimedia lectures were staged in churches, like the Simpson Memorial Church.[39]

## Early Films of San Francisco and Chinatown

Films showing the city of San Francisco and its surroundings before the earthquake and fire were few. A small amount of film material had been shot in San Francisco by traveling cameramen like James White and Frederick Blechynden (Edison) and Raymond Ackerman (American Mutoscope and Biograph Company).[40] These short films showed views of San Francisco's places of touristic appeal, like Ocean Beach and Chinatown.[41] Perhaps the first documentary-style film of the neighborhood was *Parade of Chinese*. Edison cameraman James White shot the film in 1898 during the Golden Jubilee, a fiftieth anniversary of the California gold rush. San Francisco was White's first stop on a tour to film life in East Asia. The parade gave White an opportunity to capture an exotic glimpse of the Chinese in America before his departure. However, the film does not account for the violence and racial abuse the participating Chinatowners endured during the parade. Film historian John Haddad wrote in an essay on the history of representations of Chinese in U.S. film history: "After receiving the go-ahead to march, the Chinese found themselves confronted by a 'crowd of toughs' intent on destroying all their floats and banners. The Chinese fought back, however, and with the help of the police managed to save their costumes, banners, and musical instruments to march in the parade as planned."[42] Another film of note that survives from the period is *Chinese Funeral* (1903). This forty-two-foot fragment has been preserved at the Library of Congress and shows a view of the funeral procession of Tom Kim Yung, shot from a balcony on the corner of Clay and Dupont. Like *Parade of Chinese*, the film most likely appeared to most audiences as a curiosity, showing the elaborate procession in one of America's ethnic enclaves. Similar to James White's ethnographic short, the camera did not register the grim circumstances surrounding the event. Tom Kim Yung, a military attaché of the Chinese legation in the United States and an imperial bodyguard, committed suicide after having been arrested and humiliated by members of the Chinatown Squad.[43] The policemen were initially put on trial but were later exonerated.[44] Another film shot in the Chinese neighborhood was *Scene in Chinatown* (American Mutoscope and Biograph, 1903), which showed a view of a Chinatown street policed by members of the Chinatown Squad.[45] These few early films of San Francisco Chinatown showcased the neighborhood as a novelty and served to complement and illustrate contemporary newspaper reporting about the area as a place replete with crime and cultural oddities. While Chinatown scenes were a common feature in turn-of-the-century tableau-film views of San Francisco, it seems the point of view was always that of the outsider looking in.

The most famous surviving footage of pre-quake San Francisco film culture was captured just months before the earthquake and fire. In March 1906, the *Call* reported that the Miles Brothers had asked the United Railroads for permission to mount a camera on a Market Street streetcar. The vision was to display San Francisco's main thoroughfare in full action on film. The industrious brothers made the case that the few moving pictures presently on exhibit that showed the city of San Francisco were mostly of Chinatown and the North Beach Italian area. In the Miles Brothers' local patriotic view, Market Street was "one of the greatest streets in the world, and they propose to have the world learn of its magnificence."[46] Attempts had already been made to film Market Street from an automobile, but the vibrations of the car made the films blurry. Within days, the camera was mounted and rolling on the streetcar.[47] Today, *A Trip Down Market Street* is one of the only surviving artifacts showing the hustle and bustle of Market Street before the earthquake.

In general, the pre-quake film culture in San Francisco was determined by a few entrepreneurial individuals, like the Miles Brothers, the Graumans, and Peter Bacigalupi, who exhibited film as a novelty and supplement to existing and more well-established forms of entertainment. The general view of films as a novelty also played a role. Although the Miles Brothers' company was well integrated into the emerging national film industry, film exhibition was still limited to sideshow status in San Francisco. Between Bacigalupi's introduction of the kinetoscope and the earthquake, there had been but a few theaters showing films. In early April 1906, the dominant mode of exhibition was still vaudeville and moving pictures. At this time film exhibition centered on the downtown area, with Market Street and Kearny Street as the "hot spots." After its rehabilitation, Market Street would emerge as the "Great White Way": the around-the-clock, pulsating heart of San Francisco film exhibition for the following fifty years.[48] However, this status would not remain uncontested.

## Earthquake and Aftermath

In the spring of 1906, film exhibition had been around in San Francisco for more than a decade. Yet it was only just before the earthquake and fire that business had picked up the pace and started to attract serious public attention. Therefore, the losses suffered from the disaster were limited in comparison to those experienced by more established businesses. The downtown area was hardest hit by the earthquake and fire. Jack London provided an eyewitness account of the devastation for *Collier's*: "The earthquake shook down in San Francisco hundreds of thousands worth of walls and chimneys. But the conflagration that followed burned up hundreds of millions of dollars' worth of property."[49]

The fires began to spread immediately after the earthquake on the morning of Wednesday, April 18, 1906. The flames were not contained until Friday the twentieth. At that point, they had destroyed Bacigalupi's office and the penny arcade at the old Bella Union. The Miles Brothers' new studio and exchange office were in ruins. The Graumans' Unique Theater was gone, along with the Market Street vaudeville theaters that had shown films. Furst's Cineograph and another Market Street theater close to Fifth Street were the city's only exclusive movie houses at the time of the earthquake. The flames took them both. The natural disaster dealt a devastating blow to San Francisco—and its entertainment scene was one of its biggest sufferers. These terrible circumstances made its speedy recovery all the more remarkable.

The Miles Brothers quickly got back on their feet. On May 5, the same day as *Collier's* published Jack London's story, they took out a large advertisement in *Billboard* that proclaimed in large print that their concern was "slightly bent but never broke." To capitalize on their streetcar film and the historical change in the cityscape of San Francisco that had occurred just days after filming, they now marketed the film as "the only pictures of any value ever made in San Francisco." The full 830-foot film—of which the Library of Congress has restored about thirty seconds—showed City Hall, the Palace Hotel, and offices of the

*Call*, *Chronicle*, and *Examiner*, all destroyed in the catastrophe. The only original in existence, they informed, had left the city on the night of the earthquake. Orders for the film was directed to the New York office, while the western operation had temporarily relocated to Oakland.[50]

After the earthquake, the Miles Brothers moved into a commercial space on Mission Street between Seventh and Eighth Streets, which formed the base for their San Francisco operations for the remainder of the decade.[51] While Harry's efforts remained concentrated on the Bay Area, Herbert Miles soon became manager of Laemmle, Kessel and Baumann's Motion Picture Distributing and Sales Company (Sales). In 1910, Herbert left Sales to found the short-lived Republic Film Company.[52] In the summer of 1915, *Moving Picture World* published an issue dedicated entirely to the development of the film industry on the West Coast, celebrating the Miles Brothers as pioneers of the U.S. film business.[53]

Following the fire, the Graumans reopened their business with a temporary movie theater tent in the Fillmore District. However, they were soon back on Market Street with a bigger venue than before.[54] Around the same time, another family business rose in the ranks of San Francisco film exhibition. Prussian immigrant Lesser Lesser opened the Union Nickelodeon in the Mission District. Shortly after that, his oldest son, Sol, joined his father, and together they opened a film exchange.[55] The Lessers quickly gained a significant foothold in the San Francisco film business and used the city as their base of operations until they moved their business to Los Angeles in the late 1910s.[56]

But not everyone found the way back into moving pictures. Bacigalupi lost his Edison contract and went back to focus on phonographs. Furst chose to relocate entirely to Los Angeles. The theaters and film houses on Market Street and most of the larger downtown area were gone. The earthquake had further delayed the nickelodeon boom in San Francisco. Rather, the nickelodeons arrived during the second half of 1906 in a succession of smaller bangs. As the reconstruction of the city center began in the early summer of 1906, the emerging film culture of San Francisco found new homes in other areas of the city.

## Post-quake Nickelodeon Proliferation

In 1916, Thomas A. Church, *Moving Picture World*'s designated San Francisco correspondent, reported on the development of post-quake and post-fire San Francisco film exhibition. He noted that while widespread damage to the city in 1906 did not completely quell the emergence of San Francisco's film culture, it seriously conditioned its development.[57] To investigate how this postulated "conditioning" played out in the post-quake development of local film exhibition, I begin by providing some data on the establishment of movie theaters. Although consistent information on the growth of San Francisco post-quake film exhibition is hard to secure, by studying yearly municipal reports, we can create a general outline. This outline, in turn, helps us produce a graph that comes close to the numbers disclosed in a pioneering study of San Francisco film exhibition published by the Commonwealth Club of California in 1913. By comparing the numbers of film theaters extracted from municipal reports with those provided in the Commonwealth Club report, we can establish an outline of the growth of San Francisco film exhibition. More than providing a numerical model of moviegoing in San Francisco, the Commonwealth Club of California's conclusions that film houses often became spaces that fostered indecent behavior across all age categories are approached in the context of contemporary public discussions of the debasing qualities of moviegoing across the nation. This public debate, containing locally pronounced counterviews, particularly pertains to the following investigation of film culture in Chinatown.

The graph should be approached with an error margin of plus or minus five theaters, keeping in mind that in all likelihood there were more rather than fewer actual places of exhibition. In general, the reader should view the graph as an indication of the growth of establishments that showed moving pictures in San Francisco between the years 1907 and 1917. The concurrence in numbers between the municipal data and the Commonwealth Club report lends validity to the figures presented here on the growth of places showing film following 1912. The years 1909–1910 saw the most dramatic rise in licensed establishments, partly as a result of the anomalous plummet in 1908. In the fiscal year 1910, the total number of licensed exhibition venues was 51. By 1911, the number had grown to 60.[58] The steady rise would continue until 1917, with a dip in 1915–1916.

The municipal reports show a more considerable fluctuation in the number of venues opening and closing. Between June 30, 1907, and June 30, 1908, the chief of police had granted 38 new licenses.[59] In 1909, as many as 34 venues had "retired from business," while the city supervisors had issued 28 new permits.[60] The term "retired from business" used in the reports leads to some confusion. It does not indicate whether the shutdown of theaters was due to poor economy or violation of the city's regulations. Although San Francisco was one of the biggest and most important cities on the West Coast, the annual transactions in film permits at first glance seem relatively high. However, research on nickelodeons in other cities during the period shows a similar tendency in terms of the volatility of the film business. As Ben Singer wrote about Manhattan: "Scores of exhibitors went out of business every year, while at the same time dozens of others ventured into the game. The nickelodeon business was in a state of constant upheaval during these years [1907–1910]."[61] Another locally common issue was that as theaters moved between temporary locations, they needed a new license for each new location.

In 1910, only 8 venues canceled their operations, against the issuance of 27 licenses.[62] In 1911, another 27 new permits were granted, while 18 licenses were

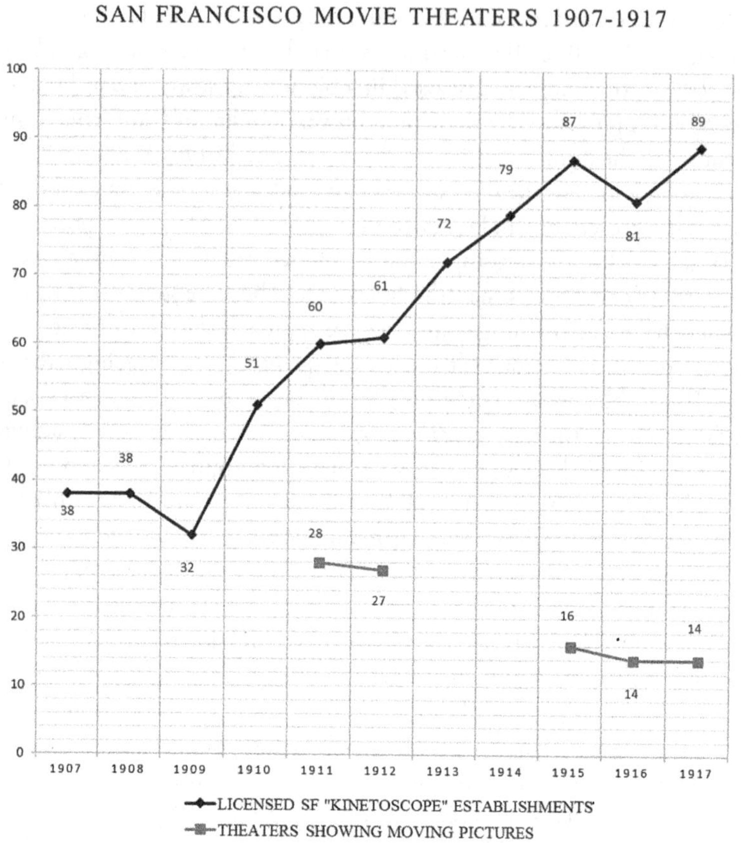


FIG. 2 Aggregated data on movie theaters from San Francisco municipal reports published between 1907 and 1917.

retired.[63] In 1912, the total numbers remained almost intact, with 18 new permits and 17 venues going out of business.[64] The reports are missing detailed numbers on the transactions of permits from 1913 to 1915, but they do provide numbers for the total number of theaters. In 1916, there were 21 new permits for film exhibition, while 27 venues were reported to have closed down.[65] The following year (1917), only 8 new permits were issued, while 7 venues were reportedly going out of business.[66]

Judging by these numbers, the film exhibition business stabilized somewhat toward the end of the 1910s, as fewer theaters were forced to close or relocate. From 1914 to 1917, the number of theaters did not fluctuate by more than 10 establishments. During the first years of the 1910s, many "film only" theaters in San Francisco were rebuilt and expanded to accommodate the acquired tastes of moviegoers, while the number of theaters that showed film as part of a more extensive repertoire was reduced by 50 percent between 1911 and 1917.

## New Exhibition

Among the essential conditions for the re-establishment of commerce in the city was the emergence of three important business districts in contrast to a single one, as in most cities. This sprawl, in turn, produced a wider variety of areas where film theaters could operate with success. The downtown district was the most important, with Market Street as its shining centerpiece. However, the augmenting industry of the Fillmore and Mission Districts provided fertile grounds for film exhibition in the ten years that followed the disaster.[67] In 1911, C. L. Mosely wrote for *Moving Picture World* that the "innate desire to be amused when not at work" was particularly strong in San Francisco, which was clear from viewing the town's entertainment offerings. He noted that all three districts had an equally high concentration of film houses.[68] To better understand the dynamics of these districts, I will provide an overview of their demographic characteristics, their most important movie houses, and the people who ran them.

The large Mission District is historically known as San Francisco's Latino neighborhood, dating back to the founding of the Misión San Francisco de Asis in 1776.[69] Before the Spanish settlers arrived, the area was inhabited by the Ohlone people, who took advantage of the valley's fortunate location, sheltered from the Pacific Ocean and with proximity to the natural riches of the San Francisco Bay.[70] Approximately one square mile in size, the district is bordered by Market and Division Streets on the north and Army Street (today Cesar Chavez Avenue) on the South. The Mission, like the Fillmore, was partially spared from the tremors and flames in the spring of 1906. In the summer, the growth started with many businesses relocating from the ruined downtown area. The northeast area, also known as the Inner Mission, was particularly bustling.

Shortly after the earthquake, Mission Street nickelodeons in the vicinity of Twenty-Second Street, such as the Peoples Theater, the Grand, and the Sherman Theater, rose to popularity along with the heightened industry of the Inner Mission. These were all smaller houses with seating capacities ranging between 300 and 700. The Victoria, which seated 800 and was located in the north end of the district, had been showing films regularly a few months after the earthquake.[71] At 2555 Mission Street, the Wigwam Theatre opened in 1907; the entire building was torn down in 1913. A new structure was erected and stood ready in the summer, when the Wigwam reopened, showing a combination of vaudeville and film.[72] Just a door down, the same year, the Kahn & Greenfield circuit opened a movie house, named the Idle Hour. In 1911, a 1,000-seater called the Majestic opened on the 2400 block of Mission Street, near the corner of Twenty-First Street. In 1910, Lesser Lesser operated the Union Nickelodeon on Mission between Nineteenth and Twentieth Streets.[73]

FIG. 3 The New Mission Theatre in 1916. From "The New Mission Theater, San Francisco," *Moving Picture World*, September 23, 1916, 1190. (Image courtesy of Media History Digital Library)

By 1916, the Mission was the biggest rival to Market Street in terms of entertainment output. By then, the Idle Hour had become the most important theater in the Mission District, relaunched as a 1,800-seater in 1916 under the name the New Mission. The southern outpost of the Mission District was the short-lived Star Theater, located between Twenty-Third and Twenty-Fourth Streets. The Star nickelodeon operated between the years 1908 and 1911. The Mission District's demography was predominantly Latino, made up of Spanish and Mexican settlers along with a few Ohlone who remained after the 150 years of western exploitation. However, the mass migration following the earthquake saw considerable numbers of Irish, Italian, German, and Polish workers relocate to the neighborhood, giving the area a predominantly Catholic working-class character.

The Fillmore District was the central thoroughfare of the Western Addition, an area designated by San Francisco city officials in the 1860s to facilitate the population boom of the gold rush. The area became known as one of San Francisco's most culturally diverse, with an ethnic population made up of

African Americans, Hispanics, and Europeans. In the 1890s, the city's Jewish community began to settle around the Fillmore District. In the summer and fall of 1906, as a consequence of the earthquake and fire, a considerable part of San Francisco's Japanese population also relocated there. Soon, four blocks centered around Post Street became known colloquially as Nihonjin-machi, or Japanese Town.[74]

The new commercial district along Fillmore Street appeared almost overnight. Many theater owners who had lost their houses and wanted to use their insurance money to rebuild with modern and fireproof standards did so in the new district. As many other businesses followed suit, the new theaters quickly became profitable.[75] Many of the theaters initially housed temporarily dispossessed theater companies, but they soon migrated into vaudeville and film screenings. In 1907, a Chutes amusement park opened in the Fillmore, covering a whole block between Fillmore and Webster Streets. Included in the grounds were several nickelodeons, to which a larger 1,600-seat theater was added in 1909. The amusement park burned down almost entirely in 1909 save for the brick-built theater, which survived and reopened as the American.[76] Initially, exhibitors capitalized on the popularity of nickelodeons, but by late 1911, only two of the dozen small movie houses remained on what used to be called "Nickelodeon Row."[77] However, this did not mean that San Francisco abandoned nickelodeons as exhibition spaces (the Haussler Theater on Fillmore, near Sutter Street, showed strictly moving pictures from its erection in 1906, as did its adjoining theater); the general movement was toward renovation and expansion.[78] In the Fillmore, no one expanded faster than Louis Greenfield and L. L. Kahn, who soon owned three theaters in the district, all within a few blocks from each other. The crown jewel of the Greenfield and Kahn circuit was the New Fillmore, located on Fillmore Street and seating 1,000.[79] *Moving Picture World* counted the New Fillmore among the city's "finest moving picture houses" and reported in 1915 that Greenfield and Kahn intended for the theater to compete with the best places downtown.[80] The duo further owned and managed the Progress, which showed feature programs "and the occasional serial."[81] They also renovated and refurbished the old Sutter Theater and relaunched it as the All Star, boasting a capacity of 700 seats.[82] Other large film venues of the area were the Garrick and the Princess Theater on Ellis Street, with 1,600 and 1,200 seats. respectively.

While the coincidence of nickelodeon popularity and post-quake displacement of established entertainment venues led to the proliferation of movie theaters in the surrounding districts, San Francisco showmen and audiences soon re-established Market Street as the city's premier destination for public amusements. Before the earthquake and fire, there were only two establishments that exclusively showed film on Market Street.[83] The first movie theater after the earthquake and fire to open on Market Street was the Silver Palace, managed by Harry Lichtenstein and Benjamin Michaels. Located at 725 Market, just above Third Street, the small theater accommodated 400 patrons.[84] The longtime acquaintance and business partner of Benjamin Michaels, N. K. Herzog, operated the Pastime Theater, located on the same block. Herzog soon also took over management of the Silver Palace.

Together with Lichtenstein, Michaels opened a second post-quake nickelodeon on Market Street in 1908, located at 1110 Market Street, just across from Sixth Street. The place was called the Gold Palace and turned out to be a short-lived venture. This setback did not deter Michaels and Lichtenstein from expanding their ventures in film exhibition toward the early 1910s. In 1913, the Silver Palace signed contracts with the then recently re-formed Warner's Features for first runs of its distribution.[85] Between the years 1912 and 1915, the Silver Palace was repeatedly in the news for violating city ordinances that banned films showing scenes that were deemed immoral.

After the earthquake, the Lessers moved their business from the Mission District to the Fillmore District and then, in 1909, onto Market Street. Lesser senior died in 1910.[86] The family nickelodeon probably remained in operation until at least 1911, as Irving, Lesser's younger son, recalled having shown some of the first Independent Motion Picture Company films starring Mary Pickford. The next address was just one block away, on Golden Gate Avenue. Around this time, the Lesser family business, now run by Sol and Irving, changed its name to the Golden Gate Film Exchange. In 1912, they once again made a short move, this time to Eddy Street, from where they continued operating until the late 1910s. Before Grauman and Lesser eventually moved their businesses to Hollywood, they jointly went into film production and distribution. Around 1911, Sid Grauman, Sol Lesser, and two young cameramen set up a small film laboratory and started producing a local newsreel, which they called The Golden Gate News Reel. The films gained popularity and were soon distributed weekly all over the West Coast.[87]

The most familiar name of the Market Street scene, and perhaps the most familiar name to appear in this book, is Sid Grauman. For the film-interested public of today, Grauman is known in relation to Grauman's Chinese Theatre, one of Hollywood's most iconic landmarks. For film historians, and particularly scholars of the American silent era, Grauman was one of the most boisterous and noticeable showmen, generally remembered for his lavish Los Angeles movie theaters, revered as monuments to the American cinema's first golden age. To this day, spectacle fills the atmosphere around Grauman's Chinese. Tourists, tour guides, sunglass hawkers, aspiring thespians, and stoned Chewbaccas flock to the theater's famous courtyard, all searching for a part of Hollywood's spiritual epicenter. But the post-quake period in San Francisco was also the time and place in which Sid Grauman laid the foundations for his successful career in show business. Grauman's Unique Theater returned in 1910 and remained one of Market Street's most up-to-date theaters until the late 1910s, in terms of both the films screened and the projection technology. The Empress, opened in 1910, was with 1,455 seats the largest theater on Market Street and became one of the pillars of San Francisco's entertainment scene.[88] It was also Sid Grauman's playground, where he laboriously developed new ways to captivate his audiences. By 1912, the Graumans had the most significant presence on Market Street with three theaters, of which two were first-run houses. Sid Grauman's Imperial opened in December 1912 at 1077 Market Street. It had an audience capacity of 1,650 and, along with the Empress, became one of the most popular attractions of the Great White Way.[89] Reviews and archived programs from Grauman's early teens suggest that the bills were evenly divided between films and short live performances, typically balanced as seven reels and seven vaudeville acts.[90] Simultaneously, he varied this format with more pointed marketing campaigns. For the Empress premiere of the 1915 scandal drama *Sin*, Grauman invested in an elaborate "four storied electrical display of 246 letters" to attract audiences from the street into his theater.[91] While at first blending variety numbers with reels of film, Grauman, like many others, gradually moved toward a focus on the feature format.[92]

In 1916, the Imperial had a Paramount distribution contract, while the Rialto showed Metro programs along with serials and news from the International Film Service. Around Seventh Street were a cluster of small nickelodeons capable of welcoming 300 patrons. These were the Màio Biograph, the Panama Theater, the Empire, and the Elite Theater. All of these were second-string houses, with film runs that lasted longer than a single day. In the summer of 1916, there were thirteen film theaters within a few intersections on Market Street, and about the same number in the blocks surrounding this stretch.[93] Another one of the area's most important film exhibitors was Eugene Roth, who controlled two of the largest theaters in the downtown area (the Portola and the Market Street Theater). Out-of-town players with considerable power were W. G. Turner and Frederick Dahnken of the Turner & Dahnken circuit, which had turned the failed Tivoli opera house on Eddy Street into a large, successful movie theater.[94] The Tivoli lay on the same block as the company's San Francisco office. Located opposite Grant Avenue, the Unique and the equal-sized Odeon were comanaged with a gentleman named Joe Huff. Between Sixth and Seventh Streets, next to the Imperial stood another of Market Street's largest theaters, the Rialto. The Rialto could welcome 1,600 patrons and had a ten-twenty-thirty cent price range.[95]

## Bold Visions and Frontier Conditions

Since the days of Eadweard Muybridge and Thomas Edison, bold visions, technological innovation, and creative experimentation have distinguished the modernity culture of greater San Francisco. In the late nineteenth century, as film arrived at the frontier of the American West, it found in San Francisco its most cosmopolitan setting. Yet despite the city's fostering of such innovation and sophistication, the rapid nationwide proliferation of public film exhibition commonly referred to as the "nickelodeon craze" was not realized in San Francisco until after the 1906 earthquake and fire. The disaster was a key reason behind this delayed emergence, but the city's geographic location was also a factor.

In the late 1800s and early 1900s, California was still a developing frontier of civilization in the United States. Most of the vital industry, economy, politics, and culture were located in the large cities of the East. While San Francisco in some aspects matched the modern infrastructure of similar-sized cities on the East Coast, its remote geographic position added a substantial delay to shipments of goods and people, whether they came from the American industrial heartland or from across the Pacific Ocean. There still existed in the city a self-image of rugged pioneerism, harking back to the gold rush days. The daily news and trade paper accounts cited in this chapter suggest that showmen and exhibitors such as Furst, Bacigalupi, the Graumans, and the Mileses also adopted a form of frontier mentality, countering the remoteness of their location with grittiness and versatility. An example of this is the Miles Brothers film exchange model, which was initially designed to make the most out of film copies distributed by companies primarily based on the other side of the continent. Another example can be found in the local showmen's response to the earthquake; faced with the fact that their places of business were in ruins, they quickly came up with alternative solutions to keep their operations afloat, such as the Graumans' makeshift tent-theater.

This versatility can also be understood as an indirect factor in the gradual shift in public amusement that occurred in the rebuilding years, away from live stage acts and toward moving pictures. The earthquake and fire effectively halted the continuity of a public amusement tradition geared toward theater and vaudeville, presented at a wide range of established theater locations. In the aftermath of the disaster, San Francisco entertainment institutions were temporarily displaced, creating a vacuum into which the film medium seeped. While the destruction briefly delayed the emergence of nickelodeons compared with in other similarly sized U.S. cities, the convenience and quick economic turnaround of film exhibition soon made film a popular alternative for seasoned showmen looking to re-establish their position, as well as for opportunistic fortune seekers who saw a chance to take advantage of the market conditions. Nickelodeons and other places showing film began popping up in perimeter neighborhoods and fringe areas. By the time the older institutions came back into place, film had gained a significant foothold where it had previously been regarded as a novelty.

As film emerged as San Francisco's preferred form of public amusement, authoritarian voices calling for control of the new mass medium also began to be heard. The brash frontier mentality of San Francisco film exhibitors was countered at first by clergy and social workers, and later by politicians and police. The city's fraught past, precarious situation in the face of rebuilding, and potential for improvement were often brought to the fore in this discourse—a triad of reasons why it was imperative to contain the negative effects film exhibition could have on the city's masses. The discussion about the harm of cinemagoing soon was annexed to the broader discussion about public health, a web of concern in which Chinatown had long figured as one of the most significant issues to be resolved. The next chapter looks closer at these debates, and at how the Panama-Pacific International Exposition, where the new San Francisco would present itself to the modern world, became a shining beacon toward which local politicians, reformists, and regulators steered the policies on local film exhibition, in the name of social improvement, public health, and cultural uplift.

# 2

# "If I Had the Power to Do So I Would Destroy Them with My Own Hands"

## Film and Politics in Post-quake San Francisco

Progressivism, more than any other social movement, conditioned the American film industry in the 1910s.[1] From early 1913 on, two-term president Woodrow Wilson introduced a number of reforms known as the "New Freedom," ensuring that the progressive political agenda set forth by the previous Roosevelt and Taft administrations would hold throughout the new decade. In an anthology tracing major developments in U.S. cinema of the 1910s, Charlie Keil and Ben Singer noted that progressivism emerged as a tool of "social policy and legislation with the goal of taming the mayhem of unchecked modernization," of which film culture was the prime example.[2] However, Moya Luckett found that American progressivism, approached through a discursive prism of 1910s film culture, encompassed a wider range of contradictory perspectives and a more ambivalent relationship to modernization, which was subject to considerable local variation. In Luckett's account, film culture "was caught up in Progressivism's sociocultural battles as the film industry attempted to align the medium with values like uplift, community, and national identity, while regulators sought to contain it through other progressive mechanisms like censorship and regulation."[3] Jennifer Peterson further distinguished between these different contemporary approaches to the effects of cinema on society, but along the lines of parallel, rather than conflicting, "'wings' of reform discourse."[4]

After the earthquake and fire, San Francisco, too, became caught up in the new direction in politics. President Roosevelt commissioned several Red Cross experts from Washington, DC, to work on disaster relief. In the words of historian Andrea Rees Davies, Roosevelt's experts formulated a common progressive agenda for San Francisco, pushing "new scientific, social work methods into the cracks and crevasses of the post-disaster city."[5] Political corruption, graft, and foul play conducted by the administrations of Mayor James Phelan (1897–1902) and Mayor Eugene Schmitz (1902–1907) tainted the general perception of the city's politics for years. However, after the catastrophe, Schmitz was replaced and prosecuted, and his successors, Edward Robeson Taylor (1907–1910) and Patrick Henry "Pinhead" McCarthy (1910–1912), both ran for office with campaigns touting social improvement along with a progressive agenda. In late 1911, reform-minded Democrat James "Sunny Jim" Rolph Jr. was elected the new mayor of San Francisco. He held the position for nineteen years. Rolph continued the progressive direction and launched several campaigns to clean up the city before the Panama-Pacific International Exposition (PPIE).

The rapid proliferation of cheap movie theaters opened up the public sphere to new and unprecedented opportunities for social experiences and interaction. Film exhibitors quickly identified and tried to monetize the potential of these new audience groups. As Richard Abel has shown, these new audience formations, along with cinema as a particular instance of modernity, "was inscribed within the discursive fields of imperialism and nationalism and their conflicted claims, respectively, of economic and cultural supremacy" during the latter period of the 1900s.[6] Immigrant and working-class citizens who frequented such establishments became easily identified as potential threats in public health improvement campaigns. At perceived risk was another significant contingent of the film audience: women and adolescents. Certain aspects of film culture now posed a potential threat not only to the welfare of the middle class but also to the health of America's future. This chapter investigates how San Francisco public discourse placed its emerging film culture alongside preexisting perceived public health hazards and disturbances of the urban milieu, and how the posited dangers of moviegoing made film exhibition suitable for local politicians to target through regulation and various uplift campaigns, formulated and carried out in anticipation of the PPIE in 1915.

## In the Name of Uplift: The California Commonwealth Club Study

In the early 1900s, the social work of reformers such as Jane Addams profoundly influenced the progressive politics on the rise nationally.[7] Following "Saint Jane's" pioneering investigations of social conditions in the growing urban

FIG. 4 The Pastime Theater on Market Street. From *Moving Picture World*, July 27, 1912, 358. (Image courtesy of Media History Digital Library)

milieu, surveys designed to facilitate social uplift in the public sphere became the fodder of political campaigns around the country.[8] As moviegoing became integrated into the social fabric of American cities, a parallel need emerged to understand the goods and evils of the public's interaction with the new medium. Between 1913 and 1915, social surveys of urban recreation became a genre in themselves, as evident in a bibliography published in 1915 by the Russell Sage

Foundation.[9] Of the fifteen studies of urban recreation included in the list, cities of a size comparable to San Francisco included Cleveland, Boston, Milwaukee, Kansas City, Detroit, Cincinnati, and Indianapolis.[10] Studies of vice and "reports of social evil" sometimes also encompassed investigations into establishments showing film.[11]

Inspired by the trend to investigate the habits and patterns of everyday life in the urban milieu, in 1911 the Commonwealth Club of California authorized an extensive study of public recreation in San Francisco. The organization, which aimed to present nonpartisan studies for the betterment of society, had been founded in 1903 by prominent San Franciscans Benjamin Ide Wheeler (president of the University of California), John P. Young (managing editor of the *San Francisco Chronicle*), Frederick Burke (president of the San Francisco Normal School), William P. Lawler (a local judge), and Edward F. Adams (an editorial writer for the *Chronicle*).[12] The foundation's first study, investigating the spreading of venereal diseases among the city's prostitutes, was published in 1911, in connection with the commencement of the recreational survey. While the executive committee at that time was made up primarily of physicians, the investigators for the recreation survey consisted of a more diverse group of illustrious and reform-minded San Franciscans. Specifically, the subcommittee that had been tasked with studying theater, vaudeville, and moving pictures included notable members such as Charles de Young (founder of the *San Francisco Chronicle* in 1865), Charles Raas (president of the First Bank of San Anselmo), J. C. Astredo (chief probation officer of the juvenile court and former chairman of San Francisco's first moving picture censorship board), and Tadini J. Bacigalupi, (attorney and business partner of Charles de Young). The survey also acknowledged the help of some of the committee members' wives, especially Mrs. Bacigalupi, Mrs. Albert Elkus, and Dr. Jessica B. Peixotto. The show committee used a questionnaire to record experiences at each establishment. The questionnaire included overall considerations of the type of show, the audience, and the level of sanitation, but it also went into detail in terms of prices, audience age and gender, and the "art grade" and "social grade" of each performance.[13]

The Commonwealth Club study offers detailed data on historical moviegoing patterns in San Francisco in the early 1910s. Unfortunately, there are no robust statistics for the latter stages of the decade. The lack of specific data prevents comparative analysis on the evolution and progress of film culture beyond the mere count of establishments with a movie projector. However, as the Commonwealth Club study provides numbers on the gender and class of audiences, as well as attempted historicization of post-quake theaters and the emergence of film, the data can be used to illustrate San Francisco moviegoing in 1912 with generous detail. More than offering a unique entry point to this specific period in local San Francisco film history, it provides a benchmark with

**Table 1.**

**Capacity and number of performances per week in San Francisco for the year 1912**

| | Capacity of Theaters | | | | | | | |
|---|---|---|---|---|---|---|---|---|
| | Capacity for One Performance | No. of Performances on Monday | Capacity on Monday | No. of Performances on Saturday | Capacity on Saturday | No. of Performances per Week | Capacity per Week | % |
| Legitimate theaters (5) | 7,185 | 5 | 7,185 | 10 | 14,370 | 48 | 68,865 | 3.5 |
| Burlesque theaters (2) | 1,934 | 6 | 5,802 | 6 | 5,802 | 42 | 40,614 | 2 |
| Vaudeville theaters (9) | 12,334 | 28 | 36,741 | 39 | 50,125 | 218 | 283,955 | 14.5 |
| Motion picture houses (69) | 28,752 | 464 | 207,975 | 651 | 277,728 | 3,588 | 1,558,848 | 80 |
| Total | 50,205 | 503 | 257,703 | 706 | 348,025 | 3,896 | 1,952,282 | 100 |

SOURCE: Data from *Transactions of the Commonwealth Club of California*, 227. Courtesy of Library of Congress.

which to compare the more inconsistent information available for the years that followed.

The show committee dedicated a considerable part of the survey to the analysis of the emerging film culture. The study placed particular emphasis on the audience, but there were also attempts to analyze and categorize the films shown in the theaters.[14] The survey results indicated that going to the movies was by far the city's preferred form of entertainment (see Table 1). In the year 1912, San Francisco had 69 film houses, 9 vaudeville theaters, 5 "legitimate" theaters, and 2 burlesque houses. The weekly capacity for San Francisco establishments showing film was 1,558,848 seats, making up 80 percent of the total theater capacity in the city as a whole. On an average Saturday throughout 1912, the keen San Franciscan moviegoer had 651 opportunities to see moving pictures. The committee noted, however, that these figures were slightly inaccurate, since some of the "legitimate" theaters had been showing moving pictures for a long time. Therefore, the committee advised, a more accurate number of establishments with "moving picture" capacity for the year 1912 would be between 70 and 75.

It remains unclear whether the statistic 651 differentiated between different film programs or whether theaters showed reruns. Because the formulation used was "shows" and "performances," it is probable that every single film title shown in a program was credited separately. If so, the number would indicate the median number of film titles shown in San Francisco on a weekly basis in 1912, rather than the number of different film programs shown by establishments licensed to show moving pictures.

The estimated weekly attendance for film houses was 373,776 patrons, and the yearly estimate was 19,436,352 (see Table 2). An inquiry commission authorized by the state of California presented a survey in early 1915 that showed similar numbers, giving film shows a 65.5 percent rating of the total estimated patronage of shows in San Francisco.[15] The second most popular entertainment form was vaudeville, which had a yearly estimate of 7,382,804, a number that corresponded to 25 percent of the audience.[16] Although the most popular form of entertainment, film was the least lucrative business in terms of how much its patrons spent on a night out. The estimated total weekly expenditure for film patrons was about $26,000, while the vaudeville shows expected about $31,000. The "legitimate theater" was still the most lucrative, having an estimated weekly patron expenditure of $41,318 and a yearly figure of $2,148,536, making up almost half of the total yearly expenditure of San Francisco shows, while the sixty-nine film houses came in at an estimated total of $1,360,520, making up 25 percent of all theater income considered.[17]

The survey ventured as far as attempting to make a generalization that classified the quality of films shown in certain types of establishments. Under the rubric "class of pictures," it was stated that films shown in vaudeville houses were deemed to be of a generally higher quality than those shown in moving

**Table 2.**
**Estimated attendance and expenditures for four different types of establishments in San Francisco throughout the year 1912**

| | Attendance | | | | | |
|---|---|---|---|---|---|---|
| | Estimated Weekly Attendance | Estimated Yearly Attendance | % | Estimated Weekly Expenditure by Patrons | Estimated Yearly Expenditure by Patrons | % |
| Legitimate theaters (5) | 34,432 | 1,790,464 | 6 | $41,318 | $2,148,536 | 40 |
| Burlesque theaters (2) | 20,307 | 1,055,964 | 3.5 | $4,467 | $232,284 | 4.5 |
| Vaudeville theaters (9) | 141,977 | 7,382,804 | 25 | $31,234 | $1,624,168 | 30 |
| Moving picture houses (69) | 373,776 | 19,436,352 | 65.5 | $26,164 | $1,360,520 | 25.5 |
| Total | 570,492 | 29,665,584 | 100 | $103,183 | $5,365,516 | 100 |

SOURCE: Data from *Transactions of the Commonwealth Club of California*, 228. Courtesy of Library of Congress.

picture houses. The explanation was that vaudeville theaters had time to pick more carefully, since they did not show as many films.[18]

The study also provided statistics on the gender and age of patrons. In 1912, male patrons over the age of sixteen were the predominant group, especially on a weekday night (see Table 3). Women in the same age bracket were the second most common patrons, with about half the attendance numbers compared with men. Child patronage was more common during the weekends, especially in the afternoons, when the count of children up to the age of sixteen surpassed that of women in the audience.[19]

A portion of the survey distinguished the "class" of people who went to the movies to further nuance the composition of audiences. It established that the majority of San Francisco's moviegoers were considered to be from the middle class. Twenty-eight percent were deemed to be in the category "struggling," while 15 percent were described as "poor," suggesting that the overwhelming majority of San Francisco movie audiences ranged from society's most disenfranchised to the "fair-to-do." These figures also suggest that the appeal of the movies had not yet reached the top flight of the urban community. The category "prosperous" was recorded as 2 percent, while the "rich" were almost absent from San Francisco movie theaters during the years of the survey.[20] Still, the

**Table 3.**
**Gender and age division for eight vaudeville establishments in San Francisco throughout the year 1912**

| | Audience | | | | | | |
|---|---|---|---|---|---|---|---|
| | Sat. Aft'n. | Tues. Aft'n. | Sat. Night. | Tues. Night. | Av'ge Satur. | Av'ge Tuesd. | Gen. Av'ge. |
| Men | 41.4 | 52.3 | 52.7 | 63. | 47.05 | 57.65 | 52.35 |
| Women | 27.2 | 34.3 | 36.4 | 30.50 | 31.80 | 32.40 | 32.10 |
| Children | 28.6 | 6. | 9.5 | 4.90 | 19.05 | 5.45 | 12.25 |
| Babies | 2.8 | 7.4 | 1.4 | 1.60 | 2.10 | 4.50 | 3.20 |

SOURCE: Data from *Transactions of the Commonwealth Club of California*, 239. Courtesy of Library of Congress.

survey authors, belonging to the highest categories of the social strata, commented that the "motion picture houses is the most democratic of the shows" in terms of diversity of attendants.[21]

The perspective and social standing of the survey authors and investigators themselves can also serve as an indicator of how the city's ruling class perceived and categorized individual citizens, but also how divisions of class played out in the urban space of movie theaters. It is also possible to detect the influence of Jane Addams's publication *The Youth and City Streets* (1909), which alarmed the country concerning the need for play and recreation programs for urban youth.[22] One of the outcomes and recommendations of the Commonwealth Club's public recreation survey was to instill further control of potentially hazardous recreational spaces to guide young San Franciscans away from moral and physical ruin. The chairman of the committee, James Edward Rogers, stated: "Our saloon, our dance hall, juvenile delinquency problem, and other social problems, arise from the wrong kind of recreation, or the lack of provision for properly supervised adequate places for good, clean, and wholesome recreation."[23] Following Addams's broad remit on recreation to include all forms of urban entertainment, the committee found the dangers of the popularity of movie houses among the younger generations to be directly linked to the corruptive influence of saloons and dance halls, which, according to the study, contaminated the public spaces of movie theaters by sheer proximity. This conclusion led the committee to recommend a prohibition of liquor sales from all places of recreation.[24] The committee also recommended the installation of a new board of supervisors, enveloping the old system of separate commissions under the new umbrella of public recreation. The question was how to enforce the new ordinances and regulations on the city's disruptive film business.

## Unwholesome Moving Pictures and Dangerous City Space

Early twentieth-century public crusades against penny arcades and moving pictures often followed a similar pattern. The sequence included, as Jan Olsson has shown, a triangulation between concerned citizens, the press, and local police and most often reached its crescendo in a self-proclaimed victory publicized in one of the crusading newspapers.[25] Editorial inroads to the influence of on-screen imagery paralleled alarming reports about the immoral activities that took place in the secrecy of the movie theater. Similar to larger East Coast cities like New York, Chicago, and Philadelphia, such issues became visible in the local press as nickelodeons started to gain footholds in various parts of the re-emerging city.[26]

Because the disaster delayed the film medium's spread in the city, it was not until 1907 that concerned voices found their way into print. In that year, a San Francisco judge, answering to a charge of the exhibition of "indecent pictures" at a Fillmore District nickelodeon, demanded to see for himself. The courthouse staff readied a projector in a clerk's office, where the films were screened before the judge. Upon his return to the courtroom, the judge denounced the film as immoral and calculated to degrade the morals of young persons. The *Chronicle* reported the extent of his indignation: "If I had the power to do so I would destroy them with my own hands."[27] In 1908, the Reverend Terence Caraher of the St. Francis Parish began a highly publicized protest against the opening of a nickelodeon across the street from his church, located two blocks north of Chinatown. According to Father Caraher, the nickelodeon attracted "fallen women and their consorts" and gave "lewdness and obscenity a place in the city of San Francisco it never had before."[28] Caraher's crusade led to the passing of a legal ordinance that forbade the establishment of nickelodeons, skating rinks, roller coasters, and "such class of amusement places" within 200 feet of any school or church building.[29]

One of the first measures taken against the presumed corruptive powers of immoral acts depicted on film was the introduction of film censors. In 1909, state assemblyman Clement Young commissioned a local board of censors to comb through the city's output of moving pictures. The board was set up the same year as the founding of the New York–based National Board of Review and was led by chief probation officer Joseph C. Astredo.[30] Not long after its installment, the censorship board clashed with many of the city's film exhibitors.[31] Among the most zealous board members was Peter Peshon, a corporal in the ranks, who continued as a censor until his death in 1931, which coincided with Rolph's final year as mayor.[32] During the years leading up to the PPIE, Peshon was often named explicitly in the film trade press as one of the driving forces behind the policing of strict regulations against film theaters.

When Astredo resigned in 1911, Mayor Rolph appointed James S. Webster in his place.[33] The board, at that time, had six members. Although the censors had managed to review 2,012 films in fiscal year 1912, they remarked in a report that the chore was overwhelming and that only 40 percent of the output had been under review.[34] In 1914, the board reported that although it was still impossible to review all films, exhibitors had grown more accustomed to their presence and increasingly submitted their films for review before showing them in the theaters.[35] While this suggested progress from the point of view of the censors, they again stressed what they perceived as a direct connection between harmful movies and vice.

From 1909 to 1911, the reporting focused mainly on the hazards of local movie theaters. Initially, the main concern was with the fire safety of the theaters.[36] The perspective on film culture expressed in the local press was often markedly different from that printed in trade papers like *Moving Picture World* and *Motion Picture News*, which generally functioned as mouthpieces for the film business. In March 1909, an alarming editorial in the *San Francisco Call* focused on the exhibition of immoral pictures as what turned movie theaters into dangerous urban spaces: "These places constitute a positive danger both to morals and life. . . . Their numbers increase day by day and they are to be found in every quarter of the city."[37] Two weeks later, an article in the *Chronicle* included comments from Joseph Astredo, who declared that he knew youths who had been "led into crime by nickelodeons."[38] Three days later, the *Chronicle* exclaimed, "All that the public asks with regard to nickelodeons is that the shows shall not be too suggestive of vice or crime and that their construction shall be such as to assure the safety of the visitors."[39] Following the creation of the censorship board, the *Call* initially made monthly updates on the progress of their work.[40]

To protect the interests of local exhibitors, a coalition of San Francisco film exhibitors had formed the San Francisco Motion Picture Exhibitors' Association in August 1908.[41] However, the organization soon concentrated its efforts on issues of local censorship. In 1912, the association was incorporated into the Motion Picture Exhibitors' League of America.[42] The Exhibitors' League, which had been initiated in 1911 by M. A. Neff, an exhibitor from Cleveland, Ohio, was "formed in part to protect exhibitors anywhere in the country from restrictive local legislation that would be hard to fight without a national organization."[43] Charles Rothschild and W. A. Cory led the San Francisco branch.

## Rolph's Crusade

When James "Sunny Jim" Rolph was elected mayor of San Francisco in 1911, he set out to prepare the city for the PPIE by way of social improvement and cultural uplift. Since the earthquake and fire, forces within the local authorities had worked to stifle the organized vice that had made the Barbary Coast the most ill-reputed and mythologized urban area of the West. Vice historian Herbert Asbury noted that although the disaster created a brief hiatus in the debauchery, the business returned faster than most other San Francisco institutions. In Asbury's words, "The opium dives and slave-dens, the cow-yards and parlor houses, the cribs and deadfalls, the dance-halls and bar-rooms, melodeons and concert saloons—all the abode and paraphernalia of vice, from the waterfront to Grant Avenue and from Morton Street to Telegraph Hill, lay a mass of smoking ruins."[44] Within months, the enterprises of the Barbary Coast had started to rebuild the quarter upon the ruins of the old, and by the beginning of 1907, the area was back in full operation.

The resurrected Barbary Coast became Rolph's first target. In 1912, police commissioners Jesse B. Cook and Max J. Kuhl decided to "nail down the lid" on the systematized illegal and immoral activities. The Board of Commissioners introduced new regulations in early 1913, especially aimed at dealing with the area's prostitution problem. The regulations effectively banned women from visiting saloons and dance halls in the area "bounded by Washington and Vallejo streets, Grant [A]venue and the Bay."[45] The new rules prohibited the sale of liquor in "questionable houses" and to women under the age of twenty-one everywhere. They also ordered establishments of the area to dim their neon lights to a softer glow. Although this represented the beginning of a stricter regime toward the area's entertainment output, it would not be until 1917 that the U.S. Supreme Court passed the Red-Light Abatement Act, which illegalized all kinds of dancing, private booths, and unescorted women in every establishment that sold liquor, effectively hindering the life source of the area's most nefarious cafés.

Another critical aspect of Rolph's campaign was to control the perceived harmful effects of the new mass medium. As moviegoing became San Francisco's most popular form of entertainment, a new battle started, with the local police and the local board of censors on one side and some adventurous San Francisco exhibitors on the other. In this long-lasting fight, the Exhibitors' League often ended up acting as a mediator. In September 1912, the California Exhibitors' League held its first statewide convention in San Francisco.[46] To bridge local politics and film exhibition, Rothschild and Cory invited Mayor Rolph as the main speaker. In his opening address, Rolph described the popularity of films in San Francisco, especially among the younger generations, saying, "When our children get lost, or if we can't find them, all we have to do is go to the moving picture show." Because of this great public interest, Rolph underlined the moral responsibility of film exhibitors and exhorted them to make a habit of displaying wholesome pictures. Rolph made it clear that an uplift in local film exhibition was to be accomplished before the beginning of the PPIE: "I believe in the uplift and moral growth of the moving picture business, and let me extend to you an invitation to meet here again in 1915 and see what we have accomplished by then."[47] In July 1914, Rothschild resigned as president of both the California state branch and the San Francisco branch of the Exhibitors' League. The next president, George R. Knowles, quickly handed over the duties to former vice president M. E. Cory, who at the national gathering of the league in July 1914 extended Mayor Rolph's invitation to reunite in 1915.[48] The Exhibitors' League agreed that the town that was going to host the PPIE was the perfect place for the next national convention.[49]

Local newspapers generally echoed Rolph's campaign to shed light on the dark spots of San Francisco. A *Call* editorial blamed previous mayors Schmitz and McCarthy for issuing permits to unsuitable establishments in the "period of confusion following the fire when anything and everything went without active objection under the plea of emergency."[50] "Girls go into these places and in the darkness meet strange men," opined Republican state senator Edward Strobridge, who in 1911 proposed a bill ordering that "every theater at all times be so light that the features of patrons may be clearly distinguished."[51] While local exhibitors fought the bill, a local ordinance was passed requiring places that showed film to keep the lights on during exhibition.[52] *Chronicle* theater critic Ralph Renaud quipped that this development would appeal to everyone "except lovin' couples."[53]

When Rolph appointed his new censorship board in the summer of 1912, the *Chronicle* reported that its efforts would focus on stricter enforcement of censorship of suggestive "pictures in moving picture shows."[54] The board reported to Rolph in 1913 that the situation was under control with the words "We receive many less complaints than formerly and the general character of pictures is more satisfactory."[55] A January 1913 *Chronicle* editorial lauded the gradual success of the local film board and the compliance of the majority of local film exhibitors: "That moving pictures in the past have not always been free from objectionable features is very true. . . . But that is no longer the condition. There may still be pictures occasionally shown that are not calculated to have good influence. But these are in the minority and can be suppressed by boards of censors just as soon as they are displayed."[56] The censorship board's report the following year confirmed this development: "There is a feeling that the type of pictures has improved materially, and it is with great pleasure that the Board is able to report an increased spirit of co-operation on the part of the majority of moving picture exhibitors."[57]

The acceptance of moviegoing as part of urban life across class boundaries gradually emerged in the local newspapers. In 1910, the *Call* announced a writers' contest aimed at its young readers on the subject "What I Like Best at the Nickelodeons."[58] Two weeks later, the paper published sixteen short essays written by children with Anglo-Saxon names between the ages eight and fifteen.

The topics of the award-winning submissions ranged from praising the educational possibility of movies to the denigration of immoral pictures such as "No Sad or Bad Ones" and "Any Pictures but Murders."[59] Early in 1913, the Reverend H. A. Jump, who, like Jane Addams, had earlier warned about the psycho-suggestive powers of cinema on young minds, gave a lecture to the Commonwealth Club. Jump underlined cinema's uplift effect on the lower classes: "Common people see in the moving pictures home life and social customs that they otherwise could never enjoy. They learn how to dress, how to be polite, how to behave in company simply from seeing it acted on the screen."[60] In the spring of 1913, a *Call* editorial proclaimed: "The moving picture business has come to stay. It is a welcome addition to urban life. Under proper regulations the moving picture entertainment is a power for good."[61] A year later, the *Chronicle* published some more favorable opinions on the growing film industry. In January 1914, San Francisco's film culture was taken to task in the *Chronicle*'s Sunday edition, featuring a three-page local movie exposé, complete with in-depth views of current affairs on exhibition, production, and distribution. In the introductory article, Joseph Northup, a local architect and writer, opened a debate on the pros and cons of contemporary moviegoing. Northup claimed that the upsurge of theaters in San Francisco was significant not only to prove that the popularity of films was not merely a "fad" but also because the electric lights from the movie theaters served to bring light to some of the city's less salubrious areas. With this sentiment, Northup knowingly went against many previous complaints of the movies as a place for vice, the corruption of young minds, and the fostering of indecent behavior.[62] Northup called these the opinions of "long haired reformers."[63] Such arguments about the potential social functioning of cinema, Lee Grieveson has pointed out, was "central for those defending the film industry and for those hoping to utilize the cinema for public good from 1907 onward."[64] In San Francisco, the inclusion of such sentiment in a Sunday feature of the *Chronicle* signaled that a new, more positive, attitude toward moviegoing was gaining traction in the public sphere.

Simultaneously, Rolph's much publicized concern about the moral quality of the city's film exhibition coincided with his general campaign to clean up the city's act before the PPIE. The mayor's office passed several local ordinances that restricted the nature of films allowed for public screening but also their manner of exhibition. The office also saw the need to rewrite some old regulations to target the newly popular medium specifically. One such complementary ordinance from 1913 prohibited the exhibition of indecent, vulgar, lewd, or obscene films.[65] The combination of suggestive movies and the darkness of the movie theater was believed specifically damaging.[66] In the view of the Commonwealth Club, the gloom of the movie theater would allow especially the younger members of the audience to "play games, or commit acts, that result in physical harm or crime."[67] A further restriction gave the police commission the right to revoke licenses on the spot if it deemed the establishment did not live up to the moral code. The targeting of the PPIE put Rolph's "uplift" campaign on a schedule. This tangible goal would also become formative for the local film culture, as regulatory measures—local and external—successively tightened the grip on film exhibition, in anticipation of the exposition.

## Exhibitors Respond

Although most San Francisco exhibitors generally tolerated the whims of the censorship board, the chief of police, and Mayor Rolph, some actively went against the promulgations of "wholesome" film culture. As a result, they suffered from crackdowns made by the local censorship board and the police, who were not afraid to arrest exhibitors even if it went against court rulings about the moral quality of local film exhibition.

In 1912, the Silver Palace proprietor Charles Kahn was found guilty in a San Francisco court for having shown the Vitascope production *The Penalty of Folly; or, The Apache's Revenge*.[68] In 1913, police arrested Benjamin Michaels for having shown the Italian import *Marquis, the Venetian Tribune*. Instead of following the officers to the police station, Michaels stood up before the Silver Palace audience and called for support on the removal of the local board of censors.[69] After his arrest, Michaels initially fought back by authoring a public petition.[70] But Michaels's attempts at rousing public outrage led nowhere, and the police court convicted him for "showing immoral pictures."[71] Given a choice between paying a fine of $200 or spending the next 100 days in the county jail, Michaels chose to pay.[72] In 1914, Michaels moved all his business to Chinatown. Management of the Silver Palace was taken over by Charles Stilwell, but legal troubles persisted. As the war in Europe unfolded, films of the fighting started appearing on American screens. In August 1914, the San Francisco Police Department issued orders "prohibiting the exhibition of any war pictures showing armies of Europe in action."[73] The chief of police, David White, justified the ban by explaining that visceral war reports from the old country might stir tensions in the highly cosmopolitan population of San Francisco.

In late August, T. A. Church of the *Moving Picture World* reported that the state of California was planning to introduce a minimum age requirement of sixteen years for viewing all moving pictures in the state. Church pointed out that the league was the only effective medium for exhibitors to "wage a fight against pernicious regulations."[74] Church noted that although most San Francisco exhibitors and exchange men believed that Chief White was overstepping his authority, their general inclination was to obey the rules. The main complaint was the seeming arbitrariness in how the local censorship board decided which films would pass muster, with "some war views being allowed to be shown unmolested, while the exhibition of others is stopped."[75] In September that year, police arrested Stilwell for showing a film titled *Faithful unto Death*, following a temporary ordinance that established that no films "dealing with wars of any nation, America included," were allowed in San Francisco theaters.[76] After protests by Stilwell, the judge permitted him to show the film. Although this was a temporary victory for the Silver Palace's ongoing fight against local censorship, Stilwell believed that the local branch of the Exhibitors' League was lenient toward the local censorship board's rulings. He expressed his indignation in an open letter published in the *Motion Picture News*: "The Silver Palace, as you are aware, has had considerable trouble with the Board of Censors in the past, and has incurred great expense as a result. In almost every case it has called upon the league for the help and moral support to which their membership entitled them. Has it, with the exception of one case ever had the assistance rendered? No! Why?"[77]

Although the general perception among local exhibitors was that the court's dismissal of the Stilwell injunction set a precedent that allowed war films in San Francisco, the Silver Palace manager was again arrested about a month later, this time for having projected *The Kaiser's Challenge*.[78] Again, the court ruled in the exhibitor's favor, instructing the police to refrain from interrupting the screening of war films and stop intimidating exhibitors and managers for the showing of these films in all of San Francisco County. At this point, however, most exhibitors had probably realized that the drawbacks of resistance were too great this close to the exposition.[79]

## Grauman's Formula

While some exhibitors actively fought Rolph's increasing restrictions, others sought to exploit the connection between San Francisco's vice district and the moving picture medium in creative ways. In 1913, Sid Grauman and Sol Lesser produced a two-reel, documentary-style exposé of the nightlife in San Francisco's most infamous areas, Chinatown and the Barbary Coast.[80] While proprietors and audiences of dance halls like Spider Kelly's, the Hippodrome, and the Thalia started preparing for business under the new rule, Sol Lesser sought to immortalize what remained of the mythologized nightspot by recording it on film. The film was shot in mid-September, before Rolph's clampdown.[81] One of the film's cameramen, Hal Mohr, later recalled the events in an interview: "They were going to have an all-out festival, a last night of excitement and immorality and hell-raising and from then on, no more Barbary Coast."[82]

The film was called *Last Night of the Barbary Coast*.[83] According to Mohr, the idea was to market the film on its sensationalist value, but to not include any pictures that could fall foul of the censors.[84] The strategy hit home, as

*Motography* reported in 1913 that, contrary to what might be imagined of a film depicting the Barbary Coast, the film was "really quite educational."[85] Released through the Progressive Film Company, a subsidiary of Lesser's Golden Gate, *Last Night of the Barbary Coast* was exported to other areas of the country through the states rights system.[86] The states rights distribution system emerged in 1909 and gave independent exhibitors the option to buy the right to be the sole distributor of a specific film title in a designated territory, often a block of American states.[87]

During Rolph's reign, Grauman rose to the top as San Francisco's most notable theater and film exhibitor. Grauman by this time regularly employed performers who frequented the establishments along the Barbary Coast.[88] He also regularly used Chinese San Franciscan actors in his vaudeville acts. According to Mohr, the documentary had been Grauman's idea.[89] For the film, Grauman procured talent from a show he had previously given at the Empress called *20 Minutes at the Barbary Coast*.[90] The majority of the stage show played out in Chinatown, including Chinese dancers performing one of the popular dance crazes to emerge from the dance halls of the Barbary Coast.[91] *Motography*'s review of the film highlighted that while it included scenes of "street life in Chinatown," it was "as harmless as the strictest of censors would wish it" and even featured an "approval by the chief of police."[92]

Grauman, more than anyone else, managed to exploit the mythology of San Francisco as the "Paris of America," while keeping his shows at a level of propriety that satisfied the political project of cleaning up the city's entertainment districts in anticipation of the exposition. In the fall of 1914, the popular San Francisco Screen Club, a social organization of local film exhibitors that worked to "make the moving picture business distinctive," elected Grauman as its president.[93] Grauman's ability to navigate San Francisco's post-quake entertainment politics is further evident by the fact that he was one of the local exhibitors to be awarded a contract to build and operate a concession in the exposition's entertainment section.[94] Keeping with his tried formula, Grauman constructed an elaborate Orientalist version of San Francisco's Chinese neighborhood, which he called "Underground Chinatown." Although he never worked at or owned a theater in Chinatown, his exploits in the area were a key component at his shows and theaters for a considerable part of his long and successful career.

## San Francisco Film Exhibition and the Panama-Pacific International Exposition

At the start of the exhibition year of 1915, it seemed as if Rolph's reign had successfully bridled the unruly film medium. At a 1915 convention of the American Association for the Advancement of Science held at Berkeley, Dr. Bascom Johnson, counsel for the American Social Hygiene Association, gave a lecture in which he argued that the film audiences of San Francisco were now of a "better class" than those of Oakland.[95] In December 1914, Rolph and his wife attended a charity ball organized by the San Francisco Screen Club. *Motion Picture News* described the evening as a great success, concluding with a short speech by Rolph. The guest list included luminaries such as Charlie Chaplin and Roscoe "Fatty" Arbuckle.[96] While local film exhibitors recognized the benefits of making peace with the mayor's methods, Rolph himself had realized the potential of fraternizing with the stars of the screen. The next chance came at the much-anticipated National Exhibitors' League Convention held at the exposition grounds in July 1915. A list of the attendees reads like a veritable menu of silent era luminaries: Carl Laemmle, Cleo Madison, Grace Cunard, and Lois Weber from Universal; D. W. Griffith and the Gish sisters from Reliance-Majestic; Cecil B. DeMille, Blanche Sweet, and Geraldine Farrar from the Lasky Feature Play Company; and Thomas Ince, Mack Sennett, and William S. Hart from the New York Motion Picture Company.[97] In his opening address, Mayor Rolph lauded the importance movies had acquired in the everyday life of San Franciscans and symbolically handed over the exposition city to the "photoplay people."[98] Rolph's embrace of moving pictures was immortalized in Mack Sennett's exposition exposé *Fatty and Mabel View the World's Fair*. In a scene shot on the steps of the unfinished San Francisco City Hall, Rolph hands an impromptu license to comedy stars Mabel Normand and Fatty Arbuckle. The card reads, "11/4/15 Permitting Mr. Arbuckle and Miss Normand to take pictures anywhere in San Francisco. James Rolph, Mayor."[99]

While Rolph expressed his belief in the future of the film industry, in his opening speech at the convention he refrained from mentioning the question of censorship. *Moving Picture World* noted the omission and added that it was one "in which he takes a keen interest."[100] During the final days of the convention, censorship and the educative potential of film were the hot topics of speeches and discussions at the Civic Auditorium of the current state of filmdom. Several speakers, including D. W. Griffith denounced the arbitrary censorship rules that pervaded the nation: "It has now come to pass that from a small beginning censorship has grown until a man of the caliber of a captain of police in Chicago can tell two million American people what they shall or shall not see on the screen."[101] W. W. Hodkinson, the president of Paramount, on the other hand, pleaded for further leniency on behalf of film producers and exhibitors, and argued for further development toward "cleaner movies."[102]

After the PPIE, Rolph's administration loosened its grip on local film exhibition. It is possible that Rolph realized the "bad will" that would be caused by keeping the crusade going against a rapidly growing industry that could greatly benefit the city. Six months after the closure of the exposition, the Board of Supervisors took the local censorship body out of operation and ordered the police to stop arresting exhibitors for showing indecent pictures. The official reason stated by the Police Committee for the inactivation of local censorship was that "it was clear a board of censorship was not wanted."[103]

Although the exposition marked a high point in the development of post-quake San Francisco, it also marked the beginning of the end for the first successful period of San Francisco film history. T. A. Church reported in the fall of 1915 that the most tangible development in the city's movie theaters was the tendency to extend runs of film programs. Church speculated that this development was due to the influx of "hundreds of thousands of strangers during the past year," meaning the tourism attracted by the PPIE, but he hastened to add that it might as well be the "natural development of the amusement trade."[104]

When the exposition closed in the middle of December 1915, many local exhibitors expressed frustration that the fair had drawn attention away from their theaters. Church noted that these complaints tended to come from exhibitors in the San Francisco suburbs and residential areas, while the downtown theaters, in general, had profited from the heightened influence of tourists. Market Street theaters even reported a 30 percent gain in income for 1915.[105] The PPIE coincided with the avalanche-like development of film production in Southern California, exemplified by the opening of Universal City in the San Fernando Valley in March 1915. The touristic appeal of Carl Laemmle's vast studio-scape drew the comparison to the San Francisco exhibition.[106] As a result of the development of the Los Angeles area as the film center on the West Coast, much of the local San Francisco talent gradually moved their businesses south. The successive departure of important film workers such as Sol Lesser and Sid Grauman did not mean a straight decline of the city as a place for film exhibition, but it did mark the end of an era in which the modus operandi interlinked production, distribution, and exhibition based from local San Francisco ventures. By the end of 1917, the most influential persons of the San Francisco transitional era film culture had gone to work in what was soon to become universally known as Hollywood.[107]

## The Emergence and Taming of San Francisco Film Culture

If the establishment of nickelodeon culture in San Francisco was replete with a form of frontier mentality among the exhibitors, the practical task of rebuilding the city was more informed by broad visions of modernity and locally specific iterations of progressive policies along with an ambition to renew its institutions and refine its reputation. The PPIE became a beacon for political players aspiring for power. These were critical external factors that conditioned local film culture between 1909 and 1915. The city's new mayor, James Rolph Jr., expressed deep concern for the hazards of film culture, set up a local censorship board, and monitored its development closely. The policing of film culture connected film's public exhibition to spaces and behaviors perceived as detrimental to the public health of the city.

The public and sometimes spectacular police interventions at movie theaters during Rolph's crusade triggered the ire of local exhibitors. While some put their trust in the diplomatic efforts of the local branch of the Exhibitors' League, others took upon themselves the quixotic mission of openly protesting the arbitrary operations of the censors. The local courts regularly ruled in favor of the movie men, but this did little to stop police meddling before the exposition. Gradually, the film exhibitors of San Francisco fell in line. By the opening of the PPIE in 1915, local film exhibitors and Rolph had formed a mutually beneficial relationship.

The showmen who became most successful had learned how to navigate local censors and the political arena, while still offering audiences sensational views of a San Francisco–specific variety. Most successful was Sid Grauman, who in shows and films such as *Last Night of the Barbary Coast* regularly activated myths and stereotypes about Chinatown and its surroundings. While reports and editorials diluted negative public perceptions of film exhibition by pointing to its virtues and educative potential, Chinatown's status as a mythical and hazardous space remained mostly unchanged.

The policies addressing local film culture interacted with a rising discontent among disenfranchised citizens who had been particularly visible in the prequake San Francisco cityscape. The Commonwealth Club study stands out as an example of concerns about the atmosphere found in modern forms of recreation like saloons, penny arcades, and moving picture theaters. The perceived darkness of San Francisco's traditional vice districts was transplanted from the alleyways and saloon backrooms of Chinatown and the Barbary Coast into the space of the movie theater from the earliest days of San Francisco film exhibition.[108] The notion of movie theaters as dangerous spaces shared key terms with the residual discourse on the polluting effects that Chinatown and Chinese San Franciscans were said to have on the rest of the city. Quotidian newspaper reports of raids on opium dens, prostitution houses, and gambling establishments shared editorial space with alarmist headlines that cast movie houses and dance halls as eyesores and places of moral corruption. At the end of the decade, the notion that Chinatown constituted an urban space where Chinese males posed a direct threat to white female virginity was reproduced nationally in newspapers, popular literature, and film.[109] But the fears of Chinatown urban space extended beyond moral corruption to concerns regarding physical health. After unsubstantiated reports of plague had caused mass hysteria in San Francisco in early 1900, the area had been subjected to periodic health investigations.[110] As film exhibition became a means to create profit in new areas of the city, the newly rebuilt Chinatown soon became a viable option. There were several ingredients for the commercial success of the film medium.

Given the proximity to the city's most popular entertainment districts, the "filmgoing" classes densely populated both Chinatown and North Beach. When the first movie theaters opened in Chinatown, they became frequent targets for such inspections.[111] As film became more popular in Chinatown, concerns about the hazards of film culture arose quickly. The perceived hazards of Chinatown that loomed large in public perception became entangled with emerging fears about illicit public recreation.

# Part II

# Chinatown Exhibition and Movie Theaters

# 3

# "The Most Cosmopolitan City in the World"

## Chinese San Francisco at the Turn of the Twentieth Century

Perched on the southern peninsula of a shallow estuary, San Francisco at the turn of the twentieth century was a gateway—a grand junction of crisscrossing traffic. Approaching from the Pacific Ocean, access to the city went through a natural passage interrupting the continuity of the Northern California coastline. This strait, known as the Golden Gate, led to the San Francisco Bay, the largest Pacific estuary of the continent. For centuries, the Bay Area, which yearly drained California's mountainous regions of nearly half their fresh water, was the home of the indigenous Ohlone. Then, in the 1770s, came Spanish colonizers, who were led by expeditions of Colonel Juan Batista de Anza and set up a mission in the name of Saint Francis of Assisi.[1] In 1835, Mexico, which had gained independence from New Spain in 1821, established a settlement called Yerba Buena on the northwestern shore of the peninsula. Only twenty-five years later, the outcome of the Mexican-American War forced Mexico to cede Yerba Buena, still a small town, to the United States; the northern Americans renamed it San Francisco. In 1849, prospectors struck gold in California. The findings spawned an incredible surge of fortune seekers from across the world, many of whom settled in San Francisco. The population boomed, increasing from 1,000 to 25,00 from 1848 to 1850. The gold and its steady influx of "forty-niners" turned the remote frontier area into a tremendous economic asset. After a brief

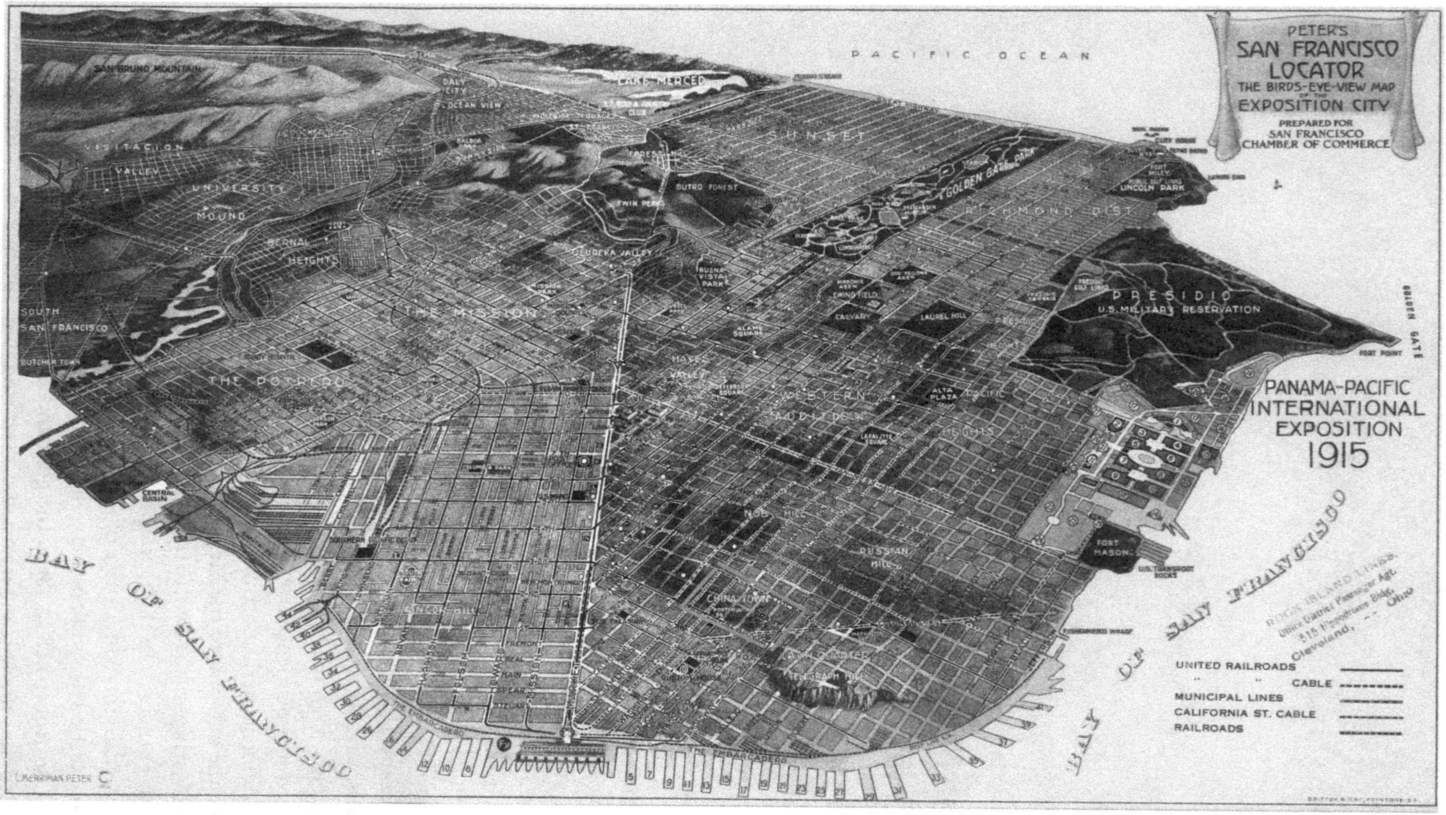


FIG. 5 Map of San Francisco, 1915. The location of Chinatown is marked off (my addition). *Peter's San Francisco locator: The bird's-eye-view of the Exposition city published by the San Francisco Chamber of Commerce, 1915*. (Image from David Rumsey Map Collection, courtesy of Cartography Associates)

period of governance by a local civil assembly, California, on September 9, 1850, became the thirty-first state of the Union..

Chinese immigrants were instrumental in the creation of San Francisco. In the late 1850s, prospectors found silver in the Comstock Lode, west of Lake Tahoe, at the foot of Mount Davidson, Nevada. Fortune seekers from all over the world came in search of their share of the bounty. San Francisco quickly became the mining industry's most convenient marketplace, attracting people from a wide range of cultures. A particular channel of immigration had opened from the southern region of Guangdong, China, from where thousands of men crossed the Pacific hoping to make their fortune. While the Chinese did become one of the pillars of the western economic infrastructure, it was not as titans of industry but as an exploited workforce. The low-paid, dangerous labor undertaken by Chinese workers was a significant factor in completing the world's first continental railroad in the 1860s, connecting the eastern United States to the western frontier. Many Chinese set up habitations around Portsmouth Square in the early 1850s. As San Francisco grew, the Chinese neighborhood gradually became the heart of the world's largest and most important Chinese community outside mainland China.

While the Chinese quickly became the largest immigrant constituency, groups of European and South American émigrés were living in close quarters in the downtown area that had developed from the old Yerba Buena settlements. San Francisco was quickly becoming one of the most diverse cities in the United States, but its existing living space could not contain the growing population. New neighborhoods were needed. The Western Addition, Haight-Ashbury, Eureka Valley, and the Mission District were added to the cityscape between 1860 and 1880. The city continued to develop, with the expanded exploitation of the area's abundant natural resources generating rapid growth. In 1870, the population had increased sixfold from 1850, to 150,000, and by 1900 that number had more than doubled, to around 350,000, making San Francisco the nation's ninth-largest city. On the maps of the western frontier, the city was the last civilized outpost. On the nautical charts of the transpacific steamers, it was the main entry point leading into the North American continent.

## Marginalized Chinese San Francisco

Scholars have studied the presence of Chinese in America ever since the Chinese became a powerful workforce on the West Coast. Most of them approached Chinese immigration as a problem to be solved by the state, or city governments, long after the Chinese Exclusion Act had effectively hampered the transpacific influx of people from the Guangdong region.[2] While some scholarship was more "pro"-Chinese, like Mary Coolidge's extensive 1909 study of Chinese immigration, the debate was rather narrow and was tinged by what Sucheng

FIG. 6 Anti-Chinese Stereotyping. "What Shall We Do With Our Boys?," George Frederick Keller, *San Francisco Illustrated Wasp*, March 3, 1882. (Image courtesy of the Bancroft Library, University of California, Berkeley)

Chan calls "partisan rhetoric."[3] A contemporary review of Coolidge's study provides an emblematic positioning on the "Chinese question." Ira B. Cross, a professor of economics at Stanford University, established that "no amount of arguing can change the attitude of the inhabitants on the Pacific Coast. . . . The Orientals are not wanted."[4]

The systemic oppression of the Chinese American community was not present only in legislation and street thuggery. Various smear campaigns depicting the Chinese as a rat-eating, opium-smoking, disease-ridden people had been launched in different versions and stuck in public media discourse, which trickled down into other forms of representation. By the turn of the century, many specific stereotypes related to Chinese Americans and Chinatowns were repeated throughout various forms of modern entertainment, such as vaudeville and "slumming tours," and were also transplanted to the newest fad around: film.

Exclusionist policies and the general dissemination of "Chineseness" as a toxic influence on U.S. public health also found support in the scientific community. Financed by organizations such as the Carnegie Fund and the Rockefeller Foundation, the American eugenics movement had gained considerable political leverage by the turn of the twentieth century.[5] Ethnic studies scholar Nancy Ordover has concluded that the eugenics movement and propagators of exclusionist policies engaged in dynamic interplay during this period: "Eugenics gave racism and nationalism substance by bringing to bear the rationalizing technologies of the day. In turn, these ideologies were prime movers of eugenic thought and its accompanying legislation."[6] The wide dissemination of eugenicist perspectives justified the passing of the Chinese Exclusion Act of 1882. Such rhetoric sustained and elaborated links between low intelligence and ethnicity, which propelled several local and federal attempts at legislating against racial mixing—or "miscegenation"—especially in the increasingly dense urban areas of modern America.[7] The influx of European refugees during the latter stages of World War I led to the passing of the Immigration Act of 1917, primarily influenced by eugenics advocates such as Madison Grant and Lothrop Stoddard.[8] In 1924, "a steady stream of false statistics" embellished the bill, underpinning the idea of a race-based "feeblemindedness" as formulated by studies conducted by eugenicist scholars.[9] While the eugenics movement on the East Coast targeted mainly Eastern European Jews and Italians, West Coast propagators focused on the Chinese as the main obstacle for racial purification of the Californian public.

The passing of the Chinese Exclusion Act in 1882 and the reinforcement of it in 1893 meant that the prejudices and racial stereotypes that had been part of the anti-Chinese sentiments of the Californian public sphere transformed into government policy. For many Chinese San Franciscans, this meant a restriction to work only in laundries, restaurants, and domestic services. Him Mark Lai has noted that the limitations not only barred Chinese immigration but also effectively reduced Chinese American participation in the mainstream of American society to a minimum, through practices of racial segregation in schools and public institutions, restrictive housing covenants, and antimiscegenation laws. This isolation, in turn, led to many Chinese Americans developing feelings of "inferiority and alienation from American society."[10]

While the present study is mainly concerned with the historical marginalization of Chinese in California, it relates to more general studies of the concept of racism and its role in the emergence of the United States as a nation. Alexander Saxton's book *The Rise and Fall of the White Republic* provides a methodological anchor. Looking beyond economic and psychological models of explanation, Saxton approached the concept of racism as a potent and malleable ideology, defined as "a system of beliefs and attitudes that ascribe central importance to real and presumed racial differences."[11] The emphasis on these differences goes beyond the physical to assert moral, intellectual, and psychological qualities as racially discernible and transmitted by heredity. For Saxton, the potential for transformation of the ideology lay in its progressive framing in social experience, resulting in an "ongoing social construction of reality" in which conflicting ideological components "must depend upon a correspondence with that ongoing construction."[12] The notion of racism as a forceful ideology has also been central for John Kuo Wei Tchen, one of the foremost scholars of Chinese American history. In his influential book *New York before Chinatown*, Tchen posited that "the use of Chinese things, ideas, and people in the United States, in various imagined and real forms, has been instrumental in forming this nation's cultural identity," at least since the end of the American Revolutionary War.[13] The ideology of white racism, according to both Saxton and Tchen, played a central role in obscuring the Chinese influence on the building of modern America, downplaying the humanity of the workers who helped shape the transcontinental U.S. infrastructure and industrialize the frontier, and instead promoting the imagery of a bucktoothed enemy that emerged in cartoons and sketches only to become fully realized in the silver screen productions of the Classical Hollywood era.[14]

While the public focus on the "Oriental threat" shifted somewhat from China to Japan after World War I, it was not until the late 1960s that Chinese American history became a recognized scholarly subject. In 1969, Thomas Chinn, Him Mark Lai, and Phil Choy published a comprehensive syllabus of Chinese American history, outlining institutions and cultural practices that had defined the Chinese communities since the 1850s.[15] The publication was the first of many tireless efforts by these three scholars to restore and reinstate the Chinese community in U.S. history. Chinn, Lai and Choy's call to revisit and retrieve Chinese American history was reflected in Alexander Saxton's important survey of the Chinese and the labor movement in California titled *The Indispensable Enemy* (1971). During the 1870s and 1880s, Chinese immigrants made up one-quarter to one-fifth of Californians working for wages.[16] Saxton identified a sharp division between California's considerable Chinese contingent and the rest of California's working class, where laborers of European descent drove the alienation of the Chinese community while being exploited within the industrial and political hegemonies of late nineteenth-century California.[17] In 1973, sociologists Victor Nee and Brett de Bary Nee sought to address the lack of voices representing the Chinatown community in U.S. historiography. In *Longtime Californ': A Documentary Study*, they compiled accounts in the form of monologues from contemporary San Francisco Chinatown inhabitants, offering firsthand accounts from participants of a wide range of ages, including labor immigrants from the early twentieth century.[18]

From these beginnings, Chinese American studies produced significant historiographical insights into the modern history of the United States by examining a range of topics. Sucheng Chan has published several influential works on the history of transpacific Chinese immigration, arguing for a historical approach that accounts for the uneven regional development of U.S. capitalism.[19] In Chan's view, asymmetrical westward expansion created ethnic enclaves in the American South and West that functioned as colonies for the industrializing East Coast and Midwest.[20] Further, Chan has, along with historian Madeleine Y. Hsu, called for a Chinese American history that accounts for the multifaceted transnational ties between members of the Chinese diaspora and their locales of origin.[21]

The transpacific perspective is more prevalent in scholarship on Chinatown. Yong Chen's 2000 study, for example, focused on the interaction of social and political changes in both Chinatown and China between 1850 and 1943. Based on a wide variety of Chinese-language sources, the study highlighted the often contradictory processes of "Americanization" and "Chinese nationalism" that permeated the Chinatown community in the post-quake period.[22] Scholars like Nayan Shah and Karen J. Leong studied the institutional suppression of Chinese Americans by investigating discursive constructions regarding Chinese Americans as public health hazards.[23] Shah's book on plague scares and racially tinged health campaigns of early twentieth-century Chinatown intersects with contemporary discourses on Chinatown theater and film venues as potential public health risks. Judy Yung's 1995 study of the physical and social "unbinding" of Chinese women in San Francisco informs this study's discussion of moviegoing as a symbol of modernity and liberation in post-quake Chinatown.[24]

Building on the foundation laid out by Chinn, Lai, and Choy, Chinese American studies has become a burgeoning scholarly field, often conceived in the intersection of common disciplinary partitions and through close readings of historical documents "against the grain." While sometimes ideologically divided, scholars have continually discovered new aspects, nuances, and alternative perspectives on the history of Chinese America in general and the social dynamics and political makeup of Chinatowns in particular.

## Social Organization of Chinatown and the Emergence of an "Alternative" Chinese American Public Sphere

In this violent and hostile environment, Chinatown became the home and political center for the Chinese population of California. In the 1860s, the Chinese Consolidated Benevolent Association—more commonly known as the Chinese Six Companies—developed from Chinese labor recruitment organizations (*huiguan*).[25] The Six Companies became Chinatown's natural governing body and continually worked to improve Chinese-American relations as well as safeguarding the rights of Chinese in America. The Six Companies were also crucial in establishing Chinese San Francisco as the "capital of Chinese America."[26]

In order to diplomatically counter the local anti-Chinese sentiments propagated by the Workingmen's Party, and echoed by many of San Francisco's social institutions, the Chinese government established a consulate on Clay Street in 1878. The Chinatown diplomatic office was the first in the United States outside of Washington, DC. The *Daily Alta California* announced the opening of the consulate in the form of a small public notice on December 12. A significantly larger column on the same page provided a commentary on the ongoing discussions of the "Chinese question" at the California Constitutional Convention in Sacramento.[27] While the convention laid the foundation for the federal Chinese Exclusion Act of 1882, the installment of what was soon to become the Chinese consul general signaled the centrality of Chinese San Francisco in the activism for the betterment of Chinese American living conditions on a national level.

The Six Companies, the consulate, and local Chinese newspapers became important administrators of social life for Chinese San Franciscans. While often working against odds of Sisyphean proportions, they arranged joint actions protesting exclusionist politics. One of these critical actions was the transpacific orchestration of the 1905 official Chinese boycott of American goods. This event, according to Yong Chen, intensified the transpacific ties between China and Chinese San Francisco and was the beginning of a new nationalist movement that advocated the modernization of social institutions on both shores.[28]

While the Six Companies and the U.S. offices of the Qing government in Beijing were of greatest importance as the spokesmen of Chinese America, the Chinese newspapers of San Francisco also held essential roles as informal social institutions of the Chinese community. Notwithstanding local Chinese-language papers in other parts of the country, nowhere were newspapers as numerous and influential as in San Francisco. The first weekly Chinese newspaper, *The Golden Hills' News*, came out as early as 1854 and was followed by several journalistic endeavors published every week. The papers were often tabloid-sized and provided the Chinese community with news items from China and the United States, as well as poems, stories, and essays by Chinese American contributors. Some of the papers included English-language sections, which sought to educate non-Chinese readers on China and Chinese America.[29] The turn of the century saw a rise in political engagement of Chinese Americans, in large part due to the societal changes that were unfolding in the empire. A growing number of local Chinese-language dailies monitored the relation between transpacific political developments and the precarious situation of the Chinese San Franciscan community. The newspapers categorized reporting into sections of international, Chinese, national, and local news. Similar to modern U.S. newspapers, the Chinese dailies were published in broadsheet format and frequently included editorials on both local and international politics.[30] Arguably, the most influential of these was the *Chung Sai Yat Po*, established by the Chinese American Presbyterian minister Ng Poon Chew. The paper favored reform, both in China and in the Chinese American community, and soon expanded to wide circulation. Ng also became a visible spokesperson for Chinese Americans in the English-language press. He had speaking engagements all over the country, advocating against Chinese exclusion, and for the modernization of the Chinese American community. Following the success of *Chung Sai Yat Po*, several of the emerging political organizations of Chinese San Francisco started daily and weekly newspapers as outlets for their political agendas. Many of the papers were reform-minded, and some, such as *Young China*, eventually became important backers of Sun Yat-sen's Chinese Nationalist Party.[31]

However, the social organization of Chinese San Francisco was not all above board. The restriction of Chinese immigration and trade by the Exclusion Act in the early 1880s paved the way for organized crime. As living conditions in Chinese America became increasingly dire, many Chinese immigrants, without eligibility for any of the larger benevolent associations, joined voluntary social organizations, which, unlike the *huiguan*, had less restrictive recruitment policies. Similarly to the Six Companies, the tongs provided their members with services denied them by federal and state jurisdictions, but their means were different. To fund their social network of member services, many of these groups turned to illegal activities.[32] Commonly, such an organization would operate illegal gambling establishments and expedite the trafficking of Chinese women for prostitution in Chinatown brothels.[33] When they grew more powerful, the rivalry between such groups occasionally developed into violent episodes that took place in the streets and establishments of Chinatown and the North Beach area. The presence of these criminal elements sometimes extended into the theaters and movie houses of Chinatown. These organizations would become known to the U.S. public as the infamous Chinatown tongs, a notion woven into the fabric of Orientalist Chinatown mythology by contemporary newspaper reports of bloody turf wars and sensationalist scholarly publications of high sensationalist value, such as Richard Dillon's book *The Hatchet Men* (1962), named after the organization's most notorious enforcers.[34] San Francisco's Chinatown became the hub for illegal transpacific business, most notably represented by the smuggling of opium and the trafficking of Chinese women. While the Six Companies actively worked to clean up its ranks, the city of San Francisco established an especially brutal police force, composed mostly of Irish Americans, to police the Chinese district. This group was known as the Chinatown Squad, a collection of baton-waving brutes who, through their violent methods, became yet another menacing presence in the everyday street life of Chinese San Franciscans.[35] The viciousness of the Chinatown Squad soon earned them a place in the American Orientalist imaginary, providing white America with a tangible and forceful response to the imagined threats of Chinatown. This imagery proliferated in early documentary-style film recordings of the neighborhood. In 1900, cameraman Raymond Ackerman filmed in San Francisco for the American Mutoscope and Biograph Company. Ackerman placed himself in the middle of Washington Street, facing Jackson Street, and had three imposing members of the Chinatown Squad walk toward the camera.[36]

Similar views of Chinese American alienation abound in early cinema. However, as we shall see, the processual marginalization of Chinese San Francisco did not so much hinder as alter the Chinatown neighborhood's immersion in contemporary modernity culture. Even before the appearance of cinema, the community had, out of necessity, developed the characteristics of an "alternative public sphere." Within cinema studies, this notion is closely linked to Miriam Hansen's pioneered usage of the term, as a way to theorize how early cinemas offered urban spaces where individual spectators could traverse dominant divisions of class and ethnicity in U.S. society. In her seminal study *Babel and Babylon*, Hansen identified a blurring of class divisions among movie theater patrons, "offering them participation in an ostensibly classless, Americanized, community of leisure."[37]

The notion of the public sphere originates from Jürgen Habermas, a Frankfurt School scholar who devised the term as a theoretical approach to studying public communications in tandem with the rise of capitalism.[38] However, Hansen's model for studying heterogeneous audience groups of the silent era relies more on Oskar Negt and Alexander Kluge's appropriation of Habermas's concept. While Negt and Kluge theorized a public sphere alternative to Habermas's conceptualization of the emergence of the bourgeois public sphere in the late nineteenth and early twentieth centuries, their adaptation focused on notions of class division rather than hegemonies of ethnic communities in modern Western nation-states.[39] Hansen took from Negt and Kluge the notion of social horizons and attributed it to contexts of early U.S. cinema audiences.[40] Hansen issued a call to study historical spectatorship in American cinema of the transitional era with an emphasis on exhibition practices as live performances, providing the "structural conditions for locally specific, collective formations of reception."[41] She reiterated the heuristic value of the historical study of shared social horizons as a window into the everyday lives of people on the fringes of the dominant public sphere: "From the perspective of the dominant pseudosynthesis, the life contexts of subordinate groups seem fragmented and disjointed.... From the perspective of the experiencing subjects, however, these life contexts, to whatever degree appropriated and/or 'othered' by dominant publicity, still constitute a *Zusammenhang*, a horizon of a different kind."[42] In *Babel and Babylon*, Hansen suggested that if approached through such a localized perspective, cinema "might have functioned as a potentially autonomous, alternative horizon of experience" for immigrant working-class audiences.[43]

As the marginalization of the Chinese community increased in the period leading up to the earthquake, the contours of an emerging Chinese American public sphere grew more well defined. It had its institutions, internal governance, and modes of communication. In many ways, the public sphere of the Chinese San Franciscan community emerged in response to the successive marginalization of the community. In this way, the Chinese American public sphere was an alternative to, but not entirely separated from, the dominant public sphere of the city.

## Industrious Chinatown

An often-overlooked aspect of the Chinese in California revolves around the group's economic industriousness and business acumen. Far from being an impoverished ghetto, Chinese San Francisco developed a notable economic infrastructure based on a wide variety of imported goods, services, and job opportunities for both immigrants and Chinese Americans. Unlike the small businesses owned by Chinese immigrants in other U.S. cities, which often sprawled over the urban areas, most Chinese San Franciscan enterprises lay in the Chinatown neighborhood.[44]

The initial emergence of the Chinese San Franciscan economy was concentrated on Sacramento Street, where small businesses—restaurants, drugstores, woodyards, and meat shops—made it possible for Chinese immigrants to transplant everyday cultural practices from ancestral Chinese regions to urban San Francisco.[45] As Chinese San Francisco grew, the commercial activities shifted toward Dupont Street, which became the area's economic center in the late nineteenth and early twentieth centuries. The *Crocker-Langley San Francisco Directory* from 1882 listed 942 Chinese businesses. Of these, around 200 were located on Dupont Street, while Sacramento Street had 56.[46] Most of the others lined the streets that crossed or ran parallel to Dupont.[47] While the official San Francisco directories are not exhaustive sources for identifying Chinese businesses, they are useful as indications of the geographic concentration of Chinese commerce in San Francisco. After the earthquake and fire, the city renamed Dupont Street after President Ulysses S. Grant. However, the Chinese name for the street, Dupont Gai, remained very much in use.

In 1839, rant had described his first experience of modern transportation technology as the "annihilation of space."[48] The emergence of modern modes of transportation such as trains, steamships, and streetcars opened up the market for the importation of Chinese goods. The establishment of the Pacific Mail Steamship Company in the late 1860s effectively cut transport time across the Pacific in half, and steamship travel quickly became an essential feature of the Chinese American community, connecting San Francisco to the native country.[49] From 1880 onward, the range of services and specialized goods offered in Chinatown expanded rapidly. The arrival of the printing press mechanized the publication of Chinese-language newspapers, while the installation of the Chinese Telephone Exchange in 1894 offered a new communicational node for

Chinese San Franciscans. Around the same time, Chinese-owned canneries opened in the East and South San Francisco Bay, and Chinese San Franciscan merchants formed the Chinese-American Bank and the Chinese Chamber of Commerce.[50]

## Demographics and Employment

According to the 1910 federal census, San Francisco, with 416,912 inhabitants, ranked as the eleventh largest city of the United States. About 96 percent of the city's population was categorized as "white."[51] This category included San Franciscan immigrants of Irish, German, and Italian descent, who made up some of the city's most significant national communities, of which many gathered in specific areas of the city. The Italian community clustered in the North Beach area, which was adjacent to Chinatown. San Franciscans of Polish and German descent were numerous in the Western Addition.

The second-largest category in the population was made up of the city's 10,582 Chinese. Of these, 9,235 were male, and only 1,347 female. While the city's "white" population was spread all over its geographic area, the Chinese, with very few exceptions, lived in the Chinatown area. The Chinese population had seen a dramatic drop since the census of 1880, when it made up 9.1 percent of the total, as the Chinese Exclusion Act effectively strained Chinese American immigration. By 1900, the Chinese population had dropped to 4.1 percent of the city total, and by 1910, the Chinese in San Francisco made up only 2.5 percent. This decline was mostly the result of the anti-Chinese movement and the federal legislation that it inspired. The downward trend in numbers continued throughout the 1910s. In 1920, San Francisco's Chinese population was at the lowest comparable rating since the 1860s. During the 1920s, the numbers turned upward again, and since 1930, the Chinese San Franciscan population has seen a steady gain.[52]

The most common employment in the turn-of-the-century San Francisco Chinese community was within trade, services, and manufacturing, with textiles, shoes, and cigars some of the most common Chinese-owned industries. In 1900, 48 percent of San Francisco's Chinese male population worked within the trade sector. Ten years later, that number had risen to around 55 percent. Within this category, the majority were merchants or grocers. Other notable occupations were business managers and salesmen.[53] In the absence of the scholarly class that usually made up the elite in Chinese society, the merchant class became the elite of Chinese San Francisco. They were a basis for the growth of the Chinese population during the exclusion era and gradually formed a middle class.[54] However, toward the end of the nineteenth century, it was within the industrial sector where Chinese entrepreneurs and laborers encountered the staunchest repugnance, as they were commonly seen to be competing with "white" firms and labor.[55]

Despite popular belief that almost all Chinese women in San Francisco during this time were prostitutes, female Chinese immigrants held a wide variety of jobs.[56] Indeed, the Chinese San Francisco community was a male-dominated society, and there were several brothels in the Chinatown area that were frequented by both Chinese and non-Chinese men. Still, the recurring contemporary framing of prostitution as part of the "Chinese problem" by both Chinese-friendly public reformers and anti-Chinese activists overshadowed the lives and social roles of the many Chinese women who were not courtesans. By the turn of the century, married women made up more than 62 percent of the Chinese community.[57] According to Yong Chen, Chinese women at this time could be found working in a wide variety of low-income jobs, such as shoe binders, servants, tailors, and launderers.[58] As Judy Yung has shown, while Chinese women in San Francisco generally were bound by both the physical and the hierarchical constraints of Confucian culture, some immigrant women, such as Maria Seise, Ah Toy, Mary Tape, and Lai Yun Oi, managed to break free from the oppressive control of male-dominated society.[59]

Other communities of non-European heritage made up smaller contingents of cosmopolitan San Francisco. The Japanese constituted 1.1 percent of the population in 1910, which amounted to about half of the city's Chinese population. However, the Japanese community had more than doubled in size since 1900. During this time, the public venom against Chinese immigration generally did not extend to the Japanese. This mentality would soon change, as China became a republic and Japan emerged as the new threat from across the Pacific Ocean.[60] The Japanese population remained at around 1 percent up until the 1960s, but this number does not account for the mass internments of Japanese Americans during the Second World War. The city's African American community was small and remained below 1 percent of the total population up until the late 1940s. Separate figures regarding the city's Spanish, Central American, and South American populations were not kept until the 1960s.

## Borders and Mobility

The social and cultural borders of Chinatown were gradually established, negotiated, and reinforced throughout the first fifty years of the city of San Francisco. Despite the drop in immigration, and insistence on social containment by anti-Chinese activists, Chinatown space gradually grew and by the early 1900s was bordered by California, Stockton, Broadway, and Kearny Streets. The public perception of this space was continually reinforced as "Chinese," to the extent that guidebooks and map companies began to include detailed sections on the neighborhood as a viable excursion for San Francisco visitors.[61] The movements of the Chinese community, on the other hand, were severely restricted by the proliferation of anti-Chinese politics, which presented Chinese urban mobility as a threat to public health and morals. Anti-Chinese sentiments were still a common underlying factor in the general public's approach to the neighborhood. The unbridled animosity was evident in the paroxysms of public fear brought on by media campaigns, such as the 1900 plague scare, during which editorials in local newspapers urged city legislators to "clean out Chinatown," even though it would mean a significant blow to the city's economy.[62] Demonstrators organized anti-Chinese marches in the surrounding neighborhoods, and violence against Chinese San Franciscans "trespassing" outside of Chinatown was common.[63]

The historian Yumei Sun argued that although no physical borders existed around Chinatown, a set of invisible demarcation lines marked out the sections where Chinese lived. According to Sun, "Chinatown was surrounded by a glass wall. Though Chinese residents in Chinatown could go outside the wall and white residents could come inside, the realm of the Chinese public life in America was constrained by this invisible barrier."[64] The invisible barrier was reinforced by the physical detainment of a large group of Chinese immigrants who did not pass the stringent requirements presented by the rigid local enforcement of exclusion laws. Initially, transpacific immigrants awaited U.S. customs inspections en masse in two sheds located at the Pacific Mail Steamship Company's wharf. The San Francisco Chinese community lodged several complaints about the unsafe and unsanitary conditions of cramming 400 to 500 people into cold wooden structures for an extended period. Finally, the U.S. Immigration Department investigated and suggested relocation. The new facilities were located at Angel Island, a small island in the San Francisco Bay.[65] The administrative wait could sometimes last several years and often ended in a return to China. Many immigrants succumbed to depression or suicide. Awaiting their fate to be decided, several men and women took to writing poetry on the walls of their barracks.[66] The "Ellis Island of the West" processed and interned approximately 175,000 Chinese immigrants during its thirty years of operation. The veritable limbo existence of Chinese immigrants detained in such proximity to Chinatown remained a defining factor of the restricted mobility for Chinese San Franciscans until 1940.[67]

While many historical accounts of Chinatown tend to frame the neighborhood as a highly segregated ethnic enclave, some scholars have underlined the multiethnic mobility that pervaded everyday street life in the area.[68] From the early 1870s, cable cars revolutionized transportation for San Francisco's citizens. Given the city's uninviting topography, with steep hills and high climbs, mobility had been conducted mainly by horse-drawn carriage.[69] In 1873, Chinatown was brought into the city's modernizing infrastructure as the Clay Street Hill

Railroad began operation, running from Leavenworth Street to Kearny.[70] The ride along Clay through Chinatown soon became a popular attraction among tourists. In 1944, urban historian Edgar Myron Kahn waxed lyrically about the moving "descent" from Nob Hill, through Chinatown, toward the Bay. Kahn wrote, "The gripman, when reaching the narrow, level strip of Dupont Street (now Grant Avenue) had to pull the brake handle with all his might to bring to a shivering stop the swiftly descending car in order to deposit his passengers at the gateway of Chinatown."[71] While employing strongly racialized prose, Kahn underlined the importance of public transportation as grounds for "inter-racial friendship" between regular commuters.[72] Somewhat contrarily, Nayan Shah and Mary Ting Yi Lui argued that streetcars, mixing the Chinese community with the rest of the city, were often seen as vehicles of transmission of disease and debauchery almost by default connected to Chinatown by social reformers, police, and the local press.[73] The increased influx of outside visitors did not dispel the myth of the Oriental city, but it did improve mobility for the Chinese community in the growing cityscape of San Francisco.

Along with Mary Louise Pratt, John Kuo Wei Tchen has underlined the historically unique status of specific intercultural border zones that appeared in cities and along the frontiers of westward expansion in turn-of-the-century America, in which white, Protestant, and European Americans interacted with various peoples of profoundly different cultures. As explained by Tchen in his book *New York before Chinatown*, "These border zones embodied various configurations of cultural mixing and hierarchy. . . . Alongside racism, the contact with non-Western peoples wrought mixed port cultures and frontier settlements in which were forged new hybrid human identities and cultures."[74] Tchen located one such contact zone in lower Manhattan. The same notion also can be used to define traits of post–gold rush San Francisco, with its reliance on the transpacific traffic of goods, ideas, and human beings. The historian Barbara Berglund wrote that San Francisco emerged as a contact zone where "peoples pushed and pulled by multiple migratory trajectories encountered each other and established relations along a continuum ranging from conflict, coercion, and exploitation to friendship, sexual liaison, and marriage."[75] In a social dynamic where European American white supremacy was the dominant ideological overtone of San Francisco's power elite, and Kearnyist agitation had intensified race hate aimed explicitly at Chinese San Franciscans, Chinatown came to function as a sort of buffer zone.

In line with Tchen's observation of New York, social intermingling and acceptance seemed to prevail most notably in connection with the commercial streetscape of Chinatown, which opened up for the development of cross-cultural interaction. As such, "these zones were not only and not always defined by hostility and exploitation, but also by friendships, interminglings, and the birth of new multicultural peoples."[76] Contemporary racial hierarchies undoubtedly dictated this intercultural mobility, but the everyday social dynamics of the Chinatown streets also opened up for interactions and exchanges beyond such rigid categorization. San Francisco's Chinatown, as noted by the theater historian Daphne P. Lei, became the first significant Sino-American contact zone in the United States.[77]

The area's entertainment scene facilitated a considerable amount of Chinatown's cross-cultural interaction. Chinatown's status as a space for cultural voyeurism was well established by the end of the nineteenth century. The flows of outside visitors created a unique dynamic for public amusements in Chinatown, as exemplified by the widespread popularity of Chinese theater. Lei wrote that the "negotiation of time and space constructed a strange niche for Chinese theatre in the contact zone. Even though the Chinese were 'imprisoned' in Chinatown, tourists were willing to cross the boundary for the thrill of the ethnic experience and take the time machine to visit an 'ancient' art."[78] The onstage and offstage performative nature of Chinatown public amusements was one of the ways through which its cross-cultural contact zones liaised with the realm of contemporary popular imagination. Other than theatergoing and people watching, parlor games and gambling were, along with the occasional visit to a brothel, the most common forms of recreation and entertainment for working-class males in the Chinese community before the earthquake and fire.[79] While Chinatown offered an urban space where Chinese San Franciscans could enjoy leisure time without daily harassment, the direct proximity to the city's famed Barbary Coast blurred the borders between San Francisco's infamous vice district and the seedier parts of Chinatown's entertainment scene. The Barbary Coast was the name of a loosely connected stretch of bars, dance halls, billiard saloons, and brothels that had made up San Francisco's red-light district since 1849. It encompassed an area of nine blocks, stretching into Chinatown, North Beach, and Jackson Square—areas occupied primarily by the city's Italian community. The main stretch of the Barbary Coast lay on Pacific Street, between Stockton and Montgomery Streets. Although this portion of the street does not seem to have had any film theaters or theaters showing film around this time, many dance halls and cheap-thrill theater houses of the Barbary Coast exerted a significant influence on the practices of contemporary theater men and film exhibitors in the city.

## Setting the Scene

Chinese immigrants played a central role in the establishment of the city of San Francisco. Workers traveling mainly from the southern parts of China provided cheap and reliable labor in the mines and on the railroads, which became the lifeblood and main arteries in the city's development from a small mining town to a western metropolis. The Chinese neighborhood that grew from the settlements around Portsmouth Square became the base for San Francisco's second-largest population group. More important, it became a spatial and symbolic point of reference for transpacific immigrants, as well as Chinese Americans at large. At the turn of the century, the enterprise and economic infrastructure of the Chinese community had turned into an integral part of San Francisco's economy.

However, the American dream never seemed to apply to members of the Chinese community. From an early stage, they, as a group, were the victims of systematic oppression. Non-Chinese labor groups, both official and unofficial, targeted the "Oriental" workforce with violence and racially tinged political campaigns, which reverberated all the way up to the city's elite. The influx of Chinese to the West Coast became a social problem to be solved. The 1882 passage of the federal Chinese Exclusion Act was the culmination of this process, ushering in a new era of social marginalization, which officially lasted until the 1940s.

As the injustices against the Chinese community grew, some diasporic organizations that initially had provided services for new immigrants began to organize to fight oppressive conditions. Several important Chinatown institutions emerged that combined Chinese cultural traditions with the developments of the modern world. While the Chinese community gradually moved toward presenting a united front in the face of political, social, and cultural exclusion and adversity, there existed a broad spectrum of diversity within the community.

Despite the anti-Chinese perceptions that recurrently appeared in San Francisco public discourse, Chinatown became a popular tourist attraction among the white middle class toward the end of the nineteenth century. Self-proclaimed Chinatown guides offered "slumming tours" that spotlighted firsthand experiences of everyday life in Chinatown through the prism of popular stereotypes of the underworld of the Oriental. However, while interracial mobility offered a common sight on the streets of Chinatown, the neighborhood was still widely regarded as an enclosed and potentially dangerous ethnic enclave.

Under continued challenging circumstances, Chinese Americans developed an alternative societal infrastructure, offering jobs, legal protection, and means of communication to a community that had been shut out or restricted from San Francisco's social and professional spheres. This "alternative" sphere extended into many dimensions of Chinese San Franciscan public life, including public amusement. Before the earthquake and fire, the most popular forms of "going out" in Chinatown included Chinese theater and gambling. Adding to Chinatown's rich history of stage performance, the neighborhood's entertainment scene mingled with the raunchy nightlife of the Barbary Coast stretch. The central location and ties to San Francisco's port culture made Chinatown popular with visitors, from aspiring performers and the local intelligentsia to the drunken sailor crowd. On evenings and weekends, this eclectic mix of people spilled onto the streets of Chinatown, mingling with its inhabitants and outside Chinese visitors, turning stretches of the neighborhood into contact zones of different cultures, experiences, and desires. It was in this setting that Chinatown's first nickelodeons and combined vaudeville and movie houses appeared between 1908 and 1915.

# 4

# "Eyes Darting Around, Spirit Dashing About"

## Mapping Chinatown Film Culture, 1906–1915

It was after the earthquake and fire that film came to Chinatown. Although scenes of Chinatown and Chinese life in San Francisco had been ubiquitous in nearly every documentary-style film showcasing the city's signifying traits, the regular exhibition of film did not emerge until after the reconstruction of the neighborhood.[1] During the years following the disaster, public amusements in Chinatown began to transform. Established popular forms of entertainment, such as vaudeville and traditional Chinese theater, gradually ceded ground to the more affordable and rapidly developing film medium. In line with developments across the United States, many storefront nickelodeons and larger, rebuilt theaters opened in the Chinatown area between 1906 and 1915. From 1908 onward, no fewer than two simultaneously operating film houses catered to local audiences and outside visitors, with shows operating from early in the afternoon until late at night.

This chapter investigates the appearance and establishment of film exhibition in San Francisco's Chinatown. It maps each theater's location in the neighborhood's densely populated and geographically condensed urbanscape. It details ownership, operations, and spatial aspects, such as proximity to shops, restaurants, other establishments of entertainment, and essential Chinatown institutions. It also evokes aspects of Chinatown's rich pre-quake theater history and looks at how the traditions and locations of former theaters were transplanted into Chinatown film exhibition.

The period 1906–1915 delimits what I call post-quake Chinatown film culture. However, because the development of this culture was so profoundly affected by its spatial setting, it is necessary to orient the reader by locating this film culture in the historical space of post-quake Chinatown. As with any form of cartography, we need to establish a perimeter, which requires first looking at the circumstances surrounding the re-establishment of Chinatown's own geographic perimeter after the neighborhood had been nearly wiped off the map.

The catastrophe forced the bulk of Chinatown's population out of the city. Many Chinese San Franciscans relocated to Oakland and the East Bay, and some remained there, as a return to Chinatown became less and less certain.[2] Populist politicians and brash public commentators suggested that the earthquake and fire provided an ample opportunity to finally move the Chinese quarters to a less central location.[3] Sydney Tyler, a newspaper correspondent who had previously published accounts of the Russo-Japanese War, wrote in a 400-page detailed report of the disaster that among the few good things that the destruction had brought to San Francisco was the removal of "the greatest pest hole of any modern city—Chinatown." Tyler asserted, "It can be taken for granted that Chinatown, which lay on the slope of Nob Hill between the best business and finest residential sections, will never be rebuilt in the center of the city."[4] On a more official level, former mayor James Phelan's committee for San Francisco's reconstruction openly discussed the idea of moving the Chinese community to away from the city.

The relocation plans led to protests from Chinese San Franciscans, as well as from the many non-Chinese property owners in Chinatown who had profited from overcharging their Chinese tenants before the catastrophe and did not intend to change their ways. A coalition of Chinese community leaders and non-Chinese property owners formed the Dupont Street Improvement Club in opposition to relocation.[5] "The business of Chinatown amounted to $30,000,000 during last year," the Improvers estimated in an article published in the *Chronicle*. They further argued that "the Chinese paid their share of the municipal taxes and should be permitted to locate wherever they desired."[6] Historian Christopher Yip has argued that there were many reasons for not moving Chinatown that influenced the final decision, among them the "understanding that the Chinese did indeed contribute to San Francisco's economy, and that moving Chinatown could adversely affect this contribution."[7] The prospect of losing important transpacific business, such as the import and retail business conducted by the Sing Fat Company, was risky for the business sector, given the deep entanglement of such Chinatown companies in the city's commercial web. Furthermore, financial assistance and support began flowing in from overseas, with the Qing government and several Chinese officials donating large amounts of money and expressing concern that the Chinese community should be thrown out of the city.[8]

These circumstances presented the committee with a dilemma. A significant reduction or outright removal of the Chinese community would risk the city's favorable trading position with China, a scenario believed likely to have "a very serious long term effect on the city's financial health."[9] Another consideration was the draw of Chinatown as a San Francisco tourist attraction.[10] Chinatown tourism had grown into an organized industry in the 1890s.[11] By the early 1900s, city guidebooks, like Charles Keeler's *San Francisco and Thereabout* (1902) as a matter of course set aside entire chapters to describe this "Corner of Cathay."[12] Days after the earthquake, in an emotional requiem to the city, local journalist Will Irwin pronounced Chinatown "chief of the foreign quarters" and stated that anyone who had ever heard of San Francisco had heard stories of this place.[13] The draw of Chinatown as a San Francisco tourist attraction was also played up by the Improvers, who considered it one of the "chief attractions for tourists," which "should be considered a valuable asset of the town."[14]

In the end, profit prevailed, and Chinatown was rebuilt in its original place, but not without significant alteration. Apart from the extravagant structures raised, then torn down for the Panama-Pacific International Exposition (PPIE), it was in Chinatown that the City Beautiful movement made its most notable and long-lasting mark on San Francisco. While the previously mentioned Burnham plan turned out to be too impractical and expensive for the majority of the city's redevelopment, aspects of it were implemented in the reconstruction of Chinatown. Herbert E. Law, chair of the subcommittee for extending, widening, and grading streets, underlined the need to "do away with the blind alleys and have the thoroughfares so arranged that the locality will be accessible in every part and easily policed."[15] While Burnham envisioned a removal of Chinatown, his plan for the area—to widen the streets and extend access to the rest of the city—was eventually transplanted onto the board's plan for the new Chinatown, complete with the infrastructural makings of a modern city, such as paved roads, plumbing, and electricity.[16]

In August 1906, construction began on the first permanent structure of the new Chinatown, a commercial building located on Grant Avenue and consigned by one of the Improvers, John H. Loeber.[17] Others soon followed suit.[18] Sing Fat, a powerful merchant, told the *San Francisco Chronicle* that the Chinese were to return to the site of old Chinatown, and estimated that it would take about two years to repopulate the new neighborhood.[19] But not all temporarily exiled Chinese San Franciscans returned to their former homes. Gradually, the population of the community declined, and this downturn seemed to increase the living space in post-quake Chinatown. Christopher Yip has pointed out that although this did not mean that Chinatown ceased to be short of space, "it probably did mean that some of the worst housing and sanitation conditions were alleviated. Bunk rooms with men sleeping in shifts were replaced by individual cubicles along hallways and residential hotels."[20] In April 1907, the *Call* reported that Chinatown was "rearing a new front rapidly and will soon be back in its old stand."[21] On May 24, the *Call* advertised that the Chinese consul, the Six Companies, and many other Chinese merchants would leave their temporary locations in Oakland and return to San Francisco during the summer.[22] By late 1907, several infrastructural pillars of Chinese San Francisco, like the Sing Fat Company, the Six Companies headquarters, and the *Chung Sai Yat Po* head office, were in place and back in operation. Chinatown's core lots along and near Grant Avenue were resettled with multistory mixed-use brick buildings. Soon, the areas west of Grant up toward and along Stockton Street again sprang to life.

## An Imaginary Movie House Stroll in Chinatown, 1906–1915

Now, let us imagine ourselves as virtual pedestrians, walking on what Giuliana Bruno called a ruined map of history.[23] "Ruined" in this case is a double entendre, since the practice of historical flânerie not only would navigate across a map pieced together by inconclusive materials but also has the literal ruins of post-quake Chinatown as its point of departure. As a visual aid, I have included a map that shows the blocks and intersections that encompassed Chinatown. On the map, I have marked the movie theaters that operated in the area starting in 1908 and continuing throughout the exposition year of 1915. These movie theaters did not operate all at the same time. Therefore, we must allow our virtual pedestrians the ability to cut across a street in 1908, glance upon a marquee in 1912, and arrive at a ticket booth in 1915.

Apart from size, management, and dates of operation, I will give extra attention to the exterior of the theaters. As we will notice during our walk through Chinatown, the storefront displays of the neighborhood's theaters, which all employed different strategies to activate the senses of passersby and lure them into the theaters, provided nodes for such a process of appropriation—a fusing of Chinatown space with the emerging U.S. film exhibition culture. Therefore, some preliminary notes regarding the distinguishing features in facade and outward appearance will be elaborated in the subsequent discussion.

The liminal spaces that connected street, sidewalk, and theater entrance during this period became of utmost importance for the visual experience and commodification of everyday life in the new Chinatown. It was here that the strategically planned vision for the new neighborhood was altered and appropriated by Chinatown pedestrianism, a process akin to what Michel de Certeau labeled the "tactics" of practicing everyday life in the modern urban milieu. In de Certeau's view, the irrational movements and interactions of pedestrians traversing streets, cutting through alleyways, occupying street corners, and pausing in front of shop windows "composed a manifold story that has neither author nor spectator, shaped out of fragments of trajectories and alterations of spaces."[24]

While de Certeau's view of the cityscape offers tempting theoretical companionship on our virtual walk, his apparent lack of interest in engaging with any of the singularities of the cityscape, rather than to theorize their movements, leaves us with a vantage point not dissimilar to the panoptical ambition he ascribes to cartographers and architects. Cultural theorist Ian Buchanan pointed out that de Certeau, in contrast to Walter Benjamin—another notable interpreter of the urban landscape—did not attempt to "romanticise the pedestrian, or reconceive commuting by foot across the city as a revolutionary act." De Certeau's notion of *wandersmänner*, Buchanan argued, was "just one possible type of city-user among countless others, and should not be accorded any special privilege for a theory of space."[25] Still, certain aspects of de Certeau's view of the cityscape bridge the gap between the Benjaminian flaneur and the notion of thirdspaces or hybrid spaces. Benjamin commented on the relation between pedestrians and flaneurs in a famous essay on Baudelaire: "There was the pedestrian who would let himself be jostled by the crowd, but there was also the flâneur, who demanded elbow room and was unwilling to forgo the life of a gentleman of leisure. Let the many attend to their daily affairs; the man of leisure can indulge in the perambulations of the flâneur only if as such he is already out of place. He is as much out of place in an atmosphere of complete leisure as in the feverish turmoil of the city."[26] For historians and avid readers of turn-of-the-century literature, the flaneur has become synonymous with the wealthy white urban classes' penchant for gawking at the daily lives of the poor and "strange" for thrills and amusement. While this study in many ways is an investigation of the (amorphous) urban crowd, and a specific crowd at that, it is often through recorded observations of flânerie, such as the one imagined in a famous short story by Edgar Allan Poe, that we glimpse the "faces in the crowd."[27] So, before we begin our walk, let us finally equip our virtual pedestrians with the ability not just to take such glimpses at face value but to approach their contents and authorship with the measured critique of historical scholarship.

Let us depart from Grant Avenue where it crosses California Street. Grant was Chinatown's main thoroughfare both before and after 1906. The quarter was geographically condensed, so chances were that if you had any business in Chinatown, let alone lived and worked there, Grant Avenue would be the street that you would walk down, or cross, at least a couple of times every day. A contemporary poem by an unknown Chinese San Franciscan gives a mesmerized street-level perspective of the area: "Everywhere, towers and terraces, all decorated in brilliant lanterns. . . . Eyes darting around, spirit dashing about, what

FIG. 7 Chinatown map with movie theaters identified by author. Illustration of Chinatown taken from *The "Chevalier" Commercial, Pictorial and Tourist Map of San Francisco from Latest U.S. Gov. and Official Surveys*. Designed, engraved and copyrighted by August Chevalier, Lithographer Publisher, San Francisco. The Exposition City 1915. (Image from David Rumsey Map Collection, courtesy of Cartography Associates)

a genuine joy—Entertaining myself, I have forgotten about going home."[28] Let us start here, and let us equip our virtual pedestrians with a similar appetite for entertainment and momentarily disregard our spatiotemporal distance from post-quake Chinatown.

We start in 1908 outside one of Chinatown's long-standing institutions, the Sing Fat Company. The newly erected bazaar was a four-story structure that occupied the entire southwestern corner of California and Grant. A large Chinese pagoda crowned its roof, and from the flagpoles waved both the Stars and Stripes and the imperial Qing Chinese flag. The building would become one of the landmarks of new Chinatown, reproduced in countless guidebooks and postcards during the 1910s. Walking northward, we would pass two more newly erected Chinese bazaars, the Sang Chong Lung Company and the Sing Chong Company. In 1910, the Western Press Association published a book that lauded the resurrection of San Francisco as the metropolis of the West, with one of its chapters dedicated to Chinatown. The writer was Look Tin Eli, a successful Chinatown merchant and the general manager of the Sing Chong Company who at the time was one of the most vocal proponents of rebuilding Chinatown as a tourist attraction conceived by non-Chinese architects.[29] Look praised the transformation of post-quake Chinatown into a "new oriental City of veritable fairy palaces." As an introduction, he imagined the perspective of an outside visitor, standing outside Look's newly built three-story enterprise, gazing northward down Grant Avenue. From there, Look described what his imaginary spectator would see.

> Let him take his stand, say at the corner of Dupont and California, and take in the fascinating vista down the former street as far as Pacific; he will enjoy a view that for fantastic Oriental architecture and color scheme cannot be duplicated anywhere in the world, not even in the Orient, because in that interesting country the contrasts are entirely too pronounced and a magnificent palace is frequently surrounded by ordinary shacks and mat sheds. Let him take his first view on any bright, sunny day, then let him return at dark and witness the wonderful transformation when the hundreds of thousands of electric lights bathe the streets and facades of the wildly fantastic buildings in a blaze of glory as bright as midday.[30]

Approaching Chinatown from the Market Street direction, this would be the default point of entry. First-time visitors to Chinatown would probably stop to admire the goods in the shop windows, which included "Ebony furniture, Silks and Linens, and Porcelain Wares."[31] If we were visitors who had been to Chinatown before the earthquake and fire, beyond the bright palette and the architecture, we would probably also notice that Grant Avenue was a good deal wider than previously.

Strolling on toward Sacramento Street, we would pass the Kong Nam Low Restaurant before arriving at our first stop, the Dragon Theater. The Dragon, located on the corner of Grant and Clay, was the smallest nickelodeon in Chinatown. It had a capacity of 142 and operated between the years 1908 and 1910 before closing due to failure to meet fire security standards.[32] Although the Dragon remains the nickelodeon we know the least about, its proximity to the most popular restaurant in Chinatown suggests a high volume of passersby. The Dragon Theater, at 739 Grant, was located in the same building as the famous Hang Far Low Restaurant, an establishment that attracted both local patrons and outside visitors.[33] Louis J. Stellman wrote in his guidebook of the area that the Hang Far Low was the only restaurant in Chinatown that served "as a showplace for tourists as well as a banqueting place for the Chinese themselves."[34] The Hang Far Low was hence one of three Chinese restaurants that provided menus in both English and Chinese.[35] As will become evident, catering to both tourists and the inhabitants of the neighborhood was a recipe that the movie theaters of Chinatown would emulate. A postcard of the restaurant published by the Pacific Novelty Company shows a picture of the movie house, with a sign above the entrance that reads "Kinetoscope." While the name of Edison's first film exhibition device would suggest an earlier provenance, the photograph could not have been taken before 1906 because the restaurant was located farther down the street after being rebuilt after the earthquake and fire.[36] Licenses from the Police Board suggest that the term "kinetoscope" was used as shorthand to describe film projectors up until the mid-1910s.[37] One of the few pieces of information we have about the Dragon is a short article from the *San Francisco Chronicle*, which mentions the theater as one of the twenty-five nickelodeons that the San Francisco fire chief had deemed hazardous in March 1909.[38] The report was published just days after a fire in another Chinatown theater, which happens to be our next stop.

To get there, we only have to walk one block down Grant, past the Gim Ho & Co. Jewelers, and stop at the crossing of Grant and Washington Street. If we look to the right, we will see how Washington continues in a steep downhill slope, past Kearny Street, toward the San Francisco Bay. In the other direction, we can see the Tai Quong Go Printers and Publishers, where some of the local Chinese press was typeset and printed.[39] If we look farther left, up Washington toward Nob Hill, we discover the marquee of the Grand Theater, just a couple of steps up the incline.

Located at 822 Washington, the Grand Theater had been in operation as a small-time vaudeville theater before the earthquake. In its post-quake iteration, the Grand expanded to show movies, and its seating capacity was 175. The Grand Theater was located on the slope of Washington Street, where, before the earthquake, Chinatown "slumming" guides used the cellars of houses built

FIG. 8 Photograph of the Hang Far Low Restaurant and Dragon Theater marked with the sign "Kinetoscope," sold as a postcard by the Pacific Novelty Company, 1908–1910. (From the author's collection)

along the incline to create an illusion of an "Underground Chinatown."[40] One of these was writer Charles Dobie, who in his book *San Francisco's Chinatown* (1936) alleged that the dimensions of the underground labyrinth grew with the legend and through word of mouth, eventually "burrowed down five, six, seven, *eight*, stories [*sic*] underground."[41] This hoax had been revealed by the earthquake and fire, which completely removed the old houses and laid bare a succession of shallow cellars following the natural downslope.[42] An advertisement for the Grand Theater before the earthquake suggests that it had offered a similarly staged "slumming" experience, as it advertised the inclusion of underground apartments.[43] Reinstated as a film house, the Grand, together with the Dragon, became Chinatown's first nickelodeon.

For now, we leave the Grand behind. As we again merge into the crossing streams of people moving along Grant Avenue, we can hear bright melodies and crashing cymbals through the evening sounds of Chinatown. Tracking the tune, we end up outside the fulgent neon sign of the Oriental Theatre. The Oriental's storefront was dominated by the source of the soundscape that had guided us here, a giant Wurlitzer PianOrchestra, installed as a centerpiece next to the small glass-enclosed ticket booth.[44] From the ceiling hung Chinese lanterns, and the arches above the entrance featured decorative elements that contributed to the aggregated Oriental "look" of the theater's street front, similar to the visual styling of the Hang Far Low's impressive facade but on a smaller scale.

In 1903, German sociologist Georg Simmel conceptualized the "blasé attitudes" of city dwellers as the neurological defense mechanism of human survival in the metropolis.[45] With the Oriental, we see early examples of how Chinatown film exhibitors developed a range of strategies to pierce through such defense mechanisms. The busy street scene in front of the theater, bustling with pedestrians and small-scale enterprises, made it an urban space imbued with the promise of considerable daily profit. But as theaters offered their main product inside, unlike the shop windows of Chinatown bazaars, managers and promoters came up with ways to create a liminal relation between interior and exterior that extended onto the street. By disrupting the movements of the everyday life of passersby, they could lure them into the theater. At the Oriental, the idea was to merge the actual space of the movie theater storefront with the notion of mythical Chinatown space circulated in countless contemporary literary descriptions of the area. Another strategy, also seen at the Oriental, was to catch the attention of pedestrians by occupying the soundscape of the street. The impressive and loud PianOrchestra installed in the storefront stretched out aural tentacles into the street to grasp the attention of passersby and pull them from the crowd into the theater. The instrument had been outfitted with an Oriental design to seamlessly blend in with the rest of the visual display of the theater front.[46]

The Oriental is our last stop on Grant Avenue, but if we walk up along the dance halls of the by now declining Barbary Coast on Pacific Street, and then take a right on Stockton, where it intersects with Broadway Street, we will happen upon the Acme Theater. The Acme, which marks the northwestern corner of Chinatown, opened at 1249 Stockton Street in early 1910.[47] Viewed from across Stockton Street, the arches, lanterns, and other embellishments provided an Oriental frame to the ticket booth and film posters that announce the program. The initial audience capacity was 300.[48] A renovation in 1914 added seats and a balcony to the theater.[49]

Shaped by another form of liminality, located where city areas of different ethnic designation intersected, the Acme Theater became an attractive spot for moviegoers from the surrounding neighborhoods. The crossing of Stockton and Broadway was a cosmopolitan carrefour, where Chinatown bordered with the Italian North Beach area to the northeast, and the upper-class apartments of Nob Hill, crowned by the Fairmont Hotel, one of the few downtown buildings to survive the earthquake and fire, to the west. Into this wide spectrum of established class and ethnic division wandered the disenfranchised and scandalized who frequented the dance halls and pool halls on Pacific Street. While the Acme's management attempted to benefit commercially from the diversity of its audiences by branding itself as the "the most cosmopolitan theater in the world," it drew the lion's share of its patrons from Chinatown.[50]

If we temporarily leave the cosmopolitan crowds of the Acme behind and continue just a few steps down Broadway, we will soon find ourselves standing in the middle of another sonorous crossfire, this time between two brass bands, blowing their penny's worth outside two large theaters facing each other. Bad blood between the two theater owners had instigated a furious competition for the patrons, many of them from Chinatown, who frequented Broadway's many restaurants and entertainment venues. This battle intensified when a third moving picture theater, the Broadway, opened just a couple of doors down from the Royal Palace in 1910. The Broadway exhibitors' strategies to attract patrons from the surrounding neighborhoods ranged from intrusion on the senses of passersby to the realm of bargain deals, literary supplements, and translation of film text. Later I will investigate how this bout affected Chinatown film culture. But for now, let us leave the noise behind and continue our walk along Broadway toward the docks.

Unwilling to leave the general Chinatown area, we will take a right on Kearny Street, which ran along the eastern perimeter of the neighborhood. Walking south for two blocks, back toward Market Street, we will stop and lock eyes with one of the two grinning dragons whose faces adorn the outside wall of the Shanghai Theatre. The Shanghai was probably the gaudiest of all Chinatown movie theaters and represented Benjamin Michaels's most daring financial gamble. The theater opened in the summer of 1911 and employed the features of a Qing imperial palace, with a pagoda-like awning crowned by a third ornamental dragon head. Wooden stucco embellished the ticket booth and entrances, and Chinese lanterns hung everywhere.

After this brisk walk, we would probably have to sit down and collect our thoughts and impressions. Just around the corner from the Shanghai was Portsmouth Square, Chinatown's historical center. This place seems like a good spot to process our impressions of Chinatown film culture. Let us leave our virtual flânerie there and begin to ponder the numerous questions that this tentative mapping provokes.

Let us begin with questions about the daily operation of the Chinatown movie theaters. Who went there? What films were shown? Who managed the venues, and who worked at them? How did these theaters strategize to attract patrons from Chinatown, and in what capacity did they cater to outside visitors? How did preexisting forms of neighborhood entertainment, such as the Chinese theater, condition the way in which film was introduced in Chinatown? To be sure, this ruined map will never be entirely clear, but by piecing together information from contemporary sources such as newspaper articles, trade magazines, advertisements, postcards, and sociological surveys, we can slowly begin to make out its finer details. Following the larger trends in San Francisco film business during the transitional era, I will also consider how original business practices, such as local film exchanges, and the combined perception of Chinatown and the "cheap" film medium as a possible public health hazard made up important coordinates that not only film exhibitors and moviegoers but also projectionists, theater producers, police brass and beat cops, and local politicians had to navigate.

## The First Nickelodeons: New Opportunities, Old Chinatown Hazards

The first theater to be rebuilt after the earthquake and fire was the Grand on Washington Street. It was rebuilt on the same spot as one of Chinatown's previously most popular theaters, also called the Grand. As such, the theater's name provided one of many palpable links between the old Chinatown and the new.

The old Grand had opened as Chinatown's third Chinese playhouse in 1877.[51] Before the earthquake and fire, it had been known among the locals as one of the "low" theaters, as opposed to the two theaters on Jackson Street, which were deemed of higher artistic merit.[52] During its forty-year pre-quake history, a wide variety of Chinatown theater entrepreneurs operated the old Grand, among others, the most notorious Chinese pre-quake gangster, Fong Ching, aka "Little Pete." Apart from his interest in blackmail, bribery, and murder, he nursed a particular fondness for the dramatic arts.[53]

Some years before the earthquake, the previously rich and burgeoning theater scene in Chinatown, where many Chinese theater troupes received their introduction to the U.S. theater circuit, began to decline. One of the problems was that the venues like the Grand on Washington had been previously associated with tong-related violence. In 1903, musician Gee Ah Gong was brutally murdered in the middle of a performance in front of a shocked capacity audience at the Grand. The *Chronicle* reported on how the midnight concert had taken an unexpected Grand Guignol–like turn, when "an unknown Chinese man stepped out on the stage from a side door, and fired four shots."[54] According to theater historian Lois Foster, similar events at other theaters, along with the effects of continuing anti-Chinese agitation and steadily tightening immigration restrictions, were detrimental to Chinatown theaters at the beginning of the twenty-first century. By the eve of April 18, 1906, the Grand on Washington had been the last bastion of a theater tradition rooted in the early days of the gold rush.[55]

In April 1907, a year after the earthquake, Louis J. Stellman reported that the Grand would be the first theater to reappear after the destruction of Chinatown. The new theater, Stellman wrote, was being "built entirely along the lines of the latest and most improved American playhouses." The American/Oriental dichotomy was omnipresent in the reporting on the rebuilding and redevelopment of Chinatown. By evoking "old Chinatown" as a point of departure, Chinatown building and business owners eagerly stressed the safety and solidity of their new houses by underlining the "Americanness" of their construction. For example, one of the Grand's newly acquired "American" attributes was its upgraded fire safety, which Stellman assured would be "as nearly fireproof as it can be made." The initial plans for the Grand made it out to be a 1,000-seat theater that would "contain a large stage with complete scenic equipment and produce plays of a much more modern character than those which formerly held board there."[56] While this would be true in terms of the modernity of the views put on display at the new Grand—as moving pictures would soon be added to the entertainments—its later documented capacity as a theater and nickelodeon was a more modest 175.[57]

While the construction of the first Chinatown movie theaters, at least initially, was made within the constraints of contemporary building codes, their operation and success challenged another essential aspect of the emerging film exhibition. Deducing from the records at hand, it seems that most of the films exhibited in Chinatown followed the general trend for San Francisco film exhibition during the nickelodeon era, which was toward the "independents." Given San Francisco's geographic distance from the centers of national film circulation, small nickelodeons and combined film and vaudeville houses received their films from local exchanges. Between 1908 and 1909, when the Grand and the Dragon commenced operation, the Trust was represented by the Miles Brothers Company, the George Breck Company (which supplied Edison films), the Theater Film Service Co., the Novelty Moving Picture Company, and Turner & Dahnken.[58] First among the post-quake independents were Sol Lesser's Golden Gate Film Exchange and the Pacific Coast Film Exchange.[59] These were joined by the Miles Brothers, who by 1911 had gone independent to distribute Sales films.[60] The first movie theaters in Chinatown had their films supplied from exchanges outside the circuit of the Motion Picture Patents Company. In November 1909, *Billboard* published a list of fourteen unlicensed film theaters in San Francisco, of which three—the Grand, the Dragon, and the Oriental—were located in Chinatown proper.[61]

## Incendiary Issues

The Grand Theater and the Dragon Theater were only in operation for a little more than eighteen months, between 1907 and 1909. Although it is difficult to find evidence of what these places looked like inside, one incident, which in a sense spelled out the beginning of the end for both theaters, provides a glimpse of the filmgoing experience at these small showplaces.

On the night of March 16, 1909, a fire broke out during an intermission at the Grand as patrons were making their way out onto Washington Street. Far from matching Stellman's imagined 1,000-seater, or previous versions of the theater, which at its opening boasted a 2,500-seat auditorium, the space was described in the *Chronicle* as cramped and windowless, with only two exits "located along the same wall."[62] The projector had been set up in the back, which probably meant that the screen was located on the same wall where people left and entered the theater. Reports in the *Chronicle* vividly described how panicked Chinatown filmgoers fought their way out into the street, while theater employees managed to quell the fire before the arrival of the fire department.[63] Irrespective of the swift and skillful intervention of the Grand staff, the theater could not be saved for long, as concerned citizens and the local press had started to clamp down on the many dangers of the nickelodeons.

Both the Grand and the Dragon, just days after the March 16 fire, were included on a list of twenty-five potentially dangerous moving picture houses that Bill Shaughnessy, the San Francisco fire chief, presented to the city board of supervisors at the end of March. To his annoyance, Shaughnessy's report—with strict instructions ordering the closing of the Grand and the Dragon—was met with skepticism by the board, led by supervisor Ralph McLeran. According to McLeran, Shaughnessy was "always too enthusiastic in these matters"; moreover, the implementation of the report as it stood would put "half the nickelodeon proprietors in this town out of business."[64] The vote went in McLeran's favor, which irked Shaughnessy. According to the *Chronicle*, as the fire chief left the room, he blurted out, "You know what the matter is with McLeran, don't you? He is building nickelodeons."[65]

The fight continued into the following week when, after the Board of Works had inspected the fire chief's report, an ordinance was passed regulating the "construction, erection, alteration, maintenance, and use of" moving pictures in San Francisco. The ordinance stated that nickelodeons, except for complying with the general fire ordinances of the city, "had to sheathe with metal the walls for a space of at least ten feet on each side of the picture box" to prevent the spread of projector fire. Answering McLeran's call for a more nuanced inspection of the existing movie houses, the Grand and the Dragon fell under the second category, which was designated by the fire wardens as "unsafe on account of insufficient exits," and were singled out for their lack of rear or side exits. However, John P. Horgan, chief inspector at the Board of Works, declared that these theaters were considered reasonably safe and should be allowed to continue operation if the ordinance was followed.[66] But the stipulated changes must have been too costly for the Grand and Dragon to take on. In late May, both the *Chronicle* and the *Call* reported that the theaters were among the ones that had been forced to shut down as a result of the new ordinance.[67]

The short life spans of the Grand and Dragon nickelodeons exemplify one of the main issues for the establishment of film exhibition throughout the nickelodeon era in Chinatown. As evidenced by the March 1909 press campaign on the multiple dangers of the moving picture theater, the attention to the dangerousness of movie theater spaces was citywide. But the neighborhood's theaters had an especially long-standing reputation as firetraps, which in turn made the audiences of the Chinatown theaters more prone to panic. According to Lois Foster, this started with the intensification of police raids against Chinese theaters during the anti-Chinese movement of the 1870s.[68] In 1876, a tragic accident took place at the Royal Chinese Theater on Jackson Street. A false fire alarm started a stampede, which ended up killing nineteen patrons—the youngest of whom was only seventeen.[69] In 1880, a can of burning phosphorus was hurled at the stage of the Grand on Washington in a bid to put an end to the theater's latest successful run. According to the *Chronicle*, the culprits were associated with a rival Jackson Street theater.[70] This time, the evacuation left no casualties, but the damages were costly. In 1900, fire again broke out at the Grand, this time originating from one of the actor's living quarters in the back of the building. The fire was put out before anyone was hurt.[71]

The notion of movie theaters as fire hazards, quite common among contemporary concerns regarding the dangers of nickelodeon culture nationwide, was interwoven in the fabric of contemporary anti-Chinese sentiment and fit the description of Chinatown as an overpopulated, riotous, and malefic place—a place foreign to the societal norms to which the rest of San Francisco was expected to conform. According to Jan Olsson, the dangers of Chinatown and the hazards of the nickelodeons first became interlinked in turn-of-the-century American press campaigns against arcade culture. In 1899, the *Call* launched a moralist crusade against Peter Bacigalupi's arcade on Market Street. Frequent references to Chinatown permeated the discourse to illustrate the level of degradation and danger inherent in the pictures put on display. Olsson wrote that "the focus on eyesores and places spreading corruption along the main pedestrian arteries was grounded in a notion of unsuccessful containment, a leakage of evil from the unequivocally infected site for vices writ large—Chinatown."[72] The perceived dangers of the Chinatown cityscape, the combustible nature of movie projection, and the inferred corruptive powers of moving pictures created potent avenues for the idiosyncrasies of media crusades against the vices of modernity in post-quake San Francisco.

Between the local authorities and the press's high-pitched intervention against nickelodeons, and the historical scrutiny and harassment of Chinatown's public institutions (legal or not), the early post-quake Chinatown movie theater navigated a tricky situation. The first casualties of the vagaries of film exhibition were small movie houses like the Grand and the Dragon, which lacked the economic muscle to meet the requirements implemented by the city's 1909 nickelodeon ordinance. The management of other theaters, like the Royal Palace on Broadway and the Oriental Theatre on Grant, which opened around the same time as the ordinance passed, might have learned from the mistakes of their predecessors. As we will see, their operations were far more long-lived, and they managed to cope with incendiary incidents as well as public outrage and stricter regulatory measures.

Of course, there is also the possibility that the managers of the Grand and the Dragon did not have any long-term plans for their operations, and thus bowed out at the first obstacle. The early nickelodeon period was rife with reports on the cheapness of nickelodeon operation, which attracted "entrepreneurs bent on quick returns rather than long-term involvement."[73] The proprietor of the Dragon Theater, Charles Ricketson, who briefly also managed a nickelodeon on Powell Street, left the city after the closure of his theaters.[74]

## Accounts of the Oriental Theatre

As competition from the other nickelodeons along Grant Avenue faded, a new establishment took center stage. The Oriental Theatre opened in January 1909. It counted 700 seats and was located between Jackson and Pacific Streets, close to the Chinatown end of the infamous Barbary Coast.[75] From the start, the Oriental's olio consisted of vaudeville performances by Chinese San Franciscans or overseas Chinese, interspersed with moving pictures. According to Nancy Rao, a gradual tightening of exclusionary laws in the

1900s had seen the traditional Chinese theater scene diminish significantly.[76] At first, the general categorizations barring Chinese laborers from entry, as defined by the Exclusion Act and its amendment, did not include Chinese actors and opera performers. But a U.S. Supreme Court decision made in 1905 erased such loopholes from legislation and gave the Immigration Bureau final say on all ambiguous cases, effectively strangling the influx of overseas actors. The earthquake and fire dealt another harsh blow to the local theater scene. As noted by Rao, "The catastrophic fire ended even the slim possibility of decent Chinatown opera theaters for at least fifteen years."[77] In this vacancy, movie theaters found footing. Following the general trend in post-quake San Francisco, the Oriental, with its combined vaudeville and film programs, offered accessible and novel entertainment in a time defined by upheaval, uncertainty, and reconstruction. Furthermore, the cheap admission, priced at five cents, made the amusements available to a broader spectrum of the predominantly low-income Chinese San Franciscan community. At the Oriental, hours ran from early in the afternoon, starting at 1:00 p.m.; the theater closed briefly between 5:00 and 6:00 for an early dinner hour and then continued service until 11:00 p.m., and sometimes even later.[78] The Oriental advertised its program in both English and Chinese.[79]

It is hard to establish an unbroken lineage within the management in charge at the Oriental. In the theater's initial bout of publicity, *Billboard* listed Ben Wiseman as its manager. A search in census and license records does not yield any information about this theater manager, but the *Crocker-Langley* directory for the years of the Oriental's operation suggests that he was either a former clerk who took a brief interlude in the exhibition business, before continuing as a traveling sales agent in Los Angeles from 1910 onward, or else was a Union Street bookbinder who combined his handicraft with the part-time management of the movie theater.[80] By the end of 1910, *Billboard* recorded real estate brokers Maurice Solomon and Arthur Gosliner as owners of the theater.[81]

Despite the sparsity of information regarding the ownership and proprietors of the Oriental, other sources suggest that the Oriental was the centerpiece of post-quake Chinatown film exhibition. Among these source materials are the observations of the Italian American feminist author and journalist Adriana Spadoni. In the late summer of 1910, Spadoni, by this time an aspiring essayist, wrote a long piece about her adventures in San Francisco's "ethnic" movie theaters. The key source for her experiences was the Oriental Theatre, which, along with the theaters of the North Beach area, she considered the most exciting places to visit for a young, single female. Spadoni's essay on moviegoing predates the contemporary and a more frequently cited essay "Some Picture Show Audiences," by Mary Heaton Vorse, whose observations about the Italian patronage of New York's Bleecker Street have illustrated several studies of "ethnic" moviegoing in large U.S. cities in the transitional era.[82]

According to Spadoni, the Wurlitzer installed in the storefront was the Oriental's main attraction. The Oriental made pointed efforts for the afternoon shows to cater to Chinatown women and children; Spadoni, meanwhile, made a habit of visiting the theater on the way home from her factory job. As an agent of historical information, Spadoni's movements in Chinatown film culture more resemble those of the flaneur described by Benjamin and Baudelaire than those of de Certeau's irrational pedestrian. Similar to contemporary flânerie reporting, her writing is evocative and seems to blend observation with imagination. The experience began outside the Oriental, in the liminal space of Grant Avenue. Spadoni described her enchantment with movie theaters as most fully realized "at night when they are all lit up with colored lights outside and the electric piano plays the loudest." One night, as Spadoni was walking through Chinatown, "all of a sudden I heard an electric piano break out into the merriest waltz, such a fine, rattling piano." The piano was, of course, the Wurlitzer orchestrion, which had cost the theater $6,000.[83]

While Spadoni's 1910 article perhaps cannot be trusted as a reliable inventory of film culture in post-quake Chinatown and the North Beach area, the text, along with its photographs from outside and inside some of the theaters, demonstrates a firsthand familiarity with the Chinatown and North Beach entertainment scene. In Spadoni's account, the Oriental offered vaudeville skits as well as acrobatic acts in Chinese, combined with the kind of movies that were standard fare on U.S. screens in 1910.[84] Spadoni offered descriptions of a few of the films she had seen at the Oriental. Most of them are too vague to identify any specific film. However, it is probable that one of them, about the French Revolution, was the Italian-produced *Under the Reign of Terror* (*Fra le spire della Rivoluzione Francese*, Aquila Films, 1910), released in the United States in late June 1910 by the independent American Kinograph exchange.[85]

Similarly to the old Chinatown playhouses, the stage was set up with a minimum of decor. According to Foster, the stage in the Chinese drama tradition was considered "an ornamented playing space on which the Chinese actors and their audiences were intended to bring to bear the necessary imagination to transform it into a palace, a forest, or a high-mountain top."[86] Behind the stage at the Oriental, films were projected onto a white sheet.

The Oriental faced the same problems as other nickelodeons of the era. In 1911, the theater's projectionist, Harry Wolff, badly burned his face and hands when the projector caught fire during a screening. While the material damages were relatively minor and extended to scorched walls inside the theater, there were reported bruises and blisters of audience members as they had scrambled for the exit in terror.[87] Wolff, on the other hand, had to be taken to the Harbor Hospital, where he was treated for severe injuries.

But the Oriental's problems did not end with the projector fire. In September 1910, about a month after the publication of Spadoni's article in the *Call*, a

FIG. 9 Inside the Oriental Theatre, 1910. *San Francisco Call*, August 21, 1910, 12. (Image courtesy of University of California, Riverside, Riverside, California)

Chinese San Franciscan man was shot dead during a screening at the Oriental. The man, Low Sing Chow, had reportedly been a key witness in a murder trial, which had sent another Chinese San Franciscan, Gee Gong, to prison for life. The two perpetrators were caught by the police when fleeing down Sullivan Alley and were brought back to the Oriental, where members of the audience identified them as the killers. The *Chronicle*, eager to sensationalize the killing, reported the murder as the first in a coming tong war.[88] Four years later, Lee Seung, allegedly tied to the Bow Leong-gang, was killed while watching a film at the Oriental. The assassin had sneaked up behind Lee and shot him in the back of his head. Again, local newspapers speculated about an onslaught of gang-related murders in Chinatown, but the Six Companies stymied any such development.[89]

But murders and the occasional fire did not seem to affect the operation of the Oriental gravely. The theater continued to cater to Chinatown audiences throughout the transitional era. However, the opening of new Chinatown theaters and the proliferation of the nearby Broadway stretch between Grant and Stockton as a local entertainment strip in the mid-1910s probably served to water down the influx of audiences at the Oriental. The Oriental played an important role in the emergence of post-quake Chinatown film culture, one

I will return to, but it probably could not compete with the emerging Broadway movie palaces that sought out Chinese San Franciscans as part of their run for dominance on the strip. The Oriental closed its doors in 1917, as it could not muster the financial backing to make necessary alterations to bring the building up to code, after yet another inspection by the San Francisco fire and electrical departments.[90]

## Advertising War: The Broadway Cluster

While trade press writings indicate that Benjamin Michaels had been one of the active "moving picture promoters" on Broadway Street as early as 1907, records of his activities in the area become more continuous beginning in 1909.[91] Michaels, a Russian-born immigrant, came to San Francisco in the early 1900s. Similar to the exploits of Ukrainian-born "Chinese film pioneer" Benjamin Brodsky, Michaels's approach to the business of public entertainment was through brash and boisterous interaction with the local newspapers and trade press correspondents.[92] Michaels became the most well-known and, to some, the most notorious proprietor of vaudeville and movie theaters in the North Beach and Chinatown area. Between 1909 and 1916, his operations resulted in his arrest or appearance at the courthouse several times, whether for the illegal duplication and spreading of films, the showing of illicit images, or failure to pay his debts.[93] As we shall see, Michaels had a penchant for seemingly endless controversy, and he routinely exploited Orientalist aesthetics for business purposes. But he also became one of the most important and innovative figures of the early North Beach and Chinatown film exhibition scene.

Michaels's first Broadway theater, the Royal Palace, was located on the north side of the street and probably began operation in the summer of 1909.[94] On November 28, Michaels opened a new theater, just across the street from the Royal Palace, called the New California.[95] It had more than 1,000 seats and had been completed under the auspices of Michaels and investor Harry Lichtenstein.[96] After a slow start, Michaels and Lichtenstein were behind on their payments for the lease. Some months of creative bookkeeping followed until another entertainment entrepreneur, Edward Brown, agreed to buy out the theater and the debt and keep Michaels as a partner. However, Brown chose to partner with Henry Levy Estes instead, angering Michaels, who went to *Variety*'s San Francisco correspondent with the story.[97] The New California became the Liberty Theater, and both Brown and Estes took over as the proprietors of the theater.[98] Adding to the competition was the Broadway Theater, located a couple of doors down from the Royal Palace on the north side of the street.

The Broadway was smaller than its adversaries, capable of welcoming "only" 550 moviegoers. Sam Gordon, also the proprietor of a popular penny arcade next door to the movie house, managed the theater.[99] The Liberty, the Royal Palace, and the Broadway Theater, due to their proximity and the internal rivalry of their managers, created a dynamic triangle for the development of film exhibition strategies throughout the 1910s. Edward Brown took the first action in a series of call-and-response marketing coups by installing a loud brass band outside the Liberty. *Variety* reported that, within days, Michaels had retaliated with ballyhoo of a similarly loud nature. During the following years, the street in front of the theaters turned into advertising space and the setting for a turf war. The short stretch between Stockton and Columbus became an arena in which the entertainment culture of the Broadway theaters played out in the form of opposing marketing strategies. In this battle, the cosmopolitan passerby, like Spadoni, was simultaneously audience, participant, and prize.

Information about which film exchanges supplied the Broadway theaters is sparse, especially for the first years, from 1909 to 1911. During this initial period, the management at the New California/Liberty, the Royal Palace, and the Broadway Theater sought to establish the block between Stockton and Columbus as the central entertainment strip in the Chinatown and North Beach areas. The two largest theaters, the New California/Liberty and the Royal Palace, were marketed as vaudeville theaters that also showed film, while the Broadway Theater kept strictly to film. I have been unable to find any records of which exchanges provided films to the New California and the Royal Palace. The New California opened as a vaudeville theater with bookings through the Sullivan-Considine circuit, but it soon added film to its program.[100] When Brown and Estes took over, the house continued with its film and live show repertoire. A 1910 *Variety* report on the Brown versus Michaels case indicated that it was not until the latter two were pushed out from the New California that Michaels and Lichtenstein added vaudeville to the roster across the street at the Royal Palace Theater.[101] The Liberty, under the new rule, took up with Bert Levey, a local independent vaudeville agent who during the latter part of the 1910s represented Jelly Roll Morton.[102] A *Moving Picture World* article from 1912 revealed that the Liberty exhibited licensed pictures, with a change of program on Tuesdays, Thursdays, and Saturdays.[103]

The Broadway started with films distributed by San Francisco's Sales agent and continued their independent film service soon after the establishment of Universal in 1912. In mid-July 1912, Sam Gordon announced that the Broadway had abandoned the "trust."[104] The first film to be screened under the new regime was the Danish-produced *Dead Man's Child* (*Bedraget i døden*, Nordisk Films, 1911), a three-reel "special feature" imported by the Great Northern Special Feature Film Company. The plot involved a dysfunctional family of nobility and a murderous "oriental doctor." While the Oriental in this Danish production seemed more Arab than Chinese, his modus operandi involving the procurement of deadly weapons from behind secret panels plays into the stereotype of Orientalist master criminals that just months later would become the newest fashion with the publication of Sax Rohmer's first installment of the Fu Manchu character.[105]

The destruction of the Royal Palace in the fall of 1912 temporarily halted the rivalry and intense competition. The *Call* reported on October 18 that a fire had started the previous afternoon, caused by defective wiring in the attic of the theater. As usual for the matinee hours, the Royal Palace had been only half full, and the 200 patrons consisted mostly of women and children. When the fire was discovered, it had engulfed the entire ceiling, and it was only through the swift actions of Nellie Harris, the theater's impromptu manager and Benjamin Michaels's romantic partner, and Frank Lee, its projectionist, that all the patrons were able to reach the street in safety. By the time the fire marshals arrived, the Royal Palace had burned down to its frame structure.[106] *Variety* reported the damages and the narrowly averted disaster on October 25.[107]

While the destruction of the Royal Palace temporarily put the Liberty in the leading position as Broadway's largest film house, and the Broadway Theater as its premier nickelodeon, it would not be long until Michaels rebounded. In January 1913, the *Call* reported that Michaels would rebuild the Royal Palace on the same spot for the total sum of $60,000.[108] The news was reprinted in the same month's edition of the California monthly *Architect and Engineer*, which announced that architect Ralph Warner Hart had been commissioned to design the Class A theater, this time by Nellie "Michaels."[109] Nellie Michaels was, of course, Nellie Harris, who, although never legally married to Benjamin Michaels, often used his last name and sporadically substituted as a caretaker of his Chinatown endeavors throughout the 1910s. While at this point she was an experienced movie theater manager, it is probable that the new theater was in her name for financial reasons. At this time, Benjamin Michaels also ran the Shanghai Theatre on Kearny Street and had put significant efforts and probably also significant amounts of money into the importation, nationwide marketing, and distribution of a Japanese-produced a documentary-style film titled *The Chinese Revolution* the previous year. Although Michaels could have gained financially from this new venture, his previous business dealings at the Silver Palace and the New California suggest that his figures seldom were in the black. Corroborating this suspicion is the fact that the rebuilding of the Royal Palace took much longer than initially planned. In the fall of 1913, *Architect and Engineer* reported that architects Rosseau and Rosseau of the Monadnock Building Company had taken over the contract.[110] It would not be until January 1914 that construction of the new theater building began.[111] The new theater finally opened in March 1914 and was named the Verdi after a publicly held naming contest.[112] The naming competition provided Michaels with an opportunity to win sympathies in North Beach's Italian community. A continuous campaign ensued, with promotional strategies like those adopted by the Oriental Theatre in Chinatown, including translation and interpretation, which served to brand the Verdi as the Italian alternative on the Broadway strip.[113]

In April 1914, the *Chronicle* announced a collaboration with Universal over the weekly published installments of the serial *Lucille Love: Girl of Mystery*. Simultaneously, the *Chronicle* launched a half-page daily movie directory, which for the first month included listings from the Acme, the Shanghai/Chinese Lyceum, and the Broadway Theater, under the subheading North Beach theaters.[114] Within days, the movie section had shrunk from a half page to a quarter page, and the North Beach listings had been slashed to include only the Acme's output.[115] As the *Lucille Love* installments came to an end, so did the *Chronicle*'s Chinatown/North Beach movie listings.

With the return of Michaels and the opening of his new 2,000-seat film and vaudeville palace, making it one of San Francisco's largest theaters, the fierce competition also returned to Broadway. In November 1914, *Moving Picture World* announced that the Liberty had changed management; a week later, it reported that the theater had closed to be refurbished, redecorated, and given a new marquee.[116] When the Liberty reopened, the competition intensified. The competing Broadway theaters sought new ways to engage and attract the North Beach and Chinatown communities. When the Stockton Street tunnel opened in early 1915, connecting Chinatown with Union Square and Market Street, the municipality held a street carnival. Michaels grabbed the opportunity for public exposure and arranged the crowning of the "Carnival Queen" at the Verdi. At the same time, Michaels complained about the conditions on Broadway to *Moving Picture World*'s San Francisco correspondent, Thomas Church, claiming that the stiff competition hampered his efforts to "better" the climate for moving pictures in the area.[117]

From late February until late March, Michaels directed his attention toward the PPIE, where he, together with Sid Grauman and Sam Wolff, ran the Underground Chinatown concession at the exposition's entertainment section. The section, where several other local showmen had opened temporary theaters and amusement stands, was called the "Joy Zone." The Underground Chinatown concession, at which Michaels ran the Chinese Theater, was closed after a public outcry from the Chinese San Franciscan community. The venture with the Underground Chinatown concession must have kept Michaels away from the day-to-day operation of the Verdi, which probably was taken over by Nellie Harris.[118]

As the summer approached, Sam Gordon of the Broadway nickelodeon acquired ownership of the Liberty Theater, which might still have been struggling as a result of the audience appeal of the monumental Verdi across the street. Gordon came up with a cunning strategy to attract patrons back to the Liberty while also keeping them at the Broadway. In July 1915, Gordon designated a "double-venue" plan in which the purchase of a ticket for either of his theaters granted access to shows at both of them. The scheme effectively slashed the admission price by half for one show, while the moviegoer had the opportunity to see fourteen reels of film for five cents, given that shows at both the Broadway and the Liberty usually consisted of seven reels.[119] Michaels's initial response seems to have been to match these prices. The low admission, in turn, as reported in racist vernacular by Thomas Church, led to a moviegoing climate in which "the dusky natives of foreign climes, who chiefly inhabit this section, have been enjoying entertainments at a lower price than prevail anywhere else in the city, perhaps in the entire country."[120]

While Gordon's stunt initially seems to have worked, his revenues likely fell behind. Church, in his reporting of the Broadway feud, also hinted that the increased movement of people between the Broadway theaters threatened to create a traffic situation on Broadway Street. A "peace conference" was arranged between the two Broadway exhibitors, who reached a deal. The Liberty would concede evening hours during the week and remain open late only on Sunday evenings, when film and vaudeville were shown. In exchange, the Verdi would give up vaudeville, and concentrate entirely on film exhibition.[121]

## The *North End News*: Broadway's Polyglot Paper

In September 1915, Michaels announced a new strategy to attract audience members from the surrounding neighborhoods' diverse communities. A month later, *Moving Picture World* reported that Michaels had ventured into publishing as part of his drive to make the Verdi number one in the Chinatown and North Beach areas. According to Church, Michaels's weekly paper, the *North End News*, was "not only newsy, but is distinctive for the energetic manner in which it attacks public questions and policies, as well as for way [*sic*] in which moving pictures are brought to general notice."[122] The film commentary, naturally focusing on the films booked for the Verdi, was described as "interesting" and "much more comprehensive than those usually given in the press." For one dollar, patrons of the Verdi would get a full year's subscription to the *North End News* and twelve movie tickets.[123] More than launching a "house organ" that dealt with local issues and at the same time advertised his movie theater, Michaels came up with the idea of offering sections of his paper translated into the languages most commonly spoken in the neighborhoods surrounding the Verdi. These were Spanish, Italian, and Chinese.

In November, Michaels wrote a letter to *Moving Picture World*'s designated marketing expert, Epes Winthrop Sargent, offering a brief and very one-sided historical account of the clamor for customers among the Broadway theaters. Sargent, in turn, published the whole thing verbatim in his "Advertising for Exhibitors" section. Michaels's letter was a philippic directed at his competitors and "friends," who, in his view, had colluded to drive him out of business after the opening of the Verdi. Michaels brought the injustice to attention before the Exhibitors' League, but he was scorned and voted down. According to Michaels:

> At a meeting at the Local League, I voiced my complaints regarding the tactics which they adopted and advocated unity of action. I was laughed at by them, and when I realized that they wanted a scrap I gave it to them. Brass bands, eight, nine, and sometimes ten reels for a nickel, a set of silver-ware every night, money to the kids from the top of the house—in fact I used every weapon that I could think of, fair or foul, to accomplish my purpose. . . . After whipping my competitors into line by giving them, first of all, all the fight they wanted, then as a victor I sent emissaries to the vanquished, not in a dictatorial manner, but in a conciliating one, asked for a meeting and organized one of the most efficient and beneficent arrangements to film exchange and exhibitor alike ever formed.[124]

Sargent commented, tongue in cheek, that while the *North End News* had yet to live up to Michaels's description, he believed that Michaels possessed the right kind of "aggressive personality" to get the attention of his intended readership and patrons.[125] While the others involved in the Broadway rivalry probably would not have corroborated Michaels's version of the events leading up to the launch of the *North End News*, it seems that, at least briefly, there was a certain sense of unprecedented harmony and spirit of collaboration on the strip. In late November, Michaels attended a dinner arranged by the San Francisco Exhibitors' League, headlined by the famous New York exhibitor Samuel "Roxy" Rothafel as guest speaker.[126] Sid Grauman also addressed the assembly, which included most of San Francisco's film exhibitors at that time.[127] But if Michaels briefly had changed his ways to a route of consolidation, in Sargent's view, this was bound to change as he, in a late November update on the *North End News*, presaged "a couple of libel suits" as part of the local paper's natural progression, given the aggressive tone of both the paper and its editor.[128] In December 1915, the *North End News* had reportedly acquired its own sports editor and had started to look for a society reporter.[129] Michaels had also started to experiment with live text translations during his film screenings at the Verdi. Live translation into Italian was, quite naturally, the Verdi's first choice, but Michaels told *Moving Picture World* that he was also working out a way to provide written translations into Chinese.[130]

Unfortunately, I have been unable to find out whether such shows materialized, as Michaels died just a few months after his last interview with Church. Michaels's apparent fancy for modern thrills ultimately also became his bane. In April 1916, after having enjoyed an afternoon at the upscale Cliff House restaurant, Michaels was driving his car back to the city along Ocean Beach when "the steering broke and caused the machine to swerve into a sandbank." The car's passenger, probably Nellie Harris, escaped the wreckage with a broken arm. However, Michaels suffered severe internal injuries and passed away a few hours later. Thomas Church eulogized Michaels as a "prominent figure in local moving picture circles and a commanding figure in the North Beach district."[131]

After Michaels died, his colleagues and competitors generally believed that Nellie Harris would take over the operation of the Verdi. Harris managed the nearby Shanghai Theatre, and Michaels had instructed her to take over in his will. However, soon the local press reported that Michaels's sister, Ida, had traveled from New York to claim her wealthy brother's estate.[132] She claimed heirdom on the legal grounds that Nellie Harris and Benjamin Michaels had never been legally married, and filed a lawsuit. Ida Michaels lost the case, and Nellie Harris hired a man named Roy Howard to operate the Verdi.[133] Sometime later, Verdi's longtime projectionist, L. C. Johnson, took over the reins. Johnson and Harris married in 1918.[134] By that time, Sam Gordon had sold the Broadway Theater, leased his interests in the Liberty, and moved away from Chinatown and North Beach to the Portola Theater on Mission and Fourth Street.[135]

## Shanghai Theatre and the Lyceum: Chinoiserie and Burlesque

In the summer of 1911, Benjamin Michaels opened a new theater on Kearny Street called the Shanghai Theatre.[136] When the Royal Palace on Broadway burned down in 1912, the Shanghai became Michaels's prime venture, together with his interest in the Silver Palace on Market Street. The Shanghai was an elaborate attempt at recuperating some of the lost glory from the golden days of "old Chinatown" drama. However, this revival was not intended to reawaken Chinese San Franciscans' interest in traditional live theater. Instead, a *Variety* article from 1911 revealed that Michaels's intention with the Shanghai was to cater to tourist audiences.[137] During the first months of operation, both *Billboard* and *Moving Picture World* praised the Shanghai for its exotic exterior and interior.[138]

Two pictures captured for promotional purposes give us a better idea of the Shanghai Theatre's appearance. In July 1912, *Moving Picture World* published a photo in its San Francisco column that showed the front of the theater. Outside the theater was a row of twenty-six people, both men, and women, some dressed in what looks like stage clothing. One can surmise that this was the Shanghai's vaudeville troupe. Stylistically, the theater, much like the reconstructed bazaars of new Chinatown, was reminiscent of a Chinese temple, with lanterns and ornamental heads adorning the front of the building.[139]

An undated postcard from the period shows a similar view but from a different angle. The picture probably was not taken at the same time as the one

FIG. 10 Front of the Shanghai Theatre. *Moving Picture World*, June 8, 1912, 925. (Image courtesy of Media History Digital Library)

depicting the line of people, and the banners outside the theater look different. On the postcard, a large banner hanging over the front entrance reads: "Chineese [*sic*] theatre." In the *Moving Picture World* picture, there are two small banners on the sides of the front, reading "China Theatre"; in the postcard picture, the side banners are similar, but instead they read, "Shanghai Theatre."

The other side of the postcard shows the theater's interior. In the absolute center of the picture is the film screen with the words "Chinese Theatre" printed in bold letters over it. Two pillars and drop curtains frame the screen. Below the screen, twelve people stand on a stage. Ten men are positioned in the foreground, dressed in embroidered "Oriental" clothing. Some of the men carry spears and other weaponry, and many of them wear elaborate headgear. In the background, closer to the screen, stand two people. To the right stands a man in a Western suit, possibly Benjamin Michaels. To the left is a woman in a Western dress, possibly Nellie Harris.

The overall appearance of the Shanghai Theatre calls to mind the notion of "chinoiserie," a term that has been most commonly used to describe an eighteenth-century Western fascination with Chinese designs evident primarily in European interior design, furniture, pottery, and textiles. Interpretations of Chinese aesthetics in American material culture became prevalent in the early to mid-nineteenth century. According to transpacific trade historian Jonathan Goldstein, the style found its most "grandiose expression" in architecture, especially through the repeated usage of the pagoda motif.[140] John Kuo Wei Tchen connected this early fascination for Chinese things seen in the American societal elite to the politically oriented stereotyping of Chinese people and culture prevalent in the United States around the turn of the twentieth century. Each of these processes "began with some admiration or fascination for an actual Chinese thing, idea, or, person, that went through a phase of emulation and mimesis, and ended with European American mastery and dominance."[141] It should also be noted that the process of casting Chinese culture through a kaleidoscopic lens of romanticism and derogation had been especially impactful in San Francisco Chinatown since its formation. However, as with the rest of San Francisco, the reimagination and reconstruction of the city after the earthquake and fire also brought on new iterations of chinoiserie in the appearance of Chinatown. In their bids for dominance, Michaels and other exhibitors liberally tapped into and developed such practices to suit their operations.

Michaels tried to market the Shanghai as a fancier alternative to live attractions at the Oriental on Grant and might have been successful in drawing tourist audiences. Chinese San Franciscans, on the other hand, seem to have been less interested in the stage action and preferred the movies.[142] As with the other Chinatown theaters, detailed information about film programming and the source of the movies is scant. Throughout his career, Michaels seemed to switch between licensed and independent film providers depending on who could give him a better deal. Around the time of the Shanghai's opening, he even started his own short-lived independent distribution company to try his luck with the emerging states rights system. It is therefore likely that the Shanghai acquired films following the same unpredictable pattern.[143]

Located next door to the Shanghai was one of the area's most infamous establishments, the Lyceum Theater. The Lyceum offered vaudeville and

FIG. 11 Reverse of the postcard from ca. 1912 showing the interior of the Shanghai Theatre on Kearny Street. From the private collection of Phil Choy. (Image by the author)

"burlesque" primarily for an audience of men between the ages of eighteen and twenty-five.[144] The burlesque turns were entr'actes of the racy variety, peppered with indecent behavior and full of risqué comedy. The routines and the shady clientele at the Lyceum reminded San Franciscan moralists of the bawdy days of the Barbary Coast, which led to recurrent indignation in the local press and arrests of the management by the local police.[145] The proximity between the two theaters led to constant mix-ups in the press, which often referred to the Shanghai as the "Chinese Lyceum." The Lyceum remained a popular establishment among the Chinatown clientele throughout the 1910s. Among the oral accounts collected for the book *Longtime Californ'*, Chinatown residents reminisced about the popularity of the Lyceum's dance shows and the Shanghai Theatre's movie output, especially among the abundant number of single males. One resident, named Fong, recalled that "Kearny street used to have a regular show. It wasn't a burlesque, but they did have dancing girls and all that, and next-door was the regular movie house, for five cents. We'd go there all the time."[146] Ironically, both theaters were located across the street from the San Francisco courthouse on Kearny Street. After Michaels's death in 1916, *Moving Picture World* listed "Nellie Michaels" as the manager of the Shanghai.[147] The new management refurbished the Shanghai and renamed it the Kearny.

## Grind House: The Acme Theater

Located in the northwest corner of Chinatown, where Broadway Street intersected with Stockton Street, the Acme Theater opened in the spring of 1910.[148] The theater was a family business operated by I. L. Marks and his son Ralph. At the time it was, along with the Oriental, the largest movie theater in the Chinatown/North Beach area, able to seat 300 people. When the competition between the theaters on the Broadway strip intensified and the exhibition spaces started to expand, the Acme's strategy seems to have been to keep out of the fierce competition and concentrate solely on film exhibition and on building a strong core audience among the diverse inhabitants of the surrounding neighborhoods. Marks senior also garnered a reputation among producers and exchanges as a strong-willed and idiosyncratic exhibitor. In 1922, *Film Daily* commemorated him and the consistency of his mode of operation at the Acme as follows: "All these years there have been rows.... But there is one showman. Who doesn't give a sou markee. Or anything else. For such ideas. He has his own."[149] These ideas often revolved around the number of reels included in one sitting. As films became longer, plots were stretched out over several reels. As the rest of the U.S. industry entered the "feature film" era, Marks kept the reel count for the price of admission at one or two per show. To keep audiences coming back to the Acme, Marks divided the screening of longer films into daily installments, reminiscent of the serial format. When Sam Gordon launched his plan to offer fourteen reels for the price of five cents, Marks offered two reels for that price; the strategy was to screen safe bets, films that had previously proved successful among the Chinatown and North Beach crowds.

Further, Marks did not seem to place any specific value on being part of the first-, second-, or even third-run theaters. In an interview with *Film Daily*, Irving Lesser recalled how Marks booked the Golden Gate Film Exchange's old copies of previous audience sensations. One of these was the Italian eight-reel adaptation of Henry Sinkiewicz's *Quo Vadis*, produced by Cines in 1912 and brought across the Atlantic and distributed by George Kleine in April 1913, becoming one of the first breakaway multireel hits on the U.S. film market.[150] According to Lesser, Marks acquired the film "at a rental of $10" and showed one reel a day for eight days.[151] While his competitors and business partners would remember Marks as one of San Francisco's most unorthodox exhibitors, the suggestion that admission to the Acme paid for the screening of only one reel sounds unlikely. It is more probable that Marks, by showing his main attraction one reel per day, included other less popular films to fill the program.

The Acme Theater soon acquired a reputation for being run-down. As the Verdi and the Liberty became gaudy film palaces, Marks too attempted to renovate his theater. In 1914, he added a balcony and a Powers Cameragraph No. 6 projector.[152] However, according to Irving Lesser, these changes did not sit well with the Acme's regulars: "He had it all painted up nice, and when he reopened, his business went to hell. . . . Failing, he closed one night, got the wrecking crew in there, busted down enough of the seats for it to look bad and slung enough mud around to imitate tobacco juice and put the map on the house again."[153] Marks, who regularly shopped around for bargains at the local independent film suppliers, would also never hesitate to reuse an old success. Lesser recalled that Marks rebooked the Italian-produced "circus story" *The Burning Train* (*Il treno ardente*, 1914) more than "25 times."[154] According to Lesser, Marks would come in "about nine o'clock in the morning and take his film and paper [poster] and go out and open up about 10.30."[155] If no new films were available, Marks would inquire about the status of *The Burning Train*. By this, Marks was referring to the current quality of the film's poster, rather than the state of the two-reel copy. If the poster appeased Marks that day, he would book the film.[156]

Marks's unorthodox strategies seem to have endeared local moviegoers to the theater. Instead of competing with the Broadway theaters on their terms, the Acme took on the role of the local grind house.[157] While the Acme increasingly was seen as an eyesore, it did not hinder Ralph Marks from becoming secretary of the Exhibitors' League of San Francisco and its state organization, and a cofounder of the Screen Club.[158]

## Fong Get at the Grand

Before ending this chapter, we shall look a bit closer at the man listed as the manager of the Grand. His name was Fong Get, a groundbreaking actor, popular community photographer, and, to boot, Chinatown's first Chinese American film exhibitor. Born in Ningyang Province of the Guangdong region in 1859, Fong Get emigrated to California sometime in the mid-1870s.[159] In the late 1890s, he became a well-known and respected member of the Chinatown community, primarily through his photography studio on Stockton Street.[160] Although Chinese photographers have generally been omitted from scholarship on the illustrious history of photography in the American West, a few scholars, such as Peter Palmquist, Anna Pegler-Gordon, and John Kuo Wei Tchen, have made inroads into examining the role of photography in the San Francisco's community.[161] Fong was one of around twenty-five professional Chinese photographers active in Chinatown between 1860 and the 1920s.

The photographic historian Peter Palmquist credits the arrival of photography in the American West to the population boom brought on by the gold rush. As San Francisco became the metropolis of this development, it also became "the most photographed city in America.[162] Portrait studios began to appear all over the city. When the need came for inexpensive darkroom assistants, San Franciscan photographers (primarily of European descent) did like most other budding industries and turned to the city's Chinese community. Initially, the Chinese were hired to perform menial, repetitive tasks such as developing, printing, and print mounting, but eventually some of them moved on to more advanced work. As early as the 1850s, a few studios even sought to realize the untapped potential of the Chinese community by advertising in the Chinese newspapers.[163] By the 1860s, Chinese photographers had begun to set up their operations. One of them was Lai Yong, whose portrait gallery on 743 Washington Street catered primarily to Chinatown.[164] While photographic scholars, such as Anna Pegler-Gordon, have shown that Chinese photographers were prolific in turn-of-the-century San Francisco, they were rarely included in the city's business directories or advertised in the city's English-language press. This omission provides a partial explanation for the historical obscurity of Chinatown's photographers. Occasionally, non-Chinese journalists would visit the Chinatown studios of prominent photographers such as Ka Chau or Ann Ting Gock and return to their editorial offices to write stories filled with an exoticism, ethnic essentialism, and casual derision similar to contemporary American travel writers' accounts of visits to Tianjin, Shanghai, or Hong Kong.[165]

One of the San Francisco studios that routinely employed Chinese workers since the beginning of the 1860s was that of photographic pioneers William Rulofson and Henry Bradley. After Rulofson's death in 1878, his oldest son, William Henry Rulofson, opened a portrait gallery named the Elite Photo Studio, located on Market Street, between Stockton and Grand.[166] Here, Fong Get began working at some point after his arrival to San Francisco.[167] In the 1890s, the Elite Studio began to specialize in celebrity portraits and became popular among San Francisco's performers.[168] Through his profession, Fong met hundreds of people, many of them San Francisco "stage folk."[169] Among them was playwright Francis Powers, who was working on a new play, set out to depict "real" life in an American Chinatown; Fong was called in to consult.[170]

The play was set in Chinatown and included several local Chinese San Franciscan actors, among them Fong Get and his oldest son, Kim Poon.[171] When the play premiered at the Alcazar on Market Street in May 1897, Fong's name appeared at the top of the Chinese names credited in the playbill. According to theater historian Sheryl Nadler, this made him the first "Asian American actor on the American stage."[172] Although contemporary reviewers saw *The First Born* as a true dramatic showcase of life in Chinatown, the play was replete with the typical tropes and stereotypes of slave girls, coolies, and joss houses.[173] Fong, his son, and the Chinese actors with credited roles played minor parts, while Powers, May Buckley, and George Osbourne—all white actors in yellowface and Oriental garb—played the leading roles. But what separates *The First Born* from similar Chinatown stories of the era is that the production hired a prominent member of the local Chinese community as a consigliere on

Chinese American culture for the play's preparation and rehearsals. In a 1922 interview, Fong related to the *Chronicle* that he had translated, supervised, and stage-managed all scenes involving Chinese actors. Fong even claimed that he was the one who came up with the title for the play.[174] The first performances at the Alcazar included not only Chinese actors onstage but also members of the upper echelons of the Chinese San Franciscan community in the audience.[175] Fong's contributions to *The First Born* are noteworthy for several reasons. Beyond providing a temporary, albeit contrived, bridge between local Chinese theater and the conservative theater circuit and San Francisco, he created a network of contacts in the entertainment business that transcended the established network and exchange of theaters, performers, and audiences in Chinese America.[176] After the play's San Francisco success, Fong and his son went on the road with the theater company to East Coast cities such as Boston and New York, and across the Atlantic Ocean, to London. By late 1897, the *Call* reported that father and son were returning to San Francisco, both "in good health and delighted with the histrionic profession."[177]

After his return, Fong Get was a public Chinatown persona, even outside of the Chinese community. In 1907, Fong leased a building at 914 Stockton Street, together with two partners.[178] There, he set up shop and ran one of the neighborhood's most successful photo studios. The building was located between Sacramento and Clay Streets, just a stone's throw from the location of the destroyed Grand Theater. Whether due to proximity or previous entertainment contacts, Fong became involved in the new iteration of the Grand when it was rebuilt to show movies. Although the Grand operation as a movie theater was brief, *Billboard* listed Fong as the theater's manager throughout 1910.[179] Given his profession and contacts, there is reason to believe that Fong could have used his photo studio to double as a makeshift film exchange in order to procure moving pictures for this Chinatown theater.

According to Palmquist and Pegler-Gordon, Fong was one of Chinatown's most prolific photographers throughout the 1910s. His studio became a neighborhood institution, and his craft would eventually pique the interests of the Chinese consul general, who hired Fong as an official photographer of pictures used by Chinese immigrants to gain access to the United States.[180] Along with a few other photographers, he was someone people would go to create a portrait for the mandatory identity certificates stipulated by the Immigration Office, but also for portraits for more personal use, such as for sending home to family in China.

Fong's short-term stint with the Grand earned him another historical title in the book of "firsts." Following Nadler's reasoning, Fong was not only the first Chinese American credited on an English-language playbill but also the first immigrant of Chinese descent to have his name listed as a San Francisco movie house manager. Whether Fong had any further direct contact with Chinatown film exhibition remains to be found out, but clearly he was a notable figure in the development of Chinese San Franciscan modernity and resistance to systemic oppression.

## Film Culture in a New Chinatown

The initial attempts to operate nickelodeons in Chinatown were conditioned by lingering concerns about new widespread fires in the wake of the 1906 catastrophe, changing regulations on the operation of film projectors, and residual public notions of the inherent dangers of Chinatown theater space. Theaters that opened after the new regulations too effect were more long-lived. Such movie houses, like the Oriental, the Broadway, and the Acme, operated from 1909 or 1910 until the late 1910s without having to make any large-scale adjustments. As the number of theaters showing film increased in 1910, competition tightened, resulting in an intensification of marketing strategies targeting audiences from nearby neighborhoods. Exhibitors started creating strategies that would make their movie theaters part of the everyday life of the Chinatown and North Beach communities. Further, some local exhibitors attempted to utilize Chinatown's position as one of San Francisco's leading tourist attractions by tapping into outside visitors' preconceived notions of Chinatown space. Such efforts manifested in the "Orientalized" storefronts of the Oriental, the Acme, and the Shanghai Theatre.

Benjamin Michaels's rise to prominence as a San Francisco exhibitor occurred when he moved his operation to the North Beach neighborhood, which is also when he started to cater to the city's Chinese and Italian populations. Before his North Beach days, he was a small-time movie and vaudeville man, operating in the shadow of men like the Graumans and the Lessers. Although Michaels's move to North Beach was probably motivated more by his difficulties establishing himself on Market Street than by a burning desire to bring movies to Chinatown and the Italian quarters, the result was a small but vibrant, highly competitive and idiosyncratic local film culture. While it seems that Michaels's competitors were often quick to keep up, the general picture emanating from the materials assembled here is of Michaels as the outstanding driving force behind the development of the Broadway strip. In 1910, when Benjamin Michaels was forced to concede his interests in one of the newly built theaters on Broadway, a five-year war for patrons commenced between the three nearby theaters. This war was fought with equal measures of ferocity and innovation and identified the lower-class inhabitants of North Beach and Chinatown as the theaters' most important customers. In the next chapter, I look more closely at these audience formations, examining how they interacted and how they shaped film exhibition and the moviegoing experience at the neighborhood's movie theaters.

# 5

# The Chinesque Aesthetic

## Orientalist Stereotypes in Post-quake Film Culture

In 1910, renowned Texan architect James Riely Gordon wrote an article for *Architect and Engineer* on the rebuilding of San Francisco. There he introduced a parable comparing the city's rise from the ashes with that of the mythical Phoenix. Especially fitting to the parable, according to Gordon, was the transformation of the city's most mythicized enclave. To differentiate between perception and experience, Gordon tapped into the Orientalist discourse shared by many of his American contemporaries: "The old Chinatown was a rookery that defied all diagram and description full of smoke-stained, odorous cliff dwellings, reeking of murder and mystery." The new Chinatown, on the contrary, was in Gordon's experience a space of cultural hybridity primed for commercialism. It was, in Gordon's words, "not quite Chinese, but certainly Chinesque . . . oriental color and Pagoda effects, grafted on the very American groundwork."[1]

Gordon's convoluted observation, alongside Benjamin Michaels's exploitation of the political culture of Chinatown, opens the door for analysis of another outstanding dynamic of post-quake Chinatown film culture: that between "on-site" manifestations of Orientalism in Chinatown and U.S. film culture at large. In contrast to the developments within the Chinatown community toward modernization and adaption of contemporary American urban life, much of Chinatown's new look relied on the employment of Orientalist stereotypes. The proliferation of the "Chinesque" visual aesthetic reflected a semiofficial strategy adopted by local merchants to attract tourists to the rebuilt, post-quake Chinatown. While being actively resisted by local institutions, Orientalist symbols of "Chineseness" were one of the most recurring elements of Chinatown film culture.

In this chapter, I look closer at how such a combination of "American groundwork" and Oriental finish permeated Chinatown film culture. More precisely, I show how Chinatown and North Beach exhibitors routinely employed tropes and manifestations that by the end of the 1910s would become central to cinematic Orientalism.[2] Finally, I offer a case study of an instance in which the Chinesque aesthetic became an exportable commodity. By looking at the exhibition practices of Sid Grauman's Underground Chinatown concession at the Panama-Pacific International Exposition (PPIE) in 1915, and the cultural-political brouhaha surrounding its opening, I follow a historical trajectory that leads from Chinatown post-quake film culture to Hollywood practices of Orientalist stereotypes.

Before I investigate post-quake Chinatown in search of Orientalist stereotypes, it might be wise to recalibrate the perspective. The notion of Orientalism as a point of departure for critical studies of Western historiography has diverged into a multivalent field straddling a wide variety of disciplines. Studies of Chinese American film history generally concentrate on the cinematic representations of Orientalism in classic Hollywood cinema. Edward Said categorized the different stages of Orientalism on the scale of latent to manifest—where the manifest is the rationalization and execution of latent Orientalism.[3] The focus here is on the process of interplay between such stages. To paraphrase Jeanette Roan, I place the prism of Orientalism within an already established exploratory space of "geographical and historical specificity."[4] Adding the "third" aspect of geographic and historical specificity to this interpretive approach aligns the emphasis on the various stages of Orientalist manifestations with Edward Soja's notion of Thirdspace. John Kuo Wei Tchen and art scholar Anthony Lee are forerunners in this direction. In his work on the Orientalism in San Francisco photography, Lee localized in the images of Arnold Genthe and Louis J. Stellman a "strange mix of tourism and revolution," particular to Chinatown.[5] Similar to Lee, my discussion of Orientalist tropes originates from the streets of post-quake Chinatown, not Hollywood writers' rooms and sound stages.

By considering articles, pictures, and descriptions of Chinatown film exhibition, I specifically target visual elements of post-quake Chinatown movie theaters as part of contemporary transmedial Orientalist discourse and pose questions around their specific employment in the context of Chinatown film exhibition, as well as their relation to the architecture of the new Chinatown at large. Seen against contemporary commentary on the development of the visual style of Chinatown, Gordon's off-the-cuff notion of the Chinesque aesthetic reappears as a problematic yet productive critical vector to approach the dynamics of exploitation, fabrication, and resistance in post-quake Chinatown.

## The Chinesque Aesthetic as Orientalist Manifestation

As established previously, the rebuilding of Chinatown was guided by an ambition to accommodate more tourism. Many Chinatown experts on the period have argued that the new Chinatown was in many ways built as a theme park grounded in shallow Chinese exoticism and primed for commercial exploitation of Orientalist stereotypes. Phil Choy, for example, noted that the vision of Chinatown merchants such as Look Tin Eli deliberately "promoted Chinatown as a tourist mecca, in the hopes that its improved image would help ameliorate the relationship with the community at large."[6] The initial reconstruction of Sing Fat Co.'s bazaar on Grant set the example for a pseudo-Oriental architectural style backed by the San Francisco Real Estate Board. Conceived of by non-Chinese architects trained in the Beaux Arts tradition, the result was a hybrid of Western methods of construction adorned with Oriental features. According to Christopher Yip, "Classical elements were combined with the 'oriental' and a variety of standard building parts from the catalogs of the day. It was in large measure the juxtaposition rather than any single element that created the picturesque effects that gave the rebuilt community its sense of identity and uniqueness."[7] Choy, drawing on his expertise as an architect and Chinatown historian, gives a more detailed account on the more and less visible changes in the new Chinatown cityscape:

> The size and lots and their location were determining factors in the outcome of the design. Corner lots lent themselves to the adaptation of the multi-tiered eaves to simulate the multi-storied pagoda. Since the building code allowed 100% coverage of the lots, the idle lots left only the street façade for design. The ground floor was maximized for storefront usage, leaving minimal room for a front entrance to the upper stories. Therefore fire escapes were turned into balconies decorated with Chinese design motifs, such as the stylized "double happiness" character. The top-floor balcony was recessed, with the roof extended to create the illusion of the massive roof prevalent in Chinese architecture. Columns, indiscriminately surmounted by capitals, supported the roof, creating an "exotic" appearance. The eclectic use of standard classical building elements—brackets, cornices, parapets, Ionic, Doric, and Corinthian capitals, antefix, and acanthus—combined with an oriental roofline, furthered the exotic image. However, only the use of the colors red, yellow and green was authentically Chinese. Where buildings abutted each other, the contiguous pattern gave the illusion of an "Oriental" streetscape. . . . The illusion created is

> a masterful design solution, unique and indigenous, for it is neither East nor West but decidedly San Francisco.[8]

Yong Chen notes that the outward appearance of Chinatown space was of great importance for non-Chinese visitors to the area, even before the 1906 disaster. According to Chen, tourists centered their attention on Chinatown's visual milieu in search of transpacific ties in Chinese American life.[9] Erica Pan pointed out that the reconstruction of Chinatown represented an effort to mix standard commercial buildings with the "fantasy of the Far East."[10] After the earthquake, as tourists returned to the reconstructed Chinatown in increasingly large numbers, "nostalgic non-Chinese tourists came in search of its exoticized past, which had been embedded in their minds for decades."[11] This act of interpretive inscription of the myth of "old Chinatown" on the outward appearance of its new incarnation is evident in two photographic volumes published by Arnold Genthe in 1908 and 1913.[12] Written commentaries by San Francisco journalist Will Irwin accompanied the books. Irwin had already mythologized Chinatown in a sentimental requiem to the city written in the summer of 1906.[13]

In 1984, John Kuo Wei Tchen offered a counterreading of Genthe's photographs. Beyond critiquing Genthe's and Irwin's exoticizing views, Tchen drew on research on the social history of the people and places pictured to give Genthe's photographs new historical contextualization and new meaning.[14] In a related analysis, theater and art historian James Moy read the emergence of touristic post-quake Chinatown as a textual geography that had to be "like, yet unlike, China (Canton); dirty, yet clean as a whistle; terribly careless, but always beautiful; pedestrian (from every doorstep), but perfect in line and color; and finally, a mystery."[15] Whereas Tchen described Genthe along the lines of a starry-eyed visitor, keen on mystery, and oblivious to the struggles and hardships that had shaped life in turn-of-the-century Chinatown, Moy postulated that Genthe and Irwin inscribed their photo-texts with a vision of Chinese America as "never assimilable, always alien to American contemporary life."[16]

James Riely Gordon was not the only contemporary observer to focus on the interplay between latent and manifest Orientalism. A 1912 San Francisco guidebook written by Helen Throop Purdy underlined how tourists and guides had projected the Orientalist fantasy onto the Chinese neighborhood. Interestingly, Purdy argued that it was primarily a question of choice on behalf of the visitor. She demonstrated this by citing two articles published in local newspapers shortly after the 1906 earthquake and fire. The first article proposed that the catastrophe had revealed the intricate underground network of secret tunnels and opium dens. The second article, a short piece published in the *Chronicle* about three weeks after the fire, directly refuted the claims made by the earlier article.[17] Purdy professed that the visitor "may take his choice of tales."[18] In the 1930s, Herbert Asbury emphasized the negotiation between fabrication and authenticity in his historical chronicle of the Barbary Coast as omnipresent. Asbury, better known to the general public for having authored *The Gangs of New York*, described the decade that followed the rebuilding of the area as one of "synthetic sin and imitation iniquity," where everything that occurred in its infamous dives was "deliberately planned to impress, and if possible, to shock, the tourist and the sightseer."[19] In Asbury's view, if the pre-quake debauchery of the Barbary Coast and Chinatown was the organic product of decades of vice, alienation, and systemic corruption, its post-quake reincarnation was guided by the attempt to capitalize on the myth.

While it is impossible to gauge the contemporary impact of this Chinesque aesthetic on the everyday lives of Chinese San Franciscans, several cultural historians have emphasized the emergence of Chinatown tourism in the 1910s as a recurring defining factor of the public image of Chinese in America in the century that followed. Anthony Lee argued that for Chinese San Franciscans, Chinatown's reconstruction for the pleasure of someone else generated a forced attentiveness to another's desires that was "interpreted as evidence of Chinatown's Westernization."[20] Christopher Yip advanced a discussion of what Gordon called the Chinesque aesthetic as representing the progress of modern capitalism in Chinatown. Yip maintains that the outward appearance of the new Chinatown "represented a merging of the new economic realities with the established nineteenth-century social order. New association buildings appeared along the main streets in Chinatown adding modest grandeur and festivity to the urban landscape. Orientalized commercial buildings were interspersed in recognition of the shifting economic reality."[21] Others, like Raymond Rast, emphasized the fact that this development was propelled by some of Chinatown's most significant institutions as a strategy to retake control of the neighborhood's public image.[22]

More than adding perspective to the racialized link between the physical appearance of the new Chinatown and the ambiguous social status of Chinese Americans in the exclusion era, Gordon's view on architectural aesthetics appears couched in an American Protestant tradition of racialization and the idea of manifest destiny. As the work of John Kuo Wei Tchen reminds us, manifest destiny was not only a colonizing vision of the frontier but also "an occidentalist view of extending European American Protestant civilization into the Pacific."[23] For Gordon, a devout Episcopalian, the hybridity of the new Chinatown seemed located in a contradictory balancing act of the Protestant virtues of capitalism ("American groundwork") and the otherness of Chinese Americans and the things that surrounded them ("pagoda effects"). The degree to which Gordon subscribed to the tenets of the contemporary Social Gospel movement remains unclear, but his analysis of the new Chinatown cityscape shared fundamentals with that movement's prescription for curing societal ills through salvation of the "unchurched," as well as its positive view of consumerist culture.[24] A few quirks and idiosyncrasies could be allowed, as long as the groundwork was solidly Christian. As the designer of several Texas landmarks in the Neo-Romanesque and Beaux Arts classicist tradition, Gordon also had a long-standing connection to the vision of modern America envisaged at turn-of-the-century world's fairs.[25] In 1893, Gordon designed the Texas pavilion for the World's Columbian Exposition in Chicago, overseen by chief architect Daniel Burnham.[26] Like Burnham, Gordon was a vocal supporter of the City Beautiful movement, which functioned as the conceptual framework for the plans to rebuild San Francisco as well as for the PPIE.[27]

In the next section, I adopt the notion of the Chinesque aesthetic as shorthand for describing these localized manifestations of Orientalism in post-quake Chinatown film culture. Granted, the notion of the Chinesque is flawed, rife with the contradictions typical of U.S. Orientalism; it also serves as a productive point of intersection for this study.[28] The contrived notion of the Chinesque aesthetic can be useful for several reasons: (1) it is conceived of through the eyes of a non-Chinese Chinatown tourist; (2) it encompasses the manifestations of Orientalism encountered in Chinatown space during my period of investigation; (3) it freely associates the post-quake Chinatown visual milieu with the mythicized neighborhood encountered in Genthe's photography and Irwin's commentary, while simultaneously recognizing these as literary constructs; and (4) it simultaneously perceives the new Chinatown cityscape as a commercially viable cultural hybrid, full of "oriental color and pagoda effects." As such, it gives us a contemporary local perspective on the manifestations of Orientalism encountered in post-quake Chinatown film culture.

## The Chinesque Aesthetic in Chinatown Film Culture

Images and contemporary descriptions of post-quake Chinatown movie theaters alongside the notion of the Chinesque aesthetic suggest that Chinatown film exhibitors heavily employed Orientalist symbols of commercial buildings as a branding strategy. The semiotics of such a construct of cultural hybridity—American by the foundation, Chinese by appearance—drew from the discursive pool of contemporary stereotypes of Chinese American attributes. The Chinesque aesthetic in Chinatown film culture, as I approach the notion, encompassed a range of Orientalist manifestations, from stage show costumes and yellowface performances to chinoiserie knickknacks sold in the bazaars of Grant Avenue. Further, its interplay between latent and manifest Orientalism activated a contemporary discourse on Chinatown as an exuberant and uncanny spectacle. Despite the active promotion of Chinatown as "new" after its rebuilding, the dominant view of it was still that of a "city within a city, a world of its

FIG. 12 The front of the Oriental Theatre showing its $6,000 Wurlitzer organ. *Moving Picture World*, February 24, 1912, 719. (Image courtesy of Media History Digital Library)

own."[29] Again, we return to street level, this time to investigate how the Chinesque aesthetic manifested at the Chinatown movie theaters.

As alluded to in the previous chapter's movie house walk fantasy, the Oriental Theatre's "aggregated Oriental" look merged with other Chinesque features on the 1000 block on Grant Avenue. The PianOrchestra, which was the dominating visual feature of the storefront, is an outstanding example of such Chinesque elements. The instrument's most striking detail was perhaps the wooden ornament placed on its crown, which was composed of two Chinese characters. Unfortunately, the deteriorating quality of the photograph renders the characters unreadable. Manufactured by the Ohio-based Rudolph Wurlitzer Company, but adorned with Orientalist symbols, the instrument essentially manifested Gordon's description of Orientalist features "grafted onto the very American groundwork."[30] Viewed from the street, the Wurlitzer adorned the space between the entry and the sidewalk, with lanterns hanging from the ceiling and a ticket booth plastered with handwritten placards in both Chinese and English. This space, in turn, was framed by a doorway of decorative brackets and a neon sign that read "ORIENTAL THEATRE." However, while the Oriental indeed showcased what Phil Choy has called the "illusion of an oriental streetscape," it clearly advertised its program toward both Chinese and non-Chinese visitors.[31]

The images that remain of the Shanghai Theatre on Kearny Street show no trace of the bilingual approach. Yet its storefront was the most grandiose of all Chinatown theaters of the 1910s. As visible in a postcard (figure 13), it utilized what Choy described as the eclectic mix of standard classical building elements combined with an Oriental roofline. As such, the Shanghai corresponded more directly to the touristic demand of fabricated authenticity. More than any other Chinatown or North Beach movie theater, the Shanghai showcased the visual stylings of the Chinesque aesthetic. An ornamental dragon's head, reminiscent of roof decorations common to the Chinese imperial period, protruded from the roof, and two flagpoles flanked the dragon's head. Similar to the Oriental Theatre, decorative brackets and lanterns framed the entry of the theater, yet the Shanghai storefront was almost double the Oriental's size.[32] Along the two sides of the entrance, two more ornamental dragon heads protruded from the sidewalls; these read, on both sides, "Shanghai Theatre." In the two photographs I have been able to find, the Shanghai Theatre troupe and management lined up in front of the building, blocking the view of the entrance and ticket booth. However, in both pictures, the banners and placards visible outside the theater announce the name and identity of the establishment in English only.

The text included beneath the picture on the front side of the postcard provides another piece of evidence that Michaels specifically targeted tourists with the Shanghai Theatre. Formulated as a set of directions, it instructs visitors how to get to the theater from Market Street, which would have been the most obvious point of reference for anyone visiting San Francisco. Specifically, the postcard urges visitors to take the streetcar—itself a symbol of modern San Francisco tourism—that conveniently ran up Kearny Street and to alight outside the recognizable theater building. As if to cement the theater's position as part of the Chinatown tourism industry, the instructions recommend that visitors who might get lost looking for the Shanghai should ask for assistance from any of the Chinatown guides. While the Chinesque features of the Shanghai's outward appearance might have symbolized a tourist trap for contemporary moviegoing Chinese San Franciscans, they impressed Sid Grauman to the degree that he hired Michaels to oversee the Chinese Theatre at his Chinatown concession at the PPIE in early 1915. I shall return to the Underground Chinatown concession later in this chapter.

Images of the Broadway theaters and the Acme bear no visible traces of the Chinesque aesthetic, keeping with the stated ambition to attract primarily the multicultural audiences frequenting Broadway, rather than branding

FIG. 13 Front of the postcard from ca. 1912 showing the front of Benjamin Michaels's Shanghai Theatre and its staff. From the private collection of Phil Choy. (Image by the author)

themselves as strictly Chinatown theaters. Yet the frequency of Chinese San Franciscan patrons and the occasional yellowface vaudeville performance offered between film screenings suggest that the movie house managers recurringly thought of ways to monetize the proximity of Chinatown.[33]

The strategic Orientalization of the theaters proved an effective way to align visitors' experiences with popular fantasies about Chinatown. This is evident in contemporary trade press descriptions. In 1909, *Billboard* correspondent Rube Cohen emphasized the opening of the Oriental Theatre on Grant Avenue in the weekly "San Francisco Letter." Cohen considered the Oriental a "very unique affair," which looked like "a big winner." The new theater, with its Oriental front and its $6,000 Wurlitzer organ, was "intended to cater to the Chinese and Japanese, who simply go into ecstasies over the exhibition."[34] While Cohen's wording could, and to some extent should, be interpreted as a disparagement of Chinese and Japanese San Franciscans and their perceived inability to function normally in public situations, the rhetoric can also be read as a display of the hyperbole often used by the trade press. The same year, Cohen again used the term "unique" to describe the newly opened Shanghai Theatre. In Cohen's view, Chinatown's latest movie house presented a "perfect dream of beauty all Oriental in design." Cohen marveled at the "illuminated dragons," the "several China devils with electric eyes," and the "rich, gold Chinese carvings" that gave the Shanghai its "strictly Chinese" touch.[35] In 1911, Ona Otto described the Shanghai Theatre as "most unusual."[36] While writers like Cohen and Otto did not represent the majority audience at the Shanghai or the Oriental at the time, their astonishment at the visual features of these theaters exemplifies the theaters' exotic appeal to Chinatown tourists and patrons visiting from other neighborhoods. James Riely Gordon similarly labeled its outward appearance "at once bizarre and bazaar."[37]

The logic of the uncanny and "weird" in the transitional era "often centered on the power of those typically deemed powerless" in early twentieth century America, as Kendall Phillips has pointed out. According to Phillips, women, people of color, and foreigners were "often portrayed as wielding mysterious power beyond those possible in the real rational world. . . . The term 'weird' encompassed the experience of a culturally repressed past."[38] Although Phillips traced the phenomenon of the "weird" in developments of narrative cinema, based on my research findings, I would suggest that this symbolism also extended to cinematic epiphenomena, such as marketing displays, advertising materials, and theater architecture.[39] Moviegoers' fascination with the weird and exotic, as seen in the employment of the Chinesque aesthetic in post-quake Chinatown film culture, points to a process that confirmed the thrust of American progressivism by way of referencing what it opposed. While conceived as opposites, both notions encompassed the contradictory logic of Chinatown modernity. The Chinesque aesthetic, in a sense, thus represented a material culture through which the perceived "weirdness" of Chinatown was domesticated and commodified.

Manifestations of the Orientalist fantasy at the Chinatown post-quake movie theaters became the most lasting visible remnant of post-quake Chinatown film exhibition in the bourgeoning first century of U.S. film culture. However, in the years leading up to the PPIE, the contradictory perception of the exotic, dangerous, and unavailable Chinatown (and the agenda of countering such views set forth by Chinatown community leaders) led to considerable public friction in San Francisco.

## Exporting the Chinesque Aesthetic: Underground Chinatown at the Panama-Pacific International Exposition

In February 1915, San Francisco opened the doors to the Panama-Pacific International Exposition, a world's fair honoring the apparent connection of East and West: the human-made canal linking the Atlantic and the Pacific Oceans. A whole new district had been created to accommodate the exposition grounds, stretched over landfills and solidified marshlands. From Van Ness Avenue in the east to Hunters Point overlooking the Golden Gate in the west, displays from each of the booming North American states presented the virtues of the New World. Among the faux colonnades and the palaces made of plaster, a contender to be the latest addition to the New World, China, participated with a display showcasing the country's rich history as well as the progress and modernization of the nascent republic. The official Chinese pavilion was built to represent the Forbidden City, with the famed Chinese wall surrounding it. Inside were copies of the Imperial Audience Hall and the Hall of Eternal Peace, as well as a model of a "Chinese home," which, according to the official souvenir guide, was furnished with "tapestries, lacquer furniture, magnificent carvings and works of art."[40] It cost around $750,000 to assemble by artisans brought from China. However, the Chinese pavilion was not the only version of China on display as the world's attention turned to San Francisco.

In the Joy Zone, the exposition's entertainment section, for ten cents visitors could walk through the Underground Chinatown concession, a slumming tour staged by Sid Grauman and Benjamin Michaels that put on public display some of the most common fantasies about San Francisco's "oriental colony," complete with opium smokers, hatchet men, and sing-song girls.[41] Non-Chinese performers in yellowface enacted the scenes. Within days, Chinatown luminaries lodged a highly coordinated protest against the display, and the protest continued until the exposition offices ordered Grauman to alter the display or close. The final section of this chapter investigates how several defining aspects of Chinatown film culture clashed at the PPIE. Drawing on their experience of exploiting Chinatown culture for entertainment purposes,

Grauman and Michaels exported their repertoire and practices to the world stage. Simultaneously, the organized protests from the Chinatown community showcased a strategical countering of stereotypes orchestrated by important Chinese San Franciscans' social institutions.

By the early twentieth century, the fascination with mythical "Chineseness" was a common feature of world's fair exhibitions. The Centennial Exhibition in Philadelphia in 1876 included an exhibit created by Chinese customs officers.[42] A decade after the passing of the exclusion act, no Chinese participated within the formal confines of the 1893 World's Columbian Exposition in Chicago.[43] However, a commodified vision of "Chineseness," including a theater, a joss house, a bazaar, and a tea garden, was on offer at the adjunct fairgrounds called the Midway Plaisance.[44] In 1894, several of the sights and attractions from the Columbian Exposition were brought to San Francisco for the California Midwinter International Exposition to be held in 1898. Construction of a Japanese Village, including several designs derived from traditional Chinese architecture, added local flavor to the entertainments.[45] Even in 1915, a Chinatown concession appeared at the Isthmus, the rival San Diego Panama-California Exposition's equivalent of the Joy Zone.[46]

While the Underground Chinatown concession had its predecessors at earlier world's fairs, the Joy Zone installment was in many respects a local version. Grauman had frequently employed the ties to the Orientalist fantasy of San Francisco's Chinatown in the early stages of his career. Later, when Grauman's Chinese Theatre had become an iconic landmark on Hollywood Boulevard, he related to publicity man Brig Townsend that much the "authenticity" seen at the Chinese Theater came from his experiences as a Chinatown guide in San Francisco. According to Townsend, Grauman had invited tourists into an opium den. Then, he had told Townsend, "I had a fellow on the outside hammer on the door. 'The cops!' I would yell, 'Let's get out of here!' And the tourists would come boiling out with a great experience to tell the folks back home."[47] Whether this account was true or just an example of Grauman's famed knack for storytelling is hard to verify. But what is clear is that Grauman, in his San Francisco days and after, routinely drew inspiration and talent from Chinatown while also frequently utilizing Orientalist tropes in his shows and at his theaters. For example, he often included Chinese dance acts in his vaudeville shows at his Empress Theater, like his popular 1909 presentation, *A Smashup in Chinatown.*[48] In 1912, he conceived a highly popular variety display titled *20 Minutes at the Barbary Coast.* Aiming to revive the fading and dubious glory of San Francisco's most notorious entertainment district, the show included many acts and scenes set in Chinatown. The Barbary Coast had been connected to Chinatown by the neighborhood's main thoroughfare at Pacific Street. In Grauman's stage version, Chinatown encompassed a Chinese theater, an opium den, and a scene outside a dancehall on Pacific Street.[49] The show also included a Chinese dance troupe doing one of the latest dance crazes, "The Texas Tommy."[50] Grauman's take on Chinatown street life as a blend of performance and authenticity was again evident in 1913, when he coproduced the film *Last Night of the Barbary Coast*. The film included street scenes from both Chinatown and the adjacent North Beach area, but it also employed actors and performances from Grauman's Chinatown number.[51]

In late 1914, Sid Grauman acquired the rights to operate in the Joy Zone. Here, within the confines of what was called the Oriental Village, Grauman had assembled a version of Chinatown with a close resemblance to his earlier depictions of Chinese culture. To further emphasize the local connection, Grauman put Chinatown "expert" Benjamin Michaels in charge of operating the Chinatown Theater. The concession presented fairgoers with a smorgasbord of Yellow Peril stereotypes, quickly becoming popular and drawing more visitors than the official Chinese pavilion. The Underground Chinatown included a guided tour through an imaginary Chinatown, during which actors in yellowface displayed various scenes. According to Chen Chi, China's official representative at the PPIE, who visited the concession, one such scene showed two non-Chinese actors seeking entry to an opium den. Another scene showed "white men prepared in Chinese costumes carry on imaginary conversations for the delectation of the visitors." Chi had also learned that "when Chinese are not present among the visitors, the slave-girl drama is enacted and a revolting scene in which women are inducted into slavery is made clear to the crowd."[52] Another account described "shrieking hatchet men, bleary eyed addicts, bookmakers with sing-song voices, and, most popular of all, prostitutes 'imported' from China who called to customers from behind prison bars."[53]

Years later, when Grauman presided over the first-run Chinese Theatre in Los Angeles, he routinely returned to similar practices. Among Grauman's signature features were his long "prologues," stage spectacles that essentially were elaborate versions of the type of vaudeville shows he had put together in the few years leading up to and following the PPIE, such as *Last Night of the Barbary Coast* and the *Midnight in Frisco'*.[54] In the late 1920s, Grauman's practices met with derision from some of the Los Angeles–based trade press (as well as a few Hollywood directors). But the critics focused their snide remarks on the longueurs of the acts rather than the misrepresentation of Chinese Americans.[55] Despite Grauman's emerging position as one of cinema's most visible showmen, the mutterings of the Hollywood crowd paled in comparison to the protests against the Orientalist spectacles on display at the PPIE. In 1915, a series of public protests orchestrated by San Francisco Chinatown institutions and high-ranking officials from the Chinese Republic immediately countered the opening of Underground Chinatown.

As letters started flooding the offices of exposition president Charles C. Moore, it was evident that many of the protesters were already familiar with

FIG. 14 Photograph of Grauman's concession at the Panama-Pacific International Exposition, taken after alterations made in response to protests. (Image courtesy of Anne T. Kent California Room, Marin County Free Library)

Grauman's and Michaels's quotidian exploitation of Orientalist stereotypes. In 1908, Benjamin Michaels received numerous letters of complaint about a yellowface act from the opening night of his California Theater. *Billboard* reported that a Chinese newspaper had published an image of the scene accompanied by a story describing how the performance ridiculed the Chinese, calling the Chinatown community to boycott the theater to change or get rid of the number. The paper, probably *Chung Sai Yat Po*, also expressed the protest in a letter directly to Michaels. Realizing the losses a boycott would mean for his theater, Michaels readily agreed to the demand and changed the costumes for the act.[56] Around this time, editors of the San Francisco Chinese newspapers, among them Ng Poon Chew, formed a joint grassroots movement called the Shen Gong Li Hui (SGLH) to effectively counter negative stereotypes. In the group's first official statement in 1909, it announced its mission as being to "protect the reputation, lives, and property of the overseas Chinese community."[57] The nationwide popularity of a play titled *The Chinatown Trunk Mystery* put the SGLH's resolve to the test immediately. The play was a fictionalization of a widely publicized 1909 murder case in New York in which a Chinese man stood accused of killing his teenage Euro-American lover. Before the play arrived in San Francisco, the Chinatown intelligentsia lodged a campaign advocating its banishment. The strategy was similar to the organized protests against Michaels's racist play. Scores of letters of protest, written in both Chinese and English, were sent to newspapers and legislators across the country.[58] *The Chinatown Trunk Mystery* came to the Princess Theatre in San Francisco in February 1911. In response, the *Chinese Defender* called the play "a disgrace to the American stage, an insult to the Chinese people, and a blot upon the record of any community that allows it to be presented."[59] The play had been stopped in Portland, but the editors of the *Defender* expressed concern that San Francisco was under "too much Union Labor domination to see the justice of the Chinese side of the matter."[60] As it turned out, these suspicions were well grounded. While representatives of the Six Companies, the Chinese vice-consul, and the Chinese San Franciscan press protested the San Francisco premiere of the play, it was allowed to continue with minor alterations.[61] However, as Lui notes, the joint effort of the SGLH resulted in the formation of a San Francisco–based Chinese American advocacy group with its sights set on countering popular Orientalist stereotypes.[62] In one of the earliest letters of protest that landed on Moore's desk, the Six Companies expressed familiarity with Grauman and Michaels, describing them as "theatrical people whose only interest in the matter is the making of money out of it. That the Chinese are humiliated and disgraced is immaterial to them."[63] It is against this background that I approach the events and protests surrounding the Underground Chinatown concession at the PPIE.

## Protests and Resistance

Just days after the opening of the Underground Chinatown pavilion, a swift and well-organized protest from the Chinese community was set in motion, starting with a letter from the Chinese commissioner-general at the PPIE, Chen Chi, addressed directly to the president of the exposition, Charles C. Moore. In the letter, Chen voiced a protest on behalf of the Six Companies against the Underground Chinatown, calling for its immediate suppression. Chen slammed the concession as a "disgrace to the Exposition and a slander of the Chinese people." He continued: "It has long been the custom in this country to exploit the frailties and peculiarities of the Chinese race," calling the concession "an exaggerated picture of all the weaknesses and degrading influences which it is hoped that the new Chinese civilization may be able to stamp out."[64] Interestingly, Chen went to great rhetorical lengths to point out the absurdity of these stereotypes as representative of the Chinese by imagining the "vices of the American society" put on "public display." The letter continued:

> Certainly a concession in a foreign country which would represent as a part of ordinary American civilization the police murders of New York City, the life of the brothel in every port city in America, and other countries, the drinking of absinthe and its attendant horrors, the dancing of practically nude women as they appear in the Hippodrome of New York City, the fashionable and exclusive gambling clubs of this and other prominent cities and the besotted and blur eyed opium and morphine fiends, and alcoholic degenerates who

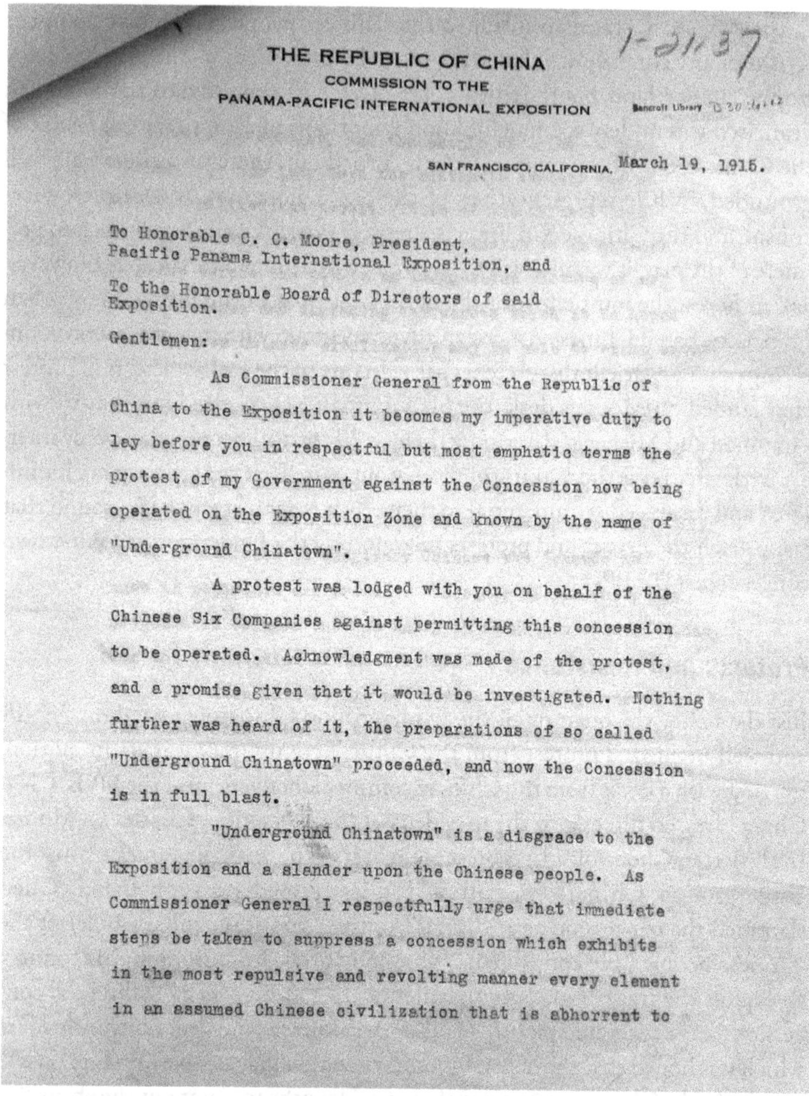

THE REPUBLIC OF CHINA
COMMISSION TO THE
PANAMA-PACIFIC INTERNATIONAL EXPOSITION

1-21137

SAN FRANCISCO, CALIFORNIA, March 19, 1915.

To Honorable C. C. Moore, President,
Pacific Panama International Exposition, and

To the Honorable Board of Directors of said
Exposition.

Gentlemen:

As Commissioner General from the Republic of China to the Exposition it becomes my imperative duty to lay before you in respectful but most emphatic terms the protest of my Government against the Concession now being operated on the Exposition Zone and known by the name of "Underground Chinatown".

A protest was lodged with you on behalf of the Chinese Six Companies against permitting this concession to be operated. Acknowledgment was made of the protest, and a promise given that it would be investigated. Nothing further was heard of it, the preparations of so called "Underground Chinatown" proceeded, and now the Concession is in full blast.

"Underground Chinatown" is a disgrace to the Exposition and a slander upon the Chinese people. As Commissioner General I respectfully urge that immediate steps be taken to suppress a concession which exhibits in the most repulsive and revolting manner every element in an assumed Chinese civilization that is abhorrent to

FIG. 15 Chen Chi's letter to Charles Moore. Carton 33, PPIE Records, Bancroft Library, University of California, Berkeley. (Image by the author)

> crowd the dock in the Police-court every morning of the week, would rouse the American government to instant and justifiable protest.[65]

Chen finished the letter by asserting that this protest was made on the behalf of his government, his people, and every Chinese civic organization, every governmental agency, and the great mass of the commercial life of the Chinese residents of the United States.[66]

During the following days, similarly formulated letters from Chinese American luminaries continued to flood the exposition offices. In one letter, the Chinese Six Companies noted that after the PPIE administration had taken notice of the initial complaint and promised to investigate, there had been no further communication. Since then, Grauman's concession had been allowed to open and was being "widely advertised to the disgrace of the Chinese residents in San Francisco." The letter continued to characterize the views on display at the Underground Chinatown as calculated to "impress one who is a stranger to Chinese habits and civilization with disgust and abhorrence for our people."[67] In a letter to Moore, H. G. Chu, the consul general of China, relayed that he had spoken to Grauman three weeks before the opening of the concession. At that point, Grauman had assured Chu that he would remove any objectionable features. But when Chu visited the Joy Zone in mid-March, he discovered that Grauman had not kept his word: "The guide at the place gives assurance to all visitors that the scenes are true to life and are not imaginary, and the impression left is indeed a terrible one as far as the character of Chinese persons is concerned."[68] The Chinese Chamber of Commerce professed that "never in the history of our state has a more dispicable [*sic*], outrageous, untrue, and libelous picture or portrayal of supposed Chinese conditions been presented for exhibition."[69] Chan Sing Kai, president of the Chinese Christian Union, presented a list of protests signed by twenty-three pastors, elders, and other members of the Chinese Christian churches across the United States.[70] Hsuwen Tsou, a Cornell and University of Illinois alumni and future Kuomintang official, remonstrated: "With my knowledge of the United States, I am able to picture the Americans to you much blacker than the display of 'Underground Chinatown' can picture my undesirable compatriots—for instance, the police system of Chicago, the ignorant people of Tennessee mountains and the Virginia whiskey distillers."[71] The Chinese newspapers of San Francisco and some Chinese Republican newspapers, such as the *Chinese Republic Journal* and the *People's Tongue*, drew the connection between the Underground Chinatown concession and the white Chinatown guides that they had fought so hard to get rid of. The newspapermen, led by Ng Poon Chew, wrote that the concession was a threat not only to the reputation of China but also to the city of San Francisco for "permitting such things to exist."[72]

The campaigns against the Underground Chinatown concession continued in the Chinese press. *Chung Sai Yat Po* reported that three Westerners who had visited the concession had been so agitated that they later went into Chinatown and attacked a Chinese San Franciscan, who had to be taken to the hospital. This incident had direct similarities to the societal repercussions the New York Chinese community had suffered following the yellow press reports of the death of Elsie Siegel and the dramatization of the *Chinatown Trunk Mystery*.[73] The article also gave the concession a new name, calling it "The

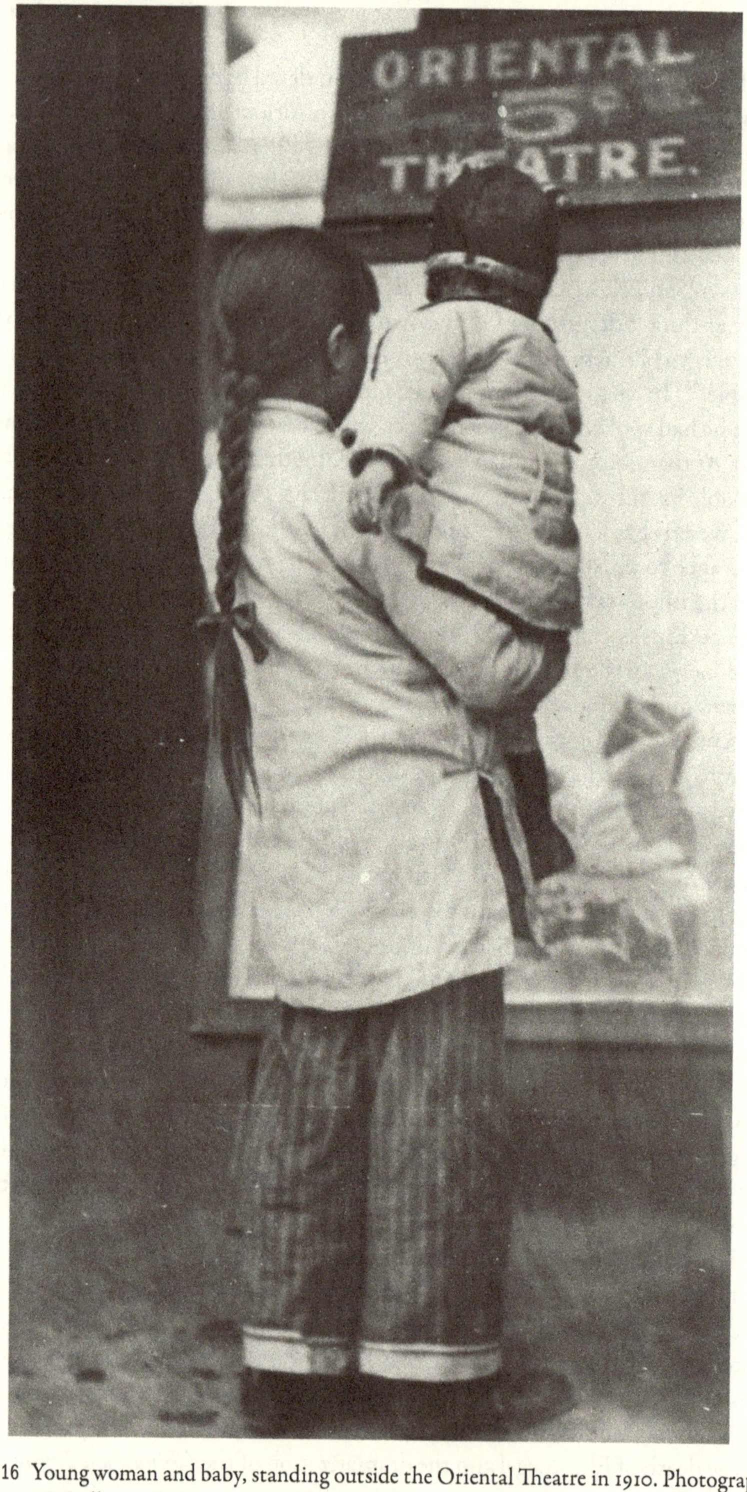


FIG. 16 Young woman and baby, standing outside the Oriental Theatre in 1910. Photograph by Louis J. Stellman. Image courtesy of the California State Library.

Chinatown Hell."[74] The reporting continued until March 27, when the paper triumphantly reported that the joint protests had paid off.[75] On the night of March 26, Charles C. Moore, accompanied by several police officers, had ordered the immediate closure of the Underground Chinatown. Grauman protested and threatened to take legal action, but the exposition president persisted in his orders, and the Underground Chinatown concession was forced to close. Grauman initially fought back, but then backed down. He had to make changes in the display to appease the Chinese community. Similar to Michaels's previous bout with the Chinatown community, Grauman made superficial changes. He removed the yellowface makeup and renamed the concession "Underground Slumming." The rest of the display remained essentially the same. A contemporary photograph of the front entrance of the concession shows a new welcome sign. Instead of "Underground Chinatown," the marquee above the entrance reads, "Slumming. Go Slumming," framed by Chinese calligraphy. Also similar to the Chinatown theaters operated by Michaels, Chinese lanterns adorn the building. Another sign, supposedly above the theater part of the building, reads "Chinatown" in stylized letters. For more than these very slight changes to the concession, Grauman demanded that the PPIE reimburse him for the expenses incurred by the changes required to comply with the Chinese protesters. As per the instructions of the PPIE's assistant director, the Joy Zone subcommittee unanimously agreed on reimbursement for Grauman in the stipulated sum of $854.81.[76] In the summer of 1916, *Billboard* praised Grauman for his "industriousness" in the face of adversity.[77]

When the exposition closed, Grauman sold parts of his decor.[78] A trade press report from December 1915 indicated it had been relocated and erected for display in the small beach town of Venice, just outside Los Angeles.[79] Grauman too relished the prospects of the emerging entertainment industry farther south and soon left San Francisco for San Jose and Los Angeles. His first roadshow, *Midnight in Frisco'*, opened at the Victory in San Jose in late September. The show consisted of fifteen scenes "opening on Market Street, to the Barbary Coast and Chinatown, through the famous music halls and much-talked-of opium dens."[80] A short time after that, Grauman and his troupe changed the title of the show and went down to Los Angeles. At the Majestic Theater, Grauman put on *A Night at the World's Fair*, which, again, included scenes from his Underground Chinatown repertoire.[81] Henry Christeen Warnack, a theater critic at the *Los Angeles Times*, who had probably not visited the PPIE, found it hard to understand why the Chinatown slumming scenes had been included: "The opium smoking scene should be eliminated and the sob stuff of the dope fiend cut out. This is farce of the worst taste. . . . Neither Coffee Dan's place nor Chinatown had anything to do with the World's Fair, and there is plenty of the programme without dragging in either of these locations."[82]

While some trade critics, especially at *Variety*, at times seemed to tire of Grauman's continual reuse and transposing of materials and performances between presentation forms, it seems that the strategy was largely successful.[83] In a 1916 article, Grauman suggested to the *San Francisco Chronicle* that he had now perfected his vaudeville and film format and was ready to try it elsewhere. "It would seem I have found what the public wants," declared Grauman. "Since what San Francisco approves should be good enough for any other city, I am confident that these productions will prove as popular on the road as they have been here."[84]

## Grauman Takes the Chinesque Aesthetic to Hollywood

For the remaining years of the 1910s, Grauman gradually shifted his attention from San Francisco to Los Angeles. In 1918, he opened the Million Dollar Theater, his first Los Angeles venue, located at Third Street and Broadway.[85] In 1922, Grauman opened the Egyptian, Hollywood's first premiere theater on Hollywood Boulevard. While Grauman briefly changed the exploitative influence to a mythical version of the Middle East, the Orientalist influence remained intact. According to Charles Beardsley, Grauman's exploitation of San Francisco's Chinese American culture was already visible in his first venture with the Unique Theater. The ornate facade and "uniformed Chinese usher to greet arriving patrons" were Orientalist ingredients of visual stimuli which Grauman kept employing as he drew up the plans to build his most majestic movie house, the Chinese Theatre, which opened on Hollywood Boulevard in Los Angeles in the spring of 1927.[86] Raymond Kennedy, one of the architects Grauman hired to work on the ornamental details of the construction, later admitted that the gaudy designs of the theater were not "an authentic representation of traditional Chinese architecture," which would have given the theater too "heavy" a feeling. Instead, the designs were influenced by the British eighteenth-century furniture designer Thomas Chippendale's appropriations of Chinese handicraft.[87]

Grauman's continued reliance on the Chinesque aesthetic throughout his career was not visible only in the architecture and decoration of his movie theaters but also in his atmospheric film prologues. Popularized by Grauman and Sam "Roxy" Rothafel, the prologues were often elaborate live stage performances designed to get the audience "in the mood for the film to come."[88] In Hollywood, Grauman's premiere theaters became synonymous with lavish prologues and public spectacles. But the short-lived prologue practice, its life span commonly dated to the 1920s and early 1930s, was not conceived out of a creative vacuum. For example, in 1918, just three years after the Underground Chinatown affair, Grauman presented a prologue for the premiere of *City of Dim Faces*

(George Melford, 1918), in which the Japanese American movie star Sessue Hayakawa played a Chinese San Franciscan child of "miscegenation," torn between his "Oriental" and "Western" culture. According to Beardsley, the set design for the stage version again evoked the Chinesque aesthetic: "The main set was a San Francisco Chinatown street façade that rose realistically three floors above the stage, with entrances on both wing stages."[89] To highlight the beginning of construction of the Chinese Theater in 1926, Grauman created a highly publicized groundbreaking ceremony, decorating several blocks of Hollywood Boulevard with banners and Chinese emblems.[90] The ballyhoo was centered around actresses Anna May Wong and Norma Talmadge digging the first shovelful. Wong, by 1926 a fashion icon and Hollywood's foremost dragon lady, had been born and raised in Los Angeles Chinatown. Vinzenz Hediger has noted that the employment of ethnic actors and creation of exotic settings brought "the prologue in line with yet another popular form of turn-the-century spectacle: The display of indigenous people at world's fairs, in zoos and in variety theaters.... The prologues featuring ethnic minority actors can thus be seen as an echo, or a prolongation, of this particular strand of turn-of-the-century visual culture."[91] Grauman's personal strategy, as evident from the Underground Chinatown concession to the Chinese Theater, seems to have been to augment this formula by tying a locally anchored Orientalist framework to the cinematic realms of the fantastical and spectacular.

## Friction and Diverging Paths

Given the long history of oppression of Chinese Americans, why did the Underground Chinatown concession matter so much to Chinese San Franciscans? And why does it matter historically? The few historians who have written on the controversy have underlined the importance of the fair to the public self-image of contemporary San Franciscans. The general view of prequake San Francisco as the Sodom of the American frontier was to be countered by the realization of the *rêve* of a Paris of the West. Anthony Lee noted the significance of the spectral relationship of the exposition to the rebuilding city outside: "It was an almost dreamlike double or wish image for San Francisco itself."[92] In 1916, Louis J. Stellman conserved the vision of the PPIE as a model for the new and improved city in a pamphlet, in which he waxed lyrically that the PPIE was "a dream worth building."[93] These ideas of improvement, modernization, and beautification were shared and appropriated by many Chinese San Franciscans. Charged by the political awakening of Chinatown and its ties to reform movements in China, the community sought to imagine and create a new Chineseness. Modernity in all its "amorphousness," as noted by Leo Ou-fan Lee, became the guiding ethos for such visions.[94]

Stellman, through his paternalist perspective, wrote about this experienced kinship in the late 1910s:

> Since Chinatown has been rebuilt—into one of the most substantial, modern, and sanitary foreign colonies in America—its people have associated pretty freely with the balance of San Francisco's inhabitants, have assimilated to a remarkable extent into that general life from which they previously held themselves aloof. One sees Chinese ladies in the big department stores constantly, many of them dressed in the height of fashions of the western world. Chinatown's young men go to the movies, walk and ride about with their sweethearts—something which the ancient decorum of Chinatown would not for a moment have permitted—use the latest slang, and lead the life of the average young American.[95]

The early American film industry held up a mirror to this development, in the words of Sabine Haenni, eagerly seizing upon Chinatown for "structures of experience that negotiated and pleasurably produced its modernity," which, in turn, resulted in Asian Americans claiming that same modernity.[96] However, a public display like the Underground Chinatown all too visibly confirmed that Chinese San Franciscans still played the villain in that imaginary. This, while the PPIE displayed San Francisco's recovery and China's awakening to modernity, it also, according to Andrea Rees Davies, "revealed the widening social divide in the post-disaster city."[97] The participation of the newly Republican China clashed with a touristic gaze that kept looking for the "quaint and fascinating."[98] Here was an instance when the increasing contradictions surrounding the representation of Chinatown became visible at a national, and to a degree international, level.

The movie houses in Chinatown functioned in the community as contested sites of modernity. The cultural hybridity of post-quake Chinatown movie audiences provided grounds for perception in the trade press of the theaters as some of the most cosmopolitan in the country. More than being the nightmare of contemporary segregationists and antimiscegenation propagators, the continuation of cultural clashes provided by the Chinatown movie theaters played into anxieties within the Chinese San Franciscan community, which perceived that the price of modernization was paid with a loss of cultural heritage. However, the management of the Chinatown movie theaters, much like the rest of the United States, was less perceptive to the development of a Chinese American middle class and the heightened vigilance against stereotypes advocated by the Six Companies. In many ways, Chinese audiences were alienated from these spaces by continuous stereotyping in local entertainment culture by the likes of Sid Grauman and Benjamin Michaels. Both Grauman and Michaels relied on Chinatown as a source of talent and audiences, but the relationship lacked reciprocity. Neither Grauman nor Michaels flinched at exploiting stereotypes of Chineseness when the opportunity presented itself. The extent of their employment of Orientalist imagery derived from their experiences as film exhibitors in San Francisco. The characterization of Chinatown was particularly obvious at their concession at the 1915 Panama-Pacific International Exposition. Benjamin Michaels's exploits would end a year later in a violent car crash, not far from the site of the Underground Chinatown concession. Sid Grauman, however, would go on to inscribe the Chinesque aesthetic into American film history.

# Part III

# Chinese American Audiences

# 6

# "Where the People Aren't All American"

## Chinatown Audiences and Spectators

Film screenings became readily available to Chinese San Franciscans in the wake of the earthquake and fire. Introduced alongside new and established forms of entertainment, moviegoing quickly became Chinatown's favorite. This chapter looks closer at who went to these theaters, how the theaters operated, and how they connected to Chinatown's urban culture. By examining newspaper articles, trade press accounts, guidebooks, social surveys, and police reports, I present a general appreciation of the audience composition of various theaters, in terms of age, gender, and ethnicity. In dialogue with previous scholarship on exhibition practices in early U.S. cinema, I investigate to what extent the social marginalization of Chinese Americans played out in the space of the movie theater, but also how the Chinese community influenced and directed exhibition practices.

The contemporary accounts of moviegoing I have been able to locate range from detailed descriptions to the discursively suggestive. Most of them contain problematic and complex historical biases. The writings of Adriana Spadoni provide a good example. As historical informants, Spadoni's accounts are rich but flawed. They contain a mélange of firsthand observation, flânerie-imagination, and Orientalist stereotypes, addressing Chinatown's modernity but also its social marginality. They employ othering discourse but also show a keen eye for that which transgresses the common stereotype, and an ambition to capture the transcultural milieu of Chinatown's streets and movie theaters. All are written from the precarious vantage point of a young woman exploring the city's most infamous immigrant neighborhoods in the early 1910s. These strands are taken to task, something that can rarely be said of other contemporary accounts of cine-reporting, as well as of more recent scholarly analyses of Chinese American film history.

Like Spadoni's accounts, several of the other sources on which this chapter is based, in one way or another dwell upon the intersection between Chinatown's street culture and the space of the movie theater. In this way, they locate the transcultural contact zones and thirdspaces of Chinatown as integral to the emergence of its film culture. Miriam Hansen asserted that moviegoing during this time offered the possibility of a public sphere of a different kind, "epitomizing the multiplication and interpenetration of spaces advanced by other media of urban commercial culture."[1] Following Hansen, I explore how the liminality of street culture and the movie theater enveloped and activated other historical forms of spectatorship in post-quake Chinatown, such as the touristic gaze fostered by Chinatown guided tours and the metaspectatorial experience at the local Chinese theater.[2]

## Audience Composition and Division

Although they are scarce, accounts of frequent Chinese American moviegoing can be found for all of Chinatown's movie theaters. Newspapers and trade magazines often made a point of mentioning any Chinese presence in the audience, even though a theater lay within the geographic confines of the Chinese community. The unfortunate night of the fire at the Grand on March 16, 1909, the audience rushing for the street was described as "Oriental" in the majority.[3] The Oriental Theatre, which seated at least 700, was, with its central location on Grant Avenue, the most heavily patronized by the Chinese community. In March 1909, *Billboard* reported that the newly opened Oriental intended to cater to entertainment-seeking Chinese San Franciscans and that the interest from the Chinatown community was high.[4] The Acme Theater on the corner of Broadway and Stockton Street made no secret of the fact that it drew the majority of its audiences from Chinatown.[5] In December 1909, the California on Broadway drew "considerable patronage from among the Chinese."[6] In 1913, the Commonwealth Club survey described the audience at the Liberty Theater on Broadway as "largely composed of foreigners, including Chinese."[7] The Verdi and Sam Gordon's Broadway Theater had so many Chinese-speaking visitors that they printed marketing materials, such as advertising pamphlets and handbills, in Chinese along with their supplements in Italian and Spanish.[8] In 1911, *Moving Picture World*'s Ona Otto claimed that both staff and the majority of the audience at the Shanghai Theatre on Kearny Street were Chinese.[9] The Commonwealth Club survey noted that 25 percent of the audiences at the Lyceum Theater on Kearny Street was composed of Chinese males between the ages of eighteen and twenty-five.[10]

Chinese American movie audiences did not consist only of people who lived in Chinatown. The long-standing position of the neighborhood as the economic and cultural hub of the Chinese transpacific also attracted out-of-town Chinese American visitors to the neighborhood restaurants, theaters, and brothels. People from the nearby regions, as far away as Stockton and Sacramento, frequently traveled to San Francisco for both business and pleasure.[11]

It would also be inaccurate to propose that Chinatown audiences consisted nearly or entirely of Chinese Americans. While Chinese San Franciscans made up the core audience, most sources report highly mixed audience demographics. Patrons from nearby neighborhoods such as North Beach and Nob Hill regularly appeared in the crowds. In 1911, *Billboard* reported that at the Shanghai the audience "not only Chinese but other nationalities patronize it liberally."[12] In 1912, *Moving Picture World* reported that the regular patrons at the Broadway nickelodeon included "English, Spanish, Italian, and Chinese" nationalities.[13] The eclectic audience at the Acme Theater was in 1915 reported to consist of "Chinese, Japanese, French, Italians, Filipinos, Hindus, and Spanish."[14]

Scholars of early U.S. film exhibition have shown that movie theaters often mirrored regional demographic politics and social marginalization. Practices such as selective admission, segregated seating, and a racially biased division of labor exemplify racial prejudice in the social microcosm of the movie theater. As has been amply demonstrated in scholarship by Mary Carbine, Gregory Waller, and Jacqueline Najuma Stewart, segregation practices were particularly aimed at African American moviegoers in the Jim Crow South and the Chicago area.[15] This segregation, in turn, led to the emergence of theaters that specifically catered to brown-skinned patrons and African American communities in such areas. Los Angeles and San Francisco public establishments also employed public racial division, especially in the theaters and dance halls of the Fillmore District, which had the city's largest population of black citizens.[16]

Racial segregation against Asian Americans in theater seating was also enforced in several locations along the West Coast, as Denise Khor's research shows.[17] However, in contrast to this world order, Chinatown, especially during the post-quake period, provided urban spaces where Chinese Americans had a different social status. This was mirrored at the neighborhood's movie theaters, where seating was not segregated by either ethnicity or gender. While Chinese San Franciscans encountered quotidian racism and the audiences of Chinatown movie theaters consisted of a mix of ethnicities, the theaters were too dependent on majority audiences to attempt to introduce blunt racial segregation. The Oriental, the Grand, and the Acme were all described in the trade press and local newspapers as theaters that catered to the movie interests of Chinese San Franciscans as the staple for their daily operation.[18] Paraphrasing Mary Carbine, in the face of historical discrimination and marginality, it is wholly conceivable that Chinese San Franciscans enjoyed a certain autonomy in constructing a cultural "Chinese world" relatively free from overt white intervention.[19] This sense of ownership was reflected in Chinatown movie theater audiences, with Chinese San Franciscans making up the majority of the urban mix, as well as in the marketing strategies of the theaters to which Chinese San Franciscans were the bread and butter of the daily operation. Exhibitors like Benjamin Michaels, Sam Gordon, and Ralph Marks Sr. of the Acme Theater knew this and, as we will see in following sections, catered directly, and especially, to the Chinatown contingent of their audience groups.

Gender divisions of audiences had been the customary practice in Chinatown theaters before the earthquake.[20] This rule, relating to traditions of imperial China, does not seem to have been carried into the post-quake theaters. Although audiences at the post-quake Chinatown theaters were still predominantly male, a growing number of the moviegoers were female. The 1913 Commonwealth Club survey showed that women made up 23 percent of the audience at the Liberty Theater; the ratio of women making up a quarter of the movie audiences was higher than Chinatown's overall male to female ratio, which in 1910 was 6.8 to 1.[21] Several press reports about the Chinatown movie houses also mentioned the presence of women and children in the audience. *Moving Picture World* wrote that the Acme Theater was popular among Chinese San Franciscans, especially with Chinese women and children. Ralph Marks Sr. told the paper's correspondent that Chinese women "thronged" the theater and that their preferred time to visit was during the afternoons.[22] After the film projector at the Oriental caught fire in 1911, the *Call* reported that many women and children were trampled during the scramble for the exits. Again, the film screening had taken place in the afternoon.[23] As we will see, Chinatown movie theaters sought to attract women and children, especially to the afternoon shows. This strategy aligns with broader national trends in large to midsize U.S. cities, where film exhibitors targeted women and children from the beginning of the nickelodeon era.[24]

The mixing of men and women in the secluded spaces of the movie theaters was something that the conservative factions of Chinese San Francisco singled out as a potentially corrupting element of Chinatown film culture. Women at pre-quake theaters were often assumed to be prostitutes.[25] Judy Yung wrote that the movement toward Chinese women's liberation was paralleled by the struggles of reformers and Christian missionaries: "Regardless of the reformers' respective motives, Chinese women in both China and the United States benefited from their combined efforts," which encouraged them to free themselves from patriarchal oppression.[26] Prostitution in Chinatown was mainly a result of the bachelor society of former railroad workers and forty-niners. The storied brothel madam Ah Toy was the first and, for long, the most famous prostitute of San Francisco's Chinatown.[27] In the 1890s, Christian missions organized a crackdown on Chinese brothels, which reduced the number of Chinatown prostitutes significantly. Erica Pan wrote that after the earthquake, San Francisco Chinese organizations reached an accord with Chinese brothel owners for the liberation of former prostitutes. In the summer of 1906, *Chung Sai Yat Po* reported that prostitutes older than twenty-five could choose to quit their trade if they so wanted.[28] Chinatown prostitution declined drastically after 1906, and the presence of Chinese San Franciscan wives and families served to diminish the bachelor society that had permeated Chinese San Francisco since its earliest days.[29] The modern post-quake era in Chinatown, just like in China, also saw unprecedented social opportunities for women to segue into the role of the "new woman."

Literary scholar Ying Hu has noted that the emergence of the concept of the new woman appeared in Chinese society in the late Qing and early Republican periods.[30] However, the model "immigrant wife" in San Francisco Chinatown society was still very much framed by traditional ideas of domesticity. It was, according to Yung, still a widely held belief in the Chinatown community that Chinese women who were old enough to marry should refrain from leaving the confines of their homes. "Since their first responsibility was to their families," Yung wrote, "immigrant wives . . . found themselves housebound, with no time to take advantage of English classes offered by the churches or to engage in leisure activities outside the home."[31] Yung's general observation, however, is contradicted by contemporary reports such as the Commonwealth Club survey and several trade press accounts from between 1909 and 1915 that underline the popularity of Chinatown movie theaters among women and children.

While such accounts might contradict Yung, the findings do not make for a significant challenge to her overall scholarship on women's role in historical Chinese America. In line with Yung's study, my research suggests that the predominant role for women in Chinese San Francisco was that of the marginalized within a community already marginalized. However, it seems that the movie theater presented a communal space that, at least initially, was less racially segregated than elsewhere in the United States, and even in San Francisco, and less dictated by the gender traditions of Chinatown pre-quake movie theaters.

William Uricchio and Roberta Pearson have claimed that the audience body of neighborhood theaters in large U.S. cities was seldom uniformly made up of that neighborhood's inhabitants.[32] The same can be said about the Chinatown movie theaters not only in terms of ethnicity but also regarding age, gender, and class. However, as Michael Aronson observed in his study of Pittsburgh moviegoing, it is crucial to recognize that in cities with sharply defined geographic and cultural landscapes, "each theater's patrons would have been overwhelmingly from the surrounding community, and that the theater would have been understood as an object collectively belonging to that community."[33] Similarly, the Chinatown theaters, although visited by moviegoers from a wide range of demographic categories, was constantly reaffirmed as being a product of the neighborhood's unique characteristics, not only through their placement and design but also by the unusually large number of Chinese American patrons in the audience.

Theaters like the Oriental and the Shanghai employed Chinese San Franciscan staff for their daily upkeep. Adriana Spadoni's account of the Oriental describes a succession of Chinese girls working at the "little glass box office" and a Chinese man in "white man's clothes" at the door.[34] In 1911, Ona Otto noted that the cashier and the doormen at the Shanghai Theatre were "all Oriental."[35] While such work provided Chinatowners with paid jobs in the emerging structure of San Francisco film exhibition, the division of labor was clear. Low-income jobs, like ticket sellers, ushers, janitors, and actors, were open to Chinese San Franciscans, while more prestigious positions, like manager and projectionist, always seemed to be filled by non-Chinese men.[36] Thus, Chinatown movie theaters' employment politics followed a regime similar to practices by white-owned "black movie theaters" in Chicago in the transitional era. Douglas Gomery noted that exhibitors Balaban & Katz had specific racial policies regarding employment, "relegating blacks to more servile jobs such as messengers, maids or porters."[37] Carbine concluded that such employment practices reinforced a "caste hierarchy of jobs and service based on white physiognomic ideals."[38]

Despite the organizational hierarchy of the movie theaters, in which Chinese San Franciscans generally held low-status jobs, there were instances suggesting a more profound involvement. For example, in the advertising campaign launched for the opening of the Oriental, Chinese San Franciscans employed by the theater were involved in shaping its public profile, not only as ushers or ticket girls but also by contributing to the marketing strategies. In formulating and printing the Chinese advertisement, the Oriental's non-Chinese manager, Ben Wiseman, had relied on the expertise of his Chinese San Franciscan employees to attract Chinatown audiences. Next, we shall look closer at these strategies.

## Catering to the Chinatown Community

Chinatown movie theaters adopted several creative strategies to attract Chinese San Franciscan moviegoers from the street into the theater. Some of these practices were similar to contemporary marketing of film exhibition elsewhere in San Francisco, as well as certain tendencies in U.S. film exhibition of the era at large. Others were more idiosyncratic and appear as the product of a careful analysis of audience demography and local competition, mixed with a good deal of experimentation.

As mentioned previously, *Billboard* published a reproduction of one of the Oriental Theatre's "circulars" in May 1909. The bill had been handed out to promote the shows among Chinatown moviegoers, but in *Billboard* it was presented as a curiosity without translation. In this manner, *Billboard* brought attention to the existence of Chinese American patrons in U.S. audience composition. At the same time, it served to underscore the estrangement and alienation of these audiences, giving no further explanation as to the advertisement's content. This is probably also how most of *Billboard*'s readers perceived it. However, a closer look at the semantics of this advertisement suggests cunning strategies to familiarize movies for Chinese San Franciscan audiences at the Oriental. Two expressions especially stand out. First, the word used for film, *yǐng huà* (影畫), was a colloquial term, originating from San Francisco's Chinatown. The use of this term, according to Phil Choy of the Chinese Historical Society, suggests that the Oriental advertised this show as a local appropriation of U.S. film exhibition.[39]

The second point of interest in the advertisement shows a different strategy of illustration that grounded the advertisement in the context of contemporary Chinatown, as it described the Wurlitzer PianOrchestra by comparing it to an ancient Chinese instrument. Here, instead of using transliteration, the Oriental advertisement called the automated Wurlitzer a *diànqì yángqín* (電氣洋琴), which roughly translates to "electrified yangqin." The yangqin was a dulcimer-like instrument with no real similarities to the Wurlitzer, except for its ability to produce sound.

Seen in hindsight, the colloquial word for "movie" provides the advertisement with a spatiotemporal dimension that hints at the cultural perimeters of moviegoing in Chinatown in the spring of 1909. These two wordings suggest that the Oriental's approach to attracting Chinese San Franciscan audiences was by way of appropriating film exhibition to the cultural references of their intended audiences. In this way, the Oriental facilitated moving picture exhibition for Chinatown. As such, the advertisement appears to be a San Francisco Chinatown–specific iteration of what Miriam Hansen has called "vernacular modernism."[40] The second wording, the symbolic electrification of a well-known ancient Chinese instrument, suggests that the exhibitions at the Oriental promised a fusion of traditional and modern cultural practices. Whoever formulated the advertisement was trying to familiarize Chinese San Franciscans with the Oriental's film programs by evoking a common cultural heritage and the local, shared experience of modernity.[41]

The handbill also appears as a compelling example of post-quake Chinatown film exhibition functioning as what Mary Louise Pratt has conceptualized as

IN SAN FRANCISCO.

# 影畫新張

啟者本戲院在都板街一千零三十七號定期是禮拜日下午两点鐘開演上等新奇活動畫影能擴人眼界激人腦海幷有新欵電氣洋琴一架值銀六千元所彈之音更能震人耳鼓華人到觀優禮相迎開演之日華人婦孺來看者則賞以物爲

每位收銀五仙

日午後一点至五點鐘

晚六點至十一點鐘

宣統元年正月廿二日

柯李烟度戲院公司啟

國魂日報印

FIG. 17 Chinese handbill for the Oriental Theatre. *Billboard*, May 29, 1909. (Image courtesy of Proquest Historical Newspapers)

a "trans-cultural contact zone," a space in which disparate cultural practices fused into expressions of cultural hybridity.[42] The advertisement indicates that Chinatown film exhibition constituted such a dynamic transcultural space. However, this potential is complicated by the advertisement's subsequent appropriation as a film cultural curiosity and artifact of face-value chinoiserie in *Billboard*, hinting at the multiple layers and frequently encountered "asymmetrical relations of power" Pratt delineated as inherent in the transcultural contact zone.[43]

Other theaters also made attempts to attract Chinatown audiences by offering translated promotional materials and films. In 1912, *Moving Picture World* reported that the Broadway Theater's change from licensed to independent film service, beginning with the screening of *Dead Man's Child*, was to be advertised in Chinese as well as Spanish and Italian. When, in 1915, Benjamin Michaels started the *North End News* to promote his new Verdi Theater, he outlined for *Moving Picture World* his plans to provide sections of the papers translated into Italian, French, and Chinese.[44] Michaels also related how he had had to employ the "assistance of several interpreters" operating in the lobby of the Verdi to explain to the cosmopolitan moviegoers the finer details of his subscription-based deal. In late 1915, Michaels expanded his translation efforts to his shows. Thomas Church reported for *Moving Picture World* in December that Michaels, "after having experimented in a quiet way for two years, had perfected a system of translating the English intertitles of his films into other languages." According to Church, Michaels's first effort to translate into Italian had proved successful, as there had been a "noticeable increase in the number of elderly persons" from the Italian North Beach area since its installment. The linguistic divide between generations of Italian San Franciscans provides an explanation for this, where "most of the young generation read English, but a great many of the older ones read Italian only." Michaels hired a translator to go through the intertitles of each new film that was received. The translated versions were copied onto separate slides and projected onto a second screen, placed above the regular one. Michaels admitted that the chief difficulty with this system was finding a slide operator with knowledge of both languages, but he told Church that he had plans to do translations into Chinese to cater to the Chinatown contingent of his audience.[45]

## Lecturers and Interpreters

The Oriental Theatre advertisement from 1909 suggests that translation and interpretation played a key role in attracting audiences to the theaters. Furthermore, the practice was part of a continual strategy to facilitate film experiences specifically for Chinatown audiences, once they had entered the theaters. The local appropriation of film culture extended from luring people from the street to pay the price of admission and enter the theater, to the ambition to cater to them inside the theater. An example of such pandering is the use of performers who translated and interpreted the movies for Chinese audiences. In its coverage of the Oriental in the spring of 1909, *Billboard* noted that a "Chinese lecturer" accompanied all the screenings.

The practice of lecturing and interpreting the action on the movie screen might bring to mind the performances of Japanese benshi lecturers.[46] However, including spoken commentaries by onstage lecturers was a widespread nickelodeon practice in the United States and elsewhere.[47] Charles Musser has argued that the early film exhibitor or lecturer executed final control over the individual show and programming, providing a "dominant narrating presence, shaping, if not creating meaning" of films at each theater.[48] Germaine Lacasse outlined three periods in which the lecturer's role shifted during the first twenty years of cinema: first, when moving pictures were incorporated into "various earlier practices involving commentary;" second, when narrative commentary became "a factor in the film's appeal as a specific attraction"; and, third, and most pertinent to our lecturer at the Oriental, "when the lecturer gradually disappeared."[49] This last stage began sometime in the mid-1900s when films on U.S. screens gradually became more narratively self-sufficient at the expense of the lecturer. However, as Lacasse and others have argued, exceptions to the evanescence of lecturers could be found in local contexts, especially when the lecturer adapted foreign films to the exhibition cultures of specific localities.[50] In post-quake Chinatown, literacy and the ability to read intertitles either in English or in Chinese were still relatively uncommon; therefore, a Chinese San Franciscan lecturer/interpreter would be all the more important. Paraphrasing Lacasse, the hegemony of the U.S.-produced films shown at the Oriental could be "attenuated by the intervention of a local agent who not only adapted the film to their audience's language and culture but who could intervene at another level through their own performance."[51]

In line with the Oriental advertisement's juxtaposition of traditional Chinese references and modern vernacular, the lecturer/interpreter familiarized and facilitated moviegoing for Chinese San Franciscans by way of negotiating the English intertitles and plots of American, French, and Italian films in the form of translation. While the scarce information on the practices of the Chinatown lecturer/interpreter gives us little to work with to analyze specific modes of operation, the mere confirmed existence of such practices suggests a variety of cunning strategies of local appropriation of film culture in Chinatown, which facilitated access to the medium not only as a new and popular technology but also within a new exhibition context.

It is also possible, as Lacasse has pointed out, that the lecturer, through translation and interpretation of films, acted as a mediator for the audiences between tradition and modernity.[52] Between the years 1899 and 1918, the translation of texts became a figurative realm for the emergence of modern identities in the late nineteenth-century and early twentieth-century Chinese society. While translation came to play a more direct role in reforming Chinese society in big cities like Shanghai and Beijing, this process also gained importance for the Chinese transpacific community.[53] Yong Chen has argued that while cultural conservatism to a degree tempered the formation of such modern identities in post-quake Chinatown, the "changing mentality" of the era was indeed spurred on by a steady transpacific exchange of ideas.[54] As Ying Hu pointed out, "Translation is fundamentally comparative, bringing the self and other face to face, as it were, and subjecting both to multiple transformations."[55] In the movie theater, then, the lecturer/intepreter could have functioned as a guide for this interchange of residual and emergent forms of cultural expression, facilitating the experience through live translation juxtaposed with moving images.

The practice of simultaneous translation was not new to Chinatown. Daphne Lei, in an essay on the historical production and consumption of Chinese theater in San Francisco, suggested that as early as the late 1860s the Royal Chinese Theatre on Jackson Street had incorporated Chinese interpreters in its shows as well as its preshow Chinese banquets. There the interpretations were offered to tourists to accommodate non-Chinese-speaking theatergoers.[56] While it remains unclear whether the Oriental offered interpretations of its "Chinese vaudeville" acts to visitors who were not familiar with Chinese drama, an advertisement from a 1909 English-language Chinatown guidebook announced the Oriental's offerings to tourist audiences.[57]

Here, the lecturer/interpreter, if translating from English to Cantonese, could have been understood by tourist audiences as a performative element that added to the local color and metaspectatorial experience of Chinatown film exhibition. Lei labels the open catering to tourist audiences by way of translation an event of "self-Orientalizing gesture," but notes that it could simultaneously be seen as a "canny use of exoticism, tourism, and capitalism."[58] Similar practices became common outside of the Chinatown theaters as well. According to tourism historian Raymond Rast, Chinese San Franciscans' responses to touristic interest in Chinatown ranged from accommodation to resistance. Among those who accommodated tourists were men and women "who put themselves on display for profit," often playing within common stereotypes about Chinatown. Such practices of self-Orientalization had become prevalent during the rise of Chinatown tourism in the 1890s, and ranged from the working class, who pretended to smoke opium, plot kidnappings, and barter slaves while tourists watched, to Chinatown merchants, who spoke "pidgin" English while bartering although they actually were "fluent in standard English."[59]

Another possible scenario was that audience members regarded the Oriental's lecturer as part of the vaudeville performances, which interacted with the film screenings. The vaudeville and film format had proved a successful combination in East Coast nickelodeons around the same time.[60] As Adriana Spadoni wrote about the Chinatown and North Beach theaters in 1910, "In one place they talk while the pictures are going. Sometimes the man can't make it up fast enough and has to say the same thing twice to use up the time. It makes it awfully real, though, when he does it as well. They put all sorts of outside things in, too, ring bells and blow horns when an automobile starts off."[61] Showmen like Benjamin Michaels employed the combination of "small time" vaudeville and film throughout the 1910s at the Chinatown Broadway theaters. Similarly, Sid Grauman offered combined vaudeville and film shows at his popular Empress Theater.[62] As mentioned previously, these two showmen frequently used "Chinese" acts, sometimes in yellowface, to add to the local color of their exhibitions. These practices open a wider spectrum of cultural functions fulfilled by the Chinatown film lecturer. At the Oriental, he surely enhanced the experience of the film for Cantonese-speaking audiences by facilitating an interpretation of its story, but his performance might just as well have been understood as a vaudeville act by audiences who did not speak the language or had seen "Chinese vaudeville" put on display by the likes of Michaels and Grauman.

## Metaspectatorship and Transcultural Audiences

Notwithstanding the sharp geographic and cultural demarcations between Chinatown and the rest of San Francisco that existed throughout the nickelodeon era, the neighborhood's movie theaters drew attention for their cosmopolitanism in a city that regularly prided itself on being the most multicultural in the country. Local journalist Hugo Hertz wrote in the *Call* in 1909, after having spent a day with the box office man at a local theater: "There are so many classes and nationalities in San Francisco that the theatergoers are especially hard to handle. I speak three languages and understand about a million dialects, and I can assure you I need all of them."[63] Not only the patrons but also the location mattered within this small cluster of theaters. Theaters like the Oriental, the Grand, and the Shanghai, located in Chinatown proper, were understood as objects belonging to the Chinese San Franciscan community. Here moviegoers from Chinatown were the norm against which "outside" visitors were identified.[64] The theaters along the Broadway strip, beginning at the intersection with Stockton and ending where Columbus Avenue made an incision through the grid, from Washington Street to Washington Square Park, were singled out for the multicultural profile of their clientele and as being representative of cosmopolitan San Francisco.

While it is possible or even likely that Chinatowners occasionally went outside their neighborhood to attend the movies, reports of such activity are scarce. The lack of Chinese San Franciscans' patronage of non-Chinatown theaters might be explained by the potential dangers for Chinatowners to leave the area after dark throughout the nickelodeon era. From the few pieces of information I have discerned, it seems that cinematic excursions outside Chinatown most often went past the Broadway theaters and farther into the Latino-dominated areas of North Beach. For example, in January 1912, the *Chronicle* reported on an altercation between a Mexican and a Chinese patron in an unnamed North Beach theater. With a great deal of derision, the story recounted how the sentiments of the two immigrant patrons were stirred by films showing pictures from revolutions going on in their respective countries:

> Came darkness, and then somebody beneath the screen began to beat a tin can and a tom-tom. Another whirring and the walls of Hankow gleamed in the sunlight. The slant-eyed revolutionists were making a charge. Instantly Sam Lee leaped to his feet and cried like an excited horse. Chaves (awfully disgusted) grabbed Sam Lee by the blouse and pulled him to his seat. Sam Lee, not noticing this check, leaped up again with his eyes wildly directed toward the screen. Chaves not wishing to tamper too much with Sam Lee's warlike enthusiasm slid down in his seat and closed his eyes. Soon he was fast asleep.[65]

Two cartoons illustrating the event complemented the story. While it is hard to confirm the veracity of this report, between the lines comes the suggestion that these San Franciscans, due to their simple, racialized nature, were perhaps not fit for the experiences of the modern world and its inventions, such as democracy and moving pictures. In the next chapter I will further investigate the important role of the 1911 Xinhai Revolution in Chinatown film culture.

The Broadway exhibitors approached the multiculturalism of the crowds on the strip with strategies of inclusion rather than segregation. While an interest in profits, rather than altruism, guided such strategies, this made for a dynamic exhibition climate where the area's diversity was one of its main selling points. Marks senior, for instance, called the Acme Theater the "most cosmopolitan theater in the world."[66] *Moving Picture World* highlighted how the liminality of the area affected the theater's clientele: "It is just beyond Chinatown, and not quite in Little Italy, with the French section on one side, the Spanish quarter just around the corner, with Nob Hill, the home of millionaire merchants, but a few steps away."[67] *Film Daily* also described the cultural mix as the defining trait of audiences on the Broadway strip: "Out in the North Beach district of Frisco there are bootleggers. And every other nationality in the world. The chop suey palace adjoins the spaghetti joints, and the clamor of the pianners. Mingles discontent with dyspepsia. It's the finest collection of polyglots in the world."[68] In this outsider's view, Chinatown and North Beach film culture encompassed the commodified immigrant cultures of North Beach and

FIG. 18 Cartoons published in the *San Francisco Chronicle* of an altercation between a Mexican and Chinese patron in a North Beach movie theater in January 1912. (Image courtesy of Proquest Historical Newspapers)

Chinatown. The street and its pedestrians became exotic artifacts on display, which movie theaters, by proximity, promotion, and interaction, attached to the spectacle offered inside the theaters.

The Orientalization of Chinatown also extended beyond material objects to people. The postcard of the Shanghai provides an example, with the actors' troupe dressed in full costume lined up outside the theater to announce its exoticness. However, the process of exoticizing Chinatown's inhabitants did not end with actors onstage.[69] Metaspectatorship—the observation of fellow audience members—had been part of the non-Chinese audience behavior since the glory days of its Chinese theater.[70] Yong Chen noted that because most non-Chinese observers were unable to appreciate the artistic quality of the Chinese theater, they became "simply spectators, driven by curiosity to gaze on the strangeness of a nonwhite race represented by the Chinese in the audience."[71]

As a general tendency, the interrelation between street culture, audience interaction, and film exhibition was not specific to San Francisco but was somewhat symptomatic of transition era film culture in general. Jan Olsson has noted how metaspectatorial accounts published in local U.S. newspapers during the nickelodeon era established liminality between street and screen. Comparing metaspectatorial accounts of Los Angeles' Main Street with Chicago's Halsted Street, Olsson described the formation of a discursive genre of "flaneurian fact-fiction" that often merged observations of street culture with the fantasies on display in film exhibition.[72] However, highlighting of Chinese audience members also traces back to the contemporary discourse of Chinatown as a tourist attraction. Around the turn of the century, a wide array of tourist literature about Chinatown had emerged, constructing a standardized tourist itinerary of the neighborhood, including exotic sites such as restaurants, joss houses, opium dens, and theaters.[73] As has been shown by several scholars, this discourse penetrated modes of spectatorship among Chinatown tourists, who entered saw the neighborhood with what tourism historian John Urry has labeled a "tourist gaze," looking to experience stereotypical Chinatown scenery in real life.[74] Because the social makeup and visual experience of Chinatown's streets were far too complex and congested to correspond to the racialized visions reproduced in articles, books, plays, and even films, tourists needed guidance. When film exhibition emerged in the neighborhood, a small industry of licensed Chinatown guides had already existed there for decades.

Tourism historians such as Barbara Berglund and Raymond Rast have written about this turn-of-the-century phenomenon. Berglund has shown how guided tours of Chinatown presented the neighborhood through the lens of Orientalist tropes established in contemporary travel literature, arguing that they equipped outside visitors with a tourist gaze, rendering Chinatown and Chinese San Franciscans exotic objects to look at.[75] Rast confirms this general tendency but puts greater emphasis on more ambiguous interactions and various forms of everyday strategies employed by Chinese San Franciscans to resist, oppose, and control touristic practices in the neighborhood.[76]

Reports of metaspectatorship inside Chinatown theaters reaffirm the liminal connection between the street and the theater interiors. Sabine Haenni has argued that Chinatown during this time was often seen as a sort of amusement park whose inhabitants performed, in part, in a fantasy production of everyday Chinatown.[77] The Orientalist fantasy of Chinatown was constantly imagined and actively sought after by out-of-town tourists as well as by non-Chinese San Franciscans. According to Rast, the promotion of Chinatown "as a bounded quarter that contained the culture of the authentic 'other'" had become part of the dynamics of the city. In Rast's view, "it promised a means by which white San Franciscans might reimagine a sense of distance and reaffirm a sense of difference between themselves and the Chinese men and women in their midst."[78] The notion that the fantasy of Chinatown extended from the streets into the movie theaters was key for their appeal to non-Chinese audiences. For the non-Chinese proprietors, the metaspectatorial experience, along with the Orientalist ornaments of their movie theater storefronts, formed an essential part of the theaters' touristic allure.[79] Orientalism at the Chinatown movie theaters thus appeared in several interrelated manifestations. It was visible in the outward appearance of theaters. It was also present—as seen through a tourist perspective—in the onstage performances of Chinese plays and live translations of movies into Chinese. The third manifestation of Orientalism can be identified in the metaspectatorial exoticization of Chinese San Franciscan moviegoers, evident in trade press descriptions of the Chinatown movie theaters, which highlight the peculiarity of the outward appearance of both theater and audience. In this manner, the act of moviegoing became embedded in these San Francisco–specific manifestations of Orientalism.

However, the notion of metaspectatorship also suggests interactions between audience members that were not organized by the kaleidoscopic logic of contemporary Orientalism. Barbara Berglund acknowledges that some of the travel literature on Chinese theater "did record the way some Chinese responded to the presence of tourists." One theatergoer in 1886 revealed that a Chinese man had come over to her group and volunteered to help them understand the play. In Berglund's view, such activities were unusual and could "best be described as mutual gazing, if that."[80] In order to explore tourist-local interaction beyond the unidirectional character presupposed by Urry's conception of the tourist gaze, tourism scholars such as Darya Maoz introduced the concept of the local gaze, "based on a more complex, two-sided picture, where both the tourist and local gazes exist, affecting and feeding each other, resulting in what is termed 'the mutual gaze.'"[81] As Berglund's essay focuses on the unidirectional accounts of tourist literature, it leaves the possibility of practices of mutual gazing unexplored. The notion of the tourist gaze and investigations such as Berglund's present useful heuristics with which to place Chinatown audience practices in their historical context but do little to illuminate recorded interactions that fail to correspond to contemporary Orientalist discourse.[82] Rast noted a more complex set of dynamics between tourists and Chinatowners: "Some Chinese San Franciscans sought to profit by providing what tourists wanted and expected to see. Others treated tourists with indifference, contempt, or hostility. A third group, positioned in between, responded more creatively. Contesting white entrepreneurs' interpretations of authentic Chinatown, they publicized and presented their own."[83]

I understand metaspectatorship as a concept that takes the complexities of audience interaction and mutual gazing into consideration, albeit often structured by asymmetrical power relations inherent in Chinatown street culture. In the next two sections, to further explore the metaspectatorial complexities of post-quake Chinatown moviegoing, I consider two of the most extensive spectatorial accounts of Chinatown film culture I have been able to find. Both employ modes of spectatorship that reaffirm the notion of an "othering," touristic gaze of Chinatown. But in various ways, as I shall argue, they also transgress some of the cultural stereotypes that were so readily available in post-quake Chinatown film culture.

## An Account of Non-Chinese Moviegoing in Post-quake Chinatown

The concept of metaspectatorship returns us to Adriana Spadoni, whose article from 1910 gives a rare glimpse into the contemporary moviegoing experience in Chinatown through multiple observations from the Oriental and the Broadway theaters, which drew a recurring audience from Chinese San Francisco.[84] While Spadoni's framework of cultural reference and demographic perspective probably differed significantly from that of a Chinese San Franciscan moviegoer of a similar age, this documented experience remains one of the few rich firsthand reports from inside a Chinatown movie theater. It also portrays an elaborate scenario of how Chinatown film culture extended from inside the movie theater out onto the street.

In her 1910 moviegoing article, Spadoni offers an ambivalent account of perceptions of movie theaters as places for vice and loose women, and Chinatown as filthy and unsafe. The text begins with the words, "I'm a Nickelodeon fiend. It came upon me in less than a year. Now I am quite a hopeless case."[85] The Spadoni's narrator admits that nickelodeons used to make her cringe, especially because any San Franciscan with a cent to spare could sit down next to her. Although she initially found this strange, in her article she described how multiple experiences at the movie theater had desensitized her: "It doesn't make me sick now, not even in the small ones that get close and hot."[86] Akin to other contemporary newspaper writings on film culture during the nickelodeon era, Spadoni pays considerable attention to the space of the movie theater and its inhabitants.

Spadoni's narrator had been attracted to the theater by the moving pictures on the screen, but what kept her there was the phenomenological experience of spectating in a group: "You feel your way into your seat, and just when you've about forgotten that the pictures aren't real someone gets up and pushes his way out past you, and you remember it.... That's why I like to sit near people that show when they like a thing."[87] The transcultural contact zones of North Beach and Chinatown appear to be places where the phenomenological experience of watching movies in the dark of the theater took on an extra dimension. As Spadoni wrote, "I think I like to go best to the places where people aren't all American—to the shows in the Latin quarter and in Chinatown. It's almost like traveling. I like to hear the strange languages around me, and when the lights go up to see dark, foreign faces all about. It pushes real things out of the way."[88] For Miriam Hansen, the multidimensional juxtaposition of spatial experience offered to audiences in the movie theater was crucial for its potential to function as an alternative sphere, as it systematically intersected "two different types of space, the local space of the movie theater, and the deterritorialized space of the film projected from the screen."[89] In Spadoni's account, the transcultural localities of Chinatown and North Beach and the interplay between street culture and film exhibition were essential organizing factors of that experience.

Spadoni herself was a product of the transcultural melting pot of San Francisco. Her parents were immigrants, her father from Italy and her mother from England. After having graduated with a bachelor of letters from Berkeley in 1903, Spadoni began writing articles for local newspapers and magazines while teaching English and French to foreign students in night school, among them Chinese.[90] These articles often described the everyday intercultural meetings of the San Francisco milieu, creating a literary realm similar to Mary Louise Pratt's "transcultural contact zones." Most often focusing on the Italian immigration experience, Spadoni occasionally delved into the urban spaces occupied by immigrants from other parts of the world, such as Chinatown. When she wrote her piece on immersive moviegoing in Chinatown, she had already published three long essays about the neighborhood in local newspapers and magazines. The first one, published in *Overland Monthly* in July 1904, provided a fictional story of good and bad in the Chinese neighborhood.[91] Spadoni's second Chinatown article, published in 1905, related the difference between perception of the neighborhood and reality, as exemplified by the history of an orphanage located in the alley between Clay and Powell Streets: "To tell the truth, in comparison to the usual thrilling tales of rescues melodramatic, to the midnight prowlings in tortuous alleys, and on tops of crowded tenements, the stories of the orphanage children are hopelessly prosaic. As tragedies they have absolutely no possibilities at all."[92] In 1908, she took on the task of translating two "outlandish" cultural practices of Chinatown, singsong girls and Chinese music, to the readers of the *Call*. Chinatown and the North Beach area also made appearances in her debut novel, *The Swing of the Pendulum*, published in 1919.[93] Spadoni's pieces on the Chinese neighborhood include some of the racist lingo typical of the local English-language press of the period, but they also recurrently demonstrate an interest in looking beyond the standard tropes and stereotypes.

An example is the narrator's focus on gender dynamics in the liminal space of street and theater. The 1910 moviegoing article, subtitled "What the Pictures Mean to a Lonely Woman," highlights Spadoni's own precarious situation in a secluded room surrounded by men, not far from the infamous Barbary Coast.

For Spadoni, there seems to be a form of kinship in this vulnerability. The article emphasizes an encounter between the narrator and the Oriental's ticket girl:

> I was walking through Chinatown when all of a sudden I heard an electric piano break out into the merriest waltz, such a fine, rattling piano, and there she was sitting in the little glass box office of the new Oriental theater. She looked just like a rare flower under glass. . . . She was shy and wouldn't look up as she tore the tickets and passed them through the opening. And her hands were the tiniest, softest, most unworking hands you ever saw. I knew she wouldn't stay there long. And she didn't. In a week she was gone. I suppose she sits all day now behind a grating, high up in some tenement, looking down into the street.[94]

Read against the contemporary notion of white slavery—in San Francisco specifically attuned to the fact that girls were taken from their homes in China and "imported" into servitude and prostitution in San Francisco's Chinatown and elsewhere—Spadoni's attention to this particular ticket girl was referencing the dire conditions in which Chinese girls had been living in the San Francisco Chinese community in the late 1800s. Also, although her perspective could be conceptualized in part as contrived and fanciful, it touched on and intermingled with contemporary San Francisco–specific narratives and discourses regarding the city's Chinese population. The first of these was the trafficking and subsequent prostitution of young Chinese girls, for which San Francisco figured as the port of call, a trope often mentioned in contemporary press coverage.[95] In 1908, the *Call* published Spadoni's investigative account of the singsong girl phenomenon in Chinatown. Although Spadoni, like many of her contemporaries, stressed the cultural difference between originating cultures, and employed stereotypical tropes such as the "Oriental mind," she quickly shifted focus, to zoom in on the dire living conditions for many Chinese girls in San Francisco.[96] According to Spadoni, the East-West cultural mélange fashioned a cage-like environment for the young Chinatown girls who serviced as concubines. Relating the story of Bo Yuk, a Chinatown singsong girl who was murdered after she refused a late night visit to a man, Spadoni stressed the vulnerable position of women in Chinatown that would color her visit to the Oriental nickelodeon two years later: "It was true she was very beautiful and much sought, but after all, she was only a woman, a sing-song girl at that, and she had refused to come at first call."[97] In 1910, at the nickelodeon, Spadoni featured a long chat with the Oriental's ticket man/janitor, an old man who presented himself as Peter, asserting to be Christian, but wearing his "queue wound up under his hat." When Spadoni

FIG. 19 Photograph taken inside "one of the Broadway theatres," in late summer 1910. *San Francisco Call*, August 21, 1910, 12. (Image courtesy of University of California, Riverside, Riverside, California)

inquired into the whereabouts of her "Golden Lily," Peter retorted that "it was hard to get honest girls."[98]

Resorting to stereotypes when describing the urban landscape and the types of people who populated it was a common tendency among contemporary American newspapers. In Gregory Waller's categorization of these types, Spadoni's narrator fits the description of an "enraptured fan" and "endangered girl," surrounded by "naïve rubes" and "newly arrived immigrants" in the process of Americanization all at once.[99] Her observations often engage and play along with the Chinesque aesthetic of the movie theaters and their surroundings. But if we take into account her own background as a chronicler of multicultural San Francisco, Spadoni's musings begin to appear as those of an embedded, albeit problematic, informant from the transcultural contact zone of the Chinatown and North Beach entertainment scenes. While her writings should be approached with a good deal of caution, especially regarding the hegemonic implications of her own perspective—a middle-class, Berkeley-educated European American—one should not overlook her status as the daughter of an

Italian immigrant father and, more important, a *female* writer shining a light on contested aspects of San Franciscan urbanity about which most readers of papers such as the *Call* and the *Chronicle*, and magazines such as *Collier's* and the *Outlook*, had strong perceptions, but little to no firsthand experience.

Spadoni's early focus on the precarious conditions for immigrants in urban America gradually expanded to include the role of women in modern society.[100] Like fellow cine-reporter Mary Heaton Vorse, Spadoni contributed regularly to the socialist monthly magazine *The Masses*, published between 1911 and 1917.[101] Within American literary history, Spadoni has been largely overshadowed by her husband, muckraking journalist and author John Kenneth Turner. However, her work has seen a recent resurgence through the scholarship of feminist literary historians such as Margaret C. Jones, who has highlighted Spadoni as an important protofeminist writer of the 1910s and 1920s and noted Spadoni's repeated portrayal of her subjects as being victims of social circumstance. According to Jones, writers such as Spadoni and fellow cine-reporter Vorse provided countertexts to contemporary racist opponents of immigration, who routinely described immigrants as "crass, ignorant, idle, immoral, and lacking civic awareness." Instead, Spadoni described immigrants as "sensitive, hungry for education, hard-working, morally upright, and socially responsible."[102]

Recast in this light, an alternative perspective emerges, in which Spadoni approached the Chinesque aesthetic and its stereotypes as portals from which to depart to gain an understanding of the marginalized in the urban milieu. In the unsegregated cinemas of Chinatown, Spadoni's metaspectatorial perspective—as a marginalized person studying other marginalized people—transcends distinctions of ethnicity and class. While indeed participating in the touristic discourse of Arnold Genthe and Will Irwin, Spadoni, with considerable subtlety, highlights the vulnerability of immigrant women in the city. Following Tchen's rereading of Genthe's Chinatown photography, Spadoni's article offers a rare and valuable account of moviegoing in San Francisco Chinatown that hints at interactions between individuals who were usually marginalized in the urban landscape—interactions that transgress the stereotypes so obviously present in the space in which they took place.[103] As such, it emerges as an iteration of Edward Soja's Thirdspace, open for the possibility of hidden and unknown cultural processes to take form. Places like the Acme and the Oriental Theatre, situated within five minutes' walking distance of each other, demonstrated such liminal qualities as "contact zones" for the intermingling of contrived and clashing cultural practices, or as thirdspaces, in which enunciations of cultural hybridity, as Homi Bhabha put it, enabled "other positions to emerge."[104] Again, the asymmetrical relation of power is present, as there is embedded in Spadoni's narrative a sort of hegemonic compass. This undercurrent is discernible in the observation of the vulnerable Chinese girl, to whom Spadoni is both sympathetic and alien.

## Post-quake Spectators and Transcultural Space on Film

As Haenni and others have shown, the tendency to sensationalize and exotify Chinatown space extended from touristic practices into U.S. filmmaking at an early stage.[105] In most cases, films with a Chinatown setting were shot not on location but in a studio or some other setting where the environment could be more easily adapted to correspond to Orientalist fantasies. A few exceptions exist. The most comprehensive endeavor known to survive was made by Harry J. Lewis, one of Chinatown's most seasoned tourist guides. The film, titled *Seeing America's Greatest Chinatown, San Francisco,* was shot in Chinatown, seemingly between the years 1910 and 1915.[106] A collection of scenes from two reels of the film (which initially comprised five reels) has been preserved by the Prelinger Archives in San Francisco and made available online through the Internet Archive. Although it does not explicitly show scenes from Chinatown movie theaters, the film corresponds to several themes explored here, portraying contemporary attitudes toward Chinatown as a tourist attraction and a mediation of Orientalized space. However, the rare footage also bears qualities that are resistant of such attitudes, instances where Chinatown appears as a transcultural contact zone and a space of cultural hybridity, in which Chinese Americans play roles transgressive of stereotypical characterization.

"Captain" Harry J. Lewis was a well-known person in Chinatown who had conducted guided tours of the area since the 1880s.[107] To distinguish himself from less serious competitors, Lewis claimed to provide more authentic tours than the "rubberneck" vehicles that sped through the neighborhood, full of tourists looking for a thrill. Lewis claimed to speak Chinese fluently and often underlined his connections in the local Chinese community. In a 1912 interview with the *Call,* he exclaimed, "So many people do not see half of San Francisco's Chinatown when they set out to view it."[108] A surviving promotional leaflet from one of Lewis's tours from around 1908 detailed some of the tour's contents:

> Chinese newspaper office, Chinese family home and singing children, the old Chinese hermit, Chinese telephone exchange, Chinese drug stores, Chinese musicians, Chinese meat and vegetable markets, Chinese undertaking parlors, Chinese fortune teller, Temple of worship, Joss house, Chinese Masonic lodge room, Chinese underground tenement, Mrs. Wong's (Mrs. Howard Gould's Sister) Old Chinese curiosity shop, the famous Portsmouth square, Chinese Banquet Hall, Chinese Pawn shops, Chinese Domino games, Chinese Cigar Factories, The Chinese Horseshoe, Opium Smoking Rooms (where opium was smoked formerly), Chinese Goldsmiths and Jewelers, Chinese Six Companies Rooms, Court of Arbitration, and other sights to [*sic*] numerous to mention.[109]

Comparing the extant footage from the film to comments and reviews published in local newspapers along the film's exhibition route, it appears that the film showed many of these locations, including several scenes of Lewis guiding a group of tourists along Grant Avenue. Many of the scenes portray real Chinatown establishments, such as the Sing Fat Company and a Chinese employment office, whereas others are clearly staged to look authentic. One of these shows an interior shot of Chinese men smoking cigarettes and pipes. Another sequence re-creates a scene from a local Chinese theater. The film also includes several close-up shots of Lewis exhibiting various objects for the camera, such as raw lotus root and dried foodstuffs. The collection also contains documentary-style footage of public events, such as the 1912 parade celebrating the establishment of the Chinese Republic.

In recent years, several scholars have written about Chinatown imagery on film in the early twentieth century.[110] The only one to analyze *Seeing America's Greatest Chinatown, San Francisco* is the German film historian Björn Schmidt. In his 2017 treatise on the representations of Orientalness in U.S. cinema, Schmidt placed Lewis's documentary-style film alongside feature film productions of the Classical Hollywood era such as *A Tale of Two Worlds* (Frank Lloyd, 1921) and *Chinatown Nights* (William A. Wellman, 1929), starring Hollywood's favorite Chinese impersonator, Warner Oland. Schmidt argued, "While Lewis advertised his 'Oriental travelogue' as a realistic and authentic look into Chinatown, the visual style of his films and his method of production were largely based on a sensationalist presentation that constructed the objects of his camera as Other."[111] In Schmidt's view, Lewis's film served to perpetuate the idea of Chinatown as an essentially Oriental space, "based on the same visual *dispositif* as Chinatown tourism."[112]

Employing a set of theoretical coordinates based in apparatus theory, Schmidt perceptively picked up on the ways on which Lewis's film conformed to some of the most common Chinatown stereotypes of the era. However, his analysis left out the instances where the film and its exhibition history did not fit this description. Granted, the film contains imagery and scenarios that reaffirm contemporary sensationalist notions of Chinatown that were circulating in the contemporary American imaginary, but many scenes also exhibit the cultural hybridity of Chinatowns streets, where Chinese and non-Chinese men, women, and children occupied the busy streets, engaged each other, and patronized the various businesses, such as Main's Bar, Tuck Kee & Co. General Furnishings, and the Sing Fat Company. These are essential aspects in which the film shows scenes and images that go beyond Lewis's postulated "othering" gaze. To describe these scenes as representing only the exotic version of Chinatown corresponding with contemporary imagery would be reductive. Schmidt admitted in a footnote that the Chinatown into which Lewis led his guided tours was far more a space of cultural hybridity than the essentialist version presented in contemporary films.[113] To address only the representation that corresponds to contemporary prejudice obscures the complexity contained by the film. As Jeanette Roan put it, "Attention to both the material and textual aspects of U.S. films shot on location" allows us to examine how cinematic manifestations of Orientalism acted "in conjunction with the particularities of the Asian/American dynamic of a given era."[114]

To address this complexity, it is important to underline the film's status as a piece of ethnographic filmmaking. The ethnographic film practice was a modern iteration and continuation of the practices of illustrated travel lecturers such as Burton Holmes and Lyman Howe.[115] Charles Musser has shown that travelogue film was one of the most popular forms of cinema in is first decades.[116] Tom Gunning argued that travel films "became absorbed so smoothly into the travel lecture that the older practices of lecture and explanation adapted to the technology without a major adjustment."[117] Alison Griffiths and others have argued that ethnographic filmmaking in the early twentieth century should be understood alongside contemporary cross-cultural image-making, rather than as a distinctly medium-specific film genre.[118]

Lewis's film qualifies as a travelogue in terms of tone, structure, and subject matter, but also through its form of presentation. The title card appearing at the beginning of the Prelinger Archives version introduces the film as a travelogue, and the film's title, *Seeing America's Greatest Chinatown, San Francisco*, corresponds to contemporary naming practices of travel films. The film was shot on location, suggesting an indexical relation between the pro-filmic place of Chinatown and the audience who experienced its cinematic representation. Further asserting this indexicality was the film's original mode of exhibition: screening accompanied by a lecturer, in this case Lewis, the Chinatown guide, in person. In 1915, Lewis embarked on a nationwide tour, in which he lectured alongside the exhibition of the film. According to reports from several cities in the Midwest, Lewis was accompanied on tour by a "Chinese family," which he claimed to have brought from Chinatown.[119]

In line with the touristic discourse formulated by Urry and revisited by Rast and Haenni, scholars of the travelogue have asserted that one of its primary functions was to reinforce preconceived notions of its audiences.[120] However, film historian Jennifer Peterson has suggested a revisionist historical approach to travelogue films that, drawing on Miriam Hansen's appropriation of the Frankfurt School, focuses on the contemporary experience of travel films and illustrated lectures.[121] Peterson argued that while the appeal of travel films to contemporary audiences generally lay in their ability to reinforce clichés and stereotypes, the genre also contained the potential to elicit resistant readings.[122] Departing from the notion that the travelogue film was a closed semiotic system of representations reaffirming the preconceived notions of its intended audiences, Peterson believes that "travelogues created a unique kind of travel experience for the movie spectator that was different from the experience of actual travel but significant in its own right."[123] Peterson underlines the film camera's ability to record and reproduce scenes with a level of detail a tourist could never register. While Schmidt's postulated comparison between Chinatown tours and the cinematic apparatus hinges on the idea of a passive spectator, Peterson suggests a more active and heterogeneous viewing experience, where a wide variety of spectators saw travel films, both within and outside of a U.S. exhibition context, with many of these audience members immigrants with personal experiences of travel that were fundamentally different from contemporary cine-voyaging.[124] Further, Peterson considers the wide variety of sonic accompaniment to travel films, usually in the form of a lecturer but also sometimes through sound effects. In this context, the noise made by the theater audience also comes into play. Peterson notes that travel films often seemed to render audiences more silent than the usually boisterous nickelodeon crowd.[125] Granted that any single experiential account of audience reception cannot provide concrete historical evidence for general experience, Peterson's considerations sustain the claim that the experience and meaning-making of travel films and their exhibition in the 1910s extended far beyond the imaginative geographies they were intended to represent.

In this context, we return to consider the aspects of Lewis's film that do not correspond to the essentialist notion of Chinatown as a secluded enclave of opium dens and underground tunnels. I begin with some of the scenes included in the Prelinger Archives version. Among the earliest scenes is a shot taken from the southwestern corner of Chinatown/Nob Hill, with the camera panning over the rooftops of Chinatown. Flying from the flagpoles on top of several of these roofs is the rainbow-colored flag of the Chinese Republic, which suggests that this footage was taken sometime after the winter of 1911. Next, are several street scenes from Chinatown. We see Grant Avenue with pagoda rooftops and modern cars lining the streets. The next shot shows the intersection of Grant and Sacramento Streets, with Chinese-owned businesses such as the Bonanza Cigar Co. and the Republic Drug Co. clearly visible.[126] In several of these scenes, we see Lewis and a group of what we must presume are tourists standing in the foreground. Lewis talks and gesticulates, while the rest of the group looks around. However, most of the people seen in these scenes do not belong to the group of tourists. Instead, they are people, both Chinese and non-Chinese, seemingly going about their day, crossing the street, entering shops, and striking up conversations on street corners. Several of these street scenes include shots of children, garbed in both typically Chinese and Western clothing. In several shots, we see both Chinese Republican and American flags waving from balconies and rooftops. A few street scenes include Chinese men who, as they exit a doorway onto the street, happen upon the camera trained in their direction. However, contrary to the imagery conjured by racist rhetoric in some

FIG. 20 Street scene from Grant Avenue in *Seeing America's Greatest Chinatown, San Francisco* (1915). (Courtesy of the Prelinger Archives)

promotional writings about the film, speculating about the reaction of "Orientals" to having "the evil eye of the camera pointed at them," the men merely glance at the camera, then turn and walk out of frame.[127] If the camera, as in Schmidt's analysis, represents the tourist gaze, such moments of defiance record a returned gaze, as theorized by Fatimah Tobing Rony and Alison Griffiths, or, following Darya Maoz, a "local gaze" indicative of a more complex process of interaction, a metaspectatorial moment in the transcultural contact zone caught on film.[128]

Despite the description of Chinese San Franciscans as inherently unwise and foreign to the technology of photography and moving pictures, Lewis's Chinatown street scenes suggest that at the time of filming there existed among Chinese San Franciscans sophisticated attitudes toward the film medium. This notion is reinforced in the interior scenes that follow, staged to better conform to stereotypical views of Chinatown space, such as a gambling den, a joss house, a Chinese theater stage, and a Chinese pharmacy, as we see Chinese actors perform quite comfortably before the cameraman's lens. Seen in the context of the multiple theaters at which Chinese San Franciscans could experience cinema within the relatively safe confines of their own community, the prescience of local tourism practices, and the extent to which camera operators had

FIG. 21 Street scene from Grant Avenue in *Seeing America's Greatest Chinatown, San Francisco* (1915). (Courtesy of the Prelinger Archives)

visited Chinatown previously, this attitude of sophistication toward cinema is, of course, not surprising.

In the summer of the exposition year of 1915, Lewis took the film on tour. Promotional materials from the tour indicate that Lewis attempted to utilize the juxtaposition of the travelogue to expand his business and offer his tours to customers who could not travel to San Francisco.[129] Several of the advertisements reuse rhetoric from Lewis's Chinatown tour pamphlet, especially in terms of his ability to access and expose the neighborhood's hidden secrets. An advertisement in the *St. Petersburg Daily Times* proclaimed, "You see things you couldn't see if you went there.... Captain Lewis knows it all. He can talk Chinese and eat with chopsticks—and he can tell you things not in the books."[130] Central among these scenes was a depiction of opium smokers (incidentally, these scenes were among the most frequently commented upon in local paper reviews). A review in the *Topeka State Journal* highlighted scenes of opium smokers in Chinatown. However, by 1915, opium was practically illegal in the United States. During the screening and lecture, Lewis claimed that this footage had been taken "four and a half years ago before the Harrison act."[131] Lewis told the audience that since the price of opium had risen so drastically, the addicts of Chinatown and the Barbary Coast had switched to opium and cocaine. But Lewis did not mention that in 1913 he had led twenty addicts to a vacant lot in Chinatown and paid them to pose "in the last stages of their craving for morphine."[132] Local papers reported that they had been found there by the authorities, "going through a series of gyrations for the benefit of a moving picture man."[133] Lewis had few qualms about staging the authenticity of his guided Chinatown tours.[134]

Most reviews of the film lectures highlighted a dynamic at play between prior expectations and the experience of watching the film guided by Lewis's narrative, a dynamic that most often veered toward the reassurance that Chinatown was indeed that mystical and strange place about which audiences had read or heard. However, some reviewers also hinted at experiences that went against preconceived notions. One reviewer admitted, "One of the sights expected which is missing is that of the Chinaman and their long queues."[135] Another reviewer wrote in the *Quad-City Times* in Danville, Iowa, about a scene of "barbers cutting off queues" along with an explanation of Chinese men "wore long queues and why of late they have all had them removed."[136] Audiences of the film in 1915 probably would have been somewhat acquainted with the shift in power and governance in China, since the Chinese Revolution and its aftermath had been well covered in U.S. newspapers. If not, newspaper reports suggest that during his lectures Lewis pointed out these markers of modernization and progress and how they affected Chinatown[137] In Greenville, South Carolina, Lewis told the audience "the Chinese speak English, and send their children to English schools provided for them."[138] While most of the contents of Lewis's lecture narrative, as well as audiences' reaction to it, remains unknown, such evidenced attention to these "signs of progress" in the Chinatown milieu should be understood against other material markers of modernity included in the film, such as the widened lanes of Grant Avenue, shiny black cars parked along the curbs, a Chinese unemployment office, architectural chinoiserie, Chinese newspaper offices, and Chinese Republican and American flags.

Taking these aspects into account, the dissonance between the moving pictures, Lewis's interpretation, and spectatorial experience grows more notable. If we also consider the promotional materials, which often placed the film in an Orientalist context, but also repeatedly highlighted the cinematic medium's inherent capacity for capturing details that even the most observant traveler or tourist could not, the film appears as a far more ambiguous representation of Chinatown. Similar to Tchen's revisionist readings of Genthe's Chinatown photography, the film thus appears to contain imagery with strong links to contemporary Orientalist tropes but also is an affirmation, albeit possibly involuntary, of the cultural hybridity and thirdspace character of the neighborhood. The illusion of a Chinesque aesthetic is punctured by a scenery far more complex. Lewis attempted to shape these scenes into a marketable commodity, through interpretation and montage, but the action caught on film at times contradicted such readings, exposing Chinatown as a space of cultural hybridity and resisting Lewis's attempts to guide and influence spectators toward a more contained interpretation.

In sum, *Seeing America's Greatest Chinatown, San Francisco,* is one of the few documentary-style films of post-quake Chinatown that has partially survived. It is a film imprinted by its contemporary Orientalist discourse. However, its imagery and the history of its production and exhibition also contain aspects that transgress the common stereotypes about Chinatown. At these instances, the film shows a Chinatown caught up in ambiguous processes of modern urbanity, where the multitude and heterogeneity of the crowds were adapted and incorporated into pragmatic and cynical enterprise—a milieu in which moviegoing, film shoots, and touristic spectatorship were, if not an everyday experience, far from the rare and spectacular occurrence that people like Lewis would have their audience believe. Film culture had emerged in Chinatown. The next chapter looks closer at the various ways in which film culture played a crucial role in post-quake Chinatown modernity.

## Potentials and Limitations of Chinatown Movie Theater Space

The reconstruction of Chinatown affected its entertainment culture in several ways. First, it opened up for new businesses, like the first nickelodeons on Washington Street and Grant Avenue that quickly set up on a temporary basis. Because during the first years after the earthquake San Francisco did not have a fire code that specifically regulated film exhibition, installing a projector and putting together a couple of rows of chairs in an open space was quite simple. Second, Chinatown movie theaters could make inroads in the audience groups that had previously frequented the Chinese playhouses along Grant Avenue and Washington and Jackson Streets. These audience groups included Chinese Americans from San Francisco and its immediate surroundings, moviegoers from nearby "ethnic" working-class neighborhoods, like North Beach and Russian Hill, as well as the occasional tourist from out of town or from the upper-class Nob Hill. By creating a place-specific film culture, shaped to the tastes and abilities of Chinatown audiences, the post-quake movie theaters afforded the Chinatown community an exceptional site for Chinese American appropriation of film culture. Albeit propelled primarily by business competition, local efforts of cultural translation and interpretation in the Chinatown and North Beach entertainment scene created urban sites of transcultural exchange and hybridity that were available to and inclusive of Chinese Americans as in no other place in the city or the country.

The potentials of approaching Chinatown movie theaters as thirdspaces of transcultural fluidity are enticing and, in many ways, enlightening. Yet it is also important to stress that while the movie theaters of Chinatown might have offered alternative spaces with an inherent potential to transcend cultural stereotypes, they simultaneously reaffirmed the same stereotypes. In *Babel and Babylon*, Miriam Hansen noted the limitations to the possibility of these new "social horizons" as "the cinema lagged behind the emerging culture of consumption to the extent that the initial marginality of the nickelodeons allowed audiences—and exhibitors often of the same background—to shape modes of reception reminiscent of older forms of working-class, immigrant culture."[139] So, while Chinatown movie theaters in a sense enabled a space in which the Chinatown community could experience and shape a local version of modernity, the appropriation of film exhibition to older forms of Chinatown public entertainment at the same time limited the potential of this experience and bound it to a more traditional form of reception. Another limitation has been formulated by Yong Chen, who wrote that although the identity of Chinese San Franciscans was not fixed, it would be a misrepresentation to overstate its fluidity, as it was more of a social reality than a personal choice. Chen noted that the freedom of individual Chinese San Franciscans to form their cultural identity was significantly constrained by how others saw them: "A young Chinese man could decide to abandon everything in his consciousness and outward appearance, but in either his communities or in the anti-Chinese white society he still would not become 'American' as it was defined by the dominant blocs of the time."[140] The persistent widely held belief was that behind Chinatown's respectable storefronts were opium dens, secret societies, and organized abductions of white virgins. Despite signs of social and other mobility, old stereotypes of Chinatown still dominated "the perception of the quarters' sensational unavailability," as Sabine Haenni put it.[141]

Local film exhibitors did identify Chinese San Franciscans as a key demographic to generate more revenue from their surrounding neighborhoods. However, this did not constrain the employment of racist representations of "Chineseness" at the theaters. Metaspectatorial practices inherited from the already established guided tour industry were transplanted into film exhibition practices, as visitors would take in a film program and people-watch at the Chinatown movie theaters. This tendency to view Chinatown through a touristic gaze can be found in both Spadoni's article and Harry J. Lewis's travelogue, which used the medium of the illustrated film lecture to export and guide audiences' perceptions of the neighborhood. However, beyond the one-directional tourist gaze, the emerging Chinatown film culture encompassed other forms of imagery, interactions, and spectatorship (e.g., vernacular Chinese film advertisements, live translators, everyday strategies to defy "slummers") that resisted the Orientalist rationale of the neighborhood. I will continue to explore these complexities and dynamics throughout the remainder of this book.

This chapter has focused on what these accounts tell us about the experience of moviegoing and spectatorship in Chinatown during the years leading up to the Panama-Pacific International Exposition. However, as the majority of these accounts were authored from the perspective of "outsiders" looking in, they tell us little about what the appearance of film exhibition meant for the local Chinese community. This will be the focus of the next chapter.

# 7

# Chinatown Modernity

## Revolutions and Movie Theaters

Film was not the first modern medium to recast everyday life in Chinese San Francisco. As early as the 1860s, local Chinese newspapers provided essential sources of information and advocacy for Chinese San Franciscans. Perhaps even more influential—and historically singular—was the designation of Chinatown's telephone exchange in the late 1880s. The origination of this unusual branch was a communication breakdown between the Chinese community and the rest of San Francisco. Since the introduction of telephone service to San Francisco earlier in the decade, many Chinese businesses had signed up. However, because none of the switchboard operators spoke Chinese, calls from Chinatown were often caught up in translational limbo between caller and operator and, as a result, never reached the intended recipient. The Six Companies wrote a petition, requesting that the telephone company consider having a branch that would cater to the large number of callers who spoke Chinese. The telephone company complied and in 1887 opened its first Chinatown branch, located at 743 Grant Avenue. The manager was Loo Kum Shu, who employed six Chinese-speaking operators.

In 1901, the San Francisco Telephone Company, again answering to public demand, opened a new exchange in the neighborhood. The building was lavishly ornamented and drew the attention of tourists and contemporary press commentators. The *Telephone Magazine* labeled it "the most curious telephone office in the world."[1] The *Tatler*, a British society magazine, called it "undoubtedly the most sumptuous one in America. Its fittings are of teakwood inlaid with colored marble. Its floor is of polished oak. Vases of porcelain abound in it, and opposite the switchboard is a joss, before incense always burns."[2] Soon enough, the telephone exchange had become a regular stop for tourists and Chinatown guides.

Beyond its allure as a piece of Chinatown exotica, the telephone exchange became an important part of the neighborhood's economic and social infrastructure. More than any other communal institution, it kept Chinatown interconnected, primarily by facilitating business transactions and job opportunities. When cinema arrived in Chinatown a few years later, it shared with the telephone the promise of swift and accessible communication. The introduction of outlets for these new media around the neighborhood, in the form of telephone booths and movie houses, created new connections to the outside world. Media historians, such as Stephen Kern, have emphasized the "expansion" of time and space incurred by the emergence of the telephone as an everyday appliance.[3] In Chinatown, the Chinese telephone exchange offered a locally specific refraction of this spatiotemporal alteration, ultimately facilitating an unprecedented communications network that became integral to the social infrastructure of the community. In other words, through the local appropriation of a once alienating instrument of communication, the telephone suddenly offered ways to break the isolation of Chinatown. This practice, of making new media its own, is fundamental for a deeper understanding of post-quake film culture's role in Chinatown.

The appearance of cinema in Chinatown dovetailed with the reconstruction of the neighborhood's infrastructure, conceived and executed under the auspices of modernizing, commercializing, and commodifying the neighborhood as a tourist attraction. It also coincided with a violent push for the modernization of the Chinese nation-state across the Pacific Ocean. Chinatown scholars have noted strong links to transpacific exchanges of modernity markers such as the organization of progressive political parties, funding of oppositional warfare in China, and commercial trade. Further, the rapid rebuilding of the "new Chinatown" coincided with political developments in China, as well as the coming of age of second and third generations of Chinese immigrants, many of whom had grown up in exclusionist era San Francisco. In the words of Him Mark Lai, this was the period in which "an American-born adult generation was beginning to become a factor in the Chinese community."[4]

The close relationship between film and modernity is a well-established hermeneutic trope within studies of early cinema. Groundbreaking work by influential scholars such as Miriam Hansen and Tom Gunning has stressed the centrality of cinema to early twentieth-century "cultures of modernity."[5] Francesco Casetti considers that cinema, more than any other medium, intercepted "the impulses of twentieth-century modernity" and "gave them a model against which the spectator could compare himself or herself."[6] Simultaneously, scholars have highlighted the inherent tension between moviegoing and the contemporarily perceived "upheaval of modernity," a form social anxiety brought on by the exuberant stimuli of modern life.[7] But how did such processes unfold if seen from the limited social horizon of early twentieth-century Chinese San Franciscans? Within post-quake Chinatown community—just as elsewhere in San Francisco—going to the movies in the early 1910s was considered a popular modern amusement that came with an unknown variety of excitements and inherent dangers. While some of the concerns regarding the rising popularity of the film medium echoed nationwide, discourses on the potential hazards of moving pictures took on a distinctly local character. In these cases, fears of the corrupting powers of the movie house corresponded to a perceived loss of cultural identity for overseas Chinese immigrants.

This chapter investigates Chinatown movie theaters as nodes of the local negotiation of modernity in Chinese San Francisco. It shows how Chinatown movie theaters, beyond their function as sites of public entertainment, became synonymous with currents of modernization charging through the neighborhood. For some Chinese San Franciscans, modernization and progress came bearing a promise of opportunity and social inclusion. For others, the changes instilled anxiety and fear. The act of going to the movies, as described by contemporary commentators, represented a break with the cultural ties that were perceived as binding Chinese immigrants to their native country. This break pointed to a generational chasm within the community, linked to a broader notion of progress emerging in post-quake Chinese California. The generational chasm connected to significant social and intercommunal developments of post-quake Chinatown, which, in turn, were vital for the facilitation and appropriation of film culture in the area.[8] By analyzing a few recorded examples of contemporary Chinese San Franciscan attitudes toward Chinatown film exhibition, we approach a locally specific condition within which we can study how film theaters and exhibitors intentionally and unintentionally offered a site for experiencing and negotiating social mobility and liminal identities for Chinese San Franciscans.

## Young China and the American Way

Chinatown historian Yumei Sun described early twentieth-century Chinatown as being girdled by an "invisible barrier"—a spatial, cultural, and, political divide between Chinatown and the rest of San Francisco.[9] Another Chinatown historian, Yong Chen, presented a somewhat different view of the era. While acknowledging the deep-seated disjuncture between Chinatown and the rest of San Francisco, caused by practical injustices and xenophobia, Chen underlined the "changing mentality" that saturated post-quake Chinatown. Drawing mainly on source material from contemporary Chinese-language accounts in local newspapers and diaries, Chen described a paradigm shift in the entertainment habits of Chinatowners after the rebuilding of the neighborhood.[10] Similarly, Eve Armentrout Ma emphasized the importance of the modernized post-quake Chinatown for the emergence and success of reform-minded Chinese political parties, which operated and influenced Chinese politics on both shores of the Pacific Ocean.[11] As the rebuilding of Chinatown progressed, the reimported Western mentality became a prevalent force in the community. It also saw the introduction of social reform, which created a new existential paradox for the community. While the influence of Western culture on Chinese Americans was significant, the persistence of anti-Chinese sentiments and "American society's branding of the Chinese as undesirables generated feelings of alienation among many Chinese Americans."[12] This paradox led to a clash between ideology and everyday life, where the new nationalist winds of change blowing in mainland China rubbed up against the traditional values that had been so important for the formation of the diasporic identities in exclusion era Chinese San Francisco. The "new mentality," described by Chen, spanned from the realm of politics and cultural tradition to a younger generation's embrace of urban modernity.

To counter the challenge of Western colonialism during the nineteenth century, the Qing government evoked a form of reversed Orientalism. By situating the Chinese self "in the center and representing ethnic others as uncivilized and barbaric," Daphne Lei argued, the Chinese rulers fostered an attitude that saturated Chinese culture on the mainland and abroad, from official policies to popular imagination and local drama.[13] In the early twentieth century, as the power and sustainability of the Qing dynasty eroded, the geographic centrality of Chinese identity formation began to slide. Between 1906 and the outbreak of World War I, the transpacific ties that connected China and Chinese San Francisco became increasingly reciprocal. Yong Chen wrote that like their compatriots in China, Chinese San Franciscans regarded the West as the model for a new China and "internalized Western concepts that had a Social Darwinist veneer, believing that China must follow the path of 'progress' paved by Western nations."[14] Middle-class bourgeois organizations such as the Chinese Chamber of Commerce, the Chinese American Citizens Alliance, the Chinatown YMCA and YWCA, the Christian Union, and the Peace Society formed alliances with outside law enforcement to fight the vices long associated with Chinatown. While this initially was met with stiff resistance from the tongs, the Chinese American progressives eventually won out.[15] Sociological surveys conducted by "white" San Francisco progressives—like the one purported by the Commonwealth Club—still did not account for the class stratification within the Chinese San Franciscan community. However, community leaders of post-quake Chinatown like Wong Bock You and Wen Xiongfei, or progressive opinion makers such as like Ng Poon Chew were now becoming political animals. Wen Xiongfei, a founding member of the organization Native Sons of the Golden State (NSGS) and the pro-revolutionary Young China Association, chronicled in his memoirs the emergence of an intellectual class in Chinatown. According to Wen, the "superstitious and feudal thinking" exemplified by the Chee Kung Tong organization, in early 1909 known in Chinatown as representative of revolutionary forces among the Chinese, was in stark contrast to the "modern attitudes" held by American-born Chinese intellectuals such as Wen and Wong.[16] Addressing this divide, Wen, Wong, and two other Chinatown intellectuals formed the Chinese Revolutionary League, closely related to the Young China Association, in the spring of 1910.[17] The NSGS met daily on the second floor of a building on Clay Street. The members were all young, and favorite conversation topics included fashion and entertainment, rules of English pronunciation and errors in Chinese transliteration, the negative bias recurrently found in local English-language newspaper discourse on the Chinese, as well as the current state of the political situation overseas.[18]

The Chinatown press seldom commented on moviegoing, but a few contemporary accounts of local perspectives on the "picture houses" can be found elsewhere. In contemporary Chinatown literature, moviegoing at times was evoked as a marker of "modern" or "American" behavior. Such accounts revealed what Asian American studies professor Marlon K. Hom called a "characteristic Chinatown perspective," which included a re-examination of the Chinese San Franciscan's "traditional cultural heritage in the light of living in a new environment, punctuated with a new priority of values."[19] In 1992, Hom published an anthology of early twentieth-century poetry from Chinese San Francisco, which situates moviegoing alongside other modern ideas, such as gender equality and sex out of wedlock. A poem from the 1910s highlights the different behavior of the American-born Chinese:

> Native-borns call each other brother and sister.
> They live in the American way.
> Holding hands, they say they're off to a picture show.
> Actually, they're going to a hotel!
> Enjoying their longings and desires,
> So what if people gossip;
> The two of them entwined in deep passion;
> She may become pregnant, but that's nothing strange![20]

While Hom stressed that Chinese Americans recognized the importance of accepting some untraditional behavior as part of the formation of the contemporary Chinatown identity, "they also wanted to balance the change by holding on to the old values they brought with them from China."[21] Such sentiment was evident in another poem that describes the Chinatown film houses as places frequented by women whose behavior was shameful when seen against the values of the old country:

> What a batch of lousy broads,
> All without proper upbringing.
> They hustle in the doorways, their gold teeth on parade;
> Day and night, always going to the picture show.
> They are fearless.
> They laugh with lust and speak the barbarian tongue.
> With men, they are experts at fooling around.
> Alas, their dissipation is shameful to our China.[22]

The connection between nationwide moral panic and public health concerns about moviegoing is well-established in scholarship on the transitional era. As we have seen, alarmist press reactions routinely framed movie theaters as places of physical and moral degradation. However, in Chinatown, concerns that film houses facilitated social corruption tied into the broader web of anxieties about a perceived self-degradation of new generations of American-born Chinese. Many Chinese immigrants were alarmed and disheartened by the younger generation's new pattern of behavior, influenced by what they perceived as the vices of modern American culture. For the older immigrant generation, "these vices represented the ignorant, uncivilized side of the Western lifestyle. Ignorance and incivility were the causes of numerous discriminatory practices in America, which had victimized them as immigrants."[23] After the safeguarding of Chinatown's post-quake existence against relocation plans and populist politicians, young Chinatown's gradual adoption of the "American way" presented new threats to the shaky fundaments of diasporic living.

The "American way" of "native-borns" also caught the attention of the local press. In April 1911, the *Chinese Defender* published an editorial penned by the pseudonymous author Ah-Sing, written in the form of a letter home to his father. The text related news about Ah-Sing's brother, Ah Wing, and his sweetheart, Ah May. According to Ah-Sing, the young Chinese couple's romance followed the rituals of "white lover-man" as opposed to those of Chinese traditions. One of Ah Wing's romantic endeavors was to take Ah May to the movies. Ah-Sing wrote: "Wing he sure crazy man; he wait Ah May school come out, walk next Ah May, go Ah May house; sometimes he take Ah May go see 5-cent picture place."[24] The *Chinese Defender* was a monthly subscription bulletin, published between 1910 and 1912, whose editorial board consisted of the local merchants C. K. Toy and Fong Sing and attorney Frank Worley. The trio were also the founding members of a local Chinese American interest organization called the Chinese League of Justice of America. The stated ambition of the *Defender* was to give the Chinese an opportunity to "defend themselves before the American public."[25] While circulated on a small scale, the paper soon gained endorsements from the Chinatown intelligentsia and boasted guest editorials by the likes of Ng Poon Chew.[26]

The character of Ah-Sing first appeared in the *Chinese Defender* in February 1911. There he was introduced as an immigrant who had arrived in San Francisco late in 1910. During the following months, Ah-Sing shared his first impressions of clashing cultures between old China and new Chinatown. The Ah-Sing character was a literary construct, conceived and penned by the *Defender*'s editorial board, perhaps in cheeky reference to Bret Harte's stereotypical "Ah-Sin." However, even if Ah-Sing was fictional, the Chinatown he described was taken from the lived collective experience of his authors. The offices of the *Chinese Defender* lay on 912 Grant Avenue, one of the busiest spots in Chinatown. The mercurial reality the paper sought to capture was right outside the window. Furthermore, the *Defender*'s office was located just one block from the Oriental Theatre.[27] Ah-Sing's letter to his father did not specify which Chinatown movie theater his brother would take his girlfriend to on a date, but it is highly likely that the Oriental Theatre was where the editors of the paper found their inspiration for this reference for moviegoing. Seen in this light, the Ah-Sing character emerges as a node that links issues and anxieties facing Chinese immigrants to the United States in the early 1910s. The example of taking a girl to the movies reinforces film culture's subversive and polarizing status within the Chinatown community.

The anonymous milieu of the movie theater, the brazen ways of "young China," and the heightened romantic tension provided by the films were also elements picked up by Adriana Spadoni in her 1910 article on Chinatown nickelodeons. Spadoni noted the interaction between on-screen diegesis and off-screen romance one late night at the Oriental Theatre:

> The other night there was an awfully sad picture. The girl's father was a cruel cold man and the boy did love her so. At last the old man got sick and that made him kinder. He called them both to him and joined their hands. The boy didn't do much, only put his arms about the girl and turned her face up to his, but it made me tremble all over and look away. It was then I saw the girl and boy in front of me. He was holding her hand and he drew her closer when the old man in the picture did that. Her face brushed his coat for a second, while they just looked at each other and smiled.[28]

Spadoni also noted that there were always one or two "young Chinamen . . . with short hair and American clothes" hanging around the cute ticket girls at the box office. The implication, filtered through Spadoni's vision, was that these young Chinese San Franciscans had parted ways with the markers of their Chinese heritage, the queue and the traditional Chinese attire, to engage in the excitement of young urban life—to pursue a beautiful girl at the movies.

In the spring of 1909, Rose Fong, the teenage daughter of Fong Get, caused a stir in Chinatown as she was seen publicly riding in the same open car as her fiancé, Choa Ming, a teacher at the newly opened Chinese Central High School. Rose Fong's daring antics caught the attention of the Chinese press, which, in turn, caught the attention of the San Francisco dailies. The *Call* wrote that the Chinese newspaper the *New Era* "Orientalized a particularly occidental style of journalism and treats the outing of the young couple with the same delicate humor and insinuation that the naughty Town Topics would apply to a debonair adventure of a Newport belle."[29] Fong Get, who was asked to comment by the *Call*, bemoaned the *New Era*'s tendency toward yellow journalism but applauded his daughter's progressivity: "In China a bride is not to be seen by her husband until the day of her wedding but the young Chinese don't like that way. They want to see whom they are to marry. My daughter and this young man went out driving in the park, and it is nobody's business."[30] About a month later, Rose Fong and Choa Min were married by a Baptist minister at the newly opened Yut Tong hotel on Clay Street, just a few blocks from Fong Get's photo studio and the Grand movie theater. Dignitaries such as the Chinese consul general, and many "students and educators" attended the wedding. Again, the *Call* gave the Fongs considerable editorial space and drew attention to the fact that certain elements of the Chinatown community had opposed the spectacle by posting placards on the walls of surrounding buildings with "mendacious comments of the affair."[31] The visible public opposition, according to the *Call*, did not, however, detract from the splendor of the ceremony or the happiness of the "Americanized couple."[32]

The story of Rose Fong's public gasoline-powered buggy ride provides a complex snapshot of contemporary Chinatown modernity. Here, Rose Fong and her fiancé figure as representatives of a new Chinese American generation, eager to adopt the novelties and experiences of the modern world, such as automobiles and female emancipation. The Chinese newspaper *New Era* demonstrated a "modern" approach to journalism by adopting the perspective of the gossip columnist, but also by locating this public demonstration of affection in a localized context where the values and traditions of conservative Chinatown were put up against a younger generation's willingness to adapt to the ways of progressive America. For example, the text made a condescending comparison between the symbolism of Rose Fong's riding together with her beau in an open car and the contemporary struggle for suffrage led by Susan B. Anthony: "Miss Anthony simply wanted the ballot—Miss Fong wants the buggy."[33] Older Chinatown was claimed to fret over this public disregard of traditional courtship, while "younger Chinatown capers in glee over its emancipation."[34] While the denigrating tone of the *Call* articles displays a third aspect of Chinatown modernity's inherent power dynamic, that of the supremacist Euro-American frame of reference, it also provides a snapshot of Chinatown's "changing mentality," in which practices and attitudes generally linked to American modernity in the early twentieth century play a central role. Perhaps it was not surprising that the daughter of Chinatown's first movie theater manager and photo studio proprietor would adopt the habits and mannerisms of contemporary American youth culture, but it is clear that the appearance and actions of the Fong family came to symbolize broader developments in the post-quake Chinatown public sphere.

Young Chinatowners' adverse attitudes toward their cultural heritage also had repercussions for the Chinese theater in San Francisco. Lois Foster has noted that Chinatown was slow to revive its once-popular stage culture after the earthquake and fire.[35] Nancy Yunwha Rao, writing about the resurgence of Chinese stage drama in the 1920s, pointed out that the 1910s was a period "devoid of Chinese theater."[36] While the destruction of established theaters probably played a role in the slow regrowth of art forms such as Chinese opera, contemporary observers ascribed the development to a growing local interest in more modern forms of public amusement. Louis J. Stellman also noted a historical shift in the patronage of local theaters, as the movie houses and film culture surpassed Chinatown's traditional Chinese theaters in popularity. The few theaters that still staged Chinese drama were, in Stellman's words, "mostly for tourists, as the Chinese prefer more modern histrionics."[37] The *Call*'s snootiest drama critic, Walter Anthony, cited similar reasons for the decline of the Chinese theater in an article published in the summer of 1913. Anthony claimed that most of the actors had left San Francisco in 1906 and had yet to return, as the interest in Chinese theater in Chinatown faded. Like Stellman, Anthony noticed that the "new Chinese owns an automobile, goes to the symphony concerts and patronizes the American stage. . . . If it were possible to secure a playhouse and competent actors to do the old dramas they would be given mainly for the entertainment of the white visitor." Anthony added, "Rest assured, young China would pay but little attention to them."[38] Him Mark Lai noted, in an essay on the rise of the Chinese drama movement, that the young audiences of post-quake Chinatown preferred modern entertainment, quoting a mid-1910s editorial from *Young China* which proclaimed that "the local Chinese are now following modern world trends and . . . are gradually changing."[39]

Chinese Americans were not the only diasporic community that feared the effects the movies and urban modernity might have on their cultural roots. Jan Olsson and Lee Grieveson, among others, have noted similar tendencies in other contemporary American immigrant cultures, where the rituals of urban moviegoing came to symbolize a new, youthful culture, characterized by its disconnection from and transgression of traditional values.[40] Olsson pointed out that the decline of infrastructure in New York's Little Italy ran "in tandem with dramatic changes in the cultural arena, which, by commentators of the day, were interpreted as a result of a voluntary and self-styled brand of Americanization amongst Italians."[41] Similar to the perceived "passing" of the Chinese theater, Olsson concludes that "the artistic forms immigrants brought with them to the new country could no longer withstand the pull from *the* medium of modernity in its American inflection: cinema."[42] In Chinatown, this "Americanizing process" of the cinema seems to have been perceived as extending to the experience of the movie theater. While its audiences were not made up only of young Chinese American couples, it seems that their visibility at the theaters constituted a cultural marker of significance for the surrounding community. The augmented thirdspace nature of the movie theater and its surroundings invited the hybridity and transcultural interactions into the realm of self-perception. As Daphne P. Lei pointed out, "the chaos of the muddy contact zone" put Chinese identity at stake.[43] The Chinatown movie theaters appeared as public spaces where the perceived loss of connection to the cultural values of the homeland became closely linked to the act of moviegoing.

The stakes for this local "rebellion" against traditional values were soon to become even more magnified by a steady stream of news reports of political turbulence from across the Pacific, where a revolution intent on "modernizing" China was putting the thousand-year-old fundaments of Chinese society under tremendous strain. As the movement developed into a full-blown revolutionary war, Chinatown film culture again came to play a significant yet contradictory role: as the preferred source of news and information, as space for political organization, but also as a medium through which the ongoing revolution turned into a cinematic spectacle.

## Chinatown Film Exhibition and the Chinese Revolution

More than functioning as a shop window for the display and dismay of young Chinese San Francisco's rebellious attitudes about dating and propriety, the neighborhood's movie theaters were significant in the political awakening of Chinatown. Beyond the primary purpose of facilitating quotidian film screenings, movie theaters frequently doubled as a venue for political rallies, fundraisers, and public announcements of news from across the Pacific. While seldom actively engaging in the cause of the Republican uprising in China, the local theaters figured as important nodes for the political currents within the Chinatown community by making available their spaces for charity events and community meetings.

One frequent organizer of such political "events" was the Young China Association (YCA). Throughout the seminal year of 1911, the YCA held several benefits and fundraisers in Chinatown to aid the revolution. In February 1911, the YCA, led by Frank R. Low, arranged a fundraiser at the Acme Theater for the relief of "the starving thousands of Chinese in the Yangtze valley." The charity event consisted of "Chinese vaudeville" and "several moving pictures of life in the stricken district."[44] In late March, the YCA arranged an evening's entertainment at the Liberty Theater on Broadway, at this point run by Michael Brown. Again, Low made the arrangements. Low promised a play showing "the great advance made by China in the past few years" performed by an all-Chinese cast.[45] Three months later, the Chinese Chamber of Commerce arranged a fundraiser at the Lyceum on Kearny Street. The *Call* reported that the $1,000 raised by the benefit performance was added to a total of "more than $55,000 raised in this city by contribution and benefits," which was "the largest single amount so far raised by any country for the stricken people of the flooded Yangtze district."[46] While these fundraisers were officially organized to aid starving people in southern China, the arrangers and the performances displayed were more politically oriented than advertised. In mid-April 1911, a *Call* review reported on the benefits organized at the local theaters with the announcement that the Young China movement had "broken into dramatics." The play, by playwright Lee Se Nom, was described as a "political drama which hovered between heaven and earth, hovered between the regime of the historic Ming dynasty and the future hopes of the Chinese and hovered very sinisterly over the Manchu dynasty, which at present occupies the throne at Peking."[47] It thus appears that the YCA, a decidedly progressive voice in the Chinatown community, had taken the opportunity to supplement the charity event with a political message about the revolution brewing in the port cities of China, framing the imagined uprooting of Chinese society within the most emblematic space of contested Chinatown modernity—a local movie theater.

In the summer of 1911, when Dr. Sun Yat-sen came to Chinatown as part of his travels throughout the North American continent to raise money for the revolution, the Chee Kung Tong arranged a meeting at a Grant Avenue restaurant, where Sun spoke to a packed audience, including many members the local Chinatown intelligentsia. There, Sun announced the amalgamation of the Chee Kung Tong and the YCA as the official organ of the revolutionary cause in the United States.[48] As the Young China movement officially announced its allegiance to the revolutionary cause, its fundraisers and galas became more outspokenly political. On August 8, Dr. Sun made an appearance at a gala arranged to honor fallen soldiers on the revolutionary side. The function took place at "a Kearny Street Theater." Because this was within a month of Benjamin Michaels's grand opening of his Shanghai Theatre on Kearny, close to Washington Street, it is highly probable that the benefit took place there.[49] This event, reported to have been attended by more than 1,000 Chinese San Franciscans, might have enticed Michaels to try further to monetize the political situation in Chinatown, as six months he later imported a film depicting war scenes from the revolution and began marketing it toward Chinese Californians.[50] The film, to which we will return shortly, had direct ties to the revolutionary Dr. Sun. In October the same year, the YCA arranged a three-day benefit at a Washington Street theater to raise funds for the Republican rebels. On October 29, the *Call* reported that dispatches reporting successful imperial attacks at the strategically important city of Hankow had reached Chinatown just hours before one of the benefit performances. These events, in turn, resulted in a "perceptible falling off in attendance at last night's performance."[51]

During the final months of 1911, the fighting in China and the simultaneous campaigning for funds conducted by the growing numbers of Chinatown revolutionaries became the subject of extensive reporting in Californian newspapers from Sacramento to Los Angeles.[52] In Chinatown, the YCA arranged several street parades to celebrate good news from the battlefronts and to entice Chinatown visitors to donate money to modernizing China. According to one observer, "The banner carried by the patriots included the American and the Chinese Republican flags and the emblems of the societies represented."[53] An unknown cameraman recorded a similar sight as Chinese San Franciscans paraded around the city in the first week of January 1912 to celebrate the official victory of the Republican forces. A surviving copy of the short film shows a narrow San Francisco street, lined with people dressed in suits and hats.[54] Down the street, moving out of frame to the right, the camera captures a procession of young and old Chinese San Franciscans. The vast majority of them are men. On foot, in closed horse carriages, and in open cars, they smile, wave, and wield flags and banners. While the version of the Republican flag that was preferred by Sun Yat-sen is the dominating feature, there are many instances where the American flag is seen flying from the cars and carriages that roll past the camera.[55] "Nothing is more modern than the modern Chinese," observed a writer for the *San Francisco Call* in a full-page article that chronicled the Chinese New Year celebration in Chinatown in 1912—the first one to take place after the fall of the Qing dynasty.[56]

It was with such scenes visible on a daily basis on the streets of Chinatown and elsewhere in downtown San Francisco, as well as in the local newspapers, that Benjamin Michaels, the proprietor of several Chinatown movie theaters, formed a one-off distribution company and imported a film from across the Pacific Ocean that depicted authentic-looking war scenes from the battlefronts, titled *The Chinese Revolution*.

## Exporting and Importing Chinese Modernity

Michaels's company, the Oriental Film Company, originally registered *The Chinese Revolution* on April 12, 1912. A fragment of the film survives in the

Library of Congress.[57] The extant copy of the film displays documentary-style scenes from the uprising in Hankow in early October 1911. One of the film's most striking features is that Asians—not actors of European or other ethnic descent in yellowface—appear as its main participants. Intertitles identify locations and actions, such as "Manchu Headquarters outside the wall of Hankow," "Boy Revolutionist receiving sentence of death," "Broken hearted father viewing remains of his boy," and "Rich Mandarin attacked by a group of Revolutionists." That the intertitles on each card appear in both English and Chinese points to aspects of the film's American distribution. Evidence from the American film trade press ties *The Chinese Revolution* to the Japanese M. Pathé company, which was run by a politically engaged film entrepreneur named Shokichi Umeya from a base in Tokyo. Umeya, at this time, was a friend of Sun Yat-sen and an outspoken proponent of transforming China into a republic. Scholar Peter B. High has argued that Umeya had begun to import documentary-type films in 1906 and promoted himself and his company as public benefactors who aimed to educate the masses on contemporary events, like the Russo-Japanese War and modern science.[58] According to Joseph L. Anderson and Donald Richie, Umeya diverted some of the company's earnings to support revolutionary activities in China and Chinese political exiles living in Japan.[59] Indeed, to many observers, Umeya appeared more of a Pan-Asian propagandist than a film producer. High asserts that Umeya invested money in the establishment of a politically progressive Chinese-language newspaper, the *Minbao*, which published articles by Sun and other revolutionists and soon became popular among Tokyo's Chinese intellectuals.[60]

In a Japanese-language book-length study on the relationship between Sun and Umeya, Ayano Kosaka recounts how Umeya sent an M. Pathé production crew to record the ongoing revolution in October 1911. Led by cameramen Hagyia Kenzo, the team consisted of six employees and a journalist from the Japanese daily newspaper *To-Yo-Hinode-Shinbun*. The expedition spent the next month filming at least three successive installments of an actuality-style documentary, following the developments until Sun Yat-sen was appointed president in the final days of December 1911. Kosaka claimed that most of the scenes were shot in the vicinity of Shanghai, since the revolutionary conflict was still underway nearby at the time of filming. In Japan, the multipart film was titled *The Xinhai Revolution*.[61]

Another scholar, Akira Nagai, has written that the film's first installment screened at the Michitaza Theater in late November 1911 in Umeya's hometown of Nagasaki.[62] Around the time of the revolution, many Chinese students in Japan lived in the city due to its proximity to the Chinese coast and its established position as the former singular Sino-Japanese trading center. Nagai argued that the film played a crucial role in delivering news of the revolution to Japan, especially to groups of Chinese overseas students, many of whom returned to China during the following months.[63]

Articles and advertisements from *Billboard* and *Moving Picture World* announced in March 1912 that Benjamin Michaels's newly formed Oriental Film Company had imported *The Chinese Revolution* from "the Pathe Company of Japan."[64] Although there is no concrete evidence of where the film was screened in San Francisco, it is likely that *The Chinese Revolution* played at the Shanghai Theatre soon after it arrived in San Francisco.[65] There is also evidence that *The Chinese Revolution* played in Los Angeles in late February or early March 1912, at a theater located close to the Plaza area. In multiple works, Jan Olsson has argued that the mix of Mexican, Spanish, and Asian ethnicities around the Los Angeles Plaza area proved to be a significant factor in the emergence of film culture in Los Angeles. Olsson noted that although the early 1910s saw a gradual shift toward more prestigious venues, the oldest nickelodeons and a few new ones on North Main Street, close to the Plaza, still catered to the ethnic patrons of the vicinity, predominantly of Mexican, Japanese, and Chinese descent.[66] *The Chinese Revolution* ran for three days at the Metropolitan, a theater owned by a Russian-born immigrant film exhibitor named Abraham (A. L.) Gore and his family. The Gores opened the Metropolitan Theater at 513–515 North Main Street, directly next to the Old Plaza Church, in 1910. Ramona Curry also suggests that local LA Chinese leaders and publications that supported the 1911 revolution may have helped promote the M. Pathé film in the community and possibly even utilized the occasion to raise further funds to benefit ongoing revolutionary activities. She noted, however, that "given the ethnic mix of businesses and residents occupying the 400–600 blocks of North Main Street during the 1910s, it is likely that the Metropolitan Theater drew ethnically Japanese and Italian American as well as Mexican and Chinese customers."[67]

Michaels, in turn, sold prints to distributors who thereby secured rights to circulate the film exclusively (on a states rights basis) within one or more of twenty-two states, including Washington, California, Texas, Arizona, Louisiana, Florida, and New York.[68] Advertisements and weekly theater listings in a variety of local newspapers document that *The Chinese Revolution* was exhibited in 1912 in multiple cities in California, as well as in Georgia and Florida (and doubtless at places in between).[69] It seems that the film played or at least partially played to Chinese audiences in the United States. For example, it ran for three days in early March 1912 in San Jose, at the Garden Theater, located on West San Fernando Street close to the intersection with Market Street. According to historian Barbara Voss, this area, formerly the location of San Jose's Market Street Chinatown, formed the heart of the Bay Area's overseas Chinese community in the 1870s and 1880s.[70] Although that settlement was destroyed by anti-Chinese arson in 1887, the Chinese presence remained active in the vicinity.[71]

In April, *Billboard* reported on an interview with Benjamin Michaels held at his Van Ness Avenue office about the sales campaign for *The Chinese Revolution*. Michaels boasted that the film had sold widely and described a phone call he had just received from New Orleans that clinched the deal for distribution in both Louisiana and Texas. Michaels averred that his company's success arose from recognition of the opportunities its product offered the "states rights men" (distributors of independently secured films over a set region) and moving picture exhibitors.[72] The *Billboard* reporter painted a vivid picture of the venture, likening the Oriental Company film office to a "state arsenal, with guns, swords and all other war instruments strewn promiscuously along the floor."[73] The company offered such "props," as well as more standard posters and handbills, for sale to give the individual independent exhibitor the "strongest lobby display ever devised."[74]

The avid marketing for states rights purchase of *The Chinese Revolution* as a "war in Asia" film spectacle, complete with "war props" and somewhat Orientalist rhetoric in a national advertisement, represents one of the ways that the film became a successful commodity in the transitional American film market, precisely for being structured as a novelty.[75] Another noteworthy aspect of *The Chinese Revolution*'s circulation in the United States was its being marketed by a Euro-American-run firm to attract not only mainstream but also expressly Chinese audiences, apparent from the inclusion of the Chinese language in both the film's promotion and intertitles, as well as in the film's exhibition in urban theaters located in or near Chinese immigrant communities. Furthermore, the film arguably had an impact somewhat counter to the usual representations of Chinese in U.S.-made films at the time due to the promotional strategy to establish a link between the film and the multitude of news reports on the revolutionary events in China that had permeated the U.S. press in the months before the film's American release. Those news reports generally addressed the anti-imperial, democratically focused revolution as a liberating trend in which contemporary Chinese were engaged as admirable political actors. The overall strategy for selling the film in the United States departed from such presumed public interest in the widely reported revolution in China to promote states rights marketing to independent regional distributors and exhibitors across the land.

Thus the article in *Billboard* on March 9, 1912, foregrounded the film's news value, given that "the hostilities in the Orient still headlined in all of the big city newspapers and flaunted in public not less than twice a day."[76] The announcement emphasizes that *The Chinese Revolution* would be suitable for exhibition across the United States, for the revolution was already in the rubrics and columns of "every daily from the lowliest country weekly to the largest big

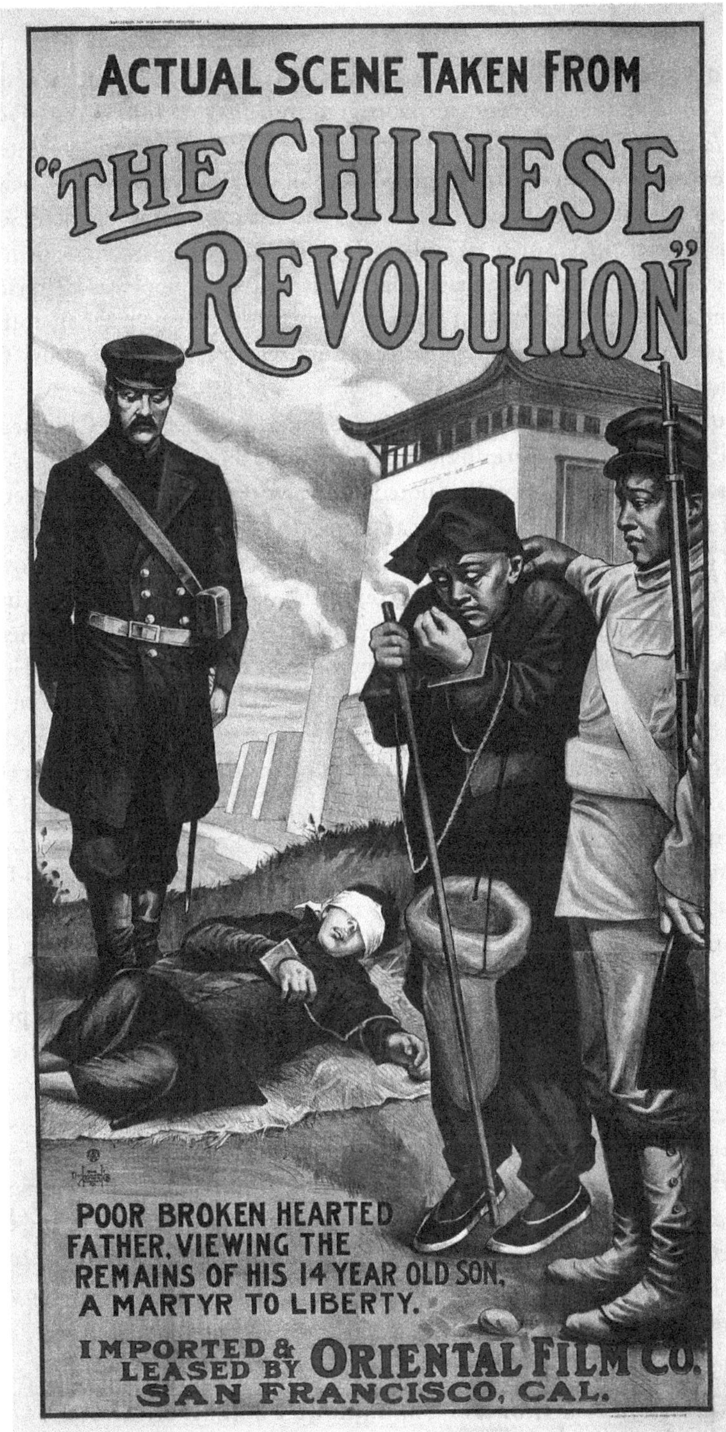


FIG. 22 Poster from the Oriental Film Company's marketing campaign for *The Chinese Revolution* (M. Pathé, 1912). (Image courtesy of Heritage Auctions/www.HA.com)

city newspapers." This film was something that they had "all been Waiting For."[77] Elaborate advertisements appeared in *Billboard* and *Moving Picture World* throughout April and May, with cartoonlike illustrations presented as scenes from the film or even from the "revolution itself." Each image includes a rubric with the film's title in block letters and also explanatory captions, sometimes written in Chinese as well as English. The images complement the aggressive promotional language, much of it written in uppercase letters. For example, one advertisement in *Billboard* displays three armed men in uniform overpowering a man dressed in plain clothing, with a caption that reads, "Capturing a Manchu Spy."[78]

Several scholars have drawn attention to the significance of the Chinese Revolution in popular American political discourse about cinematic representations. Matthew D. Johnson has noted that travelogue filmmaker and lecturer Burton Holmes "by 1913 also drew a contrast in his presentations between 'old days [and] Republican ones,' and 'the great strides made by China' toward sovereign nationhood since the 1911 Revolution."[79] Holmes was tapping into a perceived paradigm shift in popular American views on China, whereby modernization was bringing the "Oriental" closer to Western values and ideas. Sabine Haenni pointed to profound transformations during the 1910s in attitudes in the United States toward the Chinese that gave rise to increasing contradictory representations of China and Chinatown. Haenni argued that these contradictory sentiments were amplified to a national level by Republican China's participation in the San Francisco Panama-Pacific International Exposition.[80] Michaels's and the Oriental Film Company's importation and distribution of *The Chinese Revolution* were in all likelihood mostly based on commercial opportunism rather than idealism or charity. Similarly to H. J. Lewis, Michaels's involvement in the public entertainment scene around San Francisco Chinatown gave him firsthand experience of the burgeoning political activity and the emergence of Chinese American youth culture during this transformative period. Given his previous record as a Chinatown impresario, this cultural moment was surely one he was eager to exploit. But despite the underlying intentions, Michaels and the people involved in running his small entertainment empire contributed an incendiary mediation of Chinese modernity to Chinatown film culture through their facilitation of the film and their choice of language and imagery depicting iconographic events from the ongoing Chinese Revolution (and from *The Chinese Revolution* itself) in the company's marketing campaign.

## Chinatown Movie Theaters: Ambiguous Social Institutions

The modernization of Chinatown's social infrastructure coincided with the emergence of cinema as a powerful narrative medium. Between 1906 and 1915, the medium became intrinsically entangled with new ways of living and seeing the world in Chinatown. As the writings of Francesco Casetti remind us, the relation between cinema and modernity spawned a counterintuitive process, by which the "medium also gave *form* to its context."[81] In Chinatown, such a process was most evident in the cultural practices that approached cinema and moviegoing as a metaphor for modern life. However, it was also fundamentally conditioned by locally specific forces, such as diasporic reactions to the revolution overseas and attitudes born out of the neighborhood's long history of social marginalization.

While the various accounts cited in this chapter sprawl in different directions, they intersect at their connection to Chinatown movie theaters and local entertainment culture. Seen through these accounts, early Chinatown moviegoing appears intrinsically linked to a perceived societal trajectory toward Westernization, away from the traditional cultural values of the old country. The publicness and novelty of neighborhood movie theaters facilitated sites where the "Americanization" of Chinese San Franciscans was visible and enacted on an everyday basis. As younger Chinatown generations adopted and appropriated the fads and phases of modern life in the cosmopolitan city, older generations voiced concerns about where this new direction would lead. This discourse often paired moviegoing with other "Western" societal ills that plagued the Chinatown community, such as prostitution. In a more general sense, these accounts help recast the movie theaters in light of contemporary cultural and political flows—the "changing mentality" that became an inescapable aspect of everyday lives of Chinese San Franciscans in the post-quake period. Around the time of the emergence and popularization of movie shows in Chinatown, old political and societal paradigms were in notable states of transformation.

Another way in which the establishments figured in the political milieu of the rising Chinese nationalism was as venues for various events of a political character. Here, the Young China Association was among the most frequent employers of Chinatown movie theaters as stages from which to disseminate their political message. While there is no evidence to suggest that the non-Chinese proprietors of the theaters had any political leanings or alliances with the local groups tied to either side of the conflict across the Pacific, it is apparent that they recognized the commercial opportunity that arose with the emerging public interest in the Chinese Revolution. Such commercial instances are discernible through their making their facilities available to stage political plays, fundraisers, rallies, and commemorative events at various theaters in the area. It is also plausible that the popularity and heavy patronage of such events made Chinatown exhibitors look for related entertainments, to get ahead of their competitors in the ongoing fight for the local audiences in Chinatown and North Beach. Seen in this light, Benjamin Michaels's importation, exhibition, and distribution of *The Chinese Revolution* is a most elaborate example of such business acumen.

Michaels's importation and exhibition of *The Chinese Revolution* also point to a third dimension of Chinatown modernity, where complex political and social developments were repurposed to fit an American iconography dominated by fixed ideas of the Oriental. By outwardly engaging diasporic Chinese Americans in advertisements mostly published in film trade papers with little to no Chinese American readership, the film's marketing campaign, similar to that for H. J. Lewis's *Seeing America's Greatest Chinatown, San Francisco*, primarily activated tropes commonly found in Chinatown's tourism industry, where the visual presence of people and things perceived as Oriental would lend authenticity to the exotic experience. Whether this packaging was successful is hard to tell, but it provides another example of an attempt to export the experience of Chinatown's contact zones to a broader audience. Unlike Lewis, who used the camera to place himself in a position as guide and interpreter of this strange and exotic part of America, Michaels utilized a blunt marketing campaign that introduced a link between the notion of Chinese American movie audiences and the ongoing "modernization" of China. Where previous scholarship on Chinatown and cinema has concentrated on the relationship between early film production and the Chinatown conjured by the collective American imagination, the Michaels episode evidences a more direct link ,between Chinatown modernity, San Francisco Chinatown–specific film exhibition practices and contemporary U.S. film culture at large.

# 8

# Trajectories and Concluding Remarks

The space of San Francisco's Chinatown has been mapped out in the cinematic geography of twentieth-century U.S. film culture countless times, yet the film history of the neighborhood is contrived. In on-screen representations, it has often been conjured as a symbolic mutation of westward expansionism, a marginal space defined by its otherness, calling into question delimitations of criminal justice, sexual propriety, gender identity, and ultimately Americanness. Rarely has it been evoked as a space where U.S. film culture *took* place. In this study, I have found that in Chinatown during the early stages of the emergence of the U.S. film industry, there existed an alternative film culture, offering Chinese American moviegoers a place to experience and partake in U.S. film culture during its formative years.

In order to find a conceptual common ground for looking at how place-specific factors interacted with, and broke away from, more general developments, I have employed theoretical concepts developed to "localize" cultural processes in space and time. Miriam Hansen observed that immigrant moviegoing in the transitional era pointed to the formation of an alternative public sphere, positing that movie theaters provided immigrants with a window to an American society more affluent than the one in which they found themselves. Other scholars who have explored the alternative public sphere of transitional era moviegoing suggest that immigrant neighborhood movie theaters bestowed minority communities with nostalgic connections to their ethnic roots through the programming of films produced in each respective community's country of origin. While such processes might well have been underway in the Chinatown movie theaters, this did not show up in my research. Other tendencies stand out more clearly. A significant aspect was the appropriation of the moviegoing experience as a whole to attract the Chinese American community. The molding of film culture was achieved through acts of translation as well as through the monitoring of the habits of Chinese San Franciscan moviegoers. As such, like the opera and theater culture that preceded it, Chinatown film culture was influenced by the neighborhood's cultural hybridity.

Taking the notion of cultural hybridity to task, I have, with analytical heuristics of thirdspace and transcultural contact zones, approached its components and how they manifested in the limited space of post-quake Chinatown's movie theaters. In this analysis, I localized a set of paradoxes at play in the cultural contact zone of Broadway and Grant Avenue, where film exhibition and, in some respects, modernity were adopted to match the leisure practices and public amusement traditions of the Chinese San Franciscan community. Another thirdspace aspect of post-quake film culture in Chinatown can be seen in how the movie theaters both magnified and thwarted the social frictions of the neighborhood. While scholars such as Miriam Hansen, Giorgio Bertellini, and Judith Thissen all have identified the potential for a class transcendence of first- and second-generation immigrants in the relation between individual spectators and what was shown on screen, this book has evidenced, for example, through the writings of Adriana Spadoni, that in Chinatown such processes saturated the whole moviegoing experience.[1] The shared experience of Chinatown film culture is apparent from the Orientalized decor and posters outside theaters to exhibitors' efforts to cater to Chinatown audiences, and the metaspectatorial aspect of Chinese San Franciscans sharing a limited space and watching the same screen as Chinatown tourists.

In approaching these frictions, what Homi Bhabha called the "everyday of modernity," there seems to be a disconnect from the "modernity" incanted by scholars of early film, often signified by a limitless potential.[2] While the works of Miriam Hansen, Tom Gunning, and Francesco Casetti have established that the everyday experience of modernity expanded horizons and laid bare paths to new ways of experiencing the world, in Chinatown these sensations came with a set of restrictions and limitations imposed on the Chinese San Franciscan community. From this perspective, Chinatown modernity, and by extension film culture in Chinatown, held an ambiguous promise: as an alternative horizon of possibility and potential for the formation of a new Chinese American identity, but at the same time as a confirmation of the repressed reality of Chinese American existence in which the new film medium figured as a novel means of social oppression. The Janus-faced displays of Chineseness available for the world to see at the Panama-Pacific International Exposition provide a stark example of this paradox.

While cinema appeared as a popular form of entertainment in Chinatown, the Chinese San Franciscan community was undergoing a generational shift, spurred on by the neighborhood's strong transpacific connection to the revolutionary movement in China. A critical aspect of the "changing mentality" of Chinatown was the emergence of a Chinese American intellectual class, which would be a driving force behind the modernization of both China and Chinatown. In many ways, the modern institutions of new Chinatown, such as schools, local press, a hospital, a telephone exchange, as well as the strong political ties to the modernizing government in China, facilitated such development and fostered the creation of a Chinese American middle class. Here, movie theaters functioned as a multipronged site of Chinatown modernity. Within the diverse Chinese San Franciscan community, a perception emerged of Chinatown movie theaters as symbols of a growing divide between generations of Chinese Americans, threatening to curtail a shared cultural heritage. At other times, movie theaters served as venues for nationalist political rallies arranged by local political activists. Occasionally, the theaters were at the receiving end of Chinese San Franciscan ire against their populist perpetuation of distorted and fetishized imageries of Chineseness.

As the new Chinatown emerged as the cultural and economic center of Chinese America, its public perception as a node of undesirable Chineseness remained largely unaltered in the dominant public sphere. It is important to remember that immigration policies and exclusionary practices were constant forces in defining and structuring the Chinatown entertainment scene at the turn of the century. In a bid to make the space of the neighborhood more commercially available to outside visitors, Orientalist visions of Chinatown were applied onto the very streetscape of the rebuilt neighborhood through the architectural designs conceived by non-Chinese architects. Protests organized by Chinatown's intelligentsia targeted blunt misrepresentations built on the fantasy of the "Chinatown Underworld" and the exotic creatures that dwelled there, yet the more quotidian manifestations of Orientalism that were a part of the touristic appeal and visual style of new Chinatown seem to have been tolerated.

The Chinesque aesthetic, another Chinatown-specific manifestation of cultural hybridity, became for the merchant class of Chinese San Franciscans a way to capitalize on the public interest in the myth of "old Chinatown." However, it also appeared in the marketing strategies and theater designs of local film exhibitors. Non–Chinese American showmen, such as Benjamin Michaels and Sid Grauman, utilized the Chinesque aesthetic to create a symbiosis between the Orientalist fantasy of Chinatown, their public entertainment ventures, and the alluring proximity of Chinatown space.

Post-quake Chinatown film phenomena mark the trajectory of American cinema's treatment of Chinese culture in the early twenty-first century, from the on-screen Orientalism incarnations established as staples of Hollywood storytelling in the late 1910s and early 1920s, to the materialist escapism of the 1930s and 1940s. It would, of course, be absurd to claim that post-quake Chinatown exhibitors invented cinematic Orientalism. Several of the tropes employed by the likes of Grauman and Michaels long preceded their days of exploiting San Francisco's Chinatown, as demonstrated by scholars such as James Moy, John Kuo Wei Tchen, and Krystyn R. Moon.[3] However, operations such as those of Michaels and Grauman provide evidence that cultural practices tied to Chinatown during the period wielded considerable influence in merging visceral manifestations of Orientalism with film cultural practices.

Today, Grauman's Chinese Theatre stands as one of the most iconic structures of the movie palace era.[4] Sid Grauman, while not solely employing the Chinesque aesthetic in his repertoire, routinely returned to it, both in the architectural designs of his movie theaters and in his prologues. In 1932, Grauman built another dream version of San Francisco's Chinatown, this time inside the Chinese Theatre. The scenery functioned as the setting for Grauman's stage prologue to the premiere of Lewis Milestone's South Seas drama *Rain*, starring Joan Crawford. The set replicated Grant Avenue and included dancers in yellowface makeup and police raids on the neighborhood, echoing earlier Grauman exposés such as *20 Minutes at the Barbary Coast*, *Midnight in Frisco*, and Underground Chinatown.[5] Homay King wrote that the juxtaposition of the Chinatown scenery set inside theater created a dizzying *mise-en-abyme*, extending from the stage outward to the whole of Grauman's Chinese Theatre: "East and West, local and global, flat picture and live action, original and simulacrum are enfolded within one another in a way that complicates attempts to distinguish among them."[6] As if building a temple to cinema stylistically influenced by Orientalist mysticism was not enough, Grauman returned to staging Chinatown in a manner similar to his early San Francisco exploits throughout his career. Applying King's analysis as optics on Grauman's career "oeuvre," it appears as if the exhibitor repeatedly relied on this mix of nods to popular myth and immediate social reality to create a link between modern street life, architecture, stage, and cinematic representation.[7] Seen in the context of his background as a San Francisco film exhibitor and showman, the Chinese Theatre emerges as Grauman's consummate version of the Chinesque aesthetic. Teleological hindsight regarding the Underground Chinatown makes it appear as if Grauman had taken an early step toward exporting the Chinesque aesthetic to the masses; or, as Tchen puts it, "The stereotype would later be fully realized, marrying film technology with established stage conventions."[8] Through its envelopment in the internationally distributed mythologies of Classical Hollywood cinema, the proliferation of the Chinesque aesthetic overshadowed the development of vigilant Chinese

San Franciscan resistance to oppose and counter the kind of distorted views exploited by Grauman and Michaels.

Despite the relative historical obscurity, visions of Chinatown modernity and anticolonial resistance were fortified through transpacific connections in the latter part of the 1910s, suggesting that the notion of Chinatown modernity should thus be understood in liaison with scholarship on the contemporary modernity of urban Shanghai and Beijing and the anticolonial movements during the 1910s. In the wake of the failure of the Chinese Republic, intellectuals and youth organizations in Beijing and Shanghai reaffirmed the calls for reform and modernization of China's political, social, and educational infrastructure that had propelled the Xinhai revolution in the first place. The "New Culture Movement," including authors Chen Duxiu and Lu Xun, and philosopher Hu Shi led the charge against the Confucian foundations of China's ruling intellectual class. Central to the movement was a principle of enlightenment, promoting an informational and literary culture of vernacular and simplified Chinese, in contrast to the praxis of publishing in traditional Chinese. These principles and reforms were developed and discussed openly in publications such as *New Youth*, a magazine that eventually became a mouthpiece for leaders of the movement and likely inspired its Chinatown counterpart, *Young China*.[9] Another leading organization was the Commercial Press, which was the first to publish educational materials and literary works in simplified and vernacular Chinese, in an outspoken strategy to reach the masses and go against the intellectual ruling class. As the movement grew in the mid-1910s, the Commercial Press extended its communicative platform to include the film medium. The company set up a film division in 1917, with an explicit agenda to counter films that "instilled spiteful feelings toward China."[10] Matthew D. Johnson writes that the Commercial Press was the first in China to realize the film medium's possibilities as a propaganda tool, "adopting the early Republic's reformist language of culture and enlightenment to justify its commercial activities in nationalist terms, and engaging in production of nonfeature actuality films under the rubric of popular education."[11] Around the early 1920s, there were in the United States similar efforts to enlist the power of the film medium to counter negative portrayals of Chinese peoples and cultures, such as by Los Angeles director James Leong and the New York–based Li Zeyuan, two filmmakers whose work countered Hollywood's reductive view of Chineseness.[12] Lady Tsen-Mei, Anna May Wong, and Keye Luke were all actors who—while often forced to accept Orientalist roles—worked from the "inside" of the Hollywood industry to change the general public's perception of Chinese identity. As this book has shown, such organized efforts to counter stereotypes and enlighten the greater public were conceived in Chinatown as part and parcel of the neighborhood's and the community's adaptation to modernity.

## Paths Ahead

A study hypothesizing a gradual standardization in the imagery of Chinatown as a narrative milieu in early Classical Hollywood filmmaking could further investigate the connections between cinematic representation and San Francisco's Chinatown. Given the historiographical concerns of this investigation, a future discussion interlinking the spaces of representation may also be conducted within a broader framework, taking further consideration of modes of representation inherited from contemporary manifestations of Orientalism in, for example, vaudeville, burlesque, and contemporary painting.

The post-1906 proliferation of small-scale movie houses in San Francisco in many ways mirrors the development elsewhere in the United States; it is clear that the aftermath of the earthquake and fire especially conditioned the emergence of the local film industry. As I designed my investigation to frame the chapters on Chinatown, I refrained from investigating other avenues of film historical interest, such as how the Miles Brothers' early model of film rentals might have influenced San Francisco exhibitors' perceptions of the film market after the introduction of the Moving Picture Patents Company. Immigrant communities other than the Chinese also seem to have played important roles in the local film culture of San Francisco, especially the Italian community. Sometime in 1915 it seems that Michaels turned his attention to North Beach's Italian community. Around this time, leaders of that community attempted to raise funds for a *film d'art*–inspired epic produced by the California Motion Picture Company, with local movie star Beatriz Michelena playing the lead. While my investigation is among the first academic ventures to investigate how the film medium emerged as a form of public entertainment in San Francisco, the city's rich and diverse history is deserving of a more thorough treatment.

In terms of archival continuity, this is a book full of holes. As is evident in source materials, as well as in books on Chinese American history that precede it, the marginalization of Chinese Americans in the nineteenth and twentieth centuries stretches from discriminatory immigration laws to a systemic annihilation of the documented history of a community. To operate in this vast archival void, Chinese community historians have had to come up with a range of creative and painstaking strategies to safeguard, commemorate, and preserve the experience of thousands of Chinese people in the United States. Further inquiries into the cultural expressions that came out of Chinatown after the 1906 earthquake and fire will have to be creative and dig even deeper into archival resources and tools that up until now have been regarded as unconventional or anecdotal. Moving forward, we need to engage with oral histories, correspondence, family genealogies, and immigration records that will doubtless turn up more interesting aspects and stories that would help us understand the contours of this place-based culture even better, distinctive and fleeting at once, as it were.

As a microhistorical contribution to a cumulative history of film culture in the United States, this study offers an array of instances when cinema as a mass medium was appropriated to appeal to an audience seen as existing on the fringes of American society. In Chinatown, the film medium was caught up in larger ongoing cultural processes, where extreme prejudice and notions of progressivism collided with the formation of a new Chinese American identity. The appearance of film culture in San Francisco's Chinatown, as presented and discussed over these pages, points to a cultural hybridity in the public sphere that has been overlooked by scholarship on early American cinema. By extension, these findings challenge common conceptions of modernity as an inherently Western cultural and social force. While at times overused, the notion of modernity has been an essential analytical companion for revisiting early and transitional era film histories. But if it does not hold up or adapt well to investigations of marginal film cultures, such as the one presented in this book, and new studies like this one continue to unveil the complexity and inherently transnational nature of U.S. film culture in the early twentieth century, it calls for a refocusing of the concept itself, questioning some of its fundamental assumptions.[13] As historian Q. Edward Wang has pointed out, modernity's spread across many corners of the world resulted in multiple processes, some of which "challenged Western hegemony and questioned the universal application of Western model(s)."[14] For historical film studies, in moving forward with the notion of modernity as explanatory shorthand, we must consider what questions such processes pose to the concept as a whole. Going forward from this study, then, Chinatown film culture should be understood as a part of a Chinese American film culture, where the emphasis is placed on the hybrid, what binds together and exists in between. Only then, if we can see past the continued influence of monolithic concepts of modernity, monadic studies of the nation-state, and unidirectional imaginaries of westward expansion, might we begin to understand film cultures such as that which appeared in Chinatown after the earthquake and fire in 1906.

# Acknowledgments

This study would not have been possible without the lifelong efforts of historians Him Mark Lai and Phil Choy. While I never had the pleasure of meeting Professor Lai, his scholarship, archival practices, and critical focus resound throughout this book. I did have the fortune of meeting Professor Choy, who took me for historical walks through his neighborhood and invited me to his home and his impressive collection of Chinese American history. Phil gifted me insights most history books will not. The immeasurable work of these Chinatown luminaries carved out space for studies like this one to exist. This book is in honor of them.

I would like to give heartfelt thanks to my mentor Jan Olsson, whose encyclopedic knowledge, wisdom, and wit have made for a trusted compass wherever these time travels have taken me. I am also profoundly grateful to Ramona Curry for teaching me that scholarly work is passion and effort, and for extending her expertise, experience, and generosity across plains and oceans. My gratitude also goes to John Kuo Wei Tchen and Gregory Waller, whose salient readings and thought-provoking comments made this study better.

I am deeply indebted to Charles Musser, who helped me develop this study into a book manuscript during a postdoctoral period at Yale University. My gratitude also goes to Francesco Casetti and the brilliant folks at the Yale Film and Media Studies Program. In New Haven, I had the pleasure of sharing offices with Bernard Geoghegan and Daniel Steinmetz-Jenkins.

Thank you also to my editor, Lisa Banning, for her support and encouragement of this project from the first time I brought it to her. No query has been too big, no question too small. I am also grateful to my reviewers, whose critiques and suggestions have been useful toward the book's finalization.

Warm thanks to my friends, colleagues, and students at the Department of Media Studies at Stockholm University. In particular, I would like to thank

Maaret Koskinen, Tytti Soila, John Fullerton, Joel Frykholm, Kristoffer Noheden, and Nadi Tofighian, who have read and offered insightful comments at various stages. Doron Galili, Gert Jan Harkema, Laura Horak, and Elizabeth Castaldo Lundén have all been thought-provoking discussion partners. A special thanks goes to my office mate, brewmaster, and marathon companion, Ashley Smith.

Parts of this study have been presented elsewhere. A segment in the section of chapter 7 that discusses *The Chinese Revolution* was published in a different form in *Film History* in 2014, under the editorship of David Church and Gregory Waller. Aspects of this research have been presented as papers at universities and conferences. At the University of Illinois, where I had the opportunity of spending six months as a visiting scholar in the spring of 2013, discussions with Poshek Fu, Anna Stenport, and Wenshu Zhao of Nanjing University were beneficial. In other contexts, I have been lucky to discuss my research with Scott Curtis, Miyase Christensen, Ian Christie, Oliver Gaycken, Erkki Huhtamo, Yuanyuan Li, Mark Sandberg, Linda Williams, Zhang Zhen, and Jianxin Zhu. I also want to say a particular thank-you to Frank Bren, who encouraged my interests in early transpacific cinema when I was an MA student, wandering the streets of Shanghai.

I am tremendously appreciative of the financial support I have received from various institutions and organizations. A generous grant from the Sweden-America Foundation funded my time at Yale. Travel grants from Stockholm University and the Holger and Thyra Lauritzen Foundation made possible crucial research trips to San Francisco, Shanghai, Washington, DC, and New York. Stipends from Society for Cinema and Media Studies, Stiftelsen Lars Hiertas Minne, and the Royal Swedish Academy of Sciences funded my participation in conferences and workshops. I was happy to be awarded a significant grant from the Illinois-Sweden Program for Educational and Research Exchange (INSPIRE), which enabled longer research stays at the University of Illinois and in the San Francisco Bay Area.

Given the archival foundation of this study, I am indebted to the expertise and generosity of the people working in the libraries and archives I have visited. The impressive staff at the Film Library in Stockholm have responded to my every request with knowledge and interest. I am also grateful to my friends at the Swedish Film Archive and Cinemateket, who have shared their world-class insight into film history with me in movie theaters and over late-night drinks. I am indebted to the staff at the ZiKaWei branch of the Shanghai Library and at the Film Museum in Shanghai. In New York, the staff at the Elmer Holmes Bobst Library, the Museum of Modern Art, and the New York Public Library were of great assistance. The capable staff at the Library at the University of Illinois in Champaign-Urbana guided me through dusty stacks and rare documents. The Motion Pictures, Broadcasting, and Recorded Sound

Division at the Library of Congress in Washington, DC, particularly Josie Walters-Johnston, procured film materials for crucial viewing and analysis. In San Francisco, I am indebted to the Chinese Historical Society of America, particularly Sue Lee, for their assistance and collaboration. I would also like to thank the staff at the San Francisco History Center and the San Francisco Public Library, especially Christina Moretta and Susan Goldstein; the Commonwealth Club of California; the San Francisco Law Library; and the San Francisco Library of Performing Arts, particularly Kristen Tanaka. I had the pleasure of spending an afternoon in the company of Rick and Megan Prelinger, who invited me to their collections and shared some brownies at the Prelinger Library. At the University of California, Davis, I want to thank Daryl Morrison and the staff at the Special Collections unit of the General Library. At Berkeley, the staff at the Bancroft Library and University Archives made possible rigorous research on the Panama-Pacific International Exposition. In Sacramento, Karen Paige and Marianne Leach at the California State Library assisted in detective work on Louis J. Stellman. The folks at the Sterling Memorial Library and the Beinecke Rare Books and Manuscripts Library at Yale have also been of tremendous help.

I am lucky to have shared intensified moments with Alexandre Audi, Daniel Dabdoub, Jaap Verheul, my fellow blind pigs Bobby Bingle, George Duffy, and Keith Motton, Lucy Schiller, Scott Cao, Christian Lindberg, James Jacobs and ShinJoung Yeo, Elisabet Lang, Dylan Hosey and Emmet Emma Isabella Grahn, the Bingle family, and other friends from near and far who have indulged me in tirades on early film history and given me something to eat and a place to stay.

To Mom and Dad for the gift of curiosity.

Finally, I would to thank my wife and companion, Cecilia, and our beautiful boys, Joshua and Allan. You three make the world so sweet.

# Notes

## Preface

1 "Meeting of Indiana Exhibitors," *Motography*, January 1912, 18–19.

## Introduction

1 A selective bibliography of writings on representations of Chineseness in U.S. cinema includes John Haddad, "The Laundry Man's Got a Knife!," *Chinese America: History and Perspectives*, ed. Colleen Fung et al. (San Francisco: Chinese Historical Society of America, 2001): 31–47; Jeanette Roan, *Envisioning Asia: On Location, Travel, and the Cinematic Geography of U.S. Orientalism* (Ann Arbor: University of Michigan Press, 2010); Ruth Mayer, "The Glittering Machine of Modernity: The Chinatown in American Silent Film," *Modernism/modernity* 16, no. 4 (2009): 661–684.

2 See, for example, Gina Marchetti, *Romance and the "Yellow Peril": Race, Sex, and Discursive Strategies in Hollywood Fiction* (Berkeley: University of California Press, 1994); Karen J. Leong, *The China Mystique: Pearl S. Buck, Anna May Wong, Mayling Soong, and the Transformation of American Orientalism* (Berkeley: University of California Press, 2005); Yiman Wang, "The Art of Screen Passing: Anna May Wong's Yellow Yellowface Performance in the Art Deco Era," *Camera Obscura* 20, no. 3 (2005): 159–191; Ruth Mayer, *Serial Fu Manchu: The Chinese Supervillain and the Spread of Yellow Peril Ideology* (Philadelphia: Temple University Press, 2014).

3 Denise Khor, "Asian Americans at the Movies: Race, Labor, and Migration in the Transpacific West, 1900–1945" (PhD diss., University of California, San Diego, 2008).

4 See Ramona Curry, "Benjamin Brodsky (1877–1960): The Trans-Pacific American Film Entrepreneur Part One, Making *A Trip Thru China*," *Journal of American–East Asian Relations* 18, no. 1 (2011): 58–94; Curry, "Benjamin Brodsky (1877–1960): The Trans-Pacific American Film Entrepreneur Part Two, Taking *A Trip Thru China* to America," *Journal of American–East Asian Relations* 18, no. 2 (2011): 142–180.

5 Williams traces the epistemology of the noun "culture," from the early notion of cultivation and husbandry (i.e., tending to animals or crops) to more modern metaphoric usages, relating to the human mind or "an abstract process or the product of such a process." Raymond Williams, *Keywords: A Vocabulary of Culture and Society* (London: Fontana, 1976), 87.

6 Williams, 89–90.

7 The reasons for the division will be elaborated further in the section on sources.

8 Williams noted that in cultural anthropology the reference to culture or a culture is primarily to material production, whereas in history and cultural studies the reference is primarily to signifying or symbolic systems. Williams, *Keywords*, 91.

9 Robert C. Allen, "Getting to Going to the Show," *New Review of Film and Television Studies* 8, no. 3 (2010): 266.

10 Nicholas Mirzoeff and Jack Halberstam, "Decolonize Media: Tactics, Manifestos, Histories," *Cinema Journal* 57, no. 4 (2018): 120–123.

11 Lies Van de Vijver and Daniel Biltereyst, "Cinemagoing as a Conditional Part of Everyday Life," *Cultural Studies* 27, no. 4 (2013): 562. In 1986, Thomas Elsaesser used the term "New Film History" to describe interventions into early film history since the groundbreaking 1978 FIAF (International Federation of Film Archives) symposium "Cinema 1900–1906," in Brighton, where the rediscovery and restoration of a large amount of film material from before 1906 encouraged a new generation of scholars to revisit early film history. See Thomas Elsaesser, "The New Film History," *Sight & Sound* 55, no. 4 (1986): 246–251. The field has since grown into a wide-ranging set of historical inquiries, loosely organized around the principle of putting standardized film history under revisionist scrutiny. A 2004 issue of *Cinema Journal* focused on the development of New Film History See Sumiko Higashi, "In Focus: Film History, or a Baedeker Guide to the Historical Turn," *Cinema Journal* 44, no. 1 ( 2004): 94–100. A 2013 issue of *Film History* offered an update on the field, with a special focus on the emergence of new resources; see Gregory Waller, "Introduction," *Film History* 25, nos. 1–2 (2013): vii–ix.

12 Walter Benjamin, "On the Concept of History," in *Walter Benjamin: Selected Writings*, vol. 4, *1938–1940*, ed. Howard Eiland and Michael W. Jennings (Cambridge, MA: Belknap Press, 2006), 392.

13 An important exegesis was initiated by Benjamin's close friend Gershom Scholem, concerning whether or not Benjamin's theses should be considered as a turn away from history to theology. Such perspectives have been elaborated by Gershom Scholem in "Walter Benjamin," in *On Jews and Judaism in Crisis*, ed. Werner J. Dannhauser (New York: Schocken Books, 1976), 172–179; Scholem, *Walter Benjamin: The Story of a Friendship* (London: Faber and Faber, 1982); and Michael Löwy, *Fire Alarm: Reading Walter Benjamin's "On the Concept of History,"* trans. Chris Turner (London: Verso, 2005). While the theses are laden with theological concepts such as "the messianic moment," other interpreters, such as Ronald Beiner and Vanessa Schwartz, have underlined the key role the text has played for the interpretation of what Schwartz calls an "aphoristic materialist history." Vanessa R. Schwartz, "Walter Benjamin for Historians," *American Historical Review* 106, no. 5 (2001): 1724.

14 Benjamin shared Nietzsche's contempt for a historicism that admires its documented victors. However, as Michael Löwy points out, "Nietzsche's critique was made in the name of the rebellious individual, the hero—and later the overman.

That of Benjamin, by contrast, is in solidarity with those who have fallen beneath the wheels of those majestic, magnificent chariots called Civilization, Progress, and Modernity." Löwy, *Fire Alarm*, 49.

15 Ronald Beiner, "Walter Benjamin's Philosophy of History," *Political Theory* 12, no. 3 (1984): 428.

16 Benjamin, "On the Concept of History," 395.

17 John Kuo Wei Tchen and Dylan Yeats, *Yellow Peril! An Archive of Anti-Asian Fear* (London: Verso, 2014), 17.

18 Schwartz, "Walter Benjamin for Historians," 1724.

19 Beiner, "Walter Benjamin's Philosophy of History," 431.

20 Robert C. Allen and Douglas Gomery, *Film History: Theory and Practice* (New York: Knopf, 1985), 6.

21 Richard Maltby, "How Can Cinema History Matter More?," *Screening the Past* 22 (December 2007), accessed July 30, 2016, http://www.screeningthepast.com/2015/01/how-can-cinema-history-matter-more.

22 Janet Staiger, *Interpreting Films: Studies in the Historical Reception of American Cinema* (Princeton, NJ: Princeton University Press, 1992), 79–81.

23 Robert C. Allen, "Relocating American Film History," *Cultural Studies* 20, no. 1 (2006): 48–88; Robert C. Allen, "Decentering Historical Audience Studies: A Modest Proposal," in *Hollywood in the Neighborhood: Historical Case Studies of Local Moviegoing*, ed. Kathryn Fuller-Seeley (Berkeley: University of California Press, 2008), 20–34.

24 The notion of microhistory was theorized and adapted as a methodological approach by the Italian historian Carlo Ginzburg in the 1970s. His book *The Cheese and the Worms* detailed the worldview of a northern Italian miller in the sixteenth century and counts among the pioneering works within the genre. See Carlo Ginzburg, *The Cheese and the Worms: The Cosmos of a Sixteenth-Century Miller* (Baltimore: Johns Hopkins University Press, 1980). For two historiographical reviews of the topics and larger controversies of the past twenty years of microhistorical publications, see Giovanni Levi, "On Microhistory," *New Perspectives on Historical Writing* 2 (1991): 97–119; Carlo Ginzburg, John Tedeschi, and Anne C. Tedeschi, "Microhistory: Two or Three Things That I Know about It," *Critical Inquiry* 20, no. 1 (1993): 10–35.

25 The subject of local moviegoing in large U.S. East Coast cities has generated several influential articles, foremost published under the auspices of *Film History*. Summaries of developments pertaining to the "local turn" can be found in Kathryn Fuller-Seeley and George Potaminos, "Introduction: Researching and Writing the History of Local Moviegoing," in Fuller-Seeley, *Hollywood in the Neighborhood*, 3–19, and Van de Vijver and Biltereyst, "Cinemagoing as a Conditional Part of Everyday Life."

26 See, for example, Allen, "Relocating American Film History"; Maltby, "How Can Cinema History Matter More?"

27 In a more general critique of new historicism, media theorist Wolfgang Ernst has expressed concerns that the new historian's archival modus operandi is that of a selective flaneur, rather than a "rigorous" reader. Wolfgang Ernst, "Historiens textualitet? Arkiv och litteratur," in Wolfgang Ernst et al., *Sorlet Från Arkiven: Ordning Ur Oordning* (Göteborg: Glänta, 2008), 42. Charles Musser, while admitting that he has found it useful to think about cinema as an element of other histories, states that it has made him consider the term "film historian" as "at best

reductive." See "Historiographic Method and the Study of Early Cinema," *Cinema Journal* 44, no. 1 (2004): 105.

28 Maltby, "How Can Cinema History Matter More?"

29 Joel Frykholm, *Framing the Feature Film: Multi-reel Feature Film and American Film Culture in the 1910s* (Stockholm: Acta Universitatis Stockholmiensis, 2009), 74.

30 Barbara Klinger, "Film History Terminable and Interminable: Recovering the Past in Reception Studies," *Screen* 38, no. 2 (1997): 111.

31 For a particularly useful introduction to the practicalities of working in physical film and film-related archives, see Paolo Cherchi Usai, *Burning Passions: Introduction to the Study of Silent Cinema* (London: British Film Institute, 1994).

32 For a relatively "early" discussion of various archival experiences and methods of film historians working with records on microfilm, see Gordon Hendricks, *The Kinetoscope: America's First Commercially Successful Motion Picture Exhibitor* (New York: Beginnings of the American Film, 1966), xi.

33 "Digital humanities" have opened up the field to unprecedented modes and tools of inquiry. For this study, the launching of a project such as Media History Digital Library has been very important. Going online in 2011, the MHDL has continually made available source materials, primarily in the form of digitized, searchable copies of trade papers and fan magazines. While initially scrutinizing the collections in a manner similar to my method of working in physical archives, using in-text indexes, and the understanding of the editorial patterns and the visual style of the magazine that comes after some time spent on each individual publication, the ability to make in-text searches in the digitized PDF files made possible a different kind of systematic analysis of the sources. Soon, the MHDL launched its search engine, Lantern, which facilitates "searches" across individual publications. Search engines such as Lantern offer an unprecedented tool to access and analyze media history, but they also have inherent pitfalls and limitations. The possibility to "search" a digitized document relies on the quality of its textual information. While the MHDL's collections have comparatively high optical character recognition (OCR), the chances are high that documents of significant value to your study may pass through the search filters on account of a conversion incompatible with your customized term(s). The majority of source material made available through the collections is overwhelmingly in English-language publications. MHDL has pioneered the availability of historical documents worldwide, but it is not accessible through connections that "geo-block" its material. While *Lantern* is not the only database consulted, it offers some insight into the benefits and drawbacks of working with digital sources.

34 Eric Hoyt, Wendy Hagenmaier, and Carl Hagenmaier, "Media + History + Digital + Library: An Experiment in Synthesis," *Journal of E-Media Studies* 3, no. 1 (2013): 1–21; Eric Hoyt, "Lenses for Lantern: Data Mining, Visualization, and Excavating Film History's Neglected Sources," *Film History* 26, no. 2 (2014): 146–168; Richard Abel, "The Pleasures and Perils of Big Data in Digitized Newspapers," *Film History* 25, no. 1 (2013): 1–10.

35 Richard Abel, *The Red Rooster Scare: Making Cinema American, 1900–1910* (Berkeley: University of California Press, 1999), 84–85.

36 The *Chronicle* is available through Proquest, while the California Digital Newspaper Collection includes the *Call* up until December 31, 1913.

37 Jan Olsson, "Pressing Inroads: Metaspectators and the Nickelodeon Culture," in *Screen Culture: History and Textuality*, ed. John Fullerton (Eastleigh: John Libbey,

2004), 116. In articles, essays, and monographs, Olsson has developed his approach to local journalism as a gainful point of entry to studying the nuances of local film culture while offering a contemporarily palpable connection to panoramic perspectives of film history through the notion of nationwide syndication. Also see Jan Olsson, *Los Angeles before Hollywood: Journalism and American Film Culture, 1905 to 1915* (Stockholm: National Library of Sweden, 2008); Jan Olsson, "Pressing Matters: Media Crusades before the Nickelodeons," *Film History* 27, no. 2 (2015): 105–139.

38 According to Moore, "The newspaper became a tool for organizing moviegoing and leisure time—a tool transformed into a technology of great efficiency for its ability to chart an amusement 'menu' of the selections available across the entire city, which could be sampled and selected without requiring the time of travel." Paul S. Moore, "Subscribing to Publicity: Syndicated Newspaper Features for Moviegoing in North America, 1911–15," *Early Popular Visual Culture* 12, no. 2 (2014): 269–270.

39 Richard Abel, *Menus for Movieland: Newspapers and the Emergence of American Film Culture* (Berkeley: University of California Press, 2015).

40 Alexander Saxton, *The Indispensable Enemy: Labor and the Anti-Chinese Movement in California* (Berkeley: University of California Press, 1971), 46.

41 According to Saxton's survey of the Chinese Californian labor force, the Chinese constituted one-quarter to one-fifth of those working for wages during these decades; see Saxton, 258.

42 Edwin Legrand Sabin, *Building the Pacific Railway: The Construction-Story of America's First Iron Thoroughfare between the Missouri River and California, from the Inception of the Great Idea to the Day, May 10, 1869, When the Union Pacific and the Central Pacific Joined Tracks at Promontory Point, Utah, to Form the Nation's Transcontinental* (Philadelphia: Lippincott, 1919), 111.

43 An excerpt from Article IV reads, "It is further agreed that citizens of the United States in China, of every religious persuasion, and Chinese subjects in the United States, shall enjoy entire liberty of conscience, and shall be exempt from all disability or persecution on account of their religious faith or worship in either country." *Text of the Treaty between China & the United States Generally Known as the Burlingame Treaty of 1868* (San Francisco, 1879), 5.

44 Gray A. Brechin, *Imperial San Francisco: Urban Power, Earthly Ruin* (Berkeley: University of California Press, 2001).

45 For an excellent biography on Hearst, see David Nasaw, *The Chief: The Life of William Randolph Hearst* (Boston: Houghton Mifflin, 2000).

46 Alexander Saxton, *The Rise, and Fall of the White Republic: Class Politics and Mass Culture in Nineteenth-Century America* (London: Verso, 1990), 295–297.

47 Saxton, *Indispensable Enemy*, 114.

48 Chris Carlson, "The Workingmen's Party & The Dennis Kearney Agitation," FoundSF, 1995, accessed March 15, 2016, http://www.foundsf.org/index.php?title=The_Workingmen%E2%80%99s_Party_%26_The_Dennis_Kearney_Agitation.

49 I communicated inquiries into specific dates and events, mostly through e-mail, and at times in person, which Professor Choy attempted to locate in his collection of the newspaper. More than scholar with a vast knowledge of Chinatown history, Phil Choy was a prominent architect who designed and oversaw many constructions in the neighborhood, including some of the buildings that housed the area's first movie theaters.

50 Again, with the kind help of the Chinese Historical Society of America.

51 Erica Y. Z. Pan, *The Impact of the 1906 Earthquake on San Francisco's Chinatown* (New York: P. Lang, 1995); Yumei Sun, "From Isolation to Participation: 'Chung Sai Yat Po' (China West Daily) and San Francisco's Chinatown, 1900–1920" (PhD diss., University of Maryland College Park, 1999); Yong Chen, *Chinese San Francisco, 1850–1943: A Trans-Pacific Community* (Stanford, CA: Stanford University Press, 2000).

52 Rey Chow, "Introduction: On Chineseness as a Theoretical Problem," *Boundary 2* 25, no. 3 (Fall 1998): 1–24.

53 Sucheng Chan, "Chinese American Historiography: What Difference has the Asian American Movement Made?" in *Chinese Americans and the Politics of Race and Culture*, ed. Sucheng Chan and Madeline Yuan-yin Hsu (Philadelphia: Temple University Press, 2008), 1–61.

54 The cultural perspective and privilege inherent in my biography could indeed also be used to put the writing of this study into further perspective. While such analysis is probably best left to someone else, I will provide some details. I am a male from Scandinavia. The eugenics movement of the early twentieth century would have identified me as born into the "superior race," but my ancestors resisted and fled from the Nazis' occupation of Norway. I grew up in Åkersberga, in the "nice" part of what was commonly recognized as a "bad" suburb of Stockholm. I am the second child of four to secularized Protestant middle-class parents. My father is a dentist. My mother is a painter.

55 "Extending or operating across national boundaries," as defined in the *Oxford Dictionary of U.S. English*.

56 Miriam Hansen, "Vernacular Modernism: Tracking Cinema on a Global Scale," in *World Cinemas, Transnational Perspectives*, ed. Nataša Durovicová and Kathleen E. Newman (New York: Routledge, 2009), 305.

57 See, for example, Linda Tuhiwai Smith, *Decolonizing Methodologies*, 2nd ed. (London: Zed Books, 2012).

58 Olsson, *Los Angeles before Hollywood*, 16.

59 For a concise discussion of historical notions of "Chineseness," see Daphne Pi-Wei Lei, *Operatic China* (New York: Palgrave Macmillan, 2006), 6–7.

60 See, for example, Lewis Jacobs, *The Rise of the American Film, a Critical History. With an Essay: Experimental Cinema in America, 1921–1947* (New York: Teachers College Press, 1968); Robert Sklar, *Movie-Made America: A Cultural History of American Movies* (New York: Random House, 1975); Charles Musser, *History of the American Cinema. 1. The Emergence of Cinema: The American Screen to 1907*, ed. Charles Harpole (New York: Scribner, 1990).

61 Robert C. Allen, "Motion Picture Exhibition in Manhattan 1906–1912: Beyond the Nickelodeon," *Cinema Journal* 18, no. 2 (1979): 2–15.

62 This extensive debate was particularly useful in terms of defining notions of *class* and *ethnicity* in relation to film audiences of the early nickelodeon era; see Ben Singer, "Manhattan Nickelodeons: New Data on Audiences and Exhibitors," *Cinema Journal* 34, no. 3 (1995): 5–35; Sumiko Higashi, "Dialogue: Manhattan's Nickelodeons. Sumiko Higashi on Ben Singer's 'Manhattan Nickelodeons: New Data on Audiences and Exhibitors," *Cinema Journal* 35, no. 3 (1996): 72–74; Robert C. Allen, "Manhattan Myopia; Or, Oh! Iowa! Robert C. Allen on Ben Singer's 'Manhattan Nickelodeons: New Data on Audiences and Exhibitors,' 'Cinema Journal' 34, No. 3 (Spring 1995)," *Cinema Journal* 35, no. 3 (1996): 75–103; Ben Singer, "New York, Just Like I Pictured It . . . Ben Singer Responds," *Cinema*

*Journal* 35, no. 3 (1996): 104–128; William Uricchio and Roberta E. Pearson, "Manhattan's Nickelodeons. New York? New York! William Uricchio and Roberta E. Pearson Comment on the Singer-Allen Exchange," *Cinema Journal* 36, no. 4 (1997): 98–102; Judith Thissen, "Oh, Myopia! A Reaction from Judith Thissen on the Singer-Allen Controversy," *Cinema Journal* 36, no. 4 (1997): 102–107; Ben Singer, "Manhattan Melodrama: A Response from Ben Singer," *Cinema Journal* 36, no. 4 (1997): 107–112.

63 This complication was acknowledged to some degree by all sides involved and can be summed up by Ben Singer's conclusion that the neighborhood analysis method provided "no way of knowing who actually ventured into the theaters and with what frequency." See Singer, "New York, Just Like I Pictured It," 106. In a subsequent response to the critique of the demography-audience correlation, Singer defended his position by arguing that "it is simply common sense to expect that a theater's audience would bear some resemblance to the surrounding neighborhood's population. . . . Demographic generalizations are not perfectly accurate, but for certain areas, they can be *reasonably* accurate." Singer, "Manhattan Melodrama," 109–110.

64 Rebecca Solnit and Susan Schwartzenberg, *Hollow City: The Siege of San Francisco and the Crisis of American Urbanism* (Verso, 2002); Rebecca Solnit, Ben Pease, and Shizue Siegel, *Infinite City: A San Francisco Atlas* (Berkeley: University of California Press, 2010).

65 Mayer, "Glittering Machine of Modernity, 661–684; Ruth Mayer, "'The Greatest Novelty of the Age': Fu-Manchu, Chinatown, and the Global City," in *Chinatowns in a Transnational World: Myths and Realities of an Urban Phenomenon*, ed. Vanessa Künnemann and Ruth Mayer (New York: Routledge, 2011), 116–134.

66 Mayer, "The Greatest Novelty of the Age," 119–120.

67 The entire quote reads as follows: "There are also, probably in every culture, in every civilization, real places—places that do exist and that are formed in the very founding of society—which are something like counter-sites, a kind of effectively enacted utopia in which the real sites, all the other real sites that can be found within the culture, are simultaneously represented, contested, and inverted. Places of this kind are outside of all places, even though it may be possible to indicate their location in reality. Because these places are absolutely different from all the sites that they reflect and speak about, I shall call them, by way of contrast to utopias, heterotopias." See Michel Foucault, "Of Other Spaces, Heterotopias," *Architecture, Mouvement, Continuité* 5 (1984): 46–49.

68 Miriam Hansen, *Babel and Babylon: Spectatorship in American Silent Film* (Cambridge, MA: Harvard University Press, 1994), 108.

69 Hansen, 108.

70 This study's appropriation of the notion of thirdspace will henceforth be referred to as "thirdspace," to distinguish it from Edward Soja's concept, which he consistently capitalizes as "Thirdspace," and Homi Bhabha's usage of the term referred to as "third space."

71 In some instances, Bhabha's notion of the third space has been used sporadically to address notions of cultural hybridity in textual analyses of films. None of these accounts have explored the term to conceptualize film audiences or exhibition history. See, for example, Dal Yong Jin, "Critical Interpretation of Hybridisation in Korean Cinema: Does the Local Film Industry Create 'The Third Space'?," *Javnost—The Public* 17, no. 1 (2010): 55–71; Patrick F. Campos, "'Manila by Night'

as Thirdspace," *Kritika Kultura* 19 (August 2012): 139–165; Saër Maty Bâ and Kate E. Taylor-Jones, "Affective Passions: The Dancing Female Body and Colonial Rupture in Zouzou (1934) and Karmen Geï (2001)," in *De-Westernizing Film Studies*, ed. Saër Maty Bâ and Will Higbee (New York: Routledge, 2012), 53–66; Rebecca Weaver-Hightower, "The Postcolonial Hybrid," *Postcolonial Film: History, Empire, Resistance*, ed. Rebecca Weaver-Hightower and Peter Hulme (New York: Routledge, 2014), 247–266.

72 Soja refers to philosopher and sociologist Henri Lefebvre's concept of the spatial triad, outlined in *The Production of Space*. In it, Lefebvre constantly returns to three kinds of interactive concepts: *spatial practice, representation of space*, and *representational spaces*. It is the third concept, the space of "inhabitants and users . . . the dominated—and hence passively experienced—space which the imagination seeks to change and appropriate," which Soja draws extensively upon to outline the concept of Thirdspace. See Henri Lefebvre, *The Production of Space*, trans. Donald Nicholson-Smith (Malden, MA: Wiley-Blackwell, 1992), 38–40.

73 Christian Borch, "Interview with Edward W. Soja: Thirdspace, Postmetropolis, and Social Theory," *Distinktion: Scandinavian Journal of Social Theory* 3, no. 1 (January 2002): 113–115. Soja labeled the distinction of material space as "Firstspace," and mental space as "Secondspace," in Borch, 114–115. These distinctions were slight reappropriations of Lefvebre's notions of *representations of space* and *spatial practice*. See Edward W. Soja, *Thirdspace: Journeys to Los Angeles and Other Real-and-Imagined Places* (Cambridge, MA: Blackwell, 1996), 10.

74 Tchen and Yeats, *Yellow Peril!*, 34.

75 Bhabha stated his ambition as finding the instances where Western culture, "its liberalism and relativism—these very potent mythologies of 'progress'—also contain a cutting edge." Jonathan Rutherford and Homi Bhabha, "The Third Space: Interview with Homi Bhabha," in *Identity: Community, Culture, Difference*, ed. Jonathan Rutherford (London: Lawrence and Wishart, 1998), 209.

76 Rutherford and Bhabha, 209.

77 Homi K. Bhabha, *The Location of Culture* (New York: Routledge, 1994), 2.

78 Fernando Coronil, "Introduction," in Fernando Ortiz, *Cuban Counterpoint, Tobacco and Sugar* (Durham, NC: Duke University Press, 1995); Mary Louise Pratt, *Imperial Eyes: Travel Writing and Transculturation* (London: Routledge, 1992).

79 Coronil, "Introduction," xvi.

80 Ortiz, *Cuban Counterpoint*.

81 Pratt, *Imperial Eyes*, 4.

82 Edward W. Said, *Culture & Imperialism* (London: Vintage, 1994), 52, 336.

83 Sebastian Jobs and Gesa Mackenthun, eds., *Agents of Transculturation: Border-Crossers, Mediators, Go-Betweens* (Münster: Waxmann, 2013), 14.

84 Coronil, "Introduction," xvi.

85 James Hay, "Piecing Together What Remains of the Cinematic City," in *The Cinematic City*, ed. David Clarke (London: Routledge, 1997), 212.

86 Tchen and Yeats, *Yellow Peril!*, 34.

## Chapter 1 Bold Visions and Frontier Conditions

1 Geoffrey Bell, *The Golden Gate and the Silver Screen* (Rutherford, NJ: Fairleigh Dickinson University Press 1984).

2 Jack Tillmany, *Theatres of San Francisco* (Charleston, SC: Arcadia Publishing, 2005).

3 Brechin, *Imperial San Francisco*; Sarah J. Moore, *Empire on Display: San Francisco's Panama-Pacific International Exposition of 1915* (Norman: University of Oklahoma Press, 2013.

4 Tom Gunning's essays on the experience of modernity and early film have been particularly influential on this topic. A subsequent debate, on whether modernity ushered in a perceptual change in the human mind, was labeled by David Bordwell as the "modernity thesis." See Tom Gunning, "Heard over the Phone: The Lonely Villa and the de Lorde Tradition of the Terrors of Technology," *Screen* 32, no. 2 (1991): 184–196; Tom Gunning, "'Now You See It, Now You Don't': The Temporality of the Cinema of Attractions," *Velvet Light Trap* 32 (Fall 1993): 71–84; Tom Gunning, "The Whole Town's Gawking: Early Cinema and the Visual Experience of Modernity," *Yale Journal of Criticism* 7, no. 2 (Fall 1994): 189–201; David Bordwell, *On the History of Film Style* (Cambridge, MA: Harvard University Press, 1997), 141–146; Charlie Keil, "To Here from Modernity: Style, Historiography, and Transitional Cinema," in *American Cinema's Transitional Era: Audiences, Institutions, Practices*, ed. Charlie Keil and Shelley Stamp (Berkeley: University of California Press, 2004), 51–65; Tom Gunning, "Modernity and Cinema: A Culture of Shocks and Flows," in *Cinema and Modernity*, ed. Murray Pomerance (New Brunswick, NJ: Rutgers University Press, 2006), 297–315.

5 Rebecca Solnit, *Motion Studies: Time, Space and Eadweard Muybridge* (London: Bloomsbury, 2004), 3.

6 The Ottawa-based Holland Brothers were Edison's East Coast agents for the kinetoscope and also proprietors of the world's first kinetoscope parlor in New York. For a history of the Holland Brothers and early Canadian film culture, see Peter Morris, *Embattled Shadows: A History of Canadian Cinema, 1895–1939* (Montreal: McGill-Queen's University Press, 1992), 1–26.

7 "Decoyed to Death," *San Francisco Chronicle*, August 5, 1893, 16.

8 A classified listing in the *San Francisco Call* shows that Bacigalupi was trying to sell his kinetoscope parlor on Spring Street, in Los Angeles, after a couple weeks of operation. According to Bacigalupi, the establishment would bring its new owner twenty-five dollars daily. "Business Opportunities," *San Francisco Call*, October 3, 1894, 5.

9 "San Francisco, Cal., Dates Back to the Year 1894," *Moving Picture World*, July 15, 1916, 399.

10 Editorial, *San Francisco Chronicle*, March 8, 1894, 6.

11 "The Edison Kinetoscope," *San Francisco Call*, June 5, 1894, 10; "Gossip," *San Francisco Call*, August 19, 1894, 6.

12 H. S. Crocker Company, *Crocker-Langley San Francisco Directory for the Year Commencing 1898* (San Francisco: H. S. Crocker Company, 1899), 667.

13 "Toiling under the Red Cross," *San Francisco Call*, June 1, 1896, 12.

14 Bell, *The Golden Gate and the Silver Screen*, 100.

15 "San Francisco, Cal., Dates Back to the Year 1894," *Moving Picture World*, July 15, 1916, 399.

16 Cineograph program, July 1898, cited in Bell, *The Golden Gate and the Silver Screen*, 100.

17 The Los Angeles branch, as in San Francisco, started with both vaudeville and film, where Furst imported his stage talent from San Francisco. After a period of little success, Furst again settled on being film exclusive. See "New Vaudeville Theater," *Los Angeles Herald*, August 28, 1902, 7; "Cineograph," *Los Angeles Herald*, August 31, 1902, front page, part four; Olsson, *Los Angeles before Hollywood*, 105.

18 Charles Beardsley, *Hollywood's Master Showman: The Legendary Sid Grauman* (New York: Cornwall Books, 1983), 21.

19 Beardsley, 28.

20 "D. J. Grauman Early in the Game," *Moving Picture World*, July 15, 1916, 400.

21 Beardsley wrote that both the Unique and the Lyceum were "very successful houses." However, reports in the *Call* between the years 1903 and 1906 suggest that the Graumans had to give up both management and ownership of the Lyceum for some time, due to financial problems. See Beardsley, *Hollywood's Master Showman*, 29; "Grauman Sells Theater Stock," *San Francisco Call*, August 7, 1903, 14; "D. J. Grauman Demolishes Showhouse," *San Francisco Call*, January 30, 16.

22 Musser, *History of the American Cinema*, 366.

23 Musser, 367.

24 Abel, *Red Rooster Scare*, 22. Both Musser and Abel dated the Miles Brothers' operation to around late 1903. However, this does not seem to account for their early start in San Francisco.

25 Advertisement, *New York Clipper*, February 25, 1905, 22; "Miles Brothers, Pioneers," *Moving Picture World*, July 10, 1915, 248.

26 The Miles Brothers' advertisements were often "wordy" endorsements of their superiority, often owing to their status as pioneers of the film exchange system. See advertisements in *New York Clipper*, February 25, 1905, 22; *New York Clipper*, July 25, 1905, 540; *Billboard*, August 5, 1905, 26; *New York Clipper*, September 23, 1905, 794; *Billboard*, September 30, 1905, 48; *New York Clipper*, November 25, 1905, 1085; *Billboard*, December 2, 1905, 29; *Billboard*, January 27, 1906, 40; *Billboard*, February 10, 1906, 48; *Billboard*, February 24, 1906, 48; *Billboard*, March 3, 1906, 34; *Billboard*, March 17, 1906, 83.

27 "Miles Brothers Made Early Start," *Moving Picture World*, July 15, 1916, 400.

28 Advertisements seen in the *New York Clipper* throughout 1905 establishes this connection. See *New York Clipper*, January 21, 1905, 1141; January 28, 1905, 1161; April 22, 1905, 220.

29 Revisionist film historians prompted a spirited discussion in the late 1970s regarding the use of movies as a way to get audiences out of vaudeville theaters around the turn of the twentieth century. Robert C. Allen, in several installments, countered previous historians' assertion that the early development of U.S. cinema was defined by a period where movies were used as "chasers." Allen countered important film historians such as Robert Grau, Gilbert Seldes, and Lewis Jacobs, of devising a "chaser theory," unsubstantiated by historical evidence. See Robert C. Allen, *Vaudeville and Film 1895–1915: A Study in Media Interaction* (New York: Arno Press, 1980); Robert C. Allen, "Contra the 'Chaser Theory,'" *Wide Angle* 3, no. 1 (1979): 4–11. The perpetuation of the "chaser theory" was credited to Robert Grau, *The Theatre of Science: A Volume of Progress and Achievement in the Motion Picture Industry* (New York: Broadway Publishing, 1914); Gilbert Seldes, *An Hour with the Movies and the Talkies* (Philadelphia: Lippincott, 1929); Jacobs, *The Rise of the American Film*. In a series of retorts, Charles Musser, in turn, countered Allen's claims. The dialogue produced a useful discussion of source material, methodology, and historiography of revisionist forays into the history of early cinema. See Charles Musser, "Another Look at the 'Chaser Theory," *Studies in Visual Communication* 10, no. 4 (1984): 24–44; Robert C. Allen, "Looking at 'Another Look at the "Chaser Theory,"'" *Studies in Visual Communication* 10,

no. 4 (1984): 45–50; Charles Musser, "Musser's Reply to Allen," *Studies in Visual Communication* 10, no. 4 (1984): 51–52.

30 Advertisement, *Billboard*, March 24, 1906, 48.

31 *Crocker-Langley San Francisco Business Directory for the Year Ending December 31st, 1906* (San Francisco: H. S. Crocker Company, 1907), 442.

32 Musser, *History of the American Cinema*, 417–418; Abel, *Red Rooster Scare*, 32.

33 "Miles Brothers Made Early Start," *Moving Picture World*, July 15, 1916, 400.

34 Advertisement, *New York Clipper*, December 9, 1905, 1088.

35 "The Plays at the Theaters," *San Francisco Chronicle*, June 26, 7; "The Chutes," *San Francisco Call*, January 2, 1906, 14, "Chutes," *San Francisco Call*, February 20, 1906, 9; "Amusements," *San Francisco Chronicle*, March 12, 1906, 7, "Amusements," *San Francisco Chronicle*, April 5, 1906, 9.

36 "Amusements," *San Francisco Call*, February 4, 1906, 41; "California," *San Francisco Call*, February 6, 1906, 7.

37 Musser, *History of the American Cinema*, 168; Tillmany, *Theatres of San Francisco*, 106

38 Lecturers described the regional surroundings in tandem with stereopticon views at the Academy of Sciences Hall, located on Market Street, between Fourth and Fifth Streets; see "Amusements," *San Francisco Call*, January 5, 1906, 5; "Amusements," *San Francisco Call*, January 22, 1906, 5. Peter Bacigalupi remembered having seen W.K.L. Dickson's Biograph productions of Pope Leo XIII at an unsuccessful screening at the Metropolitan Hall; "San Francisco, Cal., Dates Back to the Year 1894," *Moving Picture World*, July 15, 1916, 399.

39 "Depicts Beauty of Indian Land," *San Francisco Call*, February 24, 1906, 14.

40 Musser, *History of the American Cinema*, 233.

41 See, for example, White and Blechynden's *Return of a Lifeboat* (Edison, 1898) and *Arrest in Chinatown* (Edison, 1897).

42 Haddad, "The Laundry Man's Got a Knife!," 35.

43 "Arrest and Death of Tom King Yung May Bring International Trouble," *San Francisco Call*, September 15, 1903, 3.

44 "Tom Kim Yung's Death Charged to Policeman," *San Francisco Call*, October 6, 1903, 2; "Decide Arrest Was Justified," *San Francisco Call*, February 17, 1904, 3.

45 The film's catalog entry at the Library of Congress suggests that it was shot in 1900 and that it shows what is most likely Washington Place, between Washington and Jackson Streets. See Howard Lamarr Walls, *Motion Pictures, 1894–1912, Identified from the Records of the United States Copyright Office* (Washington, DC: Library of Congress, 1953), 53; "Scene in Chinatown," Library of Congress website, accessed July 31, 2016, http://www.loc.gov/item/00694411.

46 "After Photographs of Market Street—Miles Brothers Would Show Moving Pictures in the East," *San Francisco Call*, March 29, 1906, 7.

47 David Kiehn, "Miles Brothers: Film Pioneers in SF," *The Argonaut: Journal of the San Francisco Museum and Historical Society* 20, no. 2 (2009), 72–85.

48 The Imperial immediately became one of the downtown area's most popular theaters. Tillmany, *Theatres of San Francisco*, 9.

49 Jack London, "The Story of an Eyewitness," *Collier's*, May 5, 1906.

50 Advertisement, *Billboard*, May 5, 1906, 26.

51 "Miles Brothers Made Early Start," *Moving Picture World*, July 15, 1916, 400.

52 Robert S. Birchard, "Miles Brothers," in *Encyclopedia of Early Cinema*, ed. Richard Abel (London: Routledge, 2005), 436; Tom Gunning, "Motion Picture Distributing and Sales Company," in Abel, *Encyclopedia of Early Cinema*, 447.

53 "Miles Brothers, Pioneers," *Moving Picture World*, July 10, 1915, 248
54 "D. J. Grauman Early in the Game," *Moving Picture World*, July 15, 1916, 400.
55 The film exchange was located "in the rear of the penny arcade adjoining" and was called the Nickelodium Company; "The Lessers Arrive," *Moving Picture World*, July 15, 1916, 400.
56 "The Lessers Arrive," *Moving Picture World*, July 15, 1916, 400.
57 "After the Quake and Fire," *Moving Picture World*, July 15, 1916, 400.
58 The kinetoscope licenses had brought in $6,775. Theater licenses were separate; thirty-two of them were granted in 1911, for a total amount of $5,742; San Francisco Board of Supervisors, *San Francisco Municipal Reports Fiscal Year 1910–11, Ending June 30, 1911* (San Francisco: San Francisco Board of Supervisors, 1911), 106, 720.
59 San Francisco Board of Supervisors, *San Francisco Municipal Reports Fiscal Year 1907–8, Ending June 30, 1908* (San Francisco: San Francisco Board of Supervisors, 1909), 453.
60 San Francisco Board of Supervisors, *San Francisco Municipal Reports Fiscal Year 1908–9, Ending June 30, 1909* (San Francisco: San Francisco Board of Supervisors, 1909), 1175.
61 Singer, "Manhattan Nickelodeons," 27. Earlier observations about the instability of business were made by Robert C. Allen, among others, in his dissertation, "Vaudeville and Film 1895–1915," 202–212.
62 San Francisco Board of Supervisors, *San Francisco Municipal Reports Fiscal Year 1909–10, Ending June 30, 1910* (San Francisco: San Francisco Board of Supervisors, 1910), 857.
63 San Francisco Board of Supervisors, *San Francisco Municipal Reports Fiscal Year 1910–11, Ending June 30, 1911* (San Francisco: San Francisco Board of Supervisors, 1911), 720.
64 San Francisco Board of Supervisors, *San Francisco Municipal Reports Fiscal Year 1911–12, Ending June 30, 1912* (San Francisco: San Francisco Board of Supervisors, 1912), 494.
65 San Francisco Board of Supervisors, *San Francisco Municipal Reports Fiscal Year 1915–16, Ending June 30, 1916* (San Francisco: San Francisco Board of Supervisors, 1916), 437.
66 San Francisco Board of Supervisors, *San Francisco Municipal Reports Fiscal Year 1916–17, Ending June 30, 1917* (San Francisco: San Francisco Board of Supervisors, 1917), 791.
67 "After the Quake and Fire," *Moving Picture World*, July 15, 1916, 400.
68 C. L. Mosely, "The Mercury Arc-Rectifier," *Moving Picture World*, October 14, 1911, 134.
69 The mission building was constructed in 1791 and remains San Francisco's oldest building.
70 Bernadette Hooper, *San Francisco's Mission District* (Charleston, SC: Arcadia Publishing, 2006), 7.
71 "The Mission District." *Moving Picture World*, July 15, 1916, 402.
72 Tillmany, *Theatres of San Francisco*, 82.
73 List of San Francisco theaters in *Billboard*, December 10, 1910, 101.
74 The name was later shortened to Nihonmachi, or Japantown. The Japanese presence defines the neighborhood to this day, including businesses like the Sundance Kabuki Cinema on Post Street.

75 "After the Quake and Fire," *Moving Picture World*, July 15, 1916, 401.

76 Tillmany, *Theatres of San Francisco*, 102.

77 Local writer Ona Otto reported for *Moving Picture World*; "San Francisco," *Moving Picture World*, September 16, 1911, 808.

78 Both houses had a capacity of 400 seats.

79 "The Fillmore District," *Moving Picture World*, July 15, 1916, 402.

80 "Kahn & Greenfield Circuit," *Moving Picture World*, July 10, 1915.

81 "Kahn & Greenfield Circuit," *Moving Picture World*, July 10, 1915.

82 "San Francisco," *Moving Picture World*, February 21, 1914, 981.

83 "The Downtown District," *Moving Picture World*, July 15, 1916, 402.

84 "The Downtown District," *Moving Picture World*, July 15, 1916, 401.

85 "Warner's Features Popular on Coast," *Moving Picture World*, September 12, 1913, 602.

86 Death notice for Lesser Lesser, *San Francisco Call*, May 15, 1910, 32.

87 In 1976, Hal Mohr recalled the production process of the Golden Gate newsreel: "It was sort of a one-man band. I would photograph the thing—I'd go out and cover these news events all over the San Francisco area with this camera, come in, develop the negative and make the print. Then I had a little printing press. I'd set up the titles and photograph them and assemble and cut the negative, put it together. . . . I think we made something like 20 or 25 prints, which I'd run off every Friday night. I'd run these prints through, print them and develop them, put the darn things together and then ship them out for their Saturday release all over the state. This was the Golden Gate Weekly." See George C. Pratt "Camera on the Move: An Interview with Hal Mohr," *Journal of Photography and Motion Pictures of the International Museum of Photography at George Eastman House* 19, no. 1 (March 1976): 16–19.

88 The Empress was designed by John Galen Howard, who had previously designed the Electric Tower, which had been the centerpiece at the 1901 Pan-American Exposition in Buffalo. See *Official Catalogue and Guide Book to the Pan-American Exposition: With Maps of Exposition and Illustrations, Buffalo, N.Y., U.S.A., May 1st to Nov. 1st, 1901* (Buffalo, NY: Charles Ahrhart, 1901), 7.

89 Tillmany, *Theatres of San Francisco*, 25.

90 "Empress Theatre," theater programs from 1911–1914, Folder 47, Theater, San Francisco Performing Arts Library and Museum; "Empress, San Francisco," *Billboard*, July 15, 1915, 11.

91 Stacey Endres and Robert Cushman, *Hollywood at Your Feet: The Story of the World-Famous Chinese Theater* (Universal City, CA: Pomegranate Press, 2009).

92 "Manager of Empress Becomes Producer," *San Francisco Chronicle*, August 13, 1916, 24; "Empress, San Francisco," *Billboard*, December 2, 1916, 6.

93 "The Downtown District," *Moving Picture World*, July 15, 1916, 401.

94 "Tivoli Opera-House Now Motion Picture Theater," *San Francisco Chronicle*, January 6, 1913, 26.

95 "The Downtown District," *Moving Picture World*, July 15, 1916, 401.

## Chapter 2 "If I Had the Power to Do So I Would Destroy Them with My Own Hands"

1 For two studies of the interrelated developments of U.S. Progressivism and the establishment of film culture, see Lee Grieveson, *Policing Cinema: Movies and Censorship in Early-Twentieth-Century America* (Berkeley: University of California Press, 2004), and Moya Luckett, *Cinema and Community: Progressivism,*

*Exhibition, and Film Culture in Chicago, 1907–1917* (Detroit: Wayne State University Press, 2013).

2 Charlie Keil and Ben Singer, *American Cinema of the 1910s: Themes and Variations* (New Brunswick, NJ: Rutgers University Press, 2009), 1.

3 Luckett, *Cinema and Community*, 9.

4 Peterson described these two lateral forces as one that advocated the use of "repressive forces of censorship," and one that "embraced cinema as a positive force." See Jennifer Peterson, "'The Knowledge Which Comes in Pictures': Educational Films and Early Cinema Audiences," in *A Companion to Early Cinema*, ed. André Gaudreault, Nicolas Dulac, and Santiago Hidalgo (Malden, MA: Wiley-Blackwell, 2012), 280.

5 Andrea Rees Davies, *Saving San Francisco: Relief and Recovery after the 1906 Disaster* (Philadelphia: Temple University Press, 2011), 42–43.

6 Abel, *Red Rooster Scare*, xii.

7 The turn of the twentieth century saw the emergence of a "progressive" political era in the United States. Beginning as local initiatives geared toward countering political corruption, the progressives soon developed into a broad-based movement set on modernizing the infrastructure of U.S. society through the introduction of reform policies, which were often formulated in tandem with scientific methods. For two critical studies of the Progressive Era, see Richard Hofstadter, *The Age of Reform* (New York: Vintage, 1960), and Lewis L. Gould, *America in the Progressive Era, 1890–1914* (New York: Longman, 2001).

8 Addams founded Hull House in Chicago, which became the base for her social work. For an excellent chapter on the growing influence of Addams's work as a social scholar in the early 1900s, see Allen F. Davis, *American Heroine: The Life and Legend of Jane Addams* (repr., Chicago: Ivan R. Dee, 2000), 93–109.

9 Zenas L. Potter, *The Social Survey: A Bibliography* (New York: Russell Sage Foundation, 1915).

10 Singer, "New York, Just Like I Pictured It," 124.

11 The Russell Sage bibliography included thirty-eight surveys under the heading of "Vice."

12 It was Addams who conceived of the idea of a benevolent organization, which conducted nonpartisan studies of public affairs.

13 "Appendix B," in Commonwealth Club of California, *Transactions of the Commonwealth Club of California*, 8, no. 5 (San Francisco: Commonwealth Club of California, 1913), 305.

14 The survey was presented alongside theater, opera, and vaudeville under the umbrella rubric "shows." The period allotted was from January 1912 up until its time of presentation (May 14, 1913). But for the sake of clarity, the investigators had chosen to disclose of the data only for the period January 1912 to January 1913. See Commonwealth Club of California, *Transactions of the Commonwealth Club of California*, 189.

15 The estimated yearly attendance in San Francisco movie houses in 1915 was 19,435,584; see "Report Shows How Popular Moving Pictures Are," *Moving Picture World*, February 20, 1915, 1160.

16 Commonwealth Club of California, *Transactions of the Commonwealth Club of California*, 228.

17 Commonwealth Club of California, *Transactions of the Commonwealth Club of California*, 228

18 Commonwealth Club of California, *Transactions of the Commonwealth Club of California*, 235.
19 The statistics provided were based on research into eight vaudeville houses, but the survey comments that these numbers showed uniformity with other theaters. Commonwealth Club of California, *Transactions of the Commonwealth Club of California*, 239.
20 Commonwealth Club of California, *Transactions of the Commonwealth Club of California*, 261.
21 Commonwealth Club of California, *Transactions of the Commonwealth Club of California*, 262.
21 Commonwealth Club of California, *Transactions of the Commonwealth Club of California*, 263.
22 Jane Addams, *The Spirit of Youth and the City Streets* (New York: Macmillan, 1909).
23 Commonwealth Club of California, *Transactions of the Commonwealth Club of California*, 186–187.
24 Commonwealth Club of California, *Transactions of the Commonwealth Club of California*, 291.
25 Olsson, "Pressing Matters," 105–139.
26 An early example of such press crusades against nickel culture was conducted against Peter Bacigalupi's San Francisco establishment before the earthquake. Olsson, 105–139.
27 "Say Pictures Are Immoral," *San Francisco Chronicle*, March 7, 1907, 7.
28 "Father Caraher Fights against 'Keilodeon,'" *San Francisco Chronicle*, September 13, 1908, 13
29 "Deadline for Nickelodeon," *San Francisco Chronicle*, October 10, 1908, 16.
30 San Francisco Board of Supervisors, *San Francisco Municipal Reports Fiscal Year 1910–11, Ending June 30, 1911* (San Francisco: San Francisco Board of Supervisors, 1912), 1178.
31 "Nickelodeon Proprietors Ask Supervisors to Leave Construction Order to Subordinates," *San Francisco Chronicle*, July 2, 1909, 7; "Nickelodeons and the Police Commissioners," *San Francisco Chronicle*, September 4, 1909, 5.
32 Lewis Francis Byington, "Peter A. Peshon," in *History of San Francisco*, vol. 3 (Chicago: S. J. Clarke Publishing, 1931), 295–296.
33 "Astredo Resigns Job of Reviewing Pictures," *San Francisco Call*, March 19, 1911, 53; "New Censorship Board Holds Initial Session," *San Francisco Call*, August 12, 1912, 15.
34 San Francisco Board of Supervisors, *San Francisco Municipal Reports Fiscal Year 1912–13, Ending June 30, 1913* (San Francisco: San Francisco Board of Supervisors, 1913), 438.
35 San Francisco Board of Supervisors, *San Francisco Municipal Reports Fiscal Year 1913–14, Ending June 30, 1914* (San Francisco: San Francisco Board of Supervisors, 1914), 272.
36 "Panic Follows Fire in a Nickelodeon," *San Francisco Call*, March 26, 1909, 9; "Nickelodeons Are Declared Unsafe," *San Francisco Call*, March 30, 1909, 5; "Nickelodeons Slow to Make Alterations," *San Francisco Call*, May 5, 1909, 5; "Film Theater Place Nickels above Safety," *San Francisco Call*, September 3, 1911, 8.
37 "Dangerous Moving Picture Shows," *San Francisco Call*, March 6, 1909, 2.
38 "Moral Standards Must Be Raised," *San Francisco Chronicle*, March 27, 1909, 14.

39 "The Unsafe Nickelodeons," *San Francisco Chronicle*, March 31, 1909, 6.

40 "Board of Censors for Nickelodeons," *San Francisco Call*, April 13, 1909, 25; "Board of Censors to Supervise Nickelodeons," *San Francisco Chronicle*, April 28, 1909, 38; "Censoring Moving Pictures," *San Francisco Call*, February 6, 1910, 35

41 The coalition was formed to especially guard exhibitors against the growing powers of the film exchanges; "San Francisco Exhibitors' Association," *Moving Picture World*, August 10, 1912, 629.

42 "Among the Picture Theaters," *Motography*, February 1912, 89.

43 The Motion Picture Exhibitors' League of America held its first national convention in August 1911, where Neff was elected president. "In December 1909, Neff began to push for a national trade organization because of the rental exchanges' indifference to the needs of the exhibitors. . . . Various state exhibitors' organizations existed prior to the formation of the League and continued to function during its existence, sometimes causing conflicts regarding the control and jurisdiction of the national organization." See Anthony Slide, *The New Historical Dictionary of the American Film Industry* (New York: Routledge, 2014), 132.

44 Herbert Asbury, *The Barbary Coast: An Informal History of the San Francisco Underworld* (Garden City, NY: Garden City Publishing, 1933), 279–280.

45 See "Board Divides on Subject of 'Lid,'" *San Francisco Chronicle*, February 19, 1913, 5; "Plan More Rules to Tighten 'Lid,'" *San Francisco Chronicle*, February 27, 1913, 4; "Commission Nails 'Lid' on the 'Coast': Six Months' Deliberation Ends with Drastic Measures to Eradicate the District," *San Francisco Chronicle*, September 23, 10.

46 "Call! California Convention," *Moving Picture World*, September 14, 1912, 1083.

47 "California's First Annual Convention," *Motography*, September 28, 1912, 237.

48 "San Francisco," *Moving Picture World*, July 11, 1914, 320.

49 "Pearce, of Maryland, Succeeds Neff as League Head; Latter Withdraws," *Motion Picture News*, July 18, 1914, 17.

50 "Nickelodeon Firetraps Must Obey Laws or Close Doors," *San Francisco Call*, November 21, 1911, 2.

51 "Nickelodeon Bill Is Storm Center," *San Francisco Call*, February 27, 1911, 3. The believed deleteriousness of darkened Nickelodeons emerged as an issue in national debates on unwholesome film culture around late 1909. Among suggestions to brighten the gloom of movie theaters were "daylight" screenings, mirror screens, and Snellen eye tests, mounted inside theaters. Jan Olsson offered a well-grounded orientation of these intertwined debates in a section of uplift initiatives, departing from Los Angeles nickelodeon culture. Olsson argued that projection under daylight conditions was one of the most defining aspects of the public nature of the film viewing experience of the 1910s. See Olsson, *Los Angeles before Hollywood*, 223–251.

52 Commonwealth Club of California, *Transactions of the Commonwealth Club of California*, 285.

53 Ralph Renaud, "Orpheum Offers Picture Novelty," *San Francisco Chronicle*, February 27, 1911, 5.

54 "New Censorship Board Holds Initial Session," *San Francisco Call*, August 12, 1912, 15.

55 "Moving Picture Censor Board," in San Francisco Board of Supervisors, *San Francisco Municipal Reports Fiscal Year 1912–13*, 438.

56 "Censoring the 'Movies,'" *San Francisco Chronicle*, January 1913, 6.

57 "Moving Picture Censor Board," in San Francisco Board of Supervisors, *San Francisco Municipal Reports Fiscal Year 1913–14*, 272.

58 "What I Like Best at the Nickelodeons," *San Francisco Call*, May 1, 1910, 4.

59 "Writing Contest," *San Francisco Call*, May 15, 1910, 4.

60 "Preacher Extols Moving Pictures," *San Francisco Chronicle*, January 19, 1913, 64. For an essay that frames one of Jump's earlier lectures in relation to the perceived psychological effects of cinema, see Lee Grieveson, "Cinema Studies and the Conduct of Conduct," in *Inventing Film Studies*, ed. Lee Grieveson and Haidee Wasson (Durham, NC: Duke University Press, 2008), 12.

61 "Make Nickelodeons Safe," *San Francisco Call*, April 18, 1913, 8.

62 Exemplified by the guiding hypothesis of the Commonwealth Club's survey

63 Joseph C. Northup, "Consider the 'Movies'—How They Grow! Surprising Facts and Figures from San Francisco Filmdom," *San Francisco Chronicle*, January 6, 1914, 24.

64 Grieveson, *Policing Cinema*, 196.

65 Ordinance No. 959, New Series. In Commonwealth Club of California, *Transactions of the Commonwealth Club of California*, 284–285.

66 See Olsson, *Los Angeles before Hollywood*, 230–251.

67 Commonwealth Club of California, *Transactions of the Commonwealth Club of California*, 285.

68 "Allege That Movie Is Not Film to Show," *San Francisco Chronicle*, December 22, 1912, 50; "Kahn Found Guilty," *San Francisco Chronicle*, December 24, 1912, 7; Library of Congress, Copyright Office, *Motion Pictures, 1912–1939* (Washington, DC: Library of Congress, 1951), 605.

69 "Film Man Is Arrested," *San Francisco Examiner*, March 5, 1913; "Used Uncensored Film," *Variety*, March 14, 1913, 14; "Exhibitor to Fight Censorship," *Motography*, April 5, 1913, 249.

70 "Michaels Will Start Petition for Removal," *San Francisco Call*, March 5, 1913, 13.

71 Ironically, since word stood against word, Michaels was forced to screen "Marcus, the Venetian Tribune" once again for the jury. "Free Movies for Jury," *San Francisco Examiner*, March 14, 1913; "'Movie' Manager Convicted," *San Francisco Call*, March 28, 1913, 19.

72 "Movie Man Is Convicted," *San Francisco Examiner*, March 28, 1913; "Moving Picture Man Fined," *San Francisco Call*, April 10, 1913, 10.

73 "San Francisco Police Ban War Films," *Motion Picture News*, September 5, 1914, 21.

74 "San Francisco," *Moving Picture World*, August 29, 1914.

75 "San Francisco," *Moving Picture World*, August 29, 1914.

76 The film was described by *Motion Picture News* as "a military romance of the Franco-Prussian War." See "San Francisco Police Ban War Films," *Motion Picture News*, September 5, 1914, 21.

77 "Court Lifts 'Lid' from War Films," *Motion Picture News*, September 12, 1914, 19.

78 The film was distributed by the Apex Film Company, which immediately hired a local lawyer to contest police chief White and Peter Peshon of the censorship board. "Police Censorship Breaks Out Again on Coast," *Motion Picture News*, October 10, 1914, 21.

79 "Police Censorship Breaks Out Again on Coast," *Motion Picture News*, October 10, 1914, 21.

80 "Photography Is the Star," *American Cinematographer*, November 1935, 497.

81 "Barbary Coast of San Francisco Is Blotted Out," *Sausalito News*, 27 September 1913, 6; "Big Crowd Says Good-By to Coast," *San Francisco Chronicle*, October 1, 1913, 1.

82 Pratt, "Camera on the Move," 18.

83 Like Grauman, Mohr later moved to Hollywood, where he became a successful cinematographer. But fifteen years after the production of *Last Night of the Barbary Coast*, Mohr returned to San Francisco for the filming of Alan Crosland's *Old San Francisco* (1927), perhaps the most elaborate visualization of the mythical underworld of Chinatown and the Barbary Coast of the silent era. For a comment on *Old San Francisco* and its use of the Chinatown underworld as melodramatic setting, see Kevin Brownlow, *The Parade's Gone by . . .* (Berkeley: University of California Press, 1968), 264–266.

84 Pratt, "Camera on the Move," 18.

85 "No Thrills in Last Night of Barbary Coast," *Motography*, November 15, 1913, 360.

86 "It was state-righted. I know that I personally made something over 300 prints off this negative. They were sold all over the United States." See Pratt, "Camera on the Move," 18; "Golden Gate Expands," *Billboard*, December 6, 1913, 51. Sadly, the film is believed to be lost.

87 Pratt, "Camera on the Move," 18.

88 "San Francisco," *Variety*, August 3, 1907, 19; "In San Francisco," *Billboard*, May 22, 1909, 5; "San Francisco, Cal." *Billboard*, February 1, 1913, 18.

89 Pratt, "Camera on the Move," 18.

90 "Barbary Coast Sketch Featured at the Empress," *San Francisco Chronicle*, September 23, 1912, 5.

91 Other Chinatown settings included the "Chinese Market, Barber Shop, Opium den, Etc.," *San Francisco Call*, October 2, 1912, 7.

92 "No Thrills in Last Night of Barbary Coast," *Motography*, November 15, 1913, 360.

93 "San Francisco Screen Club," *Moving Picture World*, July 10, 1915, 269.

94 "Exposition's Zone," *Variety*, March 5, 1915, 7.

95 "S. F. Movies a Subject for Discussion," *San Francisco Chronicle*, August 4, 1915, 3.

96 "San Francisco Screen Club Gives Ball," *Motion Picture News*, December 19, 1914, 53–54.

97 The first week of the convention took place at the San Francisco Exposition, while the second week was moved to the emerging studio landscape in Los Angeles. See "Surprises 'Ready for Release' at Convention," *Motion Picture News*, July 15, 1915.

98 "Convention Opens with Big Attendance," *Motion Picture News*, July 61, 1915.

99 The Library of Congress has preserved the film. A digital copy can be found at "Mabel and Fatty Viewing the World's Fair at San Francisco, Cal.," Library of Congress website, accessed December 11, 2015, https://www.loc.gov/item/00694430/.

100 "San Francisco Convention," *Moving Picture World*, July 31, 1915, 790–794.

101 "Movie Men Will Fight Censorship," *San Francisco Chronicle*, July 16, 1915, 9.

102 "Censors of Film Receive Scoring," *San Francisco Chronicle*, July 15, 1915, 8.

103 "Censorship Dead in San Francisco," *Moving Picture World*, July 27, 1916, 820.

104 "Long Runs More General," *Moving Picture World*, October 2, 1915, 114.

105 "The Exposition Closes," *Moving Picture World*, December 18, 1915, 2226.

106 William Selig's zoo in northern Los Angeles was another film industry–related attraction that competed for the attention of California tourists in 1915. Richard

Koszarski, *An Evening's Entertainment: The Age of the Silent Feature Picture, 1915–1928* (Berkeley: University of California Press, 1994), 7.

107 Richard Koszarski noted that although Southern California emerged around the mid-1910s as the U.S. center for film production, it would not be until around 1924 that a specific "Hollywood mythos" can be evidenced with substantial historical documentation. Koszarski, 99–100.

108 Olsson, "Pressing Matters," 120.

109 Mary Ting Yi Lui, *The Chinatown Trunk Mystery: Murder, Miscegenation, and Other Dangerous Encounters in Turn-of-the-Century New York City* (Princeton, NJ: Princeton University Press, 2005), 69–73.

110 Nayan Shah, *Contagious Divides: Epidemics and Race in San Francisco's Chinatown* (Berkeley: University of California Press, 2001), 17.

111 Two examples from 1910 describe how health inspectors visited "all Chinatown nickelodeons," to investigate and inform about the spread of tuberculosis. The *Call* used the evocative term "White Plague" to frame this against earlier reports of bubonic plague in the area. See "Churches Join in White Plague," *San Francisco Call*, April 22, 1910, 7; "Today Is White Plague Sunday," *San Francisco Call*, April 24, 1910, 52.

## Chapter 3 "The Most Cosmopolitan City in the World"

1 Kevin Starr, *California: A History* (New York: Modern Library, 2005), 39–40.

2 A selective bibliography of such studies includes Otis Gibson, *The Chinese in America* (Cincinnati: Hitchcock and Walden, 1877); Willard B. Farwell and John E. Kunkler, *Chinese in San Francisco* (San Francisco: San Francisco Board of Supervisors, 1885); Stewart Culin, "Social Organization of the Chinese in America," *American Anthropologist* 4, no. 4 (1891): 347–352; John Stewart Burgess, "A Study of the Characteristics of the Cantonese Merchants in Chinatown, New York, as Shown by Their Use of Leisure Time" (master's thesis, Columbia University, 1909); Mary Roberts Coolidge, *Chinese Immigration* (New York: Arno Press, 1909); George Warren Hinman, *The Oriental in America* (New York: Missionary Education Movement of the U.S. and Canada, 1913).

3 "The authors of both camps based their arguments on their assessment of Chinese civilization and perceived the immigrants as representative bearers of that culture." Chan, "Chinese American Historiography," 3.

4 Ira B. Cross, "Review," *Economic Bulletin* 3, no. 2 (June 1910): 172–174.

5 For a comprehensive exposé of the early nineteenth-century U.S. eugenics movement, see Nancy Ordover, *American Eugenics: Race, Queer Anatomy, and the Science of Nationalism* (Minneapolis: University of Minnesota Press, 2003), 3–56.

6 Ordover, 6.

7 Adam Cohen, *Imbeciles: The Supreme Court, American Eugenics, and the Sterilization of Carrie Buck* (New York: Penguin, 2016), 4–6.

8 While Grant, a lawyer, and Stoddard, a Harvard-educated sociologist, came from different academic backgrounds, their prophecies on the fall of the "dominant white race" found a large readership during the latter parts of the 1910s.

9 Ordover, *American Eugenics*, 25.

10 Him Mark Lai, "The Chinese Exclusion Act: Observations of a Centennial," *Amerasia* 9, no. 1 (1982): 2.

11 Saxton, *Rise and Fall of the White Republic*, 14.

12 Saxton, 17–18.

13 John Kuo Wei Tchen, *New York before Chinatown : Orientalism and the Shaping of American Culture, 1776–1882* (Baltimore: Johns Hopkins University Press, 2001), xv.

14 For a comprehensive historiographical review of Chinese American studies, see Sucheng Chan, "Chinese American Historiography," 1–61.

15 Thomas Chinn, Him Mark Lai, and Philip P. Choy, *A History of the Chinese in California: A Syllabus* (San Francisco: Chinese Historical Society of America, 1969).

16 Saxton, *Indispensable Enemy*, 258.

17 Saxton, 2.

18 While the study offered an unprecedented collection of firsthand accounts on the everyday experiences of members of the Chinatown community, its lack of comprehensive analysis and cohesive argumentation rendered it valuable primarily as an archive of historical sources.

19 Sucheng Chan, *This Bittersweet Soil: The Chinese in California Agriculture, 1860–1910* (Berkeley: University of California Press, 1989); Sucheng Chan, *Entry Denied: Exclusion and the Chinese Community in America, 1882–1943* (Philadelphia: Temple University Press, 1991); Chan and Hsu, *Chinese Americans*.

20 Sucheng Chan, "Contextual Frameworks for Reading Counterpoint," *Amerasia Journal* 5, no. 1 (January 1978): 115–129.

21 Madeline Yuan-yin Hsu, *Dreaming of Gold, Dreaming of Home: Transnationalism and Migration between the United States and South China, 1882–1943* (Stanford, CA: Stanford University Press, 2000); Sucheng Chan, *Chinese American Transnationalism: The Flow of People, Resources, and Ideas between China and America during the Exclusion Era*, (Philadelphia: Temple University Press, 2005); Chan and Hsu, *Chinese Americans*.

22 Chen, *Chinese San Francisco*, 125–130, 137–141, 186–216.

23 Nayan Shah's excellent study investigates the "plague scares" of San Francisco's Chinatown and details how public health discourses informed arguments for racial segregation in the late nineteenth and early twentieth centuries. See Shah, *Contagious Divides*. Karen J. Leong tracks notions of the sexless and epicene Chinese male in exclusionist debates during the Dennis Kearney era. See Karen J. Leong, "A Distinct and Antagonistic Race: Constructions of Chinese Manhood in the Exclusionist Debates, 1869–1878," in *Across the Great Divide: Cultures of Manhood in the American West*, ed. Matthew Basso, Laura McCall, and Dee Garceacu-Hagen (New York: Routledge, 2000), 131–148.

24 Judy Yung, *Unbound Feet: A Social History of Chinese Women in San Francisco* (Berkeley: University of California Press, 1995).

25 These were the Yanghe, Sanyi, Renhe, Ninyang, Shiyi, and Hehe Huiguan. Although the number of these *huiguan* changed throughout the late nineteenth and early twentieth centuries, the colloquial name remained the same. The pinyin transliteration for the collective Six Companies is the Zhonghua huiguan; Chen, *Chinese San Francisco*, 72.

26 Chen, 94–95.

27 "John Chinaman," *Daily Alta California*, December 12, 1878.

28 Chen, *Chinese San Francisco*, 153.

29 For a brief but comprehensive history of the Chinese press in North America, see Him Mark Lai, "The Chinese Press in America," in *The Ethnic Press in the United*

States: A Historical Analysis and Handbook*, ed. Sally M. Miller (New York: Greenwood Press, 1987), 27–43.

30 Lai, 31.

31 Lai, 32.

32 Robert J. Kelly, Ko-lin Chin, and Jeffrey Fagan, "Chinese Organized Crime in America," in *Handbook of Organized Crime in the United States*, ed. Rufus Schatzberg, Ko-lin Chin, and Robert J. Kelly (Westport, CT: Greenwood Press, 1994), 215.

33 Ko-lin Chin, *Chinese Subculture and Criminality: Non-traditional Crime Groups in America* (New York: Greenwood Press, 1990), 51.

34 Richard H. Dillon, *The Hatchet Men: The Story of the Tong Wars in San Francisco's Chinatown* (New York: Coward-McCann, 1962).

35 Philip P. Choy, *The Architecture of San Francisco Chinatown* (San Francisco: Chinese Historical Society, 2008), 125–127.

36 A copy of this short film has been preserved at the Library of Congress and can be viewed digitally at *Scene in Chinatown*, Library of Congress, https://www.loc.gov/item/00694411/, accessed February 12, 2020. Another cinematic appearance of the Chinatown Squad can be found in *The Chinatown Squad*, (1935), a B movie from Universal Pictures that had a small renaissance as part of the Universal Shock Theater package, released for television syndication in 1957. See "Screen Gems Issues First Pkg. of Universal Films," *Billboard*, August 19, 1957, 17.

37 Hansen, *Babel and Babylon*, 62.

38 Jürgen Habermas's important study *The Structural Transformation of the Public Sphere* examined the emergence of the bourgeois public sphere in the eighteenth century, where members of civil society, depending on education and economic assets, could articulate their interests. Habermas underlined capitalist modes of production as one of the fundamental forces, driving the emergence of the bourgeois public sphere. See Jürgen Habermas, *The Structural Transformation of the Public Sphere: An Inquiry into a Category of Bourgeois Society*, trans. Thomas Burger and Frederick Lawrence (Cambridge: Polity Press, 1992).

39 Hansen argued that while Kluge and Negt, for heuristic purposes, divided their development of Habermas's notion into three categories of public life, the categories were not isolated from each other and should be understood "in their mutual imbrication, in specific overlaps, cohabitations, and contradictions." See Miriam Hansen, "Foreword," in Oskar Negt and Alexander Kluge, *Public Sphere and Experience: Toward an Analysis of the Bourgeois and Proletarian Public Sphere* (Minneapolis: University of Minnesota Press, 1993), xxix.

40 For an intriguing discussion of how the notion of the public sphere can be applied to histories of early cinema in Asia, see Wimal Dissanayake, "Early Asian Cinema and the Public Sphere," in *Early Cinema in Asia*, ed. Nick Deocampo (Bloomington: Indiana University Press, 2017), 32–69.

41 Hansen, *Babel and Babylon*, 17.

42 Hansen, "Foreword," xxxii.

43 Hansen, *Babel and Babylon*, 17.

44 An illustrative example is that the homes and workplaces of members of New York's Chinese community were, contrary to popular belief, regularly located outside of the city's Chinese neighborhood. See Lui, *Chinatown Trunk Mystery*, 5.

45 Chinese San Franciscans of the 1850s and 1860s called Sacramento Street Tangren Jie, meaning Tang People's Street. According to historian Mae Ngai, the

contemporary historical connotation of this term alluded to the Tang dynasty (618–907), when the ancestors of the Cantonese in San Francisco became integrated with the Chinese empire. The name Tangren Jie and its etymological connection to southern China have since then become associated with the notion of Chinatowns worldwide. See Mae Ngai, *The Lucky Ones: One Family and the Extraordinary Invention of Chinese America* (Princeton, NJ: Princeton University Press, 2012), 12.

46 H. S. Crocker Company, *Crocker-Langley San Francisco Directory for the Year Commencing 1892* (San Francisco: H. S. Crocker Company, 1893), 1004–1010.

47 These were Jackson Street (about 100), Washington Street and Washington Alley (about 120), Commercial Street (67), Sacramento Street (56), Clay Street (54), Pacific Street (43), Waverly Place (29), Spofford Street (27), and Stockton Street (20). These figures are based on Yong Chen's numbers; see Chen, *Chinese San Francisco*, 61–62.

48 For a brilliant discussion of how expressions such as "annihilation of time and space" became contemporary stock phrases to describe the emergence of modern transportation technology, see Solnit, *Motion Studies*. The most important study of the railroad and the emergence of industrial modernity is still Wolfgang Schivelbusch's classic book *The Railway Journey: The Industrialization of Time and Space in the 19th Century* (Berkeley: University of California Press, 1986).

49 For a brief history of the pioneering transpacific steamship venture, see E. Mowbray Tate, *Transpacific Steam: The Story of Steam Navigation from the Pacific Coast of North America to the Far East and the Antipodes, 1867–1941* (New York: Cornwall Books, 1986), 21–43.

50 Him Mark Lai, *Becoming Chinese American: A History of Communities and Institutions* (Walnut Creek, CA: Altamira Press, 2004), 95, 151–152.

51 Campbell Gibson and Kay Jung, *Historical Census Statistics on Population Totals by Race, 1790 to 1990, and by Hispanic Origin, 1970 to 1990, for Large Cities and Other Urban Places in The United States* (Washington, DC: U.S. Census Bureau, 2005), 35.

52 These numbers are based on U.S. Census Bureau publications from 1880 to 1940.

53 Yung, *Unbound Feet*, 30.

54 The recreational habits of the Chinese merchant class in New York were the subject of study by John Stewart Burgess in 1909. See Burgess, *Study of the Characteristics of the Cantonese Merchants*.

55 Chen, *Chinese San Francisco*, 66–67.

56 A relatively late example of scholarly reiterations of such beliefs can be found in Ivan Light's article on the "moral career of Chinatowns" from the mid-1970s. See Ivan Light, "From Vice District to Tourist Attraction: The Moral Career of American Chinatowns, 1880–1940," *Pacific Historical Review* 43, no. 3 (1974): 367–394.

57 Yung, *Unbound Feet*, 41.

58 Chen, *Chinese San Francisco*, 68.

59 Maria Seise was one of the first women to immigrate to San Francisco; after having escaped slavery in Hong Kong, she settled as the servant of an American family in the San Francisco area in 1848. Ah Toy was the first, wealthiest, and most powerful brothel madam of the gold rush days. Mary Tape, whose daughter was denied entry to a school outside Chinatown, took the Board of Education to court, resulting in a ruling that stated all children, regardless of race, had the right

to public school education. After her husband's death, Lai Yun Oi moved to San Francisco, where, as a single woman, she achieved economic success in the tailoring business. See Yung, *Unbound Feet*, 47–50.

60 For a study of the changing public image of Japanese as seen through contemporary U.S. film exhibition, see Gregory Waller, "Japan on American Screens, 1908–1915," in *Early Cinema and the "National,"* ed. Richard Abel, Giorgio Bertellini, and Rob King (New Barnet, UK: John Libbey, 2008), 137–150.

61 Raymond W. Rast, "The Cultural Politics of Tourism in San Francisco's Chinatown, 1882–1917," *Pacific Historical Review* 76, no. 1 (2007): 35.

62 A *Call* editorial from May 1900 exemplifies the many violently anti-Chinese sentiments expressed following unsubstantiated rumors of a plague outbreak in Chinatown: "In no city in the civilized world is there a slum more foul or more menacing than the one which now threatens us with the Asiatic plague. Chinatown occupies the very heart of San Francisco. It is a bit of the most degraded Asiatic filth set in the center of a city of Western civilization." "Clean Out Chinatown," editorial, *San Francisco Call*, May 31, 1900, 6. For an in-depth exploration of the social and cultural significance of the several local public media campaigns that framed Chinatown as a health hazard, see Shah, *Contagious Divides*.

63 Anthony W. Lee, *Picturing Chinatown: Art and Orientalism in San Francisco* (Berkeley: University of California Press, 2001), 77.

64 Sun, "From Isolation to Participation," 66.

65 Erika Lee and Judy Yung, *Angel Island: Immigrant Gateway to America* (New York: Oxford University Press, 2010), 9–13.

66 Although guards regularly painted over the poetry, some of it remains. Angel Island of today has been transformed into a museum and a monument for the contemporary Chinese immigrant experience, and Angel Island poetry has been compiled and translated in several publications. See, for example, Him Lai, Genny Lim, and Judy Yung, eds., *Island: Poetry and History of Chinese Immigrants on Angel Island, 1910–1940* (repr., Seattle: University of Washington Press, 1991); Russell Freedman, *Angel Island: Gateway to Gold Mountain* (New York: Clarion Books, 2014).

67 Lai, Lim, and Yung, *Island*, 8.

68 Lui, *Chinatown Trunk Mystery*, 16, 63–67.

69 Choy, *Architecture of San Francisco Chinatown*, 64–65.

70 In 1877 the line was extended to Van Ness.

71 Edgar Myron Kahn, *Cable Car Days in San Francisco* (Stanford, CA: Stanford University Press, 1944), 79.

72 Kahn, 82.

73 Shah, *Contagious Divides*, 87–88; Lui, *Chinatown Trunk Mystery*, 62–73.

74 Tchen, *New York before Chinatown*, xix.

75 Barbara Berglund, *Making San Francisco American: Cultural Frontiers in the Urban West, 1846–1906* (Lawrence: University Press of Kansas, 2007), 2.

76 Tchen, *New York before Chinatown*, xix.

77 Lei, *Operatic China*, 25.

78 Lei, 83–84.

79 Victor Nee and Brett de Bary Nee, *Longtime Californ': A Documentary Study of an American Chinatown* (New York: Pantheon Books, 1973), 69–73; Chen, *Chinese San Francisco*, 75–95.

## Chapter 4 "Eyes Darting Around, Spirit Dashing About"

1 In addition to the ones mentioned in previous chapters, examples of such films are *Scene in Chinatown* (Biograph, 1900), *San Francisco Chinese Funeral* (Edison, 1903), and *Chinamen Returning to China* (Biograph, 1903).

2 "Chinese Merchants of San Francisco Now in Oakland's Oriental Quarter," *San Francisco Chronicle*, June 18, 1906.

3 "Location of the Chinese," *San Francisco Chronicle*, May 10, 1906; "Money to Go to the Chinese," *San Francisco Chronicle*, April 28, 1906; "New Chinatown Near Fort Point: Oriental Quarter Removed from Presidio Golf Links at Request of Property Owners," *San Francisco Chronicle*, April 29, 1906; "Now Fear That the Chinese May Abandon City: Citizens of San Francisco Are Now Confronted with Problem in Which Trade with Orient Is Involved," *San Francisco Chronicle*, May 2, 1906; "Plans to Move Chinese Futile: Committee Will Await the Arrival of Chinese Minister," *San Francisco Chronicle*, May 12, 1906; "Plan to Build an Oriental City: Chinese Colony at Foot of Van Ness: The Plan to Remove Celestials to San Mateo County Is Opposed," *San Francisco Chronicle*, April 27, 1906; "The Chinatown Question," *San Francisco Chronicle*, May 14, 1906.

4 Sydney Tyler, *San Francisco's Great Disaster* (Harrisburg, PA: The Minter Company, 1906), 308.

5 "To Seek Site for Chinatown: Citizens and Chinese Dignitaries Discuss Situation in Executive Session," *San Francisco Chronicle*, May 3, 1906, 13; "Oriental City Is Planned," *San Francisco Call*, May 24, 1906, 14.

6 "Want Chinatown Where It Was," *San Francisco Chronicle*, May 17, 1906, 2.

7 Christopher Lee Yip, "San Francisco's Chinatown: An Architectural and Urban History" (PhD diss., University of California, Berkeley, 1985), 173.

8 Chen, "*Chinese San Francisco*, 164–165.

9 Yip, "San Francisco's Chinatown," 174.

10 Yip, 173.

11 Rast, "Cultural Politics of Tourism," 32.

12 Charles Augustus Keeler, *San Francisco and Thereabout* (San Francisco: California Promotion Committee, 1903), 58–69.

13 Will Irwin, *The City That Was: A Requiem of Old San Francisco* (New York: B. W. Huebsch, 1906), 33–34.

14 "Want Chinatown Where It Was," *San Francisco Chronicle*, May 17, 1906, 2.

15 "Changes in Many Streets," *San Francisco Chronicle*, May 15, 1906, 5.

16 Robert W. Cherny, "City Commercial, City Beautiful, City Practical: The San Francisco Visions of William C. Ralston, James D. Phelan, and Michael M. O'Shaughnessy," *California History* 73, no. 4 (December 1994): 301–302.

17 "Will Rebuild in Chinatown: J. H. Loeber to Erect the First Permanent Structure on Old Location," *San Francisco Chronicle*, August 1, 1906, 5.

18 "Chinatown to Keep Old Site: The Wong and Lee Families Begin the Work of Rebuilding," *San Francisco Chronicle*, September 30, 1906; "First New Building on Chinatown Site: Three Stories of Mixed Spanish and Oriental Design the Plan.," *San Francisco Chronicle*, September 7, 1906; "New Building for Chinatown District: Class C Business Block with Pressed Brick Exterior Well Under Way," *San Francisco Chronicle*, September 15, 1906; "Oriental Bazar at Portsmouth Square: Structure Designed for a Chinatown Site," *San Francisco Chronicle*, September 14, 1906.

19 "Chinatown to Be as Before," *San Francisco Chronicle*, July 18, 1906, 12.
20 Yip, "San Francisco's Chinatown," 232.
21 "The Undiminished Life Atmosphere of a City Which Has Always Ranked Alone," *San Francisco Call*, April 14, 1907, 8.
22 "New Chinatown Will Be Peopled in Single Night by Celestials," *San Francisco Call*, May 24, 1907, 14.
23 Giuliana Bruno, *Streetwalking on a Ruined Map: Cultural Theory and the City Films of Elvira Notari* (Princeton, NJ: Princeton University Press, 1993).
24 "The ordinary practitioners of the city live 'down below,' below the thresholds at which visibility begins. . . . These practitioners make use of spaces which can't be seen." See Michel de Certeau, *The Practice of Everyday Life*, trans. Steven Rendall (Berkeley: University of California Press, 1984), 93.
25 Ian Buchanan, "Unknotting Place and Space," *Salt* 12, no. 1 (2000): 137–156.
26 Walter Benjamin, "On Some Motifs in Baudelaire," in *Walter Benjamin: Selected Writings*, vol. 4, *1938–1940*, ed. Howard Eiland and Michael W. Jennings (Cambridge, MA: Belknap Press, 2006), 326.
27 Edgar Allan Poe, "The Man of the Crowd," in *The Complete Edgar Allan Poe Tales* (New York: Avenel Books, 1981), 240–245.
28 Marlon K. Hom, *Songs of Gold Mountain: Cantonese Rhymes from San Francisco Chinatown* (Berkeley: University of California Press, 1992), 209.
29 Choy, *Architecture of San Francisco Chinatown*, 13.
30 Look Tin Eli, "Our New Oriental City—Veritable Fairy Palaces Filled with the Choicest Treasures of the Orient," in *San Francisco: The Metropolis of the West* (San Francisco: Western Press Association, 1910).
31 Advertisement for the Sing Chong Lung Co. in *Chinese Defender* 1, no. 1 (September 1910).
32 "Nickelodeons Are Declared Unsafe," *San Francisco Chronicle*, March 30, 1909, 5.
33 Advertisement for the Hang Far Low restaurant and tea garden in *Chinese Defender* 1, no. 1 (September 1910).
34 Louis J. Stellman, *Chinatown Photographer, Louis J. Stellman: A Catalog of His Photograph Collection: Including a Previously Unpublished Manuscript, Chinatown: A Pictorial Souvenir and Guide Written by Louis J. Stellman in 1917*, ed. Richard H. Dillon, Gary E. Strong, and California State Library (Sacramento: California State Library Foundation, 1989), 42.
35 The others were the Shanghai Low restaurant on Grant Avenue between California and Pine, and the Republic Chinese Restaurant at Grant and Sacramento, all within a block's reach of the Dragon Nickelodeon. See Stellman, 43.
36 Robert W. Bowen and Brenda Young Bowen, *San Francisco's Chinatown* (Charleston, SC: Arcadia Publishing, 2008), 89.
37 See, for example, municipal license records for "kinetoscopes" in San Francisco in 1913. *San Francisco Municipal Reports Fiscal Year 1913–14, Ending June 30, 1914* (San Francisco: San Francisco Board of Supervisors, 1914), 558.
38 "Nickelodeons Are Declared Unsafe," *San Francisco Chronicle*, March 30, 1909, 5.
39 A 1910 advertisement for the Tai Quong printing company read, "Printers and publishers for all kinds of Students and Scholars." The printing company also printed the *Chinese Defender*. Advertisement in *Chinese Defender* 1, no. 1 (September 1910).
40 Rast, "Cultural Politics of Tourism," 47.
41 Charles Caldwell Dobie, *San Francisco's Chinatown* (New York: D. Appleton-Century, 1936), 245.

42 "Fire Reveals Chinatown Fake," *San Francisco Chronicle*, May 14, 1906, 8.

43 San Francisco Tourist Agency, *A Short Story about Chinatown* (San Francisco: San Francisco Tourist Agency, 1903), 10.

44 The Wurlitzer PianOrchestra was an automatic pipe organ equipped with bells, gongs, horns, and sirens. Around this time, Wurlitzer, along with a few other companies, had realized the market potential in offering instruments to film exhibitors "designed to provide continuous descriptive accompaniment for motion pictures." Rick Altman, "Silence of the Silents," *Musical Quarterly* 80, no. 4 (Winter 1996): 703.

45 Georg Simmel, in his posthumously famous essay on the spiritual effects of urban life, wrote that it was in the blasé attitude that "the nerves reveal their final possibility of adjusting themselves to the content and the form of metropolitan life by renouncing the response to them." See Georg Simmel, "The Metropolis and Mental Life," in *On Individuality and Social Forms: Selected Writings*, ed. Donald N. Levine (Chicago: University of Chicago Press, 1971), 328.

46 The Rudolph Wurlitzer Company was so pleased with the organ's picturesque placement that it used a photograph of the Oriental Theatre storefront in its film trade press advertisements throughout 1912.

47 I. L. Marks, the Acme's manager, advertised for a business partner in the *Call* throughout March 1910 before giving the partnership to his son, Ralph. See "Classifieds," *San Francisco Call*, March 6, 1910, 56; "Classifieds," *San Francisco Call*, March 7, 1910, 11; "Classifieds," *San Francisco Call*, March 10, 1910, 13; "Classifieds," *San Francisco Call*, March 11, 1910, 13.

48 "Greeks of Bay Cities Swell the Call Fund," *San Francisco Call*, November 29, 1911, 3.

49 "The Acme Theater, San Francisco, Cal.," *Moving Picture World*, September 25, 1915, 2165.

50 "The Acme Theater, San Francisco, Cal.," *The Moving Picture World*, September 25, 1915, 2165.

51 The opening of the Washington Street theater intensified the rivalry on the Chinatown drama scene, which prior to the Grand's opening had been dominated by two theaters on Jackson and Dupont Streets. See Lois Rodecape Foster, "Chinese Theatres in America" (unpublished manuscript, 1943), 75–76.

52 "The Passing of the Chinese Theater," *San Francisco Call*, July 27, 1913, 34.

53 Little Pete was a notorious gangster, associated with the Sam Yup benevolent organization, who frequently exploited the extraordinary situation of Chinese San Franciscans. "One of his means of revenue was the exacting of fees from relatives of Chinese women arriving in America; his excellent knowledge of English (it was said he could neither read nor write Chinese) and a well-established connection with the San Francisco police enabled him to denounce immigrants as prostitutes, engineer raids of See Yup gambling halls, and otherwise persecute his enemies. . . . Little Pete wrote plays for the Jackson Street theater, which he owned in full or in large part. Since it was currently remarked that he could not write Chinese, it is to be presumed that his plots were conveyed verbally or written in the English he had learned in local schools." Shortly before his murder in 1897, Little Pete had leased the Grand in a bid to monopolize Chinatown stage drama. See Foster, "Chinese Theatres in America," 112–113, 127. For more sensationalist biographies on Little Pete, see Asbury, *Barbary Coast*, 191–196; Dillon, *Hatchet Men*, 216–249.

54 "Shot Down on Theater Stage," *San Francisco Chronicle*, December 13, 1903, 25.

55 Lois Rodecape Foster's unpublished manuscript "Chinese Theatre in America," from 1943, was a reworked account of another unpublished venture, by Foster, Peter Chu, Stephen Moy, and Nadia Lavrova, under the auspices of the Federal Research Project during the 1930s. Although mostly told from the perspectives of English-language theatergoers, it provides a rare and rather extensive orientation of pre-quake theater history in Chinatown. See Foster, "Chinese Theatres in America."

56 "Chinatown Rebuilding on the Old Site," *San Francisco Chronicle*, April 14, 1907, 6.

57 "Nickelodeons Are Declared Unsafe," *San Francisco Call*, March 30, 1909, 5.

58 "Trade Directory," *Moving Picture World*, February 15, 1908, 111; "Trade Directory," *Moving Picture World*, April 25, 1908, 378; advertisement in *Moving Picture World*, December 12, 1908, 484; "Directory of Film Exchanges," *Moving Picture World*, June 14, 1909, 232.

59 "Directory of Film Exchanges," *Moving Picture World*, June 14, 1909, 232; "A New Film Exchange," *Nickelodeon*, September 1909, 97.

60 "San Francisco," *Moving Picture World*, September 16, 1911, 808.

61 "Motion Picture Theatres. This List Comprises Only Those Exhibitors Which Do Not Use the Licensed Film of the Motion Picture Patents Company," *Billboard*, September 11, 1909, 88.

62 "New Chinese Theater, Competition in the Theatrical Circles of Chinatown," *San Francisco Chronicle*, September 25, 1879, 1.

63 "Small Panic Is Result of Fire," *San Francisco Chronicle*, March 17, 1909, 5.

64 "Nickelodeons Are Declared Unsafe," *San Francisco Call*, March 30, 1909, 5.

65 "Chief Scores Nickelodeons," *San Francisco Chronicle*, March 30, 1909, 5.

66 "Nickelodeon Men Gain Concession," *San Francisco Chronicle*, April 6, 1909, 5.

67 "Nickelodeons Slow to Make Alterations," *San Francisco Call*, May 26, 1909, 5; "Inspector Horgan Makes Report on Nickelodeons," *San Francisco Chronicle*, May 26, 1909, 11.

68 Foster, "Chinese Theatres in America," 71.

69 "The Chinese Horror," *Daily Alta California*, November 1, 1876, 1.

70 "Chinese Cussedness," *San Francisco Chronicle*, March 10, 1880, 3.

71 "Blaze in Chinatown," *San Francisco Chronicle*, December 26, 1900, 7.

72 Olsson, "Pressing Matters," 19.

73 Olsson, 3.

74 H. S. Crocker Company, *Crocker-Langley San Francisco Directory for the Year Ending August 1909* (San Francisco: H. S. Crocker Company, 1909), 1329.

75 A Chinese-language advertisement reprinted in *Billboard* dates the opening night to January 21, 1909. See *Billboard*, May 29, 1909, 12.

76 Nancy Yunhwa Rao, *Chinatown Opera Theater in North America* (Urbana, IL: University of Illinois Press, 2017), 46–47.

77 Rao, 48.

78 The operating hours have been gleaned from the Chinese advertisement reprinted in *Billboard*, May 29, 1909, 12.

79 See Chinese advertisement in *Billboard*, May 29, 1909, 12, and advertisements for the Oriental Theatre in English in *San Francisco's Chinatown—An Aid to Tourists and Others in Visiting China-Town. October 1909* (San Francisco, 1909).

80 H. S. Crocker Company, *Crocker-Langley San Francisco Directory for the Year Ending August 1909*, 1658; *Los Angeles City Directory, 1910* (Los Angeles: Los Angeles City Directory Company, 1910), 1558.

81 "San Francisco, Cal.," *Billboard*, December 10, 1910, 101.
82 Christopher Lee Yip, "San Francisco's Chinatown: An Architectural and Urban History" (PhD diss., University of California, Berkeley, 1985), 173.
83 Rick Altman noted that the placement of the mechanical instruments in theater storefronts facing the street was a somewhat customary practice in the nickelodeon (the Oriental and two other San Francisco theaters being among his prime examples). However, Altman comments, while an exterior placement was ideal for "volume and visibility," it was more common to place an instrument inside the theater and let its sounds penetrate the soundscape of the street through open doors. See Rick Altman, *Silent Film Sound* (New York: Columbia University Press, 2007), 126–129.
84 Adriana Spadoni, "An Interview with a Nickelodeon Fiend," *San Francisco Chronicle,* August 21, 1910, 12.
85 Advertisement for *Under the Reign of Terror* in *Moving Picture World*, July 2, 1910, 56. Another film depicting events during the French Revolution, *Cagliostro*, based on the work of Alexandre Dumas père was released by Pathé Frères in late July, but it is not likely it showed at the Oriental, given the theater's independent affiliation. See "Cagliostro," *Nickelodeon*, July 15, 1910, 47; *Film Index*, July 30, 1910, 13.
86 Foster, "Chinese Theatres in America," 20.
87 "Flames Cause Theater Panic," *San Francisco Call*, September 4, 1911, 2; "Film Catches Fire, Scramble Ensues," *San Francisco Chronicle*, September 4, 1911, 14.
88 "Expected Tong War Gathers One Victim," *San Francisco Chronicle*, September 8, 1910, 6.
89 "Incipient Tong War Throttled," *San Francisco Chronicle*, October 29, 1914, 2.
90 "Building Code Requirements Close Theaters," *Moving Picture World*, November 9, 1917, 745.
91 "Correspondence," *Billboard*, October 12, 1907, 8; "San Francisco Letter," *Billboard*, November 21, 1908, 11.
92 Brodsky, who in the 1910s would claim to the U.S. trade press, and just about anyone else who would listen, that he had introduced the film medium to China and at one point had owned more than eighty movie theaters across the country, had also tried his luck on the ruined streets of San Francisco after the earthquake and fire. For a comprehensive revisionist take on many of Brodsky's erroneous statements, see Curry, "Benjamin Brodsky (1877–1960): The Trans-Pacific American Film Entrepreneur Part Two," 142–180; Curry, "Benjamin Brodsky (1877–1960): The Trans-Pacific American Film Entrepreneur Part One," 58–94; Frank Bren and Law Kar, *Hong Kong Cinema: A Cross-Cultural View* (Lanham, MD: Scarecrow Press, 2004).
93 During his career as a film exhibitor, Michaels ran into trouble with the authorities several times. Perhaps most notably, he was involved in a nationally publicized court case regarding the illegal duplication and exhibition of films from the Jack Johnson–Jim Jeffries prize fight of 1910. See, for example, "Two Arrested for Fight Film Theft," *San Francisco Call*, October 26, 1910; "Michaels Arrested," *Los Angeles Times*, October 26, 1910, 6; "Three Arrested in Film Case," *Nevada State Journal*, October 27, 1910, 8; "Alleged Duping of Fight Films," *New York Dramatic Mirror*, November 9, 1910, 33; "Fight Film Cases Ordered Dropped," *San Francisco Call*, January 11, 1911, 11.
94 "San Francisco, Cal.," *Billboard*, August 7, 1909; "San Francisco, Cal.," *Billboard*, September 6, 1909.

95 "San Francisco, Cal.," *Billboard*, November 6, 1909, 11.
96 "Frisco's Latest 'Pop,' *Variety*, December 4, 8.
97 "San Francisco," *Variety*, September 3, 1910, 22.
98 See H. S. Crocker Company, *Crocker-Langley San Francisco Directory for the Year Ending August 1912* (San Francisco: H. S. Crocker Company, 1912), 337.
99 The owner of the penny arcade was another familiar figure in the early San Francisco film scene, Peter Bacigalupi. See California Block Book and Map Company, *Mery's Block Book of San Francisco: The Following Maps Were Made from the Block Books of the City and County Assessor of San Francisco* (San Francisco: California Block Book and Map Company, 1909), 39.
100 "Correspondence," *Billboard*, April 9, 1910.
101 "San Francisco," *Variety*, September 3, 1910, 22.
102 By 1910 the Bert Levey Circuit had branched out its operation to Chicago. Although Levey traveled the North American continent widely during this time, the executive office remained on Powell Street in San Francisco. See advertisement, *Variety*, October 25, 1910, 41.
103 "San Francisco, Cal.," *Moving Picture World*, September 28, 1910, 1295.
104 "San Francisco," *Moving Picture World*, July 13, 1912, 164.
105 "A Dead Man's Child," *Moving Picture World*, March 23, 1912.
106 "Theater Burns as 200 Watch Screen," *San Francisco Call*, October 19, 1912, 1.
107 "Picture Palace Burned," *Variety*, October 25, 1912, 6.
108 "Fifty Millions for Buildings Here in 1913," *San Francisco Call*, January 12, 23.
109 "Fifty Millions for Construction Work in San Francisco in 1913," *Architect and Engineer* 31, no. 3 (January 1913): 62.
110 "Work in Architects' Offices," *Architect and Engineer* 34, no .2 (September 1913): 113.
111 "Architects Rosseau & Rosseau," *Architect and Engineer* 35, no. 3 (January 1914): 113.
112 "San Francisco," *Moving Picture World*, March 7, 1914, 1255; "Exhibitors News: San Francisco," *Moving Picture World*, March 28, 1914, 1712.
113 Kathryn Fuller-Seeley has pointed out that the names of nickelodeons and picture palaces were often conceived to promote a particular experience and appeal to varying sensibilities of local audiences in order to differentiate a theater from its competitors. See Kathryn Fuller-Seeley, *At the Picture Show: Small-Town Audiences and the Creation of Movie Fan Culture* (Washington, DC: Smithsonian Institution Press, 1996), 52.
114 "Today's Feature at the Movies," *San Francisco Chronicle*, April 6, 1914, 8.
115 "At the Movies," *San Francisco Chronicle*, April 14, 1914, 8.
116 "San Francisco," *Moving Picture World*, November 21, 1914, 1105; "San Francisco," *Moving Picture World*, November 28, 1914, 1260.
117 "Other San Francisco Items," *Moving Picture World*, January 9, 1915, 233.
118 I will return to Michaels's and Grauman's exploitation of local Chinese culture and the Underground Chinatown concession in chapter 5.
119 "North Beach Price War," *Moving Picture World*, July 31, 1915, 855.
120 "Truce on North Beach," *Moving Picture World*, August 7, 1915, 1034.
121 "Truce on North Beach," *Moving Picture World*, August 7, 1915, 1034.
122 "Exhibitor Starts Paper," *Moving Picture World*, October 16, 1915, 488.
123 "Exhibitor Starts Paper," *Moving Picture World*, October 16, 1915, 488.
124 "Advertising for Exhibitors," *Moving Picture World*, November 13, 1915, 1302.
125 "Advertising for Exhibitors," *Moving Picture World*, November 13, 1915, 1302.

126 For a comprehensive study of Rothafel's exploits and importance to the development of U.S. film exhibition, see Ross Melnick, *American Showman: Samuel "Roxy" Rothafel and the Birth of the Entertainment Industry, 1908–1935* (New York: Columbia University Press, 2013).
127 "'Peace' Film on Coast," *Moving Picture World*, November 20, 1915, 1528.
128 "Going Strong," *Moving Picture World*, November 20, 1915, 1491.
129 "How About It?," *Moving Picture World*, January 1, 1916, 74.
130 "Shows Titles in Italian," *Moving Picture World*, December 4, 1915, 1876.
131 "Benjamin Michaels Killed," *Moving Picture World*, May 6, 1916, 1012.
132 "Sister Sues for Michaels Estate," *San Francisco Chronicle*, May 23, 11: "Fight Opened for Estate of Ben Michaels," *San Francisco Chronicle*, June 9, 1917, 9.
133 "San Francisco Ball," *Moving Picture World*, May 13, 1916, 1205.
134 "L. C. Johnson Weds," *Moving Picture World*, March 2, 1918, 1264.
135 "San Francisco's Market Street Theater Sold," *Moving Picture World*, June 9, 1917, 1654; "New House for North Beach," *Moving Picture World*, September 15, 1917, 1736; "Broadway Theater, San Francisco, Cal.," *Moving Picture World*, October 27, 1917, 534.
136 A *Billboard* article announced the opening of the theater in 1911, naming Benjamin Michaels as the "manager and originator," *Billboard*, July 1, 1911, 19. The San Francisco directory for 1912 lists the theater as "Chinese theatre," with the address as 813 Kearny Street. See H. S. Crocker Company, *Crocker-Langley San Francisco Directory for the Year Ending August 1912*, 414. According to San Francisco historian Jack Tillmany, the Shanghai Theatre was located on 825 Kearny Street (next door to 815) and was renamed the Kearny Street in 1913. From 1948 onward, the theater was known as the Bella Union. With Chinese films as its primary output, the Bella Union served the San Francisco community up until 1985, when the building was converted into a retail space. See Tillmany, *Theatres of San Francisco*, 70. When I last visited the address in 2018, the space hosted a ginseng import and retail company. The 800 block is located next to Portsmouth Square and across the street from the Chinese Cultural Center.
137 *Variety*, February 11, 1911, 20–21.
138 *Billboard*, July 1, 1911, 19; "San Francisco," *Moving Picture World*, September 16, 1911, 808.
139 *Moving Picture World*, June 8, 1912, 925.
140 Jonathan Goldstein, "Cantonese Artifacts, Chinoiserie, and Early American Idealization of China," in *America Views China: American Images of China Then and Now*, ed. Jonathan Goldstein, Jerry Israel, and Hilary Conroy (Bethlehem, PA: Lehigh University Press, 1991), 48–52.
141 Tchen, *New York Before Chinatown*, xx.
142 According to Louis J. Stellman, the Shanghai was mainly there for the pleasure of tourists, while Chinatowners themselves preferred the more "modern histrionics" of vaudeville and movies. See Stellman, *Chinatown Photographer*, 50.
143 Trade press reports suggest that the Shanghai, during the summer months of 1916, was showing the latest Pearl White serial, *The Iron Claw*, acquired through Pathé Exchange. However, the previously important distinction between "Independents" and the "Trust" was by this time obsolete. Advertisement for California screenings of the *Iron Claw* in *San Francisco Chronicle*, June 28, 1916, 8.
144 Commonwealth Club of California, *Transactions of the Commonwealth Club of California*, 245.

145 Apart from the more regular arrests for indecent stage performances, one episode stands out as particularly bizarre. In the early fall of 1909, the *Call* reported that the Lyceum's manager, Carl Shenecker, had been charged by the police for offering entertainment that incorporated animal cruelty. Officer Hennessy had entered the theater and discovered a pool full of fish, which visitors could try to catch with a line and hook for the modest price of a dime. After a fish had been hooked, often resulting in considerable injury, it was routinely dropped back into the pool, still hooked. This operation was much to the chagrin of Hennessy, as well as the Society for the Prevention of Cruelty to Animals. Police judge Paul Weller arrested Shenecker and fined him twenty dollars. See "Proprietor of Theater Charged with Cruelty," *San Francisco Call*, September 28, 1909, 3; "Fined for Cruelty to Fish," *San Francisco Call*, September 29, 1909, 9.

146 Nee and de Bary Nee, *Longtime Californ'*, 69–71.

147 "Benjamin Michaels Killed," *Moving Picture World*, May 6, 1916, 1012.

148 In March 1910, when Michaels, Brown, and Gordon were in the initial stages of their rivalry, Marks senior advertised in San Francisco papers that he was looking for a partner to share his new venture at Stockton Street fifty-fifty. The required sum was $4,000. "Business Chances—Continued," *San Francisco Call*, March 6, 1910, 54.

149 "Here's the Way," *Film Daily*, Monday, November 6, 1922.

150 Joel Frykholm, *George Kleine and American Cinema: The Movie Business and Film Culture in the Silent Era* (London: British Film Institute/Palgrave Macmillan, 2015), 46–70.

151 "More about Marks," *Film Daily*, November 28, 1922, 1.

152 "The Acme Theater, San Francisco," *Moving Picture World*, September 25, 1915, 2165.

153 "More about Marks," *Film Daily*, November 28, 1922, 1.

154 An advertisement in *Moving Picture World* described the film as a "two-part circus story with many big scenes and ending with a runaway train on fire." *Moving Picture World*, January 31, 1914, 611.

155 "More about Marks," *Film Daily*, November 28, 1922, 2.

156 "More about Marks," *Film Daily*, November 28, 1922, 2.

157 For a history of the "grind policy" in U.S. silent film exhibition, see David Church, "From Exhibition to Genre: The Case of Grind-House Films," *Cinema Journal* 50, no. 4 (2011): 1–25.

158 "San Francisco Screen Club," *Moving Picture World*, July 10, 1915, 269.

159 Fong Get's entry in the 1900 San Francisco census suggests that he arrived in 1877. However, I have not been able to verify this date with another source.

160 Kim Poon Fong, Passport Application, March 2, 1921. *Division of Passport Control: Emergency Passport Applications for Travel to China, 1915–1925*. Volume 44. General Records of the Department of State, Record Group 59. National Archives, Washington D.C.

161 See Box 331, Peter Palmquist Collection of Male Photographers in the American West, circa 1840–2003, Beinecke Library, Yale University; Arnold Genthe and John Kuo Wei Tchen, *Genthe's Photographs of San Francisco's Old Chinatown* (New York: Dover, 1984); Anna Pegler-Gordon, *In Sight of America: Photography and the Development of U.S. Immigration Policy* (Berkeley: University of California Press, 2009).

162 Peter Palmquist, "Asian Photographers in San Francisco 1850–1930," *The Argonaut: Journal of the San Francisco Historical Society* 9 (1998): 87–88.

163 Palmquist, 88.

164 Yong also exhibited his work at local fairs, including the 1880 San Francisco Mechanics Fair; Palmquist, 88.

165 *Daily California Chronicle*, June 8, 1954, 2; "With Asian Lens," *San Francisco Call*, March 14, 1893, 3; "The Chinese at the Photographer's," *Photographic Times and American Photographer* 12 (1882): 158.

166 Advertisement for the opening of the Elite Photo Studio on Market Street in *San Francisco Chronicle*, February 24, 1879, 3.

167 "Orient Shown 'As Is,' Says Chinese 'Fan,'" *San Francisco Chronicle*, November 5, 1922, D1.

168 The Elite Photo Studio opened in 1879 at 838 Market Street. T. H. Jones and George Robinson initially ran the studio. By the early 1890s, Robinson was gone, and Jones's apprentice, Paul Lotz, had taken over the management of the studio together with Jones. Advertisement, *San Francisco Chronicle*, February 24, 1879, 3; "Safe Crackers," *San Francisco Chronicle*, March 29, 1893, 2.

169 Under the helm of Jones and Lotz, the Elite Studio became the main producers of celebrity portraits in San Francisco, together with the Bushnell and Louis Thors Studio. Until 1902, the Elite's theatrical department was run by theater veteran Josh Davis, and it might have been through him that Fong was able to make his connections in San Francisco's theater world. For more biographical information on Lotz, Davis, and the Elite Studio, see David S. Shields, "Elite Studio | Broadway Photographs," Broadway Photographs, accessed November 1, 2017, http://broadway.cas.sc.edu/content/about-site.

170 "Orient Shown 'As Is,' Says Chinese 'Fan,'" *San Francisco Chronicle*, November 5, 1922: D1.

171 Records of performances from theaters elsewhere in the country suggest that Kim Poon played the role interchangeably with other child actors. See Sheryl Fern Nadler, "'The First Born' (1897): A Cultural, Historical, and Literary Study of Francis Powers and David Belasco's Unpublished Drama of Chinese Life in America" (PhD diss., Florida State University, 1994), 404; Charles Elwell French, *Six Years of Drama at the Castle Square Theatre: With Portraits of the Members of the Company and Complete Programs of All Plays Produced, May 3, 1897–May 3, 1903* (Boston, MA: C. E. French, 1903), 167.

172 Nadler, "'The First Born' (1897)," 2. For analysis of performances and reviews from San Francisco, New York, and London, see Nadler, 29–60.

173 After the play had become a success, Francis Powers told journalists that he had frequented the cheap haunts of Chinatown during his days as a struggling actor. These experiences would have lent authenticity to his drama set in the neighborhood. Several major U.S. newspapers recounted different versions of this story. See, for example, "Francis Powers' First Born," *Washington Post*, October 17, 1897, 23; "At the Theaters," *Los Angeles Times*, December 19, 1897, 26.

174 Orient Shown 'As Is,' Says Chinese 'Fan,'" *San Francisco Chronicle*, November 5, 1922, D1.

175 "What Is to Be Seen at the Theaters?," *San Francisco Chronicle*, May 11, 4.

176 Nancy Yunhwa Rao's investigation of Chinese opera theater on the North American continent provides a mapping of the network and circulation of performers. See Rao, *Chinatown Opera Theater in North America*, 29–33.

177 "Fong Get Will Come Back," *San Francisco Call*, December 16, 1897, 12.

178 "Real Estate and Building News," *San Francisco Call*, August 31, 1907, 7.

179 *Billboard*, December 10, 1910, 101.
180 Pegler-Gordon, *In Sight of America*, 43–44.

## Chapter 5 The Chinesque Aesthetic

1 James Riely Gordon, "San Francisco—The Phoenix City," *Architect and Engineer* 26, no. 2 (September 1911): 56.
2 The notion of different Orientalisms stems from discussion propelled by Edward Said's work of the late 1970s and early 1980s.
3 Said described the distinction as that between "an almost unconscious (and certainly an untouchable) positivity, which I shall call latent Orientalism, and the various stated views about Oriental society, languages, literatures, history, sociology, and so forth, which I shall call manifest Orientalism." Edward Said, *Orientalism*, (London: Penguin, 2003), 207.
4 Roan, *Envisioning Asia*, 4. Said stressed a similar focus in a revisitation of the notion of Orientalism published in 1985. See Edward W. Said, "Orientalism Reconsidered," *Cultural Critique*, no. 1 (Autumn 1985): 107.
5 Lee, *Picturing Chinatown*, 152.
6 Choy, *Architecture of San Francisco Chinatown*, 42–43.
7 Yip, "San Francisco's Chinatown," 204–205.
8 Choy, *Architecture of San Francisco Chinatown*, 45–46.
9 Chen, *Chinese San Francisco*, 99.
10 Pan, *The Impact of the 1906 Earthquake on San Francisco's Chinatown*, 98.
11 Chen, *Chinese San Francisco*, 187.
12 Arnold Genthe and Will Irwin, *Pictures of Old Chinatown* (New York: Moffat, Yard, and Company, 1908); Arnold Genthe and Will Irwin, *Old Chinatown* (New York: Mitchell Kennerley, 1913).
13 Irwin, *The City That Was*, 33–434.
14 Genthe and Tchen, *Genthe's Photographs of San Francisco's Old Chinatown*.
15 James S. Moy, *Marginal Sights: Staging the Chinese in America* (Iowa City: University of Iowa Press, 1996), 67.
16 Moy, 76.
17 "Fire Reveals Chinatown Fake," *San Francisco Chronicle*, May 14, 1906.
18 Helen Throop Purdy, *San Francisco: As It Was, as It Is, and How to See It* (San Francisco: Paul Elder and Company, 1912), 138–139.
19 Asbury, *Barbary Coast*, 284.
20 Lee, *Picturing Chinatown*, 174.
21 Yip, "San Francisco's Chinatown," 233.
22 Rast, "Cultural Politics of Tourism," 57.
23 See Tchen, *New York before Chinatown*, xvi.
24 Susan Curtis, *A Consuming Faith: The Social Gospel and Modern American Culture* (Columbia, MO: University of Missouri Press, 2001), xviii, 2.
25 Historian Robert Rydell described this vision as the "task of providing industrialized America with a cultural synthesis through the medium of the international exposition"; Robert W. Rydell, *All the World's a Fair: Visions of Empire at American International Expositions, 1876–1916* (Chicago: University of Chicago Press, 1984), 39.
26 For an excellent account of Burnham and his central role in the realization of the Chicago fair, see Erik Larson, *The Devil in the White City: Murder, Magic, and Madness at the Fair That Changed America* (New York: Crown, 2003).

27 Chris Meister, "The Texas State Building: J. Riely Gordon's Contribution to the World's Columbian Exposition," *Southwestern Historical Quarterly* 98, no. 1 (1994): 1–24.

28 Robert Lee wrote on the power of contradiction inherent in different historical iterations of the U.S. stereotype of the Oriental: "The Oriental is a complex racial representation, made up of contradictory images and stereotypes. This complexity and ambiguity give the Oriental its ideological power, its connection with the broadest web of social concerns. In turn, this connectedness reinforces the representation and gives the racial stereotype its power to survive, mutate, and reproduce." See Robert G. Lee, *Orientals: Asian Americans in Popular Culture* (Philadelphia: Temple University Press, 1999), 12–13.

29 Ruth Mayer, "A 'Bit of Orient Set Worn in the Heart of a Western Metropolis': The Chinatown in the United States and Europe," in Künnemann and Mayer, *Chinatowns in a Transnational World: Myths and Realities of an Urban Phenomenon*, 2013, 6.

30 Gordon, "San Francisco—The Phoenix City," 56.

31 Choy, *Architecture of San Francisco*, 46.

32 According to the Sanborn Fire Insurance Maps of San Francisco of 1913, the property for the Shanghai Theatre storefront measured forty feet in length. See Sanborn Map Company, *Sanborn Fire Insurance Map from San Francisco, San Francisco County, California, 1913–1915*, vol. 1 (New York: Sanborn Map Company, 1913), sheet 33.

33 "San Francisco., Cal.," *Billboard*, December 9, 1909, 11.

34 Rube Cohen, "San Francisco Letter, *Billboard*, March 6, 1909, 11.

35 Rube Cohen, "San Francisco, Cal.," *Billboard*, July 1, 1911, 19.

36 Ona Otto, "San Francisco," *Moving Picture World*, September 16, 1911, 808.

37 Gordon, "San Francisco—The Phoenix City," 56.

38 Kendall R. Phillips, *A Place of Darkness: The Rhetoric of Horror in Early American Cinema* (Austin: University of Texas Press, 2018), 66.

39 In fact, Phillips implies such broader connections in reference to a 1911 description of a Portland movie theater. Phillips, 72.

40 *Panama-Pacific International Exposition 1915 Souvenir Guide: Natural Color Views, Half Tones and Descriptive Text, Portraying and Interpreting the Exposition Palaces, Courts, Art and Symbolism with Summary of Attractions on the Zone* (San Francisco: Souvenir Guide Publishers, 1915), 18.

41 "Sing-song girls" was an English language expression to describe musically trained Chinese courtesans and concubines. See Peter Morris, *Cantonese Love Songs: An English Translation of Jiu Ji-Yung's Cantonese Songs of the Early 19th Century* (Hong Kong: Hong Kong University Press, 1992), 8.

42 Rydell, *All the World's a Fair*, 30–31.

43 Moy, *Marginal Sights*, 52.

44 Trumbull White and William Igleheart, *The World's Columbian Exposition, Chicago, 1893* (Philadelphia: P. W. Ziegler and Company, 1893), 580.

45 Taliesin Evans, *All about the Midwinter Fair, San Francisco, and Interesting Facts concerning California* (San Francisco: W. B. Bancroft and Company, 1894), 75–77.

46 "San Diego Expo News," *Billboard*, February 27, 1915, 28.

47 Stan Delaplane, "They Just Don't Have Premieres Like Grauman Used to Put On," *Courier-Journal*, December 23, 1959, 7.

48 "In San Francisco," *Billboard*, May 22, 1909, 5.

49 "Barbary Coast Sketch Featured at Empress," *San Francisco Chronicle*, September 23, 1912, 5.
50 Advertisement for *Twenty Minutes at the Barbary Coast* at Grauman's Empress Theater in *San Francisco Call*, October 2, 1912, 7.
51 Records and reviews of *Last Night at the Barbary Coast*, for example, include mentions of Chinese dancers performing the "Texas Tommy." See "No Thrills in Last Night of Barbary Coast," *Motography*, November 15, 1913, 360.
52 Chen Chi, letter to Charles C. Moore and the Board of Directors of the PPIE, March 19, 1915, Carton 33, PPIE Records, Bancroft Library, University of California, Berkeley.
53 Lee, *Picturing Chinatown*, 171.
54 "The prologues were often thematically related to whatever film was playing at the time; however, some departed from this model to showcase unusual novelty acts that sometimes smacked of Far Eastern flavor"; Homay King, *Lost in Translation: Orientalism, Cinema, and the Enigmatic Signifier* (Durham, NC: Duke University Press, 2010), 45.
55 While Grauman had continued the practice of prefacing moving pictures with stage performances from San Francisco days, it was not until he announced his plans build the Chinese Theater on Hollywood Boulevard in 1926 that it became a point of contention in Hollywood. In June 1926, *Film Daily* published a survey in which famous producers and directors had their say about the prologues. Marshall Neilan called them the "curse of the motion picture theater. One becomes so weary looking at them he is not able to enjoy to the utmost the picture that follows." Cecil B. DeMille expressed concern regarding how long prologues might come to influence the making of the movies they were meant to precede. Sidney Olcott offered that he saw no benefits to including a prologue unless it was "light, short and has no bearing on the production itself." Herbert Brenon believed the prologues were "hurtful to screen production." *Film Daily*, June 17, 1926, 8.
56 "San Francisco, Cal.," *Billboard*, December 9, 1909, 11.
57 Lui, *Chinatown Trunk Mystery*, 215.
58 The Chinese Justice League of America, for example, penned a letter to New York district attorney Charles Whitman to ask that the play be banned. See letter from Police Commissioner Wm. F. Bakery to Charles M. Whitman, August 19, 1910, AAS ARC 2000/43, Chinese in California Collection, Bancroft Library, Berkeley.
59 *Chinese Defender* 1, no. 6 (February 1911): 8.
60 *Chinese Defender* 1, no. 6 (February 1911): 8.
61 "Melodrama Fails to Please 'Gods,'" *San Francisco Chronicle*, February 13, 1911, 5.
62 Lui, *Chinatown Trunk Mystery*, 216.
63 Chinese Consolidated Benevolent Association, letter to Charles C. Moore and the Board of Directors of the PPIE, March 19, 1915, Carton 33, PPIE Records, Bancroft Library, University of California, Berkeley.
64 Chen Chi, letter to Charles C. Moore, March 19, 1915, Carton 33, PPIE Records, Bancroft Library, University of California, Berkeley.
65 Chen Chi, letter to Charles C. Moore, March 19, 1915.
66 Chen Chi, letter to Charles C. Moore, March 19, 1915.
67 Chinese Consolidated Benevolent Association, letter to Charles C. Moore and the Board of Directors of the PPIE, March 19, 1915.

68 H. G. Chu, letter to Charles C. Moore and the Board of Directors of the PPIE, March 19, 1915, Carton 33, PPIE Records, Bancroft Library, University of California, Berkeley.
69 Chinese Chamber of Commerce, letter to Charles C. Moore and the Board of Directors of the PPIE, March 19, 1915, Carton 33, PPIE Records, Bancroft Library, University of California, Berkeley.
70 Chinese Christian Union, letter to Charles C. Moore and the Board of Directors of the PPIE, March 24, 1915, Carton 33, PPIE Records, Bancroft Library, University of California, Berkeley.
71 Hsuwen Tsou, letter to Charles C. Moore and the Board of Directors of the PPIE, March 26, 1915, Carton 33, PPIE Records, Bancroft Library, University of California, Berkeley.
72 "The Chinese Press of San Francisco and the Chinese Press of China" (undersigned by Ng Poon Chew, Yong Kai, *Young China*, *The Chinese World*, *The Chinese Republic Journal*, and the *People's Tongue*), letter to Charles C. Moore and the Board of Directors of the PPIE, March 24, 1915, Carton 33, PPIE Records, Bancroft Library, University of California, Berkeley.
73 Lui, *Chinatown Trunk Mystery*, 204–206.
74 "Chinatown Hell Indeed Incites the Bad Impression about Chinese," *Chung Sai Yat Po*, March 27, 1915, 3.
75 "Chinatown Hell in PPIE Is Enforced to Close," *Chung Sai Yat Po*, March 27, 1915, 3.
76 Minutes from the PPIE Concession Committee, October 21, 1915, Carton 24, PPIE Records, Bancroft Library, University of California, Berkeley.
77 "San Francisco Facts," *Billboard*, June 26, 1915, 10.
78 List of Objects for Sale from the Underground Chinatown concession, 1915, Carton 33, PPIE Records, Bancroft Library, University of California, Berkeley.
79 "Get-Away Day," *Billboard*, December 18, 1915, 195.
80 "'Midnight Frisco' Will Appear at the Victory," *San Jose Enquirer*, September 29, 1916.
81 "Majestic," *Los Angeles Times*, October 23, 1916, II3.
82 Henry Christeen Warnack, "Strong in Quantity," *Los Angeles Times*, October 23, 1916.
83 Harry Bonnell, "San Francisco," *Variety* May 30, 1913.
84 "Manager of Empress Becomes a Producer," *San Francisco Chronicle*, August 13, 1916, 24.
85 Beardsley, *Hollywood's Master Showman*, 35.
86 According to Beardsley, the design of the theater was Grauman's concept, developed in association with film producer Joseph Schenck and Hollywood real estate tycoon Charles Toberman. In Beardsley's account, Toberman became so obsessed with the idea of enlarging the theater that Grauman sent him to China to gather "authentic data," in order to complete the construction in time. See Beardsley, 17–18.
87 Beardsley, 109–110; Endres and Cushman, *Hollywood at Your Feet*, 27.
88 Altman, *Silent Film Sound*, 385.
89 Beardsley, *Hollywood's Master Showman*, 45.
90 Endres and Cushman, *Hollywood at Your Feet*, 28.
91 Vinzenz Hediger, "Putting the Spectators in a Receptive Mood," in *Film's Thresholds*, ed. Veronica Innocenti and Valentina Re (Udine, Italy: Forum 2004), 303–304.

92 Lee, *Picturing Chinatown*, 170.
93 Louis J. Stellman, *That Was a Dream Worth Building; the Spirit of San Francisco's Great Fair* (San Francisco: H. S. Crocker Company, 1916).
94 Leo Ou-fan Lee, *Shanghai Modern: The Flowering of a New Urban Culture in China, 1930–1945* (Cambridge, MA: Harvard University Press, 2001), 46.
95 Stellman, *Chinatown Photographer*, 34–35.
96 Sabine Haenni, *The Immigrant Scene: Ethnic Amusements in New York; 1880–1920* (Minneapolis: University of Minnesota Press, 2008), 183.
97 Davies, *Saving San Francisco*, 141.
98 Haenni, *Immigrant Scene*, 169.

## Chapter 6 "Where the People Aren't All American"

1 Miriam Bratu Hansen, *Cinema and Experience: Siegfried Kracauer, Walter Benjamin and Theodor W. Adorno* (Berkeley: University of California Press, 2011), 55.
2 Jan Olsson noted "that the flaneur genre's incidental city reporting during the nickelodeon period provided a foundation for subsequent writings on film matters and cinema." Olsson, *Los Angeles before Hollywood*, 29. The flaneurian tendency was echoed in, for example, the early film writings of Siegfried Kracauer, which, in the words of Miriam Hansen, were "actually cinema reviews, in the sense that they include remarks on theater design, performance practices, musical accompaniment, and audience response." Hansen, *Cinema and Experience*, 6.
3 "Small Panic Is Result of Fire," *San Francisco Chronicle*, March 17, 1909, 5.
4 "San Francisco, Cal.," *Billboard*, March 6, 1909, 11.
5 "The Acme Theater, San Francisco," *Moving Picture World*, September 25, 1915, 2165.
6 "San Francisco, Cal.," *Billboard*, December 18, 1909, 11.
7 *Transactions of the Commonwealth Club of California*, 239.
8 Reading material was also printed in Italian and Spanish. "San Francisco," *Moving Picture World*, July 13, 1912, 164; "A Polyglot Program," *Moving Picture World*, November 13, 1915, 1302.
9 "San Francisco," *Moving Picture World*, September 16, 1911, 808.
10 *Transactions of the Commonwealth Club of California*, 246.
11 The diary of Chinese immigrant Ah-Quin, preserved at the San Diego History Center, exemplifies such movements. Entries between August 1879 and November 1880 describe Ah-Quin's frequent visits to Chinatown theaters, even though he lived outside the neighborhood. For example, Ah-Quin witnessed the March 1880 fire attack at the Grand Theater on Washington Street. See diary entry, 1880, MS 209, Diary 4, Ah Quin Diary Collection, San Diego History Center Document Collection, San Diego.
12 Rube Cohen, "San Francisco, Cal.," *Billboard*, July 1, 1911, 19.
13 "San Francisco," *Moving Picture World*, July 13, 1912, 164.
14 "The Acme Theater, San Francisco," *Moving Picture World*, September 25, 1915, 2165.
15 Mary Carbine, "'The Finest Outside the Loop': Motion Picture Exhibition in Chicago's Black Metropolis, 1905–1928," *Camera Obscura* 8, no. 2 (1990): 18; Gregory Waller, *Main Street Amusements: Movies and Commercial Entertainment in a Southern City, 1896–1930* (Washington, DC: Smithsonian Institution Press, 1995), 161–179; Jacqueline Najuma Stewart, *Migrating to the Movies: Cinema and Black Urban Modernity* (Berkeley: University of California Press, 2005), 149–150.

16 Elizabeth Pepin and Lewis Watts, *Harlem of the West: The San Francisco Fillmore Jazz Era* (San Francisco: Chronicle Books, 2005), 30–32.
17 Denise Khor has shown that racial segregation of Asian Americans was employed elsewhere in the theaters in the states of California and Washington in the 1920s. Khor, "Asian Americans at the Movies," 69, 74.
18 "Small Panic Is Result of Fire," *San Francisco Chronicle*, March 17, 1909, 5; Adriana Spadoni, "An Interview with a Nickelodeon Fiend," *San Francisco Chronicle*, August 21, 1910, 12 (hereafter cited as Spadoni, "Nickelodeon Fiend"); "The Acme Theater, San Francisco," *Moving Picture World*, September 25, 1915, 2165.
19 Carbine, "'The Finest Outside the Loop,'" 13.
20 Foster, "Chinese Theatres in America," 75.
21 Yung, *Unbound Feet*, 77.
22 "The Acme Theater, San Francisco," *Moving Picture World*, September 25, 1915, 2165.
23 "Flames Causes Theater Panic," *San Francisco Call*, September 4, 1911, 2.
24 See Waller, *Main Street Amusements*, 69.
25 Foster, "Chinese Theatres in America," 84. Judy Yung presented the following historical data on prostitution in San Francisco's Chinatown: "In 1870, the peak year of prostitution, 1,426 or 71 percent of Chinese women in San Francisco were listed as prostitutes. By 1900, the number had dropped to 339 or 16 percent; and by 1910, 92 or 7 percent." Yung, *Unbound Feet*, 71–72.
26 Yung, *Unbound Feet*, 54.
27 Yung, 12.
28 *Chung Sai Yat Po*, July 11, 1906, cited in Pan, *Impact of the 1906 Earthquake*, 116.
29 Yung, *Unbound Feet*, 71–72, 77.
30 Ying Hu, *Tales of Translation: Composing the New Woman in China, 1899–1918* (Stanford, CA: Stanford University Press, 2000), 12.
31 Yung, *Unbound Feet*, 80.
32 William Uricchio and Roberta E. Pearson, "Manhattan's Nickelodeons New York? New York! William Uricchio and Roberta E. Pearson Comment on the Singer-Allen Exchange," *Cinema Journal* 36, no. 4 (1997): 99.
33 Michael Aronson, *Nickelodeon City: Pittsburgh at the Movies, 1905–1929* (Pittsburgh: University of Pittsburgh Press, 2008), 92.
34 Spadoni, "Nickelodeon Fiend."
35 "San Francisco," *Moving Picture World*, September 16, 1909, 808.
36 Of the Chinatown managers, proprietors, and projectionists encountered in my research material, only Fong Get has had a Chinese name.
37 Douglas Gomery, "The Growth of Movie Monopolies: The Case of Balaban and Katz," *Wide Angle* 3, no. 1 (1979): 59.
38 Carbine, "'The Finest Outside the Loop,'" 20.
39 I am indebted to Professor Phil Choy and the Chinese Historical Society of America in San Francisco for assistance in interpreting this document.
40 Miriam Hansen developed the notion of "vernacular modernism" as a way to approach the cultural practices that "both articulated and mediated" the experience of modernity in the first decades of the twentieth century. The concept has become an influential umbrella term for the study and conceptualization of place-specific interactions with modernity and film culture in the early Classical Hollywood era. See Miriam Hansen, "The Mass Production of the Senses: Classical Cinema as Vernacular Modernism," *Modernism/modernity* 6, no. 2 (1999): 60–61; Hansen, "Vernacular Modernism," 287–314. For an excellent

utilization of the term as a perspective on early Shanghainese modernity and film culture, see Miriam Hansen, "Fallen Women, Rising Stars, New Horizons: Shanghai Silent Film as Vernacular Modernism," *Film Quarterly* 54, no. 1 (October 2000): 10–22; Zhen Zhang, *An Amorous History of the Silver Screen: Shanghai Cinema, 1896–1937* (Chicago: University of Chicago Press, 2005).

41 A few archival objects preserved by the San Francisco Performing Arts Library suggest that announcing the program in separate Chinese-language pamphlets became standard practice for the various movie operations that would succeed the Oriental in the same locale. See promotional pamphlets titled "The Mandarin Theatre," May 21, 1939, and May 27, 1939. See Folder 47, San Francisco Chinese Collection, San Francisco Performing Arts Library and Museum, San Francisco.

42 Pratt borrows the term "transculturation" from the field of ethnography, where it has been used to "describe how subordinated and marginal groups select and invent from materials transmitted to them by a dominant or metropolitan culture. While subjugated peoples cannot readily control what emanates from the dominant culture, they do determine to varying extents what they absorb into their own, and what they use it for." See Pratt, *Imperial Eyes*, 6.

43 Pratt, 7.

44 "Exhibitor Starts Paper," *Moving Picture World*, October 3, 1915, 488; "A Polyglot Program," *Moving Picture World*, November 13, 1915, 1302; "Going Strong," *Moving Picture World*, November 20, 1915, 1491; "How about It?," *Moving Picture World*, January 1, 1916, 74.

45 "Shows Titles in Italian," *Moving Picture World*, December 4, 1915, 1876. In a peculiar twist of fate, Michaels's conundrum has re-emerged at various cinematheques and silent film festivals, where silent film impresarios of the digitized age devise a separate source for projecting translated subtitles and intertitles during screenings. A common combination is PowerPoint, a digital projector, and a tech-savvy operator gifted in languages.

46 For a history of the benshi practice in Japan, see Joseph L. Anderson and Donald Richie, *The Japanese Film: Art and Industry* (Princeton, NJ: Princeton University Press, 1982); Hiroshi Komatsu and Charles Musser, "Benshi Search," *Wide Angle* 9, no. 2 (1987): 73–90; and Hiroshi Komatsu and Frances Loden, "Mastering the Mute Image: The Role of the Benshi in Japanese Cinema," *Iris* 22 (Fall 1996): 33–52.

47 For more on the early global film history and local operations of the moving picture lecturer, see See, "Le bonimenteur de vues animées—The Moving Picture Lecturer," ed. André Gaudreault and Germain Lacasse, special issue, *Iris* 22 (Fall 1996).

48 Charles Musser, "Rethinking Early Cinema, Cinema of Attractions and Narrativity," in *The Cinema of Attractions Reloaded*, ed. Wanda Strauven (Amsterdam: Amsterdam University Press, 2006), 389–416.

49 Germain Lacasse, "The Film Lecturer," in *A Companion to Early Cinema*, ed. André Gaudreault, Nicolas Dulac, and Santiago Hidalgo (Malden, MA: Wiley-Blackwell, 2012), 489.

50 Except for Lacasse and Komatsu, who have investigated the role of the lecturer in Quebecois and Japanese film exhibition, respectively, see, for example, Ansje van Beusekom, "The Rise and Fall of the Lecturer as Entertainer in the Netherlands: Exhibition-Practices in Transition Related to Local Circumstances," in Gaudreault and Lacasse, "Le bonimenteur de vues animées," 131–144; Daniel Sánches Salas, "A History of the Film Lecturer in Spanish Silent Cinema," in Gaudreault and Lacasse, "Le bonimenteur de vues animées," 171–181.

51 Lacasse, "Film Lecturer," 493. The original quote reads: "The hegemony of 'silent' films and of the countries which produced them was thus attenuated by the intervention of national and local agents who not only adapted the film to their audience's language and culture, but who could intervene on another level through their own performance."
52 André Gaudreault and Germain Lacasse, eds., *Le bonimenteur de vues animées: Le cinéma muet entre tradition et modernité* (Québec: Éditions Nota bene, 2000).
53 Ying Hu's work especially investigates the emergence of the concept of the "new woman" in the late Qing and early Republican China. See Hu, *Tales of Translation.*
54 Chen, *Chinese San Francisco,* 163.
55 Hu, *Tales of Translation*, 12–13.
56 Daphne Lei, "The Production and Consumption of Chinese Theatre in Nineteenth-Century California," *Theatre Research International* 28, no. 3 (October 2003): 295.
57 *San Francisco's Chinatown—An Aid to Tourists.*
58 Lei, "Production and Consumption of Chinese Theatre," 295.
59 Rast, "Cultural Politics of Tourism," 32.
60 David Bordwell, Janet Staiger, and Kristin Thompson, *The Classical Hollywood Cinema: Film Style and Mode of Production to 1960* (New York: Columbia University Press, 1985), 129; Robert C. Allen, *Vaudeville and Film 1895–1915: A Study in Media Interaction* (New York: Arno Press, 1980), 230–288.
61 Spadoni, "Interview with a Nickelodeon Fiend."
62 See "Correspondence: California," *Billboard,* April 9, 1910, 16; "San Francisco," *Variety*, February 11, 1911, 20; "Screeners Hold Frolic," *Moving Picture World*, January 19, 1915, 233; "Empress, San Francisco," *Billboard*, July 15, 1915, 11.
63 "Box Office Officiousness and the Puerile Public," *San Francisco Chronicle*, November 28, 1909, supplement "Dramatic and Society," 1.
64 Reports from *Billboard*, *Moving Picture World*, and various guidebooks routinely referred to these theaters as "Chinese Theaters" that attracted non-Chinese moviegoers.
65 See "Mexican and Chinese Revolutionists Clash," *San Francisco Chronicle*, January 31, 1912, 4.
66 "The Acme Theater, San Francisco," *Moving Picture World*, September 25, 1915, 2165.
67 "The Acme Theater, San Francisco," *Moving Picture World*, September 25, 1915, p. 2165.
68 "Here's the Way," *Film Daily*, November 6, 1922, 4.
69 Lei, "Production and Consumption of Chinese Theatre," 295.
70 Jan Olsson described the notion of metaspectatorship as "the double-faced reporting from visits to nickel theaters, focusing both on screen representations and audience members' bodily and physiognomic engagement with screen matters." Olsson, *Los Angeles before Hollywood*, 38. Olsson primarily located the concept in nickelodeon era newspaper reporting on film audiences, but the term is useful in this study to analyze audience accounts from other contemporary materials as well, such as guidebooks, postcards, and advertisements.
71 Chen, *Chinese San Francisco*, 92.
72 Olsson, *Los Angeles before Hollywood*, 182–183.
73 Barbara Berglund, "Chinatown's Tourist Terrain: Representation and Racialization in Nineteenth-Century San Francisco," *American Studies* 46, no. 2 (2005): 6.
74 Sociologist John Urry introduced the notion of the tourist gaze in his pioneering 1990 book of the same name. Urry described the notion as a discursively informed

mode of spectatorship through which tourists experience and consume geographic places. For example, the tourist gaze is "directed to features of landscape and townscape which separate them off from everyday experience. Such aspects are viewed because they are taken to be in some sense out of the ordinary. The viewing of such tourist sights often involves different forms of social patterning, with a much greater sensitivity to visual elements of landscape or townscape than is normally found in everyday life. People linger over such a gaze which is then normally visually objectified or captured through photographs, postcards, films, models and so on." See John Urry, *The Tourist Gaze*, 2nd ed. (London: Sage, 2002), 2–3.

75 Berglund, "Chinatown's Tourist Terrain," 5–36.

76 Rast, "Cultural Politics of Tourism," 29–60.

77 Haenni specifically connected this notion to slumming tour practices but observed that it tied into a broader perception of Chinatown as a place of sensorial overload. See Haenni, *Immigrant Scene*, 156–160.

78 Rast, "Cultural Politics of Tourism," 43.

79 See audience descriptions of the Shanghai in Rube Cohen, "San Francisco, Cal.," *Billboard*, July 1, 1911, 19; the Broadway theater in "San Francisco," *Moving Picture World*, July 13, 1912, 164; and the Acme Theater in "The Acme Theater, San Francisco," *Moving Picture World*, September 25, 1915, 2165.

80 Berglund, "Chinatown's Tourist Terrain," 26.

81 Darya Maoz, "The Mutual Gaze," *Annals of Tourism Research* 33, no. 1 (January 2006): 222.

82 In a revised edition of *The Tourist Gaze*, Urry recognizes the need for such a broadened approach. John Urry and Jonas Larsen, *The Tourist Gaze 3.0* (London: Sage, 2011), 204–205.

83 Rast, "Cultural Politics of Tourism," 32.

84 Mary Heaton Vorse's essay was initially published in the *Outlook* on June 24, 1911. Relevant studies of U.S. transition era film exhibition that cite Heaton Vorse at length include Hansen, *Babel and Babylon*; Ben Singer, *Melodrama and Modernity: Early Sensational Cinema and Its Contexts* (New York: Columbia University Press, 2001); Richard Abel, *Americanizing the Movies and "Movie-Mad" Audiences, 1910–1914* (Berkeley: University of California Press, 2006).

85 Spadoni, "Interview with a Nickelodeon Fiend."

86 Spadoni, "Interview with a Nickelodeon Fiend."

87 Spadoni.

88 Spadoni, "Interview with a Nickelodeon Fiend."

89 Hansen, *Babel and Babylon*, 55.

90 "Clubs Denied Use of School Rooms," *San Francisco Call*, July 2, 1910. Spadoni would later draw on her experiences teaching English to immigrants in San Francisco for another article. See Adriana Spadoni, "Where the Primary Pupils Wear Whiskers," *San Francisco Call*, February 19, 1911, 5.

91 Adriana Spadoni, "Devils, White, and Yellow," *Overland Monthly and Out West Magazine*, July 1, 1904, 80.

92 Adriana Spadoni, "Chinese Orphanage Founded on a Superstition," *San Francisco Chronicle*, November 12, 1905, 5.

93 The main character, Jean Norris, at first sight describes the Broadway and Stockton Street sections between Chinatown and North Beach as "the sordid section that lies between the White World and the Yellow, where mean gray

houses cling hopelessly together, like the poor for comfort and outcasts for respectability." But she then becomes sympathetic to her companion's more sophisticated perception of the place:, "It coarsened her that she had seen only the dirt and squalor of the vice, while the man beside her had grasped something beneath that linked it up with reality even as they both knew it, a kind of cosmic unity too finely tuned for her ears." Adriana Spadoni, *The Swing of the Pendulum* (New York: Boni and Liveright, 1919), 34–37.

94 Spadoni, "Interview with a Nickelodeon Fiend."

95 "Slave Girls of Chinatown Tell about Their Bondage," *San Francisco Chronicle*, February 12, 1901; "Chinatown Belle Off with Coolie: Pretty Chun Moy, an Heiress, Has Fled with a Poor Fisherman," *San Francisco Chronicle*, July 22, 1909; "Save Young Girls from Chinatown: Detectives Arrest Chinamen Who Had 15-Year-Old Christina Braun Locked in a Room," *New York Times*, September 8, 1909; "Police Rescue Slave Girl in Chinatown," *San Francisco Chronicle*, September 27, 1911; "Chinatown Girls Rescue Needs Aid: Settlement for Redeeming Whites from Evil Influence Lacks Funds," *New-York Tribune*, June 21, 1915, Woman's Page; "Girls Visit Chinatown; Two Chinese Arrested: Detectives Break into Pell Street Room to Rescue Sightseers," *New-York Tribune*, January 5, 1917.

96 Adriana Spadoni, "The Sing-Song Slaves of Chinatown," *San Francisco Call*, December 6, 1908, 3.

97 Adriana Spadoni, "The Sing-Song Slaves of Chinatown," *San Francisco Call*, December 6, 1908, 3.

98 Spadoni, "Interview with a Nickelodeon Fiend."

99 Waller, *Main Street Amusements*; Gregory Waller, *Moviegoing in America: A Sourcebook in the History of Film Exhibition* (Malden, MA: Blackwell, 2002

100 Although her first novel garnered lukewarm criticism, her second book, *The Noise of the World*, was received as the work of an accomplished and "remarkably advanced" female writer. Adriana Spadoni, *The Noise of the World* (New York: Boni and Liveright, 1921). For review examples, "Acid Test of a Hero," *New York Tribune*, March 7, 1920, 10; "O for a Real Woman as an Emancipated Heroine," *San Francisco Chronicle*, March 28, 1920, E2; "Two Points of View," *San Francisco Chronicle*, April 10, 1921, E3; "California Literary Field Yields Abundant Harvest," *San Francisco Chronicle*, October 16, 1921, B1.

101 Margaret C. Jones, *Heretics and Hellraisers: Women Contributors to* The Masses, *1911–1917* (Austin: University of Texas Press, 2014), 25.

102 Jones, 111.

103 Genthe and Tchen, *Genthe's Photographs of San Francisco's Old Chinatown*, 15–16.

104 Rutherford and Bhabha, "Third Space," 211. While Homi Bhabha's conceptualizations of cultural hybridity were often fleeting, one of his interpreters, geographer Paul Routledge, found it most visible in the concept of thirdspace, which he conceived as places of "invention and transformational encounters, a dynamic in-between space that is imbued with the traces, relays, ambivalence, ambiguities and contradictions, with the feelings and practices of both sites, to fashion something different, unexpected." Paul Routledge, "The Third Space as Critical Engagement," *Antipode* 28, no. 4 (October 1996): 406.

105 Haenni, *Immigrant Scene*, 169.

106 Dating the various recordings included in this film is tricky, since the footage was most likely collated from a variety of sources. However, newspaper articles from 1913 and 1914 contain reports from the shooting of some of the scenes from the

film. See "Paid Hop Heads to Pose," *Variety*, October 24, 1913, 17; "Mrs. Gould Enraged," *Variety*, October 3, 1913, 13; "Guide Held for Criminal Libel," *San Francisco Chronicle*, October 9, 1913, 7; "Charge Pressed by Mrs. Gould," *Los Angeles Times*, September 27, 1914, 4.

107 "Seeing Chinatown, San Francisco, Lewis' Tours" (Sierra, San Francisco, ca. 1908), Beinecke Rare Book and Manuscript Library, Yale University. This three-panel leaflet dated from around 1908 claims that Lewis had conducted tours of Chinatown for twenty-four years.

108 "Chinatown Guide Is Interesting Person," *San Francisco Call*, March 10, 1912, 33.

109 "Seeing Chinatown, San Francisco, Lewis' Tours." The 1912 interview with Lewis in the *Call* recounted a less detailed version of this tableau. "Chinatown Guide Is Interesting Person," *San Francisco Call*, March 10, 1912, 33.

110 In addition to Haenni, see Matthew Bernstein and Gaylyn Studlar, *Visions of the East: Orientalism in Film* (New Brunswick, NJ: Rutgers University Press 1997); Haddad, "The Laundry Man's Got a Knife!"; Mayer, "Glittering Machine of Modernity," 661–684; Björn A. Schmidt, *Visualizing Orientalness: Chinese Immigration and Race in U.S. Motion Pictures, 1910s–1930s* (Cologne, Germany: Böhlau Verlag, 2017), 107–194.

111 Schmidt, *Visualizing Orientalness*, 163.

112 Schmidt, 165.

113 Schmidt even acknowledges the thirdspace/heterotopic character of "real" Chinatown, as opposed to the closed-off racialized enclave described in dominant contemporary discourses on the neighborhood. Schmidt, 110.

114 Roan, *Envisioning Asia*, 16.

115 Both Holmes and Howe gradually began using moving pictures in their illustrated lectures in the 1910s.

116 Charles Musser, "The Travel Genre in 1903–1904: Moving towards Fictional Narrative," in *Early Cinema: Space, Frame, Narrative*, ed. Thomas Elsaesser and Adam Barker (London: BFI Publishing, 1990), 123–132.

117 Tom Gunning, "The Whole World within Reach: Travel Images without Borders," in *Virtual Voyages: Cinema and Travel*, ed. Jeffrey Ruoff (Durham, NC: Duke University Press, 2006), 25–26.

118 Alison Griffiths, *Wondrous Difference: Cinema, Anthropology, and Turn-of-the-Century Visual Culture* (New York: Columbia University Press, 2001); Roan, *Envisioning Asia*.

119 The film was finished in late 1914. *Moving Picture World* reported that Lewis planned to take the show east, "accompanied by a Chinese family." This was confirmed in later reports from Lewis's lecture tours. See "San Francisco," *Moving Picture World*, November 28, 1914, 1259; "At the Grand," *Topeka Daily Capital*, September 19, 1915, 6.

120 Charles Musser called the genre "a cinema of reassurance." Charles Musser, *High-Class Moving Pictures: Lyman H. Howe and the Forgotten Era of Traveling Exhibition, 1880–1920* (Princeton, NJ: Princeton University Press, 1991).

121 Peterson cites Hansen's work on the Frankfurt School in *Babel and Babylon*, as well as in Hansen's last book, *Cinema and Experience*. On the subject of multiple experiential dimensions of the travel film, Peterson quotes explicitly a passage in *Babel and Babylon*: "The reciprocity between film on the screen and the spectator's stream of associations becomes the measure of the film's use value for an alternative public sphere: a film either exploits the viewer's needs, perceptions, and wishes

or it encourages their autonomous movement, fine-tuning, self-reliance." Jennifer Lynn Peterson, *Education in the School of Dreams: Travelogues and Early Nonfiction Film* (Durham, NC: Duke University Press, 2013), 212. Quoted from Hansen, *Babel and Babylon*, 13.

122 Peterson, *Education in the School of Dreams*, 209.

123 Peterson, 217.

124 See Schmidt, *Visualizing Orientalness*, 165; Peterson, *Education in the School of Dreams*, 211–212.

125 Peterson, *Education in the School of Dreams*, 226–230.

126 I have used a Chinese business directory published in 1913 to locate and identify the street views and businesses shown in the film. See International Chinese Business Directory Company, *International Chinese Business Directory of the World: A Comprehensive List of Prominent Chinese Firms and Individuals in Parts of China, Japan, India Proper [etc.]* (San Francisco: International Chinese Business Directory Company, 1913), 1445, 1453.

127 "Pictures of Chinatown," *Topeka Daily Capital*, September 28, 1915, 10.

128 Fatimah Tobing Rony theorized the cinematic "return of the gaze" as a voyeuristic pleasure for white audiences safely removed from situations in which the subaltern looks back. This schema was criticized by the likes of Alison Griffiths, who argued that the return gaze of cinema pointed audiences toward moments of transcultural interaction, highlighting a dimension of reciprocity reminiscent of Mary Louise Pratt's contact zone. Fatimah Tobing Rony, *The Third Eye: Race, Cinema and Ethnographic Spectacle* (Durham, NC: Duke University Press, 1996); Griffiths, *Wondrous Difference*, 199–200.

129 Initial reports from the tour suggest that Lewis brought along a group of Chinese San Franciscans who worked in the lobby before and after the show. "San Francisco," November 28, 1914, 1259; "At the Theaters," *Topeka State Journal*, September 18, 1915, 7; "Chinatown Tours," *Topeka State Journal*, September 22, 1915, 7.

130 Advertisement in *St. Petersburg Daily Times*, February 3, 1920, 6.

131 The Harrison Narcotics Tax Act was passed in 1914 to regulate and control the import and distribution of opium in the United States.

132 "Drug-Users Caught Posing for Movies," *Oakland Tribune*, October 16, 6; "Arrest Drug Fiends Posing for Movies," *San Francisco Call*, October 16, 1913, 1.

133 "Drug-Users Caught Posing for Movies," *Oakland Tribune*, October 16, 6. The news also reached the trade press. See "Paid Hop Heads to Pose," *Variety*, October 24, 1913, 17.

134 Chinatown institutions, such as the Six Companies, had long protested the guided tours' insistence on entertaining "visitors with stories of the depravity among Chinese residents." See, for example, "Chinese Consul-General Complains at Exploitation of Vice in Chinatown," *San Francisco Chronicle*, September 21, 1904, 5.

135 "In Chinatown," *Topeka State Journal*, September 28, 1915, 9.

136 "China's Golden Box Is Like Fairytale," *Quad-City Times*, October 19, 1915, 3.

137 Reports from the film exhibition tour suggest that Lewis talked about how the revolution had impacted and modernized Chinese life in San Francisco. See, for example, "In Chinatown," *Topeka State Journal*, September 28, 1915, 9; "Chinatown at Burtis," *Quad-City Times*, October 18, 1915, 3; "Take a Trip through Chinatown with Guide at the Rialto Today," *Greenville News*, December 20, 1919, 10.

138 "Take a Trip through Chinatown with Guide at the Rialto Today," *The Greenville News*, December 20, 1919, 10.

139 Hansen, *Babel and Babylon*, 63.
140 Chen, *Chinese San Francisco*, 125.
141 Haenni, *Immigrant Scene*, 169.

## Chapter 7 Chinatown Modernity

1 "A Chinese Telephone Exchange," *Telephone Magazine*, September 1, 1901, 198.
2 "A Chinese Telephone Exchange," *Tatler*, no. 139 (February 24, 1904): 302.
3 Stephen Kern, *The Culture of Time and Space, 1880–1918: With a New Preface* (Cambridge, MA: Harvard University Press, 2003), 215.
4 Him Mark Lai, "A Brief Historical Overview of Wei Xiongfei's Times," in *Chinese America: History and Perspectives*, ed. Colleen Fong (San Francisco: Chinese Historical Society of America, 2005), 19.
5 Gunning, "Modernity and Cinema," 302.
6 Francesco Casetti, *Eye of the Century: Film, Experience, and Modernity* (New York: Columbia University Press, 2005), 5.
7 Lucy Fischer, "'The Shock of the New': Electrification, Illumination, Urbanization, and the Cinema," in *Cinema and Modernity*, ed. Murray Pomerance (New Brunswick, NJ: Rutgers University Press, 2006), 28.
8 Studies of early film culture often engage processes of modernity. As noted by Leo Charney and Vanessa Schwartz, various usages of the notion of modernity have been entertained by scholars in the field as a way to organize "changes in so-called subjective experience" brought on by the emergence and popularization of public film exhibition. Alternatively, modernity has been mobilized as shorthand for social, economic, and cultural transformations connected to everyday functions of early film cultures. In this study, the usage of the term falls closer to the latter categorization. The processes of modernity here investigated can be broadly defined as dealing with and commenting on the perceived effects of communications technologies in general, and cinema in particular, in the everyday lives of humans and the urban environment of Chinatown. See Leo Charney and Vanessa R. Schwartz, eds., *Cinema and the Invention of Modern Life* (Berkeley: University of California Press, 1995), 1.
9 Sun, "From Isolation to Participation," 66.
10 Chen, *Chinese San Francisco*, 162–185.
11 "As the political parties were changing, American Chinatowns were also changing. A far broader segment of the population of Chinese in America became interested in politics. Nationalism grew at a faster pace than ever before. More and more it served to break down intracommunity barriers and encouraged political activism, as individuals seeking ways to help China regain international prestige." L. Eve Armentrout Ma, *Revolutionaries, Monarchists, and Chinatowns: Chinese Politics in the Americas and the 1911 Revolution* (Honolulu: University of Hawaii Press, 1990), 125–126.
12 Lai, "A Brief Historical Overview of Wei Xiongfei's Times," 19.
13 Lei, *Operatic China*, 7.
14 Chen, *Chinese San Francisco*, 163.
15 Yung, *Unbound Feet*, 69.
16 Wen Xiongfei, "Founding of the Chinese Revolutionary League in America," in *Chinese America: History and Perspectives*, ed. Colleen Fong (San Francisco: Chinese Historical Society of America, 2005), 21.

17 Wen would go on, by way of Hawaii, to become a member of Sun Yat-sen's short-lived presidential reign. After holding various high-ranking positions in the highly unstable Chinese governments of the 1910s, Wen exited politics and became a prominent history scholar, conducting important historical work at several prominent Chinese universities. See Wen, 33.

18 Wen, 22.

19 Hom, *Songs of Gold Mountain*, 204.

20 Hom, 230.

21 Hom, 204.

22 Hom, 225.

23 Hom, 205.

24 *Chinese Defender* 1, no, 8 (April 1911): 1.

25 *Chinese Defender* 1, no. 1 (August 1910): 1.

26 Ng Poon Chew, "America's Chance in China's Commerce," *Chinese Defender* 1, no. 10 (June 1911):1.

27 *Chinese Defender* 1, no. 8 (April 1911): 1.

28 Adriana Spadoni, "An Interview with a Nickelodeon Fiend."

29 "Buggy Ride Stirs Chinese Society," *San Francisco Call*, April 12, 1909, 2.

30 "Buggy Ride Stirs Chinese Society," *San Francisco Call*, April 12, 1909, 2.

31 "Sweet Little Bridesmaids in Pantaloons," *San Francisco Call*, May 30, 1909, 17.

32 "Wedding in the Chinese Smart Set," *San Francisco Call*, May 30, 1909, 18.

33 "Buggy Ride Stirs Chinese Society," *San Francisco Call*, April 12, 1909, 2.

34 "Buggy Ride Stirs Chinese Society," *San Francisco Call*, April 12, 1909, 2.

35 Foster, "Chinese Theatres in America," 160.

36 Nancy Yunhwa Rao, "The Public Face of Chinatown: Actresses, Actors, Playwrights, and Audiences of Chinatown Theaters in San Francisco during the 1920s," *Journal of the Society for American Music* 5, no. 2 (May 2011): 236.

37 Stellman, *Chinatown Photographer*, 50.

38 Walter Anthony, "The Passing of the Chinese Theater," *San Francisco Call*, July 27, 1913, 34.

39 Him Mark Lai, "The Drama Movement in San Francisco's Chinatown," *East/West*, April 4, 1973, 9.

40 Lee Grieveson, "Why the Audience Mattered in Chicago in 1907," in *American Movie Audiences: From the Turn of the Century to the Early Sound Era*, ed. Melvyn Stokes and Richard Maltby (London: British Film Institute, 1999), 79–91.

41 See Jan Olsson, "Italian Marionettes Meet Cinematic Modernity," in *Media, Popular Culture, and the American Century*, ed. Kingsley Bolton and Jan Olsson (Stockholm: Kungliga Biblioteket, 2010), 37.

42 Olsson, 37.

43 Lei, *Operatic China*, 4.

44 "Young China Party to Aid Countrymen," *San Francisco Call*, February 20, 1911, 5. The Young China Association also arranged charity events outside of Chinatown, at the Columbia Theater, on Geary and Mason Streets, about a ten-minute walk from the Chinese neighborhood.

45 "Chinese to Give Play in Liberty Theater," *San Francisco Call*, March 28, 1911, 1.

46 "$1,000 More Is Raised for Chinese Sufferers," *San Francisco Call*, May 6, 1911, 13.

47 "Young China Play Slams Manchus," *San Francisco Call*, April 17, 1911, 2.

48 "Revolutionary Chinese Form United Party," *San Francisco Call*, July 7, 1911, 12.

49 "Chinese Honor 72 Heroes of Revolution," *San Francisco Call*, August 8, 1912, 12.

50 "San Francisco, Cal.," *Billboard*, July 1, 1911, 19,

51 "Chinese Lose Bland Smile," *San Francisco Call*, October 29, 1911, 36.

52 See, for example, "200,000 Is Sent from U.S. to Rebels—Chinese Free Masons Here Back Revolt," *Los Angeles Herald*, October 14, 1911, 2; "China Grants Provisions of Constitution," *Sausalito News*, November 11, 1911, 1; "Propose Convention for Constitution," *Sacramento Union*, November 12, 1911, 12.

53 "Greedy Lion of Gold Eats $3000," *San Francisco Call*, November 19, 1911, 45.

54 This copy is part of the Rick Prelinger collection. A digitized version of the film has been made available on the Internet Archive. See *Parade Celebrating Chinese Republic* (1912), Internet Archive, accessed February 19, 2020, https://archive.org/details/ParadeCe1912.

55 Sun Yat-sen's Republican flag, commonly known as the "Blue Sky, White Sun, and Wholly Red Earth," would later become the symbol of the Kuomintang and, subsequently, the flag of Taiwan.

56 Glenn Adams Byers, "Good-Eye to Gay Chinese New Year," *San Francisco Call*, February 4, 1912, 25.

57 Walls, *Motion Pictures, 1894–1912*, 11. The film available for viewing at the Library of Congress is a digitized version of an archival positive print. The digitized version of the fragment has the call number FLA1429; the film's accession number is 6820. The original 16mm nitrate copy was donated in 1944 as part of what is known as the Louise Ernst Collection. The catalog registers the copy as incomplete, with reel number one missing. The film's longest running time was, according to a contemporary *Billboard* article, just under an hour; the preserved section of 300 feet runs at silent speed for about eleven minutes. "The Chinese Revolution," *Billboard*, May 4, 1912, 13.

58 Peter B. High, "Shokichi Umeya: The Revolutionist as Impresario," in *Tagen Bunka to Mirai Shakai Kenkyu Project* (Nagoya: Nagoya University, 2005), 124. Accessed February 20, 2020. http://www.lang.nagoya-u.ac.jp/proj/socho/mirai/mirai-high.pdf.

59 Anderson and Richie, *The Japanese Film*, 28.

60 High, "Shokichi Umeya," 122.

61 Ayano Kosaka, *Kakumei o purodyusushita Nihonjin* [革命をプロデュースした日本人] (Tokyo: Kodansha, 2009).

62 Today this building is the Takarazuka theater of Nagasaki, located at 6–38 Motoshikui-machi, close to the Shianbashi entertainment district.

63 Akira Nagai, "Umeya Shokichi to Eizo Shiryo—Shingai Kakumei No Kiroku Film Wo Chyushinni . . ." [梅屋庄吉と映像史料〜 辛亥革命の記録フィルムを中心に], Nagai University Web Society, accessed August 1, 2016, http://tabinaga.jp/tanken/view.php?hid=20120111192403.

64 *Billboard*, March 9, 1912, 12; *Moving Picture World*, March 16, 1912, 1032.

65 Two *Billboard* articles from March 1912 suggest that the film screened in San Francisco, as well as in several other cities in California. See "Chinese Revolution," *Billboard*, March 9, 1912, 7; "The Chinese Revolution Doing Big Business," *Billboard*, March 16, 1912, 61.

66 Olsson, *Los Angeles before Hollywood*, 108.

67 Research and writings on the Metropolitan Theater and the Gore Brothers have generously been made available by Ramona Curry from her forthcoming study on the history of the transpacific flow of Chinese films into the United States.

68 *Billboard*, March 9, 1912, 12; *Moving Picture World*, March 16, 1912, 962; *Moving Picture World*, March 16, 1912, 1032.

69 Advertisements for shows at the San Jose Garden Theater can be found in *Evening News*, March 7, 1912, 8, and *Evening News*, March 9, 1912, 3. The film also seems to have played at the Bonita Theater in Augusta, Georgia; *Augusta Chronicle*, August 28, 1912, 10. In Modesto, California, the film screened at the Star Theatre. An article in the *Modesto News* described the film as having been made under the supervision of the French Pathé Company and presents a different story of origins, claiming that five men died during the film's shooting; *Modesto News*, May 15, 1912, 3. An advertisement in *Moving Picture World*, May 25, 1912, 761, implies that the film also played in Jackson, Florida. An advertisement in the *Pacific Commercial Advertiser* suggests that the film played at the Chinese Theater in Honolulu as early as December 30, 1911, which, if it was the same film, would constitute its first U.S. exhibition; *Pacific Commercial Advertiser*, December 30, 1911, 3.

70 Barbara L. Voss, "The Archaeology of Overseas Chinese Communities," *World Archaeology* 37, no. 3 (2005): 429–430.

71 R. Scott Baxter and Rebecca Allen, "Archaeological Investigations of Life within the Woolen Mills Chinatown, San Jose," in *The Chinese in America: A History from Gold Mountain to the New Millennium*, ed. Susie Lan Cassel (Walnut Creek, CA: Rowman Altamira, 2002).

72 *Billboard*, April 13, 1912, 12.

73 *Billboard*, April 13, 1912, 12.

74 *Moving Picture World*, April 6, 1912, 65.

75 I elaborate further on these aspects of the film in Kim Fahlstedt, "Marketing Rebellion: The Chinese Revolution Reconsidered," *Film History* 26, no. 1 (2014): 80–107.

76 *Billboard*, March 9, 1912, 12.

77 *Billboard*, April 13, 1912, 12.

78 *Billboard*, March 30, 1912, 65.

79 Matthew D. Johnson, "'Journey to the Seat of War': The International Exhibition of China in Early Cinema," *Journal of Chinese Cinemas* 3, no. 2 (June 2009): 115.

80 Haenni, *Immigrant Scene*, 169

81 Casetti, *Eye of the Century*, xx.

## Chapter 8 Trajectories and Concluding Remarks

1 Judith Thissen, "Jewish Immigrant Audiences in New York City, 1905–14," in *American Movie Audiences: From the Turn of the Century to the Early Sound Era*, ed. Melvyn Stokes and Richard Maltby (London: British Film Institute, 1999), 15–28.

2 In an interview with W.J.T. Mitchell, Bhabha distilled one of the larger questions from *The Location of Culture* as "what was modernity for those who were part of its instrumentality or governmentality but, for reasons of race or gender or economic status, were excluded from its forms of rationality, or its prescriptions of progress?" See Homi Bhabha, "Interview with Cultural Theorist Homi Bhabha by W.J.T. Mitchell," *Artforum* 33, no. 7 (March 1995), accessed August 1, 2016, http://prelectur.stanford.edu/lecturers/bhabha/interview.html.

3 Moy, *Marginal Sights*; Tchen, *New York before Chinatown*; Tchen, *Yellow Peril!*; Krystyn R. Moon, *Yellowface: Creating the Chinese in American Popular Music*

*and Performance, 1850s–1920s* (New Brunswick, NJ: Rutgers University Press, 2004).

4 Grauman continued to oversee the theater until his death in 1950.

5 Terry Helgesen, *Grauman's Chinese Theatre Hollywood* (Los Angeles: A Console Feature, 1969), 15.

6 King, *Lost in Translation*, 46.

7 King, 47.

8 Tchen, *New York before Chinatown*, 129.

9 Chow Tse-Tsung, *May Fourth Movement: Intellectual Revolution in Modern China* (Cambridge, MA: Harvard University Press, 1960), 41–48.

10 Johnson, "'Journey to the Seat of War,'" 117.

11 Johnson, 113.

12 Johnson, 113.

13 A small group of historians have made similar interdisciplinary observations and called for a modernization theory that looks beyond Western-centric and Eurocentric conceptualizations of modernity. In scholarship on U.S. film history, studies positing notions of "black modernity" are the most advanced; see, for example, Paul Gilroy, *The Black Atlantic: Modernity and Double-Consciousness*, reissue edition (Cambridge, MA: Harvard University Press, 1993); Stewart, *Migrating to the Movies*; Allyson Nadia Field, *Uplift Cinema: The Emergence of African American Film and the Possibility of Black Modernity* (Durham, NC: Duke University Press, 2015). In 2009, a special issue of *Chinese Studies in History* was dedicated to identify and develop the notion of Chinese modernity as one of "multiple modernities." See Q. Edward Wang, ed., special issue, *Chinese Studies in History* 43, no. 1 (September 2009.

14 Q. Edward Wang, "Modernization Theory in/of China," *Chinese Studies in History* 43, no. 1 (September 2009): 3.

# Bibliography


Abel, Richard. *Americanizing the Movies and "Movie-Mad" Audiences, 1910–1914*. Berkeley: University of California Press, 2006.

———, ed. *Encyclopedia of Early Cinema*. London: Routledge, 2005.

———. "The Movies in a 'Not So Visible Place': Des Moines, Iowa, 1911–1914." In *Hollywood in the Neighborhood: Historical Case Studies of Local Moviegoing*, edited by Kathryn Fuller-Seeley, 107–129. Berkeley: University of California Press, 2008.

———. "The Passing (Picture) Show in the Industrial Heartland: The Early 1910s." In *Allegories of Communication: Intermedial Concerns from Cinema to the Digital*, edited by John Fullerton and Jan Olsson, 321–332. Eastleigh, UK: John Libbey, 2004.

———. "The Pleasures and Perils of Big Data in Digitized Newspapers." *Film History* 25, no. 1 (2013): 1–10.

———. *The Red Rooster Scare: Making Cinema American, 1900–1910*. Berkeley: University of California Press, 1999.

Addams, Jane. *The Spirit of Youth and the City Streets*. New York: Macmillan, 1909.

Allen, Robert C. "Contra the 'Chaser Theory.'" *Wide Angle* 3, no. 1 (1979): 4–11.

———. "Decentering Historical Audience Studies: A Modest Proposal." In *Hollywood in the Neighborhood: Historical Case Studies of Local Moviegoing*, edited by Kathryn Fuller-Seeley, 20–34. Berkeley: University of California Press, 2008.

———. "From Exhibition to Reception: Reflections on the Audience in Film History." *Screen* 31, no. 4 (1990): 347–356.

———. "Getting to Going to the Show." *New Review of Film and Television Studies* 8, no. 3 (2010): 264–276.

———. "Looking at 'Another Look at the "Chaser Theory."'" *Studies in Visual Communication* 10, no. 4 (1984): 45–50.

———. "Manhattan Myopia; Or, Oh! Iowa! Robert C. Allen on Ben Singer's 'Manhattan Nickelodeons: New Data on Audiences and Exhibitors,' Cinema Journal' 34, No. 3 (Spring 1995)." *Cinema Journal* 35, no. 3 (1996): 75–103.

———. "Motion Picture Exhibition in Manhattan 1906–1912: Beyond the Nickelodeon." *Cinema Journal* 18, no. 2 (1979): 2–15.

———. "Relocating American Film History." *Cultural Studies* 20, no. 1 (2006): 48–88.

———. *Vaudeville and Film 1895–1915: A Study in Media Interaction* (New York: Arno Press, 1980).

Allen, Robert C., and Douglas Gomery. *Film History: Theory and Practice.* New York: Knopf, 1985.

Altman, Rick. "Silence of the Silents," *Musical Quarterly* 80, no. 4 (Winter 1996): 648–718.

———. *Silent Film Sound.* New York: Columbia University Press, 2007.

Anderson, Joseph L., and Donald Richie. *The Japanese Film: Art and Industry.* Princeton, NJ: Princeton University Press, 1982.

Aronson, Michael. *Nickelodeon City: Pittsburgh at the Movies, 1905–1929.* Pittsburgh: University of Pittsburgh Press, 2008.

Asbury, Herbert. *The Barbary Coast: An Informal History of the San Francisco Underworld.* Garden City, NY: Garden City Publishing, 1933.

Bâ, Saër Maty, and Kate E. Taylor-Jones. "Affective Passions: The Dancing Female Body and Colonial Rupture in Zouzou (1934) and Karmen Geï (2001)." In *De-Westernizing Film Studies,* edited by Saër Maty Bâ and Will Higbee, 53–66. New York: Routledge, 2012.

Baxter, R. Scott, and Rebecca Allen. "Archaeological Investigations of Life within the Woolen Mills Chinatown, San Jose." In *The Chinese in America: A History from Gold Mountain to the New Millennium,* edited by Susie Lan Cassel, 381–398. Walnut Creek, CA: Rowman Altamira, 2002.

Beardsley, Charles. *Hollywood's Master Showman: The Legendary Sid Grauman.* New York: Cornwall Books, 1983.

Beiner, Ronald. "Walter Benjamin's Philosophy of History." *Political Theory* 12, no. 3 (1984): 423–434.

Bell, Geoffrey. *The Golden Gate and the Silver Screen.* Rutherford, NJ: Fairleigh Dickinson University Press, 1984.

Benjamin, Walter. "On Some Motifs in Baudelaire." In *Walter Benjamin: Selected Writings.* Vol. 4, *1938–1940,* edited by Howard Eiland and Michael W. Jennings, 313–355. Cambridge, MA: Belknap Press, 2006.

———. "On the Concept of History." In *Walter Benjamin: Selected Writings.* Vol. 4, *1938–1940,* edited by Howard Eiland and Michael W. Jennings, 389–400. Cambridge, MA: Belknap Press, 2006.

Berglund, Barbara. "Chinatown's Tourist Terrain: Representation and Racialization in Nineteenth-Century San Francisco," *American Studies* 46, no. 2 (2005): 5–36.

———. *Making San Francisco American: Cultural Frontiers in the Urban West, 1846–1906.* Lawrence: University Press of Kansas, 2007.

Bernstein, Matthew, and Gaylyn Studlar. *Visions of the East: Orientalism in Film.* New Brunswick, NJ: Rutgers University Press, 1997.

Bertellini, Giorgio. "Italian Imageries, Historical Feature Films and the Fabrication of Italy's Spectators in Early 1900s New York." In *American Movie Audiences: From the Turn of the Century to the Early Sound Era,* edited by Melvyn Stokes and Richard Maltby, 29–45. London: British Film Institute, 1999.

———. *Italy in Early American Cinema: Race, Landscape, and the Picturesque.* Bloomington: Indiana University Press, 2009.

Beusekom, Ansje van. "The Rise and Fall of the Lecturer as Entertainer in the Netherlands. Exhibition-Practices in Transition Related to Local Circumstances." *Iris,* no. 22 (Fall 1996): 131–144.

Bhabha, Homi. "Interview with Cultural Theorist Homi Bhabha by W.J.T. Mitchell." *Artforum* 33, no. 7 (March 1995). Accessed August 1, 2016. http://prelectur.stanford.edu/lecturers/bhabha/interview.html.

———. *The Location of Culture.* New York: Routledge, 1994.

Biltereyst, Daniël, Richard Maltby, and Philippe Meers. *Cinema, Audiences and Modernity: New Perspectives on European Cinema History.* London: Routledge, 2013.

Borch, Christian. "Interview with Edward W. Soja: Thirdspace, Postmetropolis, and Social Theory." *Distinktion: Scandinavian Journal of Social Theory* 3, no. 1 (January 2002): 113–120.

Bordwell, David. *On the History of Film Style.* Cambridge, MA: Harvard University Press, 1997.

Bordwell, David, Janet Staiger, and Kristin Thompson. *The Classical Hollywood Cinema: Film Style and Mode of Production to 1960.* New York: Columbia University Press, 1985.

Bowen, Robert W., and Brenda Young Bowen. *San Francisco's Chinatown.* Charleston, SC: Arcadia Publishing, 2008.

Brechin, Gray A. *Imperial San Francisco: Urban Power, Earthly Ruin.* Berkeley: University of California Press, 2001.

Bren, Frank, and Law Kar. *Hong Kong Cinema: A Cross-Cultural View.* Lanham, MD: Scarecrow Press, 2004.

Brownlow, Kevin. *The Parade's Gone by. . . .* Berkeley: University of California Press, 1968.

Bruno, Giuliana. *Streetwalking on a Ruined Map: Cultural Theory and the City Films of Elvira Notari.* Princeton, NJ: Princeton University Press, 1993.

Buchanan, Ian. "Unknotting Place and Space." *Salt* 12, no. 1 (2000): 137–156.

Burgess, John Stewart. "A Study of the Characteristics of the Cantonese Merchants in Chinatown, New York, as Shown by Their Use of Leisure Time." Master's thesis, Columbia University, 1909.

Butsch, Richard. *The Making of American Audiences: From Stage to Television, 1750–1990.* New York: Cambridge University Press, 2000.

Byington, Lewis Francis. "Peter A. Peshon." In *History of San Francisco*, ed. Lewis Francis Byington, vol. 3 (Chicago: S. J. Clarke Publishing, 1931), 295–296.

Campos, Patrick F. "'Manila by Night' as Thirdspace." *Kritika Kultura* 19 (August 2012): 139–165.

Carbine, Mary. "'The Finest Outside the Loop': Motion Picture Exhibition in Chicago's Black Metropolis, 1905–1928." *Camera Obscura* 8, no. 2 (1990): 8–41.

Carlson, Chris. "The Workingmen's Party & The Dennis Kearney Agitation." FoundSF, 1995, accessed March 15, 2016. http://www.foundsf.org/index.php?title=The_Workingmen%E2%80%99s_Party_%26_The_Dennis_Kearney_Agitation.

Casetti, Francesco. *Eye of the Century: Film, Experience, and Modernity.* New York: Columbia University Press, 2005.

Certeau, Michel de. *The Practice of Everyday Life.* Translated by Steven Rendall. Berkeley: University of California Press, 1984.

Chan, Sucheng. *Chinese American Transnationalism: The Flow of People, Resources, and Ideas between China and America during the Exclusion Era.* Philadelphia: Temple University Press, 2005

———. "Contextual Frameworks for Reading Counterpoint." *Amerasia Journal* 5, no. 1 (January 1978): 115–129.

———. *Entry Denied: Exclusion and the Chinese Community in America, 1882–1943.* Philadelphia: Temple University Press, 1991.

———. *This Bittersweet Soil: The Chinese in California Agriculture, 1860–1910*. Berkeley: University of California Press, 1989.

Chan, Sucheng, and Madeline Yuan-yin Hsu, eds. *Chinese Americans and the Politics of Race and Culture*. Philadelphia: Temple University Press, 2008.

Charney, Leo, and Vanessa R. Schwartz, eds. *Cinema and the Invention of Modern Life*. Berkeley: University of California Press, 1995.

Chen, Yong. *Chinese San Francisco, 1850–1943: A Trans-Pacific Community*. Stanford, CA: Stanford University Press, 2000.

Cherchi Usai, Paolo. *Burning Passions: Introduction to the Study of Silent Cinema*. London: British Film Institute, 1994.

Cherny, Robert W. "City Commercial, City Beautiful, City Practical: The San Francisco Visions of William C. Ralston, James D. Phelan, and Michael M. O'Shaughnessy." *California History* 73, no. 4 (December 1994): 296–307.

Chin, Ko-lin. *Chinese Subculture and Criminality: Non-traditional Crime Groups in America*. New York: Greenwood Press, 1990.

Chinn, Thomas, Him Mark Lai, and Philip P. Choy. *A History of the Chinese in California: A Syllabus*. San Francisco: Chinese Historical Society of America, 1969.

Chow, Rey. "Introduction: On Chineseness as a Theoretical Problem." *Boundary 2* 25, no. 3 (Fall 1998): 1–24.

Chow, Tse-Tsung. *May Fourth Movement: Intellectual Revolution in Modern China*. Cambridge, MA: Harvard University Press, 1960.

Choy, Philip P. *The Architecture of San Francisco Chinatown*. San Francisco: Chinese Historical Society, 2008.

Church, David. "From Exhibition to Genre: The Case of Grind-House Films." *Cinema Journal* 50, no. 4 (2011): 1–25.

Cohen, Adam. *Imbeciles: The Supreme Court, American Eugenics, and the Sterilization of Carrie Buck*. New York: Penguin, 2016.

Commonwealth Club of California, *Transactions of the Commonwealth Club of California*, 8, no. 5. San Francisco: Commonwealth Club of California, 1913.

Coolidge, Mary Roberts. *Chinese Immigration*. New York: Arno Press, 1909.

Cross, Ira B. "Review." *Economic Bulletin* 3, no. 2 (June 1910): 172–174.

Culin, Stewart. "Social Organization of the Chinese in America." *American Anthropologist* 4, no. 4 (1891): 347–352.

Curry, Ramona. "Benjamin Brodsky (1877–1960): The Trans-Pacific American Film Entrepreneur Part One, Making *A Trip Thru China*." *Journal of American–East Asian Relations* 18, no. 1 (2011): 58–94.

———. "Benjamin Brodsky (1877–1960): The Trans-Pacific American Film Entrepreneur Part Two, Taking *A Trip Thru China* to America." *Journal of American–East Asian Relations* 18, no. 2 (2011): 142–180.

Curtis, Susan. *A Consuming Faith: The Social Gospel and Modern American Culture*. Columbia, MO: University of Missouri Press, 2001.

Daniels, Roger. *Asian America: Chinese and Japanese in the United States since 1850*. Seattle: University of Washington Press, 1988.

Davies, Andrea Rees. *Saving San Francisco: Relief and Recovery after the 1906 Disaster*. Philadelphia: Temple University Press, 2011.

Davis, Allen F. *American Heroine: The Life and Legend of Jane Addams*. Repr., Chicago: Ivan R. Dee, 2000.

Dillon, Richard H. *The Hatchet Men: The Story of the Tong Wars in San Francisco's Chinatown*. New York: Coward-McCann, 1962.

Dissanayake, Wimal. "Early Asian Cinema and the Public Sphere." In *Early Cinema in Asia*, edited by Nick Deocampo, 32–69. Bloomington: Indiana University Press, 2017.

Dobie, Charles Caldwell. *San Francisco's Chinatown*. New York: D. Appleton-Century, 1936.

Drichel, Simone. "The Time of Hybridity." *Philosophy and Social Criticism* 34, no. 6 (July 2008): 587–615.

Durovicová, Nataša, and Kathleen E. Newman. *World Cinemas, Transnational Perspectives*. New York: Routledge, 2009.

Elsaesser, Thomas. "The New Film History." *Sight & Sound* 55, no. 4 (1986): 246–251.

Endres, Stacey, and Robert Cushman. *Hollywood at Your Feet: The Story of the World-Famous Chinese Theater*. Universal City, CA: Pomegranate Press, 2009.

Ernst, Wolfgang, Tommy Andersson, Thomas Götselius, and Otto Fischer. *Sorlet Från Arkiven: Ordning Ur Oordning*. Göteborg: Glänta, 2008.

Evans, Taliesin. *All about the Midwinter Fair, San Francisco, and Interesting Facts Concerning California*. San Francisco: W. B. Bancroft and Company, 1894.

Everson, William K. *American Silent Film*. New York: Oxford University Press, 1978.

Ewen, Elizabeth. *Immigrant Women in the Land of Dollars: Life and Culture on the Lower East Side, 1890–1925*. New York: Monthly Review Press, 1985.

Fahlstedt, Kim. "Marketing Rebellion: The Chinese Revolution Reconsidered." *Film History* 26, no. 1 (2014): 80–107.

Farwell, Willard B. and John E. Kunkler. *Chinese in San Francisco*. San Francisco: San Francisco Board of Supervisors, 1885.

Field, Allyson Nadia. *Uplift Cinema: The Emergence of African American Film and the Possibility of Black Modernity*. Durham, NC: Duke University Press, 2015.

Fischer, Lucy. "'The Shock of the New': Electrification, Illumination, Urbanization, and the Cinema." In *Cinema and Modernity*, edited by Murray Pomerance, 19–37. New Brunswick, NJ: Rutgers University Press, 2006.

Foster, Lois Rodecape. "Chinese Theatres in America." Unpublished manuscript, 1943.

Foucault, Michel. "Of Other Spaces, Heterotopias." *Architecture, Mouvement, Continuité* 5 (1984): 46–49.

Freedman, Russell. *Angel Island: Gateway to Gold Mountain*. New York: Clarion Books, 2014.

French, Charles Elwell. *Six Years of Drama at the Castle Square Theatre: With Portraits of the Members of the Company and Complete Programs of All Plays Produced, May 3, 1897–May 3, 1903*. Boston, MA: C. E. French, 1903.

Frykholm, Joel. *Framing the Feature Film: Multi-reel Feature Film and American Film Culture in the 1910s*. Stockholm: Acta Universitatis Stockholmiensis, 2009.

———. *George Kleine and American Cinema: The Movie Business and Film Culture in the Silent Era*. London: British Film Institute/Palgrave Macmillan, 2015.

Fuller-Seeley, Kathryn. *At the Picture Show: Small-Town Audiences and the Creation of Movie Fan Culture*. Washington, DC: Smithsonian Institution Press, 1996.

———. *Hollywood in the Neighborhood: Historical Case Studies of Local Moviegoing*. Berkeley: University of California Press, 2008.

Gaudreault, André and Germain Lacasse, eds. "Le bonimenteur de vues animées—The Moving Picture Lecturer," special issue, *Iris* 22 (Fall 1996).

Genthe, Arnold, and Will Irwin. *Old Chinatown*. New York: Mitchell Kennerley, 1913.

———. *Pictures of Old Chinatown*. New York: Moffat, Yard, and Company, 1908.

Genthe, Arnold, and John Kuo Wei Tchen. *Genthe's Photographs of San Francisco's Old Chinatown*. New York: Dover, 1984.
Gibson, Otis. *The Chinese in America*. Cincinnati: Hitchcock and Walden, 1877.
Gibson, Campbell and Kay Jung, *Historical Census Statistics on Population Totals by Race, 1790 to 1990, and by Hispanic Origin, 1970 to 1990, for Large Cities and Other Urban Places in The United States*. Washington, DC: U.S. Census Bureau, 2005.
Gilroy, Paul. *The Black Atlantic: Modernity and Double-Consciousness*. Reissue edition. Cambridge, MA: Harvard University Press, 1993.
Ginzburg, Carlo. *The Cheese and the Worms: The Cosmos of a Sixteenth-Century Miller*. Baltimore: Johns Hopkins University Press, 1980.
Ginzburg, Carlo, John Tedeschi, and Anne C. Tedeschi. "Microhistory: Two or Three Things That I Know about It." *Critical Inquiry* 20, no. 1 (1993): 10–35.
Goldstein, Jonathan. "Cantonese Artifacts, Chinoiserie, and Early American Idealization of China." In *America Views China: American Images of China Then and Now*, edited by Jonathan Goldstein, Jerry Israel, and Hilary Conroy, 43–55. Bethlehem, PA: Lehigh University Press, 1991.
Gomery, Douglas. "The Growth of Movie Monopolies: The Case of Balaban and Katz." *Wide Angle* 3, no. 1 (1979): 54–63.
———. *Shared Pleasures: A History of Movie Presentation in the United States*. London: British Film Institute, 1992.
Gordon, James Riely. "San Francisco—The Phoenix City." *Architect and Engineer* 26, no. 2 (September 1911): 54–57.
Gould, Lewis L. *America in the Progressive Era, 1890–1914*. New York: Longman, 2001.
Grau, Robert. *The Theatre of Science: A Volume of Progress and Achievement in the Motion Picture Industry*. New York: Broadway Publishing, 1914.
Grieveson, Lee. *Policing Cinema: Movies and Censorship in Early-Twentieth-Century America*. Berkeley: University of California Press, 2004.
———. "Why the Audience Mattered in Chicago in 1907." In *American Movie Audiences: From the Turn of the Century to the Early Sound Era*, edited by Melvyn Stokes and Richard Maltby, 79–91. London: British Film Institute, 1999.
———. "Cinema Studies and the Conduct of Conduct." In *Inventing Film Studies*, edited by Lee Grieveson and Haidee Wasson, 3–37. Durham, NC: Duke University Press, 2008.
Griffiths, Alison. *Wondrous Difference: Cinema, Anthropology, and Turn-of-the-Century Visual Culture*. New York: Columbia University Press, 2001.
Gunning, Tom. "Heard over the Phone: The Lonely Villa and the de Lorde Tradition of the Terrors of Technology." *Screen* 32, no. 2 (1991): 184–196.
———. "Modernity and Cinema: A Culture of Shocks and Flows." In *Cinema and Modernity*, edited by Murray Pomerance, 297–315. New Brunswick, NJ: Rutgers University Press, 2006.
———. "'Now You See It, Now You Don't': The Temporality of the Cinema of Attractions." *Velvet Light Trap* 32 (Fall 1993): 71–84.
———. "The Whole Town's Gawking: Early Cinema and the Visual Experience of Modernity." *Yale Journal of Criticism* 7, no. 2 (Fall 1994): 189–201.
———. "The Whole World within Reach: Travel Images without Borders." in *Virtual Voyages: Cinema and Travel*, ed. Jeffrey Ruoff, 25–41. Durham, NC: Duke University Press, 2006.
H. S. Crocker Company. *Crocker-Langley San Francisco Directory for the Year Commencing 1892*. San Francisco: H. S. Crocker Company, 1893.

———. *Crocker-Langley San Francisco Directory for the Year Commencing 1898*. San Francisco: H. S. Crocker Company, 1899.

———. *Crocker-Langley San Francisco Business Directory for the Year Ending December 31st, 1906*. San Francisco: H. S. Crocker Company, 1907.

———. *Crocker-Langley San Francisco Directory for the Year Ending August 1909*. San Francisco: H. S. Crocker Company, 1909.

———. *Crocker-Langley San Francisco Directory for the Year Ending August 1912*. San Francisco: H. S. Crocker Company, 1912.

Habermas, Jürgen. *The Structural Transformation of the Public Sphere: An Inquiry into a Category of Bourgeois Society*. Translated by Thomas Burger and Frederick Lawrence. Cambridge: Polity Press, 1992.

Haddad, John. "The Laundry Man's Got a Knife!" in *Chinese America: History and Perspectives*, edited by Colleen Fong, Marlon K. Hom, Madeline Hsu, Him Mark Lai, Laurene McClain, and Ruthannee Lum McCunn, 31–47. San Francisco: Chinese Historical Society of America, 2001.

Haenni, Sabine. *The Immigrant Scene: Ethnic Amusements in New York, 1880–1920*. Minneapolis: University of Minnesota Press, 2008.

Hansen, Miriam. *Babel and Babylon: Spectatorship in American Silent Film*. Cambridge, MA: Harvard University Press, 1994.

———. *Cinema and Experience: Siegfried Kracauer, Walter Benjamin and Theodor W. Adorno*. Berkeley: University of California Press, 2011.

———. "Fallen Women, Rising Stars, New Horizons: Shanghai Silent Film as Vernacular Modernism." *Film Quarterly* 54, no. 1 (October 2000): 10–22.

———. "The Mass Production of the Senses: Classical Cinema as Vernacular Modernism." *Modernism/modernity* 6, no. 2 (1999): 59–77.

———. "Vernacular Modernism: Tracking Cinema on a Global Scale." In *World Cinemas, Transnational Perspectives*, edited by Nataša Durovicová and Kathleen E. Newman, 287–314. New York: Routledge, 2009.

Hay, James. "Piecing Together What Remains of the Cinematic City." In *The Cinematic City*, edited by David Clarke, 209–229. London: Routledge, 1997.

Hediger, Vinzenz. "Putting the Spectators in a Receptive Mood." In *Film's Thresholds*, edited by Veronica Innocenti and Valentina Re, 291–308. Udine, Italy: Forum 2004.

Helgesen, Terry. *Grauman's Chinese Theatre Hollywood*. Los Angeles: A Console Feature, 1969.

Hendricks, Gordon. *The Kinetoscope: America's First Commercially Successful Motion Picture Exhibitor*. New York: Beginnings of the American Film, 1966.

Higashi, Sumiko. "Dialogue: Manhattan's Nickelodeons. Sumiko Higashi on Ben Singer's 'Manhattan Nickelodeons: New Data on Audiences and Exhibitors' 'Cinema Journal' 34, No. 3 (Spring 1995)." *Cinema Journal* 35, no. 3 (1996): 72–74.

———. "In Focus: Film History, or a Baedeker Guide to the Historical Turn." *Cinema Journal* 44, no. 1 (2004): 94–100.

High, Peter B. "Shokichi Umeya: The Revolutionist as Impresario." In *Tagen Bunka to Mirari Shakai Kenkyu Project*. Nagoya: Nagoya University, 2005. Accessed February 20, 2020. http://www.lang.nagoya-u.ac.jp/proj/socho/mirai/mirai-high.pdf.

Hinman, George Warren. *The Oriental in America*. New York: Missionary Education Movement of the U.S. and Canada, 1913.

Hofstadter, Richard. *The Age of Reform*. New York: Vintage, 1960.

Hom, Marlon K. *Songs of Gold Mountain: Cantonese Rhymes from San Francisco Chinatown*. Berkeley: University of California Press, 1992.

Hooper, Bernadette. *San Francisco's Mission District*. Charleston, SC: Arcadia Publishing, 2006.

Hoyt, Eric. "Lenses for Lantern: Data Mining, Visualization, and Excavating Film History's Neglected Sources." *Film History* 26, no. 2 (2014): 146–168.

Hoyt, Eric, Wendy Hagenmaier, and Carl Hagenmaier. "Media + History + Digital + Library: An Experiment in Synthesis." *Journal of E-Media Studies* 3, no. 1 (2013): 1–21.

Hsu, Madeline Yuan-yin. *Dreaming of Gold, Dreaming of Home: Transnationalism and Migration between the United States and South China, 1882–1943*. Stanford, CA: Stanford University Press, 2000.

Hu, Ying. *Tales of Translation: Composing the New Woman in China, 1899–1918*. Stanford, CA: Stanford University Press, 2000.

International Chinese Business Directory Company. *International Chinese Business Directory of the World: A Comprehensive List of Prominent Chinese Firms and Individuals in Parts of China, Japan, India Proper [etc.]*. San Francisco: International Chinese Business Directory Company, 1913.

Irwin, Will. *The City That Was: A Requiem of Old San Francisco*. New York: B. W. Huebsch, 1906.

Jacobs, Lewis. *The Rise of the American Film, a Critical History. With an Essay: Experimental Cinema in America, 1921–1947*. New York: Teachers College Press, 1968.

Jin, Dal Yong. "Critical Interpretation of Hybridisation in Korean Cinema: Does the Local Film Industry Create 'The Third Space'?" *Javnost—The Public* 17, no. 1 (2010): 55–71.

Jobs, Sebastian, and Gesa Mackenthun, eds. *Agents of Transculturation: Border-Crossers, Mediators, Go-Betweens*. Münster: Waxmann, 2013.

Johnson, Matthew D. "'Journey to the Seat of War': The International Exhibition of China in Early Cinema." *Journal of Chinese Cinemas* 3, no. 2 (June 2009): 109–122.

Jones, Margaret C. *Heretics and Hellraisers: Women Contributors to* The Masses, *1911–1917*. Austin: University of Texas Press, 2014.

Kahn, Edgar Myron. *Cable Car Days in San Francisco*. Stanford, CA: Stanford University Press, 1944.

Keeler, Charles Augustus. *San Francisco and Thereabout*. San Francisco: California Promotion Committee, 1903.

Keil, Charlie. "To Here from Modernity: Style, Historiography, and Transitional Cinema." In *American Cinema's Transitional Era: Audiences, Institutions, Practices*, edited by Charlie Keil and Shelley Stamp, 51–65. Berkeley: University of California Press, 2004.

Keil, Charlie, and Ben Singer. *American Cinema of the 1910s: Themes and Variations*. New Brunswick, NJ: Rutgers University Press, 2009.

Kelly, Robert J., Ko-lin Chin, and Jeffrey Fagan. "Chinese Organized Crime in America." In *Handbook of Organized Crime in the United States*, edited by Rufus Schatzberg, Ko-lin Chin, and Robert J. Kelly, 213–244. Westport, CT: Greenwood Press, 1994.

Kern, Stephen. *The Culture of Time and Space, 1880–1918*. Cambridge, MA: Harvard University Press, 2003.

Khor, Denise. "Asian Americans at the Movies: Race, Labor, and Migration in the Transpacific West, 1900–1945." PhD diss., University of California, San Diego, 2008.

Kiehn, David. "Miles Brothers: Film Pioneers in SF." *The Argonaut: Journal of the San Francisco Museum and Historical Society* 20, no. 2 (2009): 72–85.

King, Homay. *Lost in Translation: Orientalism, Cinema, and the Enigmatic Signifier.* Durham, NC: Duke University Press, 2010.

Klinger, Barbara. "Film History Terminable and Interminable: Recovering the Past in Reception Studies." *Screen* 38, no. 2 (1997): 107–128.

Komatsu, Hiroshi, and Frances Loden. "Mastering the Mute Image: The Role of the Benshi in Japanese Cinema." *Iris*, no. 22 (Fall 1996): 33–52.

Komatsu, Hiroshi, and Charles Musser. "Benshi Search." *Wide Angle* 9. no. 2 (1987): 73–90.

Kosaka, Ayano. *Kakumei o purodyusushita Nihonjin [革命をプロデュースした日本人].* Tokyo: Kodansha, 2009.

Koszarski, Richard. *An Evening's Entertainment: The Age of the Silent Feature Picture, 1915–1928.* Berkeley: University of California Press, 1994.

Künnemann, Vanessa, and Ruth Mayer, eds. *Chinatowns in a Transnational World: Myths and Realities of an Urban Phenomenon.* New York: Routledge, 2011.

Lacasse, Germain. "The Film Lecturer." In *A Companion to Early Cinema*, edited by André Gaudreault, Nicolas Dulac, and Santiago Hidalgo, 487–497. Malden, MA: Wiley-Blackwell, 2012.

Lai, Him Mark. *Becoming Chinese American: A History of Communities and Institutions.* Walnut Creek, CA: Altamira Press, 2004.

———. "A Brief Historical Overview of Wei Xiongfei's Times." In *Chinese America: History and Perspectives,* edited by Colleen Fong, 19. San Francisco: Chinese Historical Society of America, 2005.

———. "The Chinese Exclusion Act: Observations of a Centennial," *Amerasia* 9, no. 1 (1982): 1–4.

———. "The Chinese Press in America." In *The Ethnic Press in the United States: A Historical Analysis and Handbook*, edited by Sally M. Miller, 27–43. New York: Greenwood Press, 1987.

———. "The Drama Movement in San Francisco's Chinatown." *East/West: The Chinese American Journal*, April 4, 1973: 9.

Lai, Him, Genny Lim, and Judy Yung, eds. *Island: Poetry and History of Chinese Immigrants on Angel Island, 1910–1940.* Repr., Seattle: University of Washington Press, 1991.

Lai, Him Mark, and Karl Lo. *Chinese Newspapers Published in North America 1854–1975.* Washington, DC: Center for Chinese Research Materials, 1977.

Larson, Erik. *The Devil in the White City: Murder, Magic, and Madness at the Fair That Changed America.* New York: Crown, 2003.

Lee, Anthony W. *Picturing Chinatown: Art and Orientalism in San Francisco.* Berkeley: University of California Press, 2001.

Lee, Erika, and Judy Yung. *Angel Island: Immigrant Gateway to America.* New York: Oxford University Press, 2010.

Lee, Leo Ou-fan. *Shanghai Modern: The Flowering of a New Urban Culture in China, 1930–1945.* Cambridge, MA: Harvard University Press, 2001.

Lee, Robert G. *Orientals: Asian Americans in Popular Culture.* Philadelphia: Temple University Press, 1999.

Lefebvre, Henri. *The Production of Space.* Translated by Donald Nicholson-Smith. Malden, MA: Wiley-Blackwell, 1992.

Lei, Daphne. "The Production and Consumption of Chinese Theatre in Nineteenth-Century California." *Theatre Research International* 28, no. 3 (October 2003): 289–302.

Lei, Daphne Pi-Wei. *Operatic China*. New York: Palgrave Macmillan, 2006.

Leong, Karen J. *The China Mystique: Pearl S. Buck, Anna May Wong, Mayling Soong, and the Transformation of American Orientalism*. Berkeley: University of California Press, 2005.

———. “A Distinct and Antagonistic Race: Constructions of Chinese Manhood in the Exclusionist Debates, 1869–1878.” In *Across the Great Divide: Cultures of Manhood in the American West*, edited by Matthew Basso, Laura McCall, and Dee Garceau-Hagen, 131–148. New York: Routledge, 2000.

Levi, Giovanni. “On Microhistory.” *New Perspectives on Historical Writing* 2 (1991): 97–119.

Light, Ivan. “From Vice District to Tourist Attraction: The Moral Career of American Chinatowns, 1880–1940.” *Pacific Historical Review* 43, no. 3 (1974): 367–394.

Lindstrom, J. A. “Where Development Has Just Begun: Nickelodeon Location, Moving Picture Audiences, and Neighborhood Development in Chicago.” In *American Cinema's Transitional Era: Audiences, Institutions, Practices*, edited by Charles Keil and Shelley Stamp, 217–238. Berkeley: University of California Press, 2004.

Look Tin Eli, “Our New Oriental City—Veritable Fairy Palaces Filled with the Choicest Treasures of the Orient.” In *San Francisco: The Metropolis of the West*. San Francisco: Western Press Association, 1910.

Los Angeles City Directory Company. *Los Angeles City Directory, 1910*. Los Angeles: Los Angeles City Directory Company, 1910.

Luckett, Moya. *Cinema and Community: Progressivism, Exhibition, and Film Culture in Chicago, 1907–1917*. Detroit: Wayne State University Press, 2013.

Lui, Mary Ting Yi. *The Chinatown Trunk Mystery: Murder, Miscegenation, and Other Dangerous Encounters in Turn-of-the-Century New York City*. Princeton, NJ: Princeton University Press, 2005.

Löwy, Michael. *Fire Alarm: Reading Walter Benjamin's “On the Concept of History.”* Translated by Chris Turner. London: Verso, 2005.

Ma, L. Eve Armentrout. *Revolutionaries, Monarchists, and Chinatowns: Chinese Politics in the Americas and the 1911 Revolution*. Honolulu: University of Hawaii Press, 1990.

Maltby, Richard. “How Can Cinema History Matter More?” *Screening the Past* 22 (December 2007). Accessed July 30, 2016. http://www.screeningthepast.com/2015/01/how-can-cinema-history-matter-more.

Maltby, Richard, Daniël Biltereyst, and Philippe Meers. *Explorations in New Cinema History: Approaches and Case Studies*. Oxford: Blackwell, 2011.

Maltby, Richard, and Melvyn Stokes. *Hollywood Abroad: Audiences and Cultural Exchange*. London: British Film Institute, 2004.

Maltby, Richard, Melvyn Stokes, and Robert C. Allen. *Going to the Movies: Hollywood and the Social Experience of the Cinema*. Exeter: University of Exeter Press, 2007.

Maoz, Darya. “The Mutual Gaze.” *Annals of Tourism Research* 33, no. 1 (January 2006): 221–239.

Marchetti, Gina. *Romance and the” Yellow Peril”: Race, Sex, and Discursive Strategies in Hollywood Fiction*. Berkeley: University of California Press, 1994.

Mayer, Ruth. “The Glittering Machine of Modernity: The Chinatown in American Silent Film.” *Modernism/modernity* 16, no. 4 (2009): 661–684.

———. *Serial Fu Manchu: The Chinese Supervillain and the Spread of Yellow Peril Ideology*. Philadelphia: Temple University Press, 2014.

Mayne, Judith. "Immigrants and Spectators." *Wide Angle* 5, no. 2 (1982): 32–40.

Meister, Chris. "The Texas State Building: J. Riely Gordon's Contribution to the World's Columbian Exposition." *Southwestern Historical Quarterly* 98, no. 1 (1994): 1–24.

Melnick, Ross. *American Showman: Samuel "Roxy" Rothafel and the Birth of the Entertainment Industry, 1908–1935*. New York: Columbia University Press, 2013.

Mirzoeff, Nicholas, and Jack Halberstam. "Decolonize Media: Tactics, Manifestos, Histories." *Cinema Journal* 57, no. 4 (2018): 120–123.

Mitchell, Katharyne. "Different Diasporas and the Hype of Hybridity." *Environment and Planning D: Society and Space* 15 (1997): 533–554.

Moon, Krystyn R., *Yellowface: Creating the Chinese in American Popular Music and Performance, 1850s–1920s*. New Brunswick, NJ: Rutgers University Press, 2004.

Moore, Paul S. *Now Playing: Early Moviegoing and the Regulation of Fun*. Albany: State University of New York Press, 2008.

———. "Subscribing to Publicity: Syndicated Newspaper Features for Moviegoing in North America, 1911–15." *Early Popular Visual Culture* 12, no. 2 (2014): 260–273.

Moore, Sarah J. *Empire on Display: San Francisco's Panama-Pacific International Exposition of 1915*. Norman: University of Oklahoma Press, 2013.

Morris, Peter. *Cantonese Love Songs: An English Translation of Jiu Ji-Yung's Cantonese Songs of the Early 19th Century*. Hong Kong: Hong Kong University Press, 1992.

Morris, Peter. *Embattled Shadows: A History of Canadian Cinema, 1895–1939*. Montreal: McGill-Queen's University Press, 1992.

Moy, James S. *Marginal Sights: Staging the Chinese in America*. Iowa City: University of Iowa Press, 1996.

Musser, Charles. "Another Look at the 'Chaser Theory.'" *Studies in Visual Communication* 10, no. 4 (1984): 24–44.

———. *High-Class Moving Pictures: Lyman H. Howe and the Forgotten Era of Traveling Exhibition, 1880–1920*. Princeton, NJ: Princeton University Press, 1991.

———. "Historiographic Method and the Study of Early Cinema." *Cinema Journal* 44, no. 1 (2004): 101–107.

———. *History of the American Cinema. 1, The Emergence of Cinema: The American Screen to 1907*. Edited by Charles Harpole. New York: Scribner, 1990.

———. "Musser's Reply to Allen." *Studies in Visual Communication* 10, no. 4 (1984): 51–52.

———. "Rethinking Early Cinema, Cinema of Attractions and Narrativity." In *The Cinema of Attractions Reloaded*, edited by Wanda Strauven, 389–416. Amsterdam: Amsterdam University Press, 2006.

———. "The Travel Genre in 1903–1904: Moving towards Fictional Narrative." In *Early Cinema: Space, Frame, Narrative,* edited by Thomas Elsaesser and Adam Barker, 123–132. London: BFI Publishing, 1990.

Nadler, Sheryl Fern. "'The First Born' (1897): A Cultural, Historical, and Literary Study of Francis Powers and David Belasco's Unpublished Drama of Chinese Life in America." PhD diss., Florida State University, 1994.

Nagai, Akira. "Umeya Shokichi to Eizo Shiryo—Shingai Kakumei No Kiroku Film Wo Chyushinni" [梅屋庄吉と映像史料～ 辛亥革命の記録フィルムを中心に]. Nagai University Web Society. Accessed August 1, 2016. http://tabinaga.jp/tanken/view.php?hid=20120111192403.

Nasaw, David. *The Chief: The Life of William Randolph Hearst*. Boston: Houghton Mifflin, 2000.

Nee, Victor, and Brett de Bary Nee. *Longtime Californ': A Documentary Study of an American Chinatown*. New York: Pantheon Books, 1973.

Negt, Oskar, and Alexander Kluge. *Public Sphere and Experience: Toward an Analysis of the Bourgeois and Proletarian Public Sphere*. Minneapolis: University of Minnesota Press, 1993.

Ngai, Mae. *The Lucky Ones: One Family and the Extraordinary Invention of Chinese America*. Princeton, NJ: Princeton University Press, 2012.

*Official Catalogue and Guide Book to the Pan-American Exposition: With Maps of Exposition and Illustrations, Buffalo, N.Y., U.S.A., May 1st to Nov. 1st, 1901*. Buffalo, NY: Charles Ahrhart, 1901.

Olsson, Jan. "Italian Marionettes Meet Cinematic Modernity." In *Media, Popular Culture, and the American Century*, edited by Kingsley Bolton and Jan Olsson, 35–61. Stockholm: Kungliga Biblioteket, 2010.

———. *Los Angeles before Hollywood: Journalism and American Film Culture, 1905 to 1915*. Stockholm: National Library of Sweden, 2008.

———. "Pressing Inroads: Metaspectators and the Nickelodeon Culture." In *Screen Culture: History and Textuality*, edited by John Fullerton, 113–135. Eastleigh, UK: John Libbey, 2004.

———. "Pressing Matters: Media Crusades before the Nickelodeons." *Film History* 27, no. 2 (2015): 105–139.

Ordover, Nancy. *American Eugenics: Race, Queer Anatomy, and the Science of Nationalism*. Minneapolis: University of Minnesota Press, 2003.

Ortiz, Fernando. *Cuban Counterpoint, Tobacco and Sugar*. Durham, NC: Duke University Press, 1995.

Palmquist, Peter. "Asian Photographers in San Francisco 1850–1930." *The Argonaut: Journal of the San Francisco Historical Society* 9 (1998): 87–88.

Pan, Erica Y. Z. *The Impact of the 1906 Earthquake on San Francisco's Chinatown*. New York: P. Lang, 1995.

Panama-Pacific International Exposition Company. *The Panama-Pacific International Exposition, San Francisco, 1915*. San Francisco: Panama-Pacific International Exposition Company, 1914.

Pegler-Gordon, Anna. *In Sight of America: Photography and the Development of U.S. Immigration Policy*. Berkeley: University of California Press, 2009.

Peiss, Kathy Lee. *Cheap Amusements: Working Women and Leisure in Turn-of-the-Century New York*. Philadelphia: Temple University Press, 1986.

Pepin, Elizabeth, and Lewis Watts. *Harlem of the West: The San Francisco Fillmore Jazz Era*. San Francisco: Chronicle Books, 2005.

Peterson, Jennifer Lynn. *Education in the School of Dreams: Travelogues and Early Nonfiction Film*. Durham, NC: Duke University Press, 2013.

Peterson, Jennifer. "'The Knowledge Which Comes in Pictures': Educational Films and Early Cinema Audiences," in *A Companion to Early Cinema*, edited by André Gaudreault, Nicolas Dulac, and Santiago Hidalgo, 277–297. Malden, MA: Wiley-Blackwell, 2012.

Phillips, Kendall R. *A Place of Darkness: The Rhetoric of Horror in Early American Cinema*. Austin: University of Texas Press, 2018.

Poe, Edgar Allan. "The Man of the Crowd." In *The Complete Edgar Allan Poe Tales*, 240–245. New York: Avenel Books, 1981.

Potter, Zenas L. *The Social Survey: A Bibliography*. New York: Russell Sage Foundation, 1915.

Pratt, George C. "Camera on the Move: An Interview with Hal Mohr." *Journal of Photography and Motion Pictures of the International Museum of Photography at George Eastman House* 19, no. 1 (March 1976): 16–19.

Pratt, Mary Louise. *Imperial Eyes: Travel Writing and Transculturation*. London: Routledge, 1992.

Purdy, Helen Throop. *San Francisco: As It Was, as It Is, and How to See It*. San Francisco: Paul Elder and Company, 1912.

Rabinovitz, Lauren. *For the Love of Pleasure: Women, Movies, and Culture in Turn-of-the-Century Chicago*. New Brunswick, NJ: Rutgers University Press, 1998.

Rao, Nancy Yunhwa. *Chinatown Opera Theater in North America*. Urbana, IL: University of Illinois Press, 2017.

———. "The Public Face of Chinatown: Actresses, Actors, Playwrights, and Audiences of Chinatown Theaters in San Francisco during the 1920s." *Journal of the Society for American Music* 5, no. 2 (May 2011): 235–270.

Rast, Raymond W. "The Cultural Politics of Tourism in San Francisco's Chinatown, 1882–1917." *Pacific Historical Review* 76, no. 1 (2007): 29–60.

———. "Tourist Town: Tourism and the Emergence of Modern San Francisco, 1869–1915." PhD diss., University of Washington, 2006.

Reed, Christopher A. *Gutenberg in Shanghai: Chinese Print Capitalism, 1876–1937*. Vancouver: UBC Press, 2005.

Roan, Jeanette. *Envisioning Asia: On Location, Travel, and the Cinematic Geography of U.S. Orientalism*. Ann Arbor: University of Michigan Press, 2010.

Rony, Fatimah Tobing. *The Third Eye: Race, Cinema, and Ethnographic Spectacle*. Durham, NC: Duke University Press, 1996.

Rosenzwieg, Roy. "From Rum Shop to Rialto: Workers and Movies." In *Moviegoing in America: A Sourcebook in the History of Film Exhibition*, edited by Gregory Waller, 27–45. Malden, MA: Blackwell, 2002.

Routledge, Paul. "The Third Space as Critical Engagement." *Antipode* 28, no. 4 (October 1996): 399–419.

Rutherford, Jonathan, and Homi Bhabha. "The Third Space: Interview with Homi Bhabha." In *Identity: Community, Culture, Difference*, edited by Jonathan Rutherford, 207–221. London: Lawrence and Wishart, 1998.

Rydell, Robert W. *All the World's a Fair: Visions of Empire at American International Expositions, 1876–1916*. Chicago: University of Chicago Press, 1984.

Sabin, Edwin Legrand. *Building the Pacific Railway: The Construction-Story of America's First Iron Thoroughfare between the Missouri River and California, from the Inception of the Great Idea to the Day, May 10, 1869, When the Union Pacific and the Central Pacific Joined Tracks at Promontory Point, Utah, to Form the Nation's Transcontinental*. Philadelphia: Lippincott, 1919.

Said, Edward W. *Culture & Imperialism*. London: Vintage, 1994

———. *Orientalism*. London: Penguin, 2003.

———. "Orientalism Reconsidered." *Cultural Critique*, no. 1 (Autumn 1985): 89–107.

Sanborn Map Company, *Sanborn Fire Insurance Map from San Francisco, San Francisco County, California, 1913–1915*, vol. 1. New York: Sanborn Map Company, 1913.

San Francisco Board of Supervisors, *San Francisco Municipal Reports Fiscal Year 1907–8, Ending June 30, 1908*. San Francisco: San Francisco Board of Supervisors, 1909.

———. *San Francisco Municipal Reports Fiscal Year 1908–9, Ending June 30, 1909*. San Francisco: San Francisco Board of Supervisors, 1909.

———. *San Francisco Municipal Reports Fiscal Year 1909–10, Ending June 30, 1910.* San Francisco: San Francisco Board of Supervisors, 1910.

———. *San Francisco Municipal Reports Fiscal Year 1910–11, Ending June 30, 1911.* San Francisco: San Francisco Board of Supervisors, 1911.

———. *San Francisco Municipal Reports Fiscal Year 1911–12, Ending June 30, 1912.* San Francisco: San Francisco Board of Supervisors, 1912.

———. *San Francisco Municipal Reports Fiscal Year 1915–16, Ending June 30, 1916.* San Francisco: San Francisco Board of Supervisors, 1916.

———. *San Francisco Municipal Reports Fiscal Year 1916–17, Ending June 30, 1917* (San Francisco: San Francisco Board of Supervisors, 1917.

Sánches Salas, Daniel. "A History of the Film Lecturer in Spanish Silent Cinema." *Iris*, no. 22 (Fall 1996): 171–181.

*San Francisco's Chinatown—An Aid to Tourists and Others in Visiting China-Town. October 1909.* San Francisco, 1909.

Saxton, Alexander. *The Indispensable Enemy: Labor and the Anti-Chinese Movement in California.* Berkeley: University of California Press, 1971.

———. *The Rise and Fall of the White Republic: Class Politics and Mass Culture in Nineteenth-Century America.* London: Verso, 1990.

Schivelbusch, Wolfgang. *The Railway Journey: The Industrialization of Time and Space in the 19th Century.* Berkeley: University of California Press, 1986.

Schmidt, Björn A. *Visualizing Orientalness: Chinese Immigration and Race in U.S. Motion Pictures, 1910s–1930s.* Cologne, Germany: Böhlau Verlag, 2017.

Scholem, Gershom. "Walter Benjamin." In *On Jews and Judaism in Crisis: Selected Essays*, edited by Werner J. Dannhauser, 172–197. New York: Schocken Books, 1976.

———. *Walter Benjamin: The Story of a Friendship.* London: Faber and Faber, 1982.

Schwartz, Vanessa R. "Walter Benjamin for Historians." *American Historical Review* 106, no. 5 (2001): 1721–1743.

Seldes, Gilbert. *An Hour with the Movies and the Talkies.* Philadelphia: Lippincott, 1929.

Shah, Nayan. *Contagious Divides: Epidemics and Race in San Francisco's Chinatown.* Berkeley: University of California Press, 2001.

Simmel, Georg. "The Metropolis and Mental Life." In *On Individuality and Social Forms: Selected Writings*, edited by Donald N. Levine, 324–339. Chicago: University of Chicago Press, 1971.

Singer, Ben. "Manhattan Melodrama: A Response from Ben Singer." *Cinema Journal* 36, no. 4 (1997): 107–112.

———. "Manhattan Nickelodeons: New Data on Audiences and Exhibitors." *Cinema Journal* 34, no. 3 (1995): 5–35.

———. *Melodrama and Modernity: Early Sensational Cinema and Its Contexts.* New York: Columbia University Press, 2001.

———. "New York, Just Like I Pictured It . . . Ben Singer Responds." *Cinema Journal* 35, no. 3 (1996): 104–128.

Sklar, Robert. *Movie-Made America: A Cultural History of American Movies.* New York: Random House, 1975.

Slide, Anthony. *The New Historical Dictionary of the American Film Industry.* New York: Routledge, 2014.

Smith, Linda Tuhiwai. *Decolonizing Methodologies.* 2nd ed. London: Zed Books, 2012.

Soja, Edward W. *Postmodern Geographies: The Reassertion of Space in Critical Social Theory.* London: Verso, 1989.

———. *Thirdspace: Journeys to Los Angeles and Other Real-and-Imagined Places.* Cambridge, MA: Blackwell, 1996.
———. "Writing the City Spatially." *City* 7, no. 3 (November 2003): 269–280.
Solnit, Rebecca. *Motion Studies: Time, Space and Eadweard Muybridge.* London: Bloomsbury, 2004.
Solnit, Rebecca, and Susan Schwartzenberg. *Hollow City: The Siege of San Francisco and the Crisis of American Urbanism.* London: Verso, 2002.
Solnit, Rebecca, Ben Pease, and Shizue Siegel. *Infinite City: A San Francisco Atlas.* Berkeley: University of California Press, 2010.
Spadoni, Adriana. *The Noise of the World.* New York: Boni and Liveright, 1921.
———. *The Swing of the Pendulum.* New York: Boni and Liveright, 1919.
Staiger, Janet. *Bad Women: Regulating Sexuality in Early American Cinema.* Minneapolis: University of Minnesota Press, 1995.
———. *Interpreting Films: Studies in the Historical Reception of American Cinema.* Princeton, NJ: Princeton University Press, 1992.
Starr, Kevin. *Americans and the California Dream, 1850–1915.* New York: Oxford University Press, 1973.
———. *California: A History.* New York: Modern Library, 2005.
Stellman, Louis J. *Chinatown Photographer, Louis J. Stellman: A Catalog of His Photograph Collection: Including a Previously Unpublished Manuscript, Chinatown: A Pictorial Souvenir and Guide Written by Louis J. Stellman in 1917.* Edited by Richard H. Dillon, Gary E. Strong, and California State Library. Sacramento: California State Library Foundation, 1989.
———. *That Was a Dream Worth Building; the Spirit of San Francisco's Great Fair.* San Francisco: H. S. Crocker Company, 1916.
Stewart, Jacqueline Najuma. *Migrating to the Movies: Cinema and Black Urban Modernity.* Berkeley: University of California Press, 2005.
Streible, Dan. "The Literature of Film Exhibition: A Bibliography: Individual Theaters, Architecture and Design, Audiences, Technical Aspects, Regional Exhibition, Alternative Exhibition, Technologies, Journals and Yearbooks, Miscellany, Biography, Theater Management, Commerce, Legal Aspects, Silent Film Accompaniment, and Drive-Ins." *Velvet Light Trap* 25 (1990): 81–119.
Sun, Yumei. "From Isolation to Participation: 'Chung Sai Yat Po' (China West Daily) and San Francisco's Chinatown, 1900–1920." PhD diss., University of Maryland College Park, 1999.
Tate, E. Mowbray. *Transpacific Steam: The Story of Steam Navigation from the Pacific Coast of North America to the Far East and the Antipodes, 1867–1941.* New York: Cornwall Books, 1986.
Tchen, John Kuo Wei. *New York before Chinatown: Orientalism and the Shaping of American Culture, 1776–1882.* Baltimore: Johns Hopkins University Press, 2001.
Tchen, John Kuo Wei, and Dylan Yeats. *Yellow Peril! An Archive of Anti-Asian Fear.* London: Verso, 2014.
Thissen, Judith. "Jewish Immigrant Audiences in New York City, 1905–14." In *American Movie Audiences: From the Turn of the Century to the Early Sound Era,* edited by Melvyn Stokes and Richard Maltby, 15–28. London: British Film Institute, 1999.
———. "Oh, Myopia! A Reaction from Judith Thissen on the Singer-Allen Controversy." *Cinema Journal* 36, no. 4 (1997): 102–107.
Tillmany, Jack. *Theatres of San Francisco.* Charleston, SC: Arcadia Publishing, 2005.

Todd, Frank Morton. *The Chamber of Commerce Handbook for San Francisco, Historical and Descriptive: A Guide for Visitors*. San Francisco: San Francisco Chamber of Commerce, 1914.
Vijver, Lies Van de, and Daniel Biltereyst. "Cinemagoing as a Conditional Part of Everyday Life." *Cultural Studies* 27, no. 4 (2013): 561–584.
Voss, Barbara L. "The Archaeology of Overseas Chinese Communities." *World Archaeology* 37, no. 3 (2005): 424–439.
Uricchio, William, and Roberta E. Pearson. "Manhattan's Nickelodeons. New York? New York! William Uricchio and Roberta E. Pearson Comment on the Singer-Allen Exchange." *Cinema Journal* 36, no. 4 (1997): 98–102.
Urry, John. *The Tourist Gaze*. 2nd ed. London: Sage, 2002.
Urry, John, and Jonas Larsen, *The Tourist Gaze 3.0*. London: Sage, 2011.
Waller, Gregory. "Introduction." *Film History* 25, nos. 1–2 (2013): vii–ix.
———. "Japan on American Screens, 1908–1915." In *Early Cinema and the "National,"* edited by Richard Abel, Giorgio Bertellini, and Rob King, 137–150. New Barnet, UK: John Libbey Publishing, 2008.
———. *Main Street Amusements: Movies and Commercial Entertainment in a Southern City, 1896–1930*. Washington, DC: Smithsonian Institution Press, 1995.
———. *Moviegoing in America: A Sourcebook in the History of Film Exhibition*. Malden, MA: Blackwell, 2002.
Walls, Howard Lamarr. *Motion Pictures, 1894–1912, Identified from the Records of the United States Copyright Office*. Washington, DC: Library of Congress, 1953.
Wang, Q. Edward. "Modernization Theory in/of China." *Chinese Studies in History* 43, no. 1 (September 2009): 3–6.
Wang, Yiman. "The Art of Screen Passing: Anna May Wong's Yellow Yellowface Performance in the Art Deco Era." *Camera Obscura* 20, no. 3 (2005): 159–191.
Weaver-Hightower, Rebecca. "The Postcolonial Hybrid." *Postcolonial Film: History, Empire, Resistance*, edited by Rebecca Weaver-Hightower and Peter Hulme, 247–266. New York: Routledge, 2014.
Wen, Xiongfei. "Founding of the Chinese Revolutionary League in America." In *Chinese America: History and Perspectives*, edited by Colleen Fong, 21–42. San Francisco: Chinese Historical Society of America, 2005.
White, Trumbull, and William Igleheart. *The World's Columbian Exposition, Chicago, 1893*. Philadelphia: P. W. Ziegler and Company, 1893.
Williams, Raymond. *Keywords: A Vocabulary of Culture and Society*. London: Fontana, 1976.
Wright, Hamilton, and Western Press Association. *San Francisco: The Metropolis of the West*. San Francisco: Western Press Association, 1910.
Yip, Christopher Lee. "San Francisco's Chinatown: An Architectural and Urban History." PhD diss., University of California, Berkeley, 1985.
Young, Robert J. C. *Colonial Desire: Hybridity in Theory, Culture and Race*. New York: Routledge, 2005.
Yung, Judy. *Unbound Feet: A Social History of Chinese Women in San Francisco*. Berkeley: University of California Press, 1995.
Zhang, Zhen. *An Amorous History of the Silver Screen: Shanghai Cinema, 1896–1937*. Chicago: University of Chicago Press, 2005.

# Index

## About the Author

KIM K. FAHLSTEDT is a postdoctoral scholar of cinema and media studies at Stockholm University.